International Financial Governance under Stress

T0312110

Persistent episodes of global financial crises have placed the existing system of international monetary and financial governance under stress. The resulting economic turmoil provides a focal point for rethinking the norms and institutions of global financial architecture and the policy options of public and private authorities at national, regional and transnational levels.

This volume moves beyond analysis of the causes and consequences of recent financial crises and concentrates on issues of policy. Written by distinguished scholars, it focuses on the growing tension between global market structures and national policy imperatives. The ongoing crises in Argentina and elsewhere dramatically illustrate these difficulties.

Accessible to both specialists and general readers, the analysis is coherent across a broad range of theoretical and empirical cases. Offering a series of reasoned policy responses to financial integration and crises, the volume grapples directly with the institutional and often-neglected normative dimensions of international financial architecture. The volume thus constitutes required reading for scholars and policy makers.

GEOFFREY R. D. UNDERHILL is Professor of International Governance in the Department of Political Science and the Amsterdam School for Social Science Research of the University of Amsterdam. He is the author of *Industrial Crisis and the Open Economy: Politics, Global Trade, and Textiles in the Advanced Economies* (1998).

XIAOKE ZHANG is Research Fellow at the Amsterdam School for Social Science Research of the University of Amsterdam. He is the author of *The Changing Politics of Finance in Korea and Thailand* (2002).

International Financial Governance under Stress

Global Structures versus
National Imperatives

GEOFFREY R. D. UNDERHILL
XIAOKE ZHANG

CAMBRIDGE
UNIVERSITY PRESS

CAMBRIDGE UNIVERSITY PRESS
Cambridge, New York, Melbourne, Madrid, Cape Town, Singapore, São Paulo

Cambridge University Press
The Edinburgh Building, Cambridge CB2 8RU, UK

Published in the United States of America by Cambridge University Press, New York

www.cambridge.org
Information on this title: www.cambridge.org/9780521817325

© Cambridge University Press 2003

First published 2003
This digitally printed version 2007

A catalogue record for this publication is available from the British Library

Library of Congress Cataloguing in Publication data
International financial governance under stress : global structures versus national
imperatives / edited by Geoffrey R. D. Underhill and Xiaoke Zhang.
    p. cm.
Based on an international conference held Feb. 3–5, 2000 in Amsterdam.
Includes bibliographical references and index.
ISBN 0 521 81732 3
1. International finance – Congresses.   2. Financial crises – Congresses.
3. Monetary policy – Congresses.   4. International finance – Asia – Congresses.
5. Financial crises – Asia – Congresses.   6. Monetary policy – Asia – Congresses.
I. Underhill, Geoffrey R. D.   II. Zhang, Xiaoke.
HG3881 .I60728   2002
332'.042 – dc21   2002067214

ISBN 978-0-521-81732-5 hardback
ISBN 978-0-521-03637-5 paperback

Contents

Figures

Tables

Contributors

Andrew Baker is a Lecturer at the Institute of European Studies, the Queen's University of Belfast.

Chris Baker is an independent researcher and writer in Bangkok.

Shaun Breslin is Reader in the Department of Politics and International Studies, University of Warwick.

Benjamin J. Cohen is Louis G. Lancaster Professor of International Political Economy, Department of Political Science, University of California, Santa Barbara.

Jean-Marc Coicaud is Senior Academic Officer, Peace and Governance Programme, United Nations University, Tokyo.

Stephen L. Harris is Associate Professor in the Department of Public Policy, National University of Singapore.

Vijay Joshi is Reader in the Department of Economics and Merton College, Oxford University.

Manmohan S. Kumar is an Advisor in the Research Department, International Monetary Fund.

Marcus Miller is Professor of Economics and Co-Director, Centre for the Study of Globalisation and Regionalisation, University of Warwick.

Luiz A. Pereira da Silva is a Visiting Scholar at the Institute for Fiscal and Monetary Policy, Tokyo, on secondment from the World Bank.

Pasuk Phongpaichit is Professor in the Faculty of Economics, Chulalongkorn University, Bangkok.

Vladimir Popov is Professor at the Institute of European and Russian Studies, Carleton University, Ottawa, and Academy of National Economy, Moscow.

Richard Robison is Professor of Political Economy, the Institute of Social Studies, the Hague.

Andrew Rosser is Research Fellow at the Institute of Development Studies, University of Sussex.

Jonathan Story is Shell Fellow in Economic Transformation and Professor of International Political Economy, INSEAD.

Masayuki Tadokoro is Professor of International Relations, Keio University, Japan.

Geoffrey R. D. Underhill is Professor of International Governance in the Department of Political Science and the Amsterdam School for Social Science Research of the University of Amsterdam.

Marc Uzan is the Executive Director of the Reinventing Bretton Woods Committee, New York.

George Vojta is President of the Financial Services Forum, New York.

John Williamson is a Senior Fellow at the Institute for International Economics, Washington, DC.

Xiaoke Zhang is Research Fellow at the Amsterdam School for Social Science Research of the University of Amsterdam.

Acknowledgements

This volume began life as an international conference ('What Is to Be Done? Global Economic Disorder and Policies for a New Financial Architecture in the Millennium', 3–5 February 2000) in Amsterdam. It was directed by Geoffrey Underhill and Karel van Wolferen and organised by the Research Centre for International Political Economy (RECIPE, now integrated into the Amsterdam School for Social Science Research or ASSR) and the Institute for Comparative Political and Economic Institutions (ICPEI), both at the Universiteit van Amsterdam (UvA). The conference was designed to address the various problems that global market integration and recent episodes of financial crises presented to public and private authorities at the national, regional and global levels. The underlying premise was that the policy debate on global financial architecture issues was lacking in important regards. It brought together a global and interdisciplinary selection of scholars and a range of practitioners from the public and private sectors alike. It provided an important forum for both academic and policy discussions across disciplinary and professional boundaries. The emphasis, as the title suggests, was on what should be done, an important part of which concerned the correct identification of the problem.

The conference received financial support from a range of internal and external sources. These were: the faculties of Economics and Econometrics and of Social and Behavioural Sciences (UvA); the Royal Netherlands Academy of Sciences (KNAW), Asia House (Amsterdam), De Nederlandsche Bank, the New York-based Reinventing Bretton Woods Committee (Director: Marc Uzan), the Netherlands Organisation for Scientific Research (NWO) and the ASSR. Paul van de Velde, from the ICPEI, and Helge Lasschuijt, headed the conference secretariat, which was central to the successful organisation of the conference. The conference participants and volume editors are most grateful to organisers and fundraisers alike for their enthusiasm and generosity. Karel van Wolferen, director of the ICPEI, was not only a skilful planner of the conference but also an insightful contributor to its intellectual exchanges. A special thanks to our keynote speaker, William Pfaff of the *International Herald Tribune*. The editors wish to acknowledge the contributions of all those who presented papers at the conference, too numerous to name here. The range of papers went well beyond those which we were able to include in the volume, to which the usual constraints of space and coherence had to apply. We are furthermore grateful to Hendrik Jan Brouwer (Executive Director, De Nederlandsche Bank), Hervé Carré (Director, Economy of the Eurozone, Directorate General of Economic and Financial Affairs, European Commission), Michael Ellman (Professor of Economics, UvA), Jacques van der Gaag (Dean, Faculty of Economics, UvA), Robert Gray (Vice-Chairman, HSBC Investment Bank and Vice-Chair, International Primary Markets Association), Richard Higgott (Director, Centre for the Study of Globalisation and Regionalisation, University of Warwick), Helge Hveem (Professor of Political Science, University of Oslo), Jorge Braga de Macedo (President, OECD Development Centre), Barbara Matthews (Regulatory Counsel, Institute for International Finance), Mar'ie Muhammad (Director, Oversight Commission for Indonesia's Bank Restructuring Agency), David Vines (Director, Global Economic Research Programme, GEI, and University of Oxford), George Vojta (Chairman, Westchester Group, NY) and Yukio Yoshimura (IMF Executive Director for Japan), all of whom took time out from astoundingly busy lives to attend as discussants and/or panel chairs. The substantial audience also added to the quality of the eventual outcome.

As editors, we wish to thank the contributors to the volume for their cooperation and efficiency, which made the editing of the volume more agreeable than has usually been the case with such large collective and interdisciplinary projects. We appreciate the penetrating and thorough commentary of anonymous reviewers for Cambridge University Press, which helped to shape the final versions of each contribution as well as to enhance the overall quality of the volume. We would also like to thank those who contributed comments, either informally or in conference settings, to our own chapters in the volume over the past year or so. The errors and omissions remain ours alone.

The ASSR and the Department of Political Science of the University of Amsterdam served as the home base for finalising the volume. David Vines, Director of the GEI research programme, funded by the Economic and Social Research Council of the UK (in which Geoffrey Underhill was a participant) and general editor of the GEI book series in which this book is included, gave essential support for the conference and the volume throughout the development of the project. The GEI programme also provided much of the funding for the research that lies behind the chapters by Geoffrey Underhill and Xiaoke Zhang (grant no. L120251029). Finally, we very much appreciate the help and expertise of Chris Harrison (economics editor for Cambridge University Press) and his staff for steering the manuscript to final completion. We also thank Jeroen Starrenburg for preparing the index. It is our hope that this volume serves to broaden and deepen the debate over global financial and monetary governance.

Amsterdam
October 2002

Introduction: global market integration, financial crises and policy imperatives

GEOFFREY R. D. UNDERHILL AND XIAOKE ZHANG

The Asian crisis was the world economy's closest shave since the Latin American debt crisis of the early 1980s and, arguably, since the Great Depression of the 1930s. A combination of currency and financial crises which erupted in east Asia during mid- and late 1997 rapidly developed into a global disturbance, engulfing not only most Asian newly industrialising economies but also Russia, South Africa and some Latin American countries. These systemic disruptions were major, but were not the only examples of financial volatility in recent years. The Asian crisis has been followed by further difficulties in Turkey and Latin America, and at time of writing it remains to be seen what the full effects of 11 September 2001 will be. Indeed, more than seventy financial and monetary crises of different proportions and characteristics have occurred in both developed and developing countries over the past two decades.[1] Large and growing amounts of public money have been committed to tackling the financial crises and their socioeconomic consequences.

A common background to these developments is the intensifying process of global financial liberalisation and integration. Starting with the introduction of floating exchange rates and financial market deregulation from the 1970s onwards, the global monetary and financial system has undergone a radical transformation. Whereas national governments were once effective at shaping socioeconomic policies and development strategies in line with the imperatives of domestic political stability and legitimacy, there is now an increasingly market-oriented and integrated global system. The deepening integration of financial markets has imposed considerable constraints on national policy choices and generated significant strains in various domestic and international policy arenas. As financial crises have become more frequent and more severe over the past two decades, this has raised the question of whether the growing frequency and severity of crises correlate with the emergence of this liberal and transnational financial order.

The root causes of financial crises are most likely to lie in a complex mix of economic, political and social variables across the domestic and international

1

domains. The recent episodes of currency and financial crises in many emerging market economies admit of no single-factor explanations. If the causes of the crises are sufficiently complex as to encourage an open mind, what is equally important is to think carefully, comprehensively and innovatively about the policy agenda. Too much is at stake for developed and developing economies alike to ignore the question of what should be the appropriate national and international responses to the growing intensity of financial crises, as the process of global market integration continues. This concerns both crisis prevention and management. The ongoing crisis in Argentina demonstrates almost daily how monetary and financial problems can spill over into social unrest and problems of governability.

This volume is designed to bring together conceptual discussions, empirical analyses and policy proposals that will collectively address the strategic dimensions, at national, regional and global levels, of managing a highly integrated and liberalised financial system characterised by considerable instability. The major focus is on the tension between the harmonising pressures of financial globalisation led by the advanced financial centres and the prevailing diversity of financial systems, corporate practices and development models throughout the international economic landscape, particularly in emerging market economies. This clear focus and its elaboration through attention to a broad range of related theoretical and policy issues will form a coherent and comprehensive treatment of the dilemmas presented by coping with the brave new world of capital mobility in the global system.

In line with this analytical focus, the volume has three principal objectives. In the first place, and cutting across the scholarly disciplines of political science, political economy and economics, it will advance a set of concepts and arguments which will help us to reflect on the central policy questions involved in the reform and development of the global financial architecture. These concepts and arguments will lend the volume underlying coherence, despite the variety of opinions and analytical approaches among its interdisciplinary contributors. The theoretical discussion will also enable us to understand better and interpret the changing dynamics of the international financial system and its impact on the policy preferences of, and power relations among, the various national and transnational actors and institutions involved in developing the global financial architecture. Similarly, the discussion will illustrate the nature of increasing tension between the rapid integration of financial markets across regulatory and political boundaries on the one hand and national and global macroeconomic policy management on the other.

Second, the volume aims to analyse a range of national experiences with global capital mobility and with currency and financial crises. There are several dimensions to this policy agenda: the effects of global market integration on the pursuit of national economic strategies, the causes and consequences of financial crises, and mechanisms for crisis prevention and management. The volume seeks to show which domestic and systemic forces have shaped responses to the policy problems inherent in the process of financial globalisation and respective attempts to adjust national policy to the new environment. The volume also draws out the policy implications of these national cases in relation to global monetary and financial governance.

Finally, this volume discusses specific policy options open to national and international policy makers in devising patterns of regional and global cooperation to reform the contemporary international financial architecture. Critical issues include how international institutions can be more accountable to domestic political and economic imperatives and how intergovernmental cooperative processes might overcome the tensions among different national value systems and economic development models. Once again, emphasis will be on the policy dilemmas of accelerated financial integration and their implications for the pursuit of domestic socioeconomic policies, the achievement of national development objectives and the management of global monetary and financial relations.

The breadth of this volume sets it apart from similar books in important ways. Recent efforts at the examination of major regional financial crises tend to focus on either macroeconomic and structural factors or on political and institutional dimensions.[2] An interdisciplinary approach sensitive to the interactive effects of economic, political and social factors is not only vital to understanding the frequency and severity of financial crises, but is also, we argue, essential to the effective governance of the global monetary and financial system. The volume has brought together contributors from various disciplines: international political economy, public policy and administration, international economics, business and management, and public and private international law.

The geographical coverage of case material in this volume is also wider than that of many similar books.[3] It presents the varied experiences of both developed and emerging market economies affected by financial crises. It also looks at a broad range of international institutions and private interests involved in the policy debates. Finally, this volume is unique in addressing explicitly the normative dimensions of monetary and financial governance. The argument is that effective financial architecture requires legitimate normative underpinnings if it is to prove acceptable to civil society, in developed and emerging market economies alike, and therefore to function effectively. The current politics of the Argentine street, as the monetary and financial system melt down, should be ample demonstration.

Central conceptual and policy issues

In keeping with the three objectives outlined above, this volume has attempted to address six interrelated conceptual and policy issues which run through its various chapters. The first set concerns the way in which national governments in emerging market economies can and should respond to growing international economic volatility in the process of financial globalisation. While governments may count on multilateral rescue packages in future cases of financial crises, they must defend themselves against financial market instabilities.[4] External rescue packages have increasingly come with often intrusive conditions attached. The modesty of current attempts to restructure the global financial system are, in this light, unlikely on their own to make the financial world a much safer place. The IMF Sovereign Debt Restructuring Mechanism proposals may prove the exception, but emerging market countries which want to avoid devastating financial crises must protect themselves; this requires policy reforms and innovations.

The various contributors to this volume have focused on three policy questions where reforms and innovations are needed, particularly with regard to national experiences following the Asian crisis. They include the proper mechanisms of exchange rate management, the desirability and viability of capital controls, and the design and implementation of sound practices in financial regulation and corporate governance.[5] These policy issues are not merely technical but are developed in a politicised environment. The analyses of national policy responses in this volume, while varied in approach and perspective, sustain the assumption that market reforms are difficult to disentangle from sociopolitical forces, and that officials invariably face political imperatives in the policy-making process. Realistic advice for sound and achievable policy reforms and innovations thus entails a full understanding of their political feasibility as well as their technocratic complexity.

The second set of issues concerns the implications for public policy of the coexistence of distinct national and regional financial system variants with accelerating global integration of these once-distinct markets. While the old distinctions between the national and the offshore have been disappearing, contrasting national or regional financial systems, corporate practices and development patterns seem likely to persist in the foreseeable future. The political, social and institutional features of national economic governance will continue to shape the responses of domestic actors and agencies to the challenges and opportunities created by globalisation.[6] Nonetheless, global financial integration and contemporary attempts at designing financial architecture appear to presume a more uniform environment than is in fact to be found. Even the most well-meaning of policies can suffer compatibility deficits when applied across a range of different national systems.

Following recent financial crises, international institutions, particularly the International Monetary Fund (IMF), prescribed structural reforms in such areas as finance–industry relations, regulatory frameworks, banking practices, bankruptcy procedures and corporate governance. These reforms emphasised the adoption in all countries of a set of codes and standards on financial regulation, policy transparency and corporate management.[7] The persistence of variations in economic and financial systems, however, are likely to pose serious questions to the IMF among others: how can uniform codes and standards of financial and corporate governance be adapted successfully to individual national jurisdictions? And how can we devise effective policies for micro- and macroeconomic management that are compatible not only with contrasting national development norms and goals but also with divergent domestic sociopolitical systems and institutional structures? Concepts such as regulation, transparency and governance do not admit of universal definition, especially at the implementation stage. The structural reforms designed to improve the workings of the international financial system may prove difficult to implement if they clash excessively with different domestic political and economic contexts.[8]

The third set of conceptual and policy issues, which follows on from the second, relates to the fact that national policy makers remain accountable to domestic constituencies and parliaments, despite the global dimensions of economic and social policy problems. Although the individual responses of national governments often make sense in their own peculiar context, which one can hardly ask them to ignore, in aggregate there is considerable room for dissonance and major errors in crisis prevention and management. The very fact that there exist no institutional arrangements for exercising anything like the centralised authority and capacity at the international level complicates the task of managing global financial integration, formulating effective macroeconomic policies, and ensuring adequate supervisory oversight of transnational financial institutions on the basis of national jurisdictions. International organisations are thus faced with the enormous challenges of devising robust strategies for policy co-ordination and global economic governance that are congruous with the priorities of national development needs and the imperatives of domestic political stability and legitimacy.

The difficulties of co-operation in the international system of competing states and jurisdictions are well known. To add to those difficulties, any international co-operative efforts at monetary and financial governance would need to be reconciled with differences in domestic market structures and financial practices, variations in national regulatory frameworks and institutional patterns, and dissimilarities in legal and accounting systems. One issue that has been given special attention in this volume relates to the feasibility of, and possible alternatives to, international co-operation in the domain of global money and finance, under the political and institutional constraints of national sovereignty, prevailing diversity and conflicting interests.[9]

The fourth set of issues examines the role of the private sector in the policy-making process in general and in crisis prevention and management in particular. The private sector is crucial to the governance of the monetary and financial system at national, regional and global levels. Given that private sector activities have increasingly dominated global financial transactions, private financial firms should be integrated into the process of crisis resolution.[10] While the proposition that the private sector is important is widely accepted, what should be the proper balance between private interests and public good? Particularly in financial sector regulatory processes, which are notoriously susceptible to particularistic rent seeking and private capture, this remains unclear. To what extent and under what conditions should governments cede their policy-making power to private market forces? What would be the consequences of private domination of public policy processes for financial stability, democratic accountability and political legitimacy?

The normative dimension of these issues needs explicitly to be recognised by policy makers. As implied above, different national systems are likely to provide contrasting answers. Therefore, a central theme developed throughout this volume is that if the policy mix is simply left to the dictates of global financial market pressures and to dominant private interests, the legitimacy and much-trumpeted benefits of financial openness may prove politically unsustainable over time. This already appears imminent in the Argentine case, and heightens the widely perceived conflicts between the globalisation of finance and democratic forms of governance. The transnational integration of financial markets has affected the changing balance of public authority versus market power in relation to public policy making in the domain of the monetary and financial system. The underlying argument is that the more market-oriented and transnational financial order which has emerged in the past three decades has increasingly aligned economic policy and regulatory processes with the preferences of powerful private interests and crucially altered the nature of public policy objectives in monetary and financial governance. If the financial sector and regulatory policy become unduly dominated by private interests, we risk not only the legitimacy deficit but also economic instability and crisis, as has been so forcefully revealed through the recent episodes of economic turmoil and sociopolitical unrest in Asian and Latin American countries.[11]

The fifth set of conceptual and policy issues is the relationship between the regulatory and prudential supervisory aspects of financial policy on the one hand, and the macroeconomic (particularly exchange rate and monetary) policy aspects on the other. Regulatory policy changes in favour of deregulation imply the liberalisation of capital accounts, with necessary effects on prudential regulation, macroeconomic management and the finance of social and health policies. Nonetheless, regulatory policy changes are typically made in considerable isolation from discussions on macroeconomic policy making and other policy domains. The exception appears to be in small, open economies such as Hong Kong and Singapore, where vulnerability to and dependence upon capital flows, yielding exchange rate volatility, link together financial regulation, macroeconomic management and government finance in the minds of policy makers.

In many developed and emerging market countries, regulatory policy changes are perceived to be necessary in order to enhance the efficiency of financial markets and to please powerful market actors and interests both at home and abroad (the latter usually relating to market access for foreign firms). But the difficulties which the transformation of financial market structures might present for the achievement of major policy commitments of democratically elected governments are given little attention. There has certainly been little consideration of the problems of political legitimacy which market preferences in terms of regulatory and macroeconomic policies may pose for domestic political regimes.[12] In the shadow of the Asian and Latin American financial crises this problem has been felt acutely. Where there are discussions in official circles about the dilemmas created by the formulation of regulatory and macroeconomic policies in isolation from each other, new approaches to the resolution of these dilemmas are still lacking. More systematic discussion of these issues seems desirable as the legitimacy of governments and effective international co-operation often depend on the success of macroeconomic policies.

The final set of policy issues to be addressed in this volume explores the nature of the public interest in the face of global financial integration. The chapters examine a number of more specific questions. What are the goals (by nature contestable) which public policy seeks to achieve in the domain of financial system and monetary management? What role should the financial system and (particularly external) financial constraints play in the process of economic development, especially where social and humanitarian issues are concerned? What should be the proper balance in crisis management between the interests of investors and those of debtor countries and between the interests of creditor countries and those of intergovernmental organisations? This in turn invites discussion of the institutional and legal frameworks for international co-operation and global financial governance. What asymmetries of power and distribution might call a global system operating through international financial institutions into dispute? Answers to those questions point once again to the unavoidable normative content of the public policy choices in financial market governance. The international financial order and the broad impact of its dramatic transformations are not merely technical matters but are essentially linked to such important questions as the global financial system for what ends and for whom.[13] These are the issues which should ultimately shape the ongoing reform and development of the international financial architecture.

The organisation of the volume

The volume has been organised around these six sets of conceptual and policy issues. It is divided into four parts. The first part presents the major intellectual and policy problems under consideration in the volume and illustrates different perspectives on the nature and process of global financial integration. It discusses the diversity of dilemmas and challenges that the globalisation of financial market structures has presented to political authorities at national, regional and global levels, and explores the policy directions which we may consider when thinking about the institutional and normative constructs of the new international financial order against the backdrop of recent financial crises in emerging market economies.

Jonathan Story's chapter leads off with a broad and critical review of the main arguments deployed in the US-centred debate on the fundamental causes of, and proper responses to, the recent financial crises. He places his review in a matrix consisting of the four dominant institutions of the contemporary global transformation – the state system, the state, world markets and multinational corporations – plotted against what he labels the liberal, the realist, the social democratic, and the 'apocalyptic' perspectives typically employed to explain the transformation. Story contends that the current debate on global financial instability has been located within a narrow ideological spectrum dominated by liberals and social democrats, and has ignored or side-tracked the insights derived from the other perspectives, most noticeably realist arguments about power structures. He suggests that an international political economy approach, sensitive to the complex interactions between the state and the market at national and transnational levels and to power clashes conducted through states and among corporations, should be given priority in the research and policy agenda on the reform of the international financial regime.

The remaining three chapters in this section pick up many of these issues, and add new insights into the nature of financial globalisation and crises from different angles. John Williamson's chapter starts by reviewing the arguments, largely developed along neo-classical lines, for capital account liberalisation. It then focuses on the costs of opening capital accounts and integrating with international financial markets, particularly against the empirical evidence derived from recent financial crises in emerging market economies. The claimed benefits and costs of free capital mobility are also evaluated by drawing upon extant cross-national studies on the correlation between capital decontrols and economic growth. The chapter concludes by discussing national policy responses to problems of capital mobility and capital account liberalisation and the role of international institutions in reducing global financial instability.

Benjamin Cohen underscores the theoretical and empirical implications of Williamson's cost-benefit analysis of capital account liberalisation by exploring the political context of the debate about capital controls. Focusing on emerging market economies, he examines how policy debates have been recalibrated as a result of the Asian financial crisis, bringing renewed attention to the old case for capital controls. Despite the shift of opinion among economists and the evidence that capital controls can contribute to domestic financial stability, few governments have opted for this policy option. The principal reason, Cohen argues, has rested with the combined resistance of the US government, international investors and powerful domestic market players. He concludes by offering some suggestions on what might be done to mobilise wide political support for capital controls as a legitimate instrument of state policy.

Geoffrey Underhill and Xiaoke Zhang bring the first section to a close with an examination of the consequences of intensifying financial integration for democratic governance and for the maintenance of a well-functioning international economic system. They argue that increased financial globalisation has severely limited the ability of states to pursue economic and social policies in line with domestic preferences expressed through democratic processes, crucially altered the power balance between public authority and private interests strongly in favour of the latter, and generated pressures for the convergence of financial systems, corporate structures and development models towards market-oriented, neo-liberal practices. They suggest that if the erosion of state policy capacity, the growing dominance of private market interests and the convergence of financial and economic institutions conflict excessively with the imperatives of national security, with the mandates of democratically elected governments and with the requirements of domestic political stability, the process of global financial integration may be called into question or even unravel. These tensions focus our attention on the key issue of political legitimacy and democratic accountability as the real bottom line when it comes to normative underpinnings of the international financial order.

The second part of the volume looks at the interactions between transnational market forces and external political constraints on the one hand, and domestic policy changes before, during and after the recent financial crises on the other, in seven developed and emerging market economies. Country case studies expand on and substantiate the arguments and themes developed in the previous section, depicting national experiences with international financial volatility and examining the role of leading industrial nations and the Bretton Woods institutions in crisis management. Pasuk Phongpaichit and Chris Baker begin by making the case that the IMF-mandated policy reforms in post-crisis Thailand, which were based on the erroneous assessments of local conditions, had negative consequences for crisis management and economic recovery. In their view, the IMF's policy prescriptions had serious flaws because the Fund reflected unduly the interests of the US government and of global investors. The authors suggest that externally imposed policies can go awry when they come into collision with domestic political and economic arrangements, and that domestic policy initiatives and regional co-operation can be an alternative to greater IMF intrusion in national economic management.

Richard Robison presents a case study of the political economy of banking recapitalisation in Indonesia in the wake of the financial crisis. The underlying argument of his analysis is that recapitalisation, involving institutional transformations of central importance to a range of domestic-level state and societal actors, is driven by changes in the architecture of power and interests at the domestic level. Following a brief review of the causes of the banking crisis in Indonesia, Robison examines how the crisis and external pressures shifted the balance of power from the old corporate and political oligarchies towards the alliance between reformist technocrats and populist elements in the major political parties. The shift, he argues, helped to thrust banking recapitalisation and the corresponding reform of the regulatory system on to the policy agenda of the government. The author asserts that the changing configuration of domestic power relations and political interests continue to shape the future course of financial restructuring in Indonesia. Echoing the findings of Phongpaichit and Baker, Robison implies that there may be serious limits to the approach adopted by international organisations to structural reforms in crisis economies, which has given little attention to the constraints of distinctive domestic political structures.

Stephen Harris's account of the South Korean financial crisis is conducted at two interrelated levels of analysis. At the domestic level, the South Korean value systems, corporate practices, regulatory processes and policy-making rules were cast from authoritarian capitalism prior to the crisis, and were not compatible with the important features of South Korea's emergent democratic system. At the international and intergovernmental level, Harris observes that vigorous external demands for financial liberalisation and South Korean state elites' desire for membership of the Organisation for Economic Co-operation and Development (OECD) created strong pressures for policy changes along the neo-liberal lines. The resulting tensions between the lingering legacies of authoritarianism and pressures for market-oriented reforms led to severe governance problems and contributed directly to the outbreak of the financial crisis in South Korea. These observations reiterate the main messages derived from the previous two chapters and heighten the dire consequences of compatibility deficits.

The chapter by Vladimir Popov takes us from the financial turmoil in east Asia to the currency crises in Russia and other transition economies. It also focuses squarely on the problems of macroeconomic management in the context of global financial integration. Rejecting the validity of such conventional explanatory variables as regional contagion and domestic institutional weaknesses, he argues that the erroneous pursuit of an overvalued exchange rate on the part of the government constituted the single most important cause of the Russian currency collapse in August 1998. He reasons that the maintenance of the strong rouble stemmed from policy makers' desire to use exchange rate policy as a nominal anchor for domestic prices and as a redistributive instrument. In his analysis of the currency crises in the other transition economies, he comes to similar conclusions in terms of the causes and the main reasons behind them. Drawing on his major empirical findings, Popov suggests that future efforts to prevent currency and financial crises in developing and transition economies should focus on the avoidance of real exchange rate appreciation and on external debt controls.

The next two chapters look at the respective experiences with and policy responses to global financial integration and instability in India and China, which escaped the Asian crisis with only minor damage. Following a review of the evolution of the international payments regime and financial reform in India, Vijay Joshi argues that the prime reason for the country being spared in the Asian financial crisis was the presence of effective capital controls. This leads him to assert that India should not rush for premature capital account convertibility and external financial liberalisation. Underscoring the arguments of Williamson and Cohen in the previous section, Joshi concludes that capital controls can be made effective under certain economic and institutional conditions and that countries with weak financial and regulatory systems should be cautious with capital account liberalisation.

Shaun Breslin observes that political factors have determined the nature and process of financial reform in China. The reform, which entails the fundamental transformation of the state-planned political economy, has confronted the government with severe sociopolitical difficulties. Particularly difficult, as Breslin emphasises, are the negative impacts of reforms on: (a) the exercise of central controls over local authorities, and (b) the maintenance of employment levels and domestic political stability. These difficulties have tempered the speed and scale of financial reform and resulted in the foreign exchange and capital regime remaining restrictive in China. The author suggests that while restrictions on capital flows largely insulated China from the regional contagion, there may be a price China must pay for export-led growth and membership of the World Trade Organization (WTO). The combination of the further opening of the economy and crippling financial sector weakness associated with incomplete reform may render the country vulnerable to future external tremors.

The final chapter, by Masayuki Tadokoro, offers a detailed analysis of how domestic constraints in Japan and changing Japan–US relations affected Japanese and regional responses to the Asian financial crisis. He argues that domestic financial problems, institutional rigidities and weak leadership limited the ability of the Japanese government to respond effectively to the crisis and to co-operate with its American counterpart to contain the tremors as they rippled across the Asian region. Equally, the same set of economic and political impediments also prevented Japan from playing a leading role in establishing the regional mechanisms for policy co-ordination and crisis management, despite the heightened need for such mechanisms in the wake of the Asian crisis. Tadokoro concludes that the prospects for closer regional collaboration on financial issues are likely to be hopeful if Japan could sort out its domestic problems.

The third part of the volume focuses on the role of market actors and private–public interactions in domestic and international policy-making processes. More specifically, the three chapters in this section explore the extent to which private market actors and interests facilitate or impede the realisation of public policy objectives in the areas of financial reform and crisis management. Xiaoke Zhang and Geoffrey Underhill present a comparative study of how the growing influence of private interests over public policy and declining state capacity severely compromised the ability of governments effectively to implement market reforms and tackle mounting economic difficulties prior to the outbreak of the crisis in South Korea and Thailand. The resulting policy failures contributed to the profound loss of investor confidence and triggered massive currency depreciation in the two countries. Their analysis draws attention to the dangers of private capture. The ongoing reform of both state and market institutions should aim to ensure the predominance of public interests in the financial system.

Through a case study of accounting reform in Indonesia, Andrew Rosser illustrates how internationally driven pressures can affect the domestic balance of power between competing private and state interests in shaping financial policy. Conducting his analysis in historical perspective, Rosser explains the nature and direction of Indonesian accounting reform as a function of changes at the global and domestic levels, shifting the preferences and resources of the coalitions central to the policy-making process. He argues that although the financial crisis of 1997–8 helped both liberal state technocrats and those who controlled financial flows to thrust the issue of accounting reform on to the policy agenda, the enforcement of new standards was opposed by powerful corporate players and their political allies, who managed to retain direct control over the state apparatus. The author concludes by suggesting that the convergence of financial systems in developing countries towards neo-liberal models is likely to be a slow and uneven process, mainly because these systems are embedded in different national sociopolitical configurations of power and interests.

Finally, George Vojta and Marc Uzan look at the role of the private sector in the development of international standards for minimally acceptable practices in financial management and corporate governance. Starting from a general premise that public officials have been caught in a tide of transnational market changes beyond their effective capacity to monitor and regulate, Vojta and Uzan argue that private sector actors and institutions, which have played an increasingly important role in shaping market practices and rules, should be incorporated into the standard-setting process. Private-sector involvement, they caution, may have its own problems. These manifest themselves mainly in the difficulty of co-ordinating different private actors in public policy and, more important, the ongoing danger of public purposes being dominated by private interests in the financial sector. Reinforcing the arguments of the previous two chapters in this section, they contend that if global reform processes are to achieve their intended policy objectives, a politically sustainable balance between private power and public authority has to be maintained.

The fourth and final part of the volume examines the norms, institutions and forms of governance on which international public and private efforts at reforming the global financial regime can be built, and assesses the prospects for the current reform of international financial architecture. While different in analytical focus and approach, the three chapters in the section pay particular attention to the critical issues of how intergovernmental co-operative processes might overcome the growing tensions between persistent national diversity and global market integration and how international financial institutions can design more effective rules and institutions to ensure better economic governance and the stability of the global financial system.

Jean-Marc Coicaud and Luiz Pereira da Silva present a generic discussion of these questions. They observe that a lack of consistency in values and policies, client-based institutional cultures and a low level of institutionalisation at the global level have all weakened the legitimacy of international organisations in general and international financial institutions in particular. Coicaud and Pereira da Silva suggest that the solution to these problems rests with the efforts of international institutions to realign their organisational structures and resources with their mandates and policy goals and to institute and implement clearly defined values and norms around the principles of inclusiveness, responsibility and accountability. Failure to do so, the authors conclude, will impair the effectiveness of any future international co-operative endeavours to establish a fair and well-functioning financial order and will undermine their contribution towards the governance of global economic relations.

Andrew Baker focuses more specifically on the role and authority of the Group of Seven (G-7) finance ministers and central bankers in global economic governance and in the reform of the international financial regime. He develops an argument that links the policy co-operation among G-7 financial authorities to their shared belief system. He demonstrates that this belief system and the dominant position of the G-7 in the global political economy account for the limitations of the evolving official consensus on the redesign of the financial architecture. Baker emphasises that this consensus, which mainly reflects the values and preferences of leading industrial nations but ignores the interests of a wide range of developing economies, has failed to address the fundamental weaknesses of existing arrangements in the global monetary and financial system. In this sense, contemporary reform of global financial architecture was almost predestined to ignore many of the issues raised by the analyses presented in this volume.

Manmohan Kumar and Marcus Miller conclude the section with a detailed analysis of how innovations in legal and institutional arrangements governing the strategic relationship between the IMF and private sector actors might improve the effectiveness of debt restructuring, a key issue in the reform of the global financial architecture. They argue that international financial architecture should be adapted to a role regularly played by public authorities in national policy-making settings. The aim is to increase the responsibility of private sector actors and institutions in crisis management through standstill and bail-in devices that can reduce the need for official support and lead to enhanced private involvement. Changing the rules of this strategic dimension of the financial architecture involves the significant strengthening of the role of international public authorities in governing the global financial system.

The conclusion summarises the major empirical findings of the volume and draws explicit attention to their implications for current international efforts to reform global financial architecture. Focusing on the six sets of conceptual and policy issues addressed in the various chapters, the conclusion argues, first, that capital controls and the consistent application of standards in financial and corporate management can provide emerging market governments with workable policy instruments to deal with market volatility. In implementing these instruments, policy makers should consider not only technical complexity but, more importantly, political feasibility and compatibility with local practices. Second, there has emerged a consensus in the volume that while the convergence of financial systems and development models may be taking place in the global economy, differences among national economic institutions and market systems are likely to persist. This implies, third, that international co-operation will continue to be difficult, and that the regional solution is perhaps a more effective alternative for managing the global monetary and financial system.

Fourth, the various contributors to the volume concur that the private sector is crucial to financial policy making and needs to be integrated into the process of crisis prevention and management. But they also emphasise that market actors can make a positive contribution towards the realisation of public policy objectives only when there is a proper balance between private power and public authority in the domain of global monetary and financial governance. Fifth, the volume emphasises that there are close and extensive linkages between regulatory changes on the one hand and supervisory and macroeconomic policies on the other. Financial architecture reform must avoid fragmenting these micro–macro linkages if important socioeconomic policy objectives are to be achieved. And finally, it is made clear in the volume that financial globalisation has enormous costs as well as benefits, with important distributional ramifications for a wide range of societal groups at national and international levels. This suggests a significant normative dimension to financial policy making, and failure to address this dimension is most likely to lead to the loss of legitimacy of global markets as a form of governance.

The empirical findings that emerge from this volume have crucial implications for current efforts to redesign the international financial architecture. These findings suggest that such efforts can stand a good chance of success if they take into account the tension between the harmonising pressures of global market integration versus the continued diversity of national financial and economic systems and if they aim to resolve the strains generated by ever increasing capital mobility in various domestic and international sociopolitical arenas. These tensions, however, have received little attention in the prevailing consensus on the reform of the global financial regime among the leading economic powers and international institutions. Despite the growing gravity of financial crises, the proposed reforms have failed to address many of the fundamental weaknesses of existing financial arrangements that threaten the world economy and therefore have not represented any significant transformation of the ways in which international financial relations are governed.

Notes

1. See Irma Adelman, 'Editor's Introduction', *World Development*, vol. 28, no. 6 (2000), p. 1053.
2. Book-length treatment of the Asian financial crisis which emphasises macroeconomic policy errors and structural weaknesses as the main causal factors can be found in: Pierre-Richard Agenor, Marcus Miller, David Vines and Axel Weber (eds.), *The Asian Financial Crisis: Causes, Contagion and Consequences* (Cambridge: Cambridge University Press, 1999); Martin Feldstein (ed.), *Economic and Financial Crises in Emerging Market Economies* (Chicago: University of Chicago Press, 2001); Tran Van Hoa and Charles Harvie (eds.), *The Causes and Impact of the Asian Financial Crisis* (London: Macmillan, 2000); Ross H. Mcleod and Ross Garnaut (eds.), *East Asia in Crisis: From Being a Miracle to Needing One?* (London: Routledge, 1998). The political and institutional analyses of the financial crisis are exemplified by T. J. Pempel (ed.), *The Politics of the Asian Economic Crisis* (Ithaca: Cornell University

Press, 1999); Richard Robison, Mark Beeson, Kanishka Jayasuriya and Hyuk-Rae Kim (eds.), *Politics and Markets in the Wake of the Asian Crisis* (London: Routledge, 2000).

3. See note 2. See also Stephan Haggard, *The Political Economy of the Asian Financial Crisis* (Washington, DC: Institute for International Economics, 2000); Gregory W. Noble and John Ravenhill, *The Asian Financial Crisis and the Architecture of Global Finance* (Cambridge: Cambridge University Press, 2000). One of the few studies that examines financial crises in a wider range of developing and emerging market economies is Miles Kahler (ed.), *Capital Flows and Financial Crises* (Ithaca: Cornell University Press, 1998).

4. The importance of self-protection, as opposed to the dependence on external assistance and architectural reform, is emphasised in Kenneth Kletzer and Ashoka Mody, 'Will Self-protection Policies Safeguard Emerging Markets from Crises?' SCCIE Working Paper 99–10 (Santa Cruz: Santa Cruz Centre for International Economics, University of California, 2000).

5. For general discussions on these policy issues, see Chapter 2 by Williamson and Chapter 3 by Cohen in this volume. National experiences with macroeconomic policy management and structural reforms are discussed more systematically in Chapter 6 by Robison, Chapter 8 by Popov, Chapter 9 by Joshi, and Chapter 13 by Rosser in this volume.

6. The point is discussed at length in Richard Higgott and Nicola Phillips, 'Challenging Triumphalism and Convergence: the Limits of Global Liberalisation in Asia and Latin America', *Review of International Studies*, vol. 26, no. 3 (2000), pp. 359–79; Louis Pauly, 'National Financial Structures, Capital Mobility, and International Economic Rules: the Normative Consequences of East Asian, European and American Distinctiveness', *Policy Sciences*, vol. 27, no. 4 (1994), pp. 343–63; Geoffrey Underhill, 'Transnational Financial Markets and National Economic Development Models: Global Structures versus Domestic Imperatives', in *Économies et Sociétés*, Série 'Monnaie', ME, n° 1–2, 9–10 (1999), pp. 37–68.

7. See International Monetary Fund, *International Capital Markets: Developments, Prospects and Key Policy Issues* (Washington, DC: IMF, 1998); *Toward A Framework for Financial Stability* (Washington, DC: IMF, 1998).

8. See Chapter 4 by Underhill and Zhang, Chapter 5 by Phongpaichit and Baker, and Chapter 13 by Rosser in this volume. See also Miles Kahler, 'The New International Financial Architecture and its Limits', in Noble and Ravenhill, *The Asian Financial Crisis*; Dani Rodrik 'Governing the Global Economy: Does One Architectural Style Fit All?' paper presented to the Brookings Institution Trade Policy Forum conference on Governing in a Global Economy, Washington, DC, 15–16 April 1999.

9. The issue is discussed in a more detailed manner in Chapter 5 by Phongpaichit and Baker and Chapter 11 by Tadokoro.

10. Useful and stimulating discussions of private-sector involvement in crisis prevention and management can be found in William R. Cline, 'The Role of the Private Sector in Resolving Financial Crises in Emerging Markets', in Feldstein, *Economic and Financial Crises*; Barry Eichengreen, *Toward a New International Financial Architecture: A Practical Post-Asia Agenda* (Washington, DC: Institute for International Economics, 1999), esp. ch. 5.

11. See Chapter 12 by Zhang and Underhill in this volume; Stephan Haggard, 'Governance and Growth: Lessons from the Asian Economic Crisis', *Asian–Pacific Economic Literature*, vol. 13, no. 2 (1999), pp. 30–42; *The Political Economy*, esp. ch. 1. For a more general and theoretically oriented discussion of this issue see Geoffrey Underhill, 'The Public Good versus Private Interests in the Global Financial and Monetary System', *International Comparative and Corporate Law Journal*, vol. 2, no. 3 (2001), pp. 335–59.

12. See Chapter 4 by Underhill and Zhang in this volume; these issues are also discussed more systematically in Geoffrey Underhill, 'Keeping Governments out of Politics', *Review of International Studies*, vol. 21, no. 3 (1995), pp. 251–78; 'Private Markets and Public Responsibility', in Underhill (ed.), *The New World Order in International Finance* (London: Macmillan, 1997), pp. 17–49.

13. The point is discussed at length in Chapter 4 by Underhill and Zhang, Chapter 15 by Coicaud and Pereira da Silva, and Chapter 16 by Baker in this volume.

Part I

Financial globalisation and policy responses: concepts and arguments

1 Reform of the international financial architecture: what has been written?

JONATHAN STORY

The financial crises of the 1990s, following two decades of financial market liberalisation and ever growing capital flows, have prompted a passionate debate about 'globalisation' as the successor world system to the Cold War. The background to these crises is a story well told, stretching from the breakdown in the Bretton Woods system in the 1960s, the confirmation of the dollar as the world's reserve and transaction currency, the recycling of funds following the rise in oil prices, and the expansion of the financial marketplaces in London and New York. This in turn prompted a scramble among developed countries to open their securities markets to institutional investors, who demanded the liberalisation of capital controls as the price for their presence. Liberalisation of capital movements then spread to developing countries.[1] Initially, resistance was loud, but as time passed and US hegemony became entrenched, even major financial meltdowns – such as the devaluations of the Italian lira and pound sterling in 1992, or the collapse of the Mexican peso in late 1994 – attracted only temporary attention. By the mid-1990s, confidence in dominant policy prescriptions reigned supreme. Asia's financial crash therefore came as a shock, the equivalent for economists of the Soviet Union's collapse for sovietologists, all the more severe in that it was unpredicted and its severity unanticipated. The crisis started with the devaluation of the Thai baht in July 1997, spread to Indonesia where General Suharto's regime was coming to a close and ricocheted into Taiwan, South Korea and Malaysia before spreading to Brazil, South Africa and then Russia.

Unlike previous meltdowns, this chain of events revived a long-dormant debate on the world's financial architecture, conducted this time principally among economists, and mainly in the United States. It therefore tended to be skewed in that politics – domestic or international – was given a back seat, or granted a walk-on role to provide light relief to a supposedly technical problem. It also meant that US opinions weighed disproportionately in the balance, seeming to reinforce the view of the post-Cold War decades as representing a unipolar moment in world affairs. Caricaturing only slightly, reform of the world financial

Table 1. *Perspectives on globalisation.*

	State system	Norms of state governance	World markets	MNCs and host countries
Liberals				
Social democrats				
Prophets				
Realists				

system was presented as a choice between more government or more market. Joe Stiglitz, the World Bank's chief economist, in one corner challenged the IMF's emphasis on the benefits of open capital movements for developing countries, and favoured Asian states' insistence on a central role for government, notably in the regulation and supervision of financial markets;[2] US Treasury Secretary Larry Summers in the opposing corner favoured open world capital markets, and argued for an ever more modest role for the IMF as developing countries' needs were met by the continued expansion of world capital markets. The IMF could not expect, he maintained, 'its financial capacity to grow in parallel with the growth of private sector capital flows'.[3]

This chapter seeks to place the debate in a wider setting. The first section presents a matrix to enable us to judge what the various explanations in the US-centred debate included and what they omitted. The second section presents the main arguments deployed in the debate as to the causes of the crisis, the criticisms about policies, and the suggestions advanced for improvements. The third section uses the matrix to illustrate how this debate is located within a rather narrow ideological spectrum and excludes, ignores or side-tracks the insights derived from other perspectives. All of these perspectives raise questions about the legitimacy of states which fail to master financial market flows and the legitimacy of the international financial system, which regularly confronts states with policy dilemmas which only a few can readily deal with.

Differing perspectives on the globalisation debate

This section presents a matrix (see Table 1), the horizontal axis of which presents four elements of the world's transformation, while the vertical axis presents different lenses through which the phenomenon of 'globalisation' is discussed. The four elements of the world's great transformation, whose formative features became visible sometime in the course of the 1970s, are predicated on Karl Polanyi's famous stylisation of the nineteenth-century world as shaped by four institutions – free trade, representative government, the gold standard and the balance of power among states.[4] In the twentieth century, states have shaped and channelled markets, in contrast to the state-imposed primacy of markets depicted in Polanyi's nineteenth century. It is pluralistic politics understood as the association of two or more wills in pursuit of common purposes that drives the world economy,[5] and not abstract 'market forces' which dictate circumstances.[6]

The first institution of the world economy is the state system. Fragmentation and hierarchy are its two central features: the Soviet Union's collapse in 1991 furthered the fragmentation of the world market space and terminated the unequal bipolar structure characteristic of the years following the end of the Second World War. In the post-Cold War world, the United States is clearly the world's leading power,[7] with a galaxy of policy instruments which were harnessed in the 1990s to keep the motor of world capitalism running, through a liberal policy of open markets and 'enlargement' of the area of Western influence to cover the globe.

The second institution is the unit of the system, the state. By the 1990s, Western norms of governance, predicated on the necessary distinction between the sphere of public power and policy and the private domain of individual conscience and rights,[8] faced no major challenge. Both communism and military dictatorships were discredited.[9] Islamic states were experimenting with theocracy, but the example of Iran, Afghanistan or Pakistan was not particularly attractive. The only serious remaining alternative was the Asian developmental state,[10] where government's role was to help chart a development course, and fashion 'an institutional framework for non-ideological and effective policy implementation'.[11]

A third institution is world markets. The rapid expansion in the scope of world business, underpinned by an integrated, around-the-clock global financial market, has resulted in an allocation of world savings to end uses on a truly international scale.[12] Developing countries were eager to tap these markets in order to finance the balance of payments, to make local capital markets more liquid or to accelerate the build-up of their productive capacity. But investors attached conditions such as 'no investment without regime change', 'no funds without structural adjustment' or 'no major investment flows without freedom of capital movements'. World financial markets could not impose policies on sovereigns who refused to comply, but they could make the cost of non-compliance very high.

The fourth institution is the multinational corporation and its relations to home or host governments. Foreign direct investment (FDI) replaced aid and credit in the 1990s as Western corporations adopted global strategies. These entailed integrated production and marketing strategies intended to reconcile the contradictory exigencies of competition in world markets, and the need to be responsive to local conditions.[13] Countries working their way up the value-added chain competed to have their own firms integrated into the networks of strategic accords between corporations, seeking to share the costs and know-how required to supply markets driven by fast-changing technologies and consumer demands.

The horizontal axis presents four different perspectives or strands in the debate about how to interpret the world beyond communism – liberal, social democrat, apocalyptic, realist. Capitalism's predominance in the 1990s left the world looking two ways: back to pre-1914 and forward to the twenty-first century. Pre-1914 seemed in many respects a golden age of civilisation, cut short and wrenched from its path by war and revolution. Was the world heading forward to a renewal of the golden age, or towards the disasters which overcame it in the past? The Asian financial crash, its aftermath and the 11 September 2001 attacks on the World Trade Center buildings in New York and the US Department of Defense in Washington, served as reminders of how integrated and how vulnerable we have become.

Classical liberals consider that trade and specialisation along the principle of comparative advantage have always led to growth, not to underdevelopment.[14] As world markets develop, a universal brotherhood emerges, binding peoples together through a web of private property rights, governed by private law, and relying on tradition and trust. Classical liberalism advocates limited government intervention on the grounds not of efficiency, but of government's clumsy inability to understand the coherence of market phenomena. An international order is perfectly compatible with an international political system of nation states, as it is built from the bottom up, on the basis of domestic national orders.[15]

Neo-liberals, like social democrats, share assumptions from welfare economics regarding market failures, which are to be corrected by government intervention. For them, a world market does not emerge spontaneously, but has to be organised 'from above', through government co-operation and through international institutions. Ultimately, a global public interest is best served by an elite of nationally rooted civil servants working together in international organisations, governments and non-governmental organisations for the good of 'the international community'.[16]

Social democrats concur that we are still in an international economy, predicated on the distinction between the world external to the state's territorial authority, and its internal realm.[17] Because states have forged different social compromises over time,[18] the workings of international markets challenge social stability,[19] which in turn may prompt beggar-my-neighbour policies.[20] Intra-national responses to social conflicts thus engender international tensions, which can only be resolved through co-operation and policy co-ordination among governments in international regimes.[21] The global 'competition system' which results is thus a negotiated construct, which reflects the institutional arrangements – national, regional or global – from which they emerged.[22] Governance in this global economy is necessarily multi-tiered, as in the Middle Ages, where nation states are one class of power in a complex system of power from world to local levels.

Apocalyptic perspectives assume a world where national economies are subsumed in global processes.[23] In particular, free capital movements have created a border-less world economy,[24] where states are less and less able to decide on behalf of their citizens.[25] The result is that power over outcomes is exercised by impersonal markets, and by those who deal in markets and often in disregard of states.[26] The 'manic logic'[27] of global capitalism makes the dreams of the European Union (EU) of continental social democracy untenable,[28] generates 'a race to the bottom' in labour and environmental standards, destroys local cultures [29] or attacks democracy and the welfare state.[30] Politics revives in such a world as the handmaiden of religion, through the delegation of legitimacy from existing states to smaller regions, or through the creation of continental Leviathans – the way of the EU.

Realists maintain that global capitalism is the instrument of the Western powers. Currencies are state-produced commodities, and replicate the hierarchy of the state system.[31] It follows that the world economy has origins and outcomes that are political.[32] In particular, the United States holds structural power, 'the power to shape and determine the structures of the global political economy within which other states, their political institutions, their economic enterprises and (not least) their scientists and other professional people have to operate'.[33]

This matrix of elements and perspectives yields sixteen categories enabling us to judge what the debate among economists in the United States included and left out in terms of possible combinatory explanations of causes, critiques and suggestions with regard to the east Asian crisis. Before exploring these possible combinations, let us present the broad themes present in the US-centred debate.

Causes, critiques, suggestions

This section presents the main arguments deployed in the US-centred debate among economists about the Asian crash debate as to the causes of the crisis, the criticisms of policies and the suggestions advanced for improvements. The debate was conducted with verve, but also with a clear recognition among the more sober-minded participants of the problems confronting reformers. Barry Eichengreen provides a sophisticated rationale for his adopting such a position of 'robust incrementalism': liberalised capital markets are beneficial and as good as irreversible; information asymmetries are unavoidable in financial markets between borrowers and lenders, so the price mechanism cannot be relied on to restore equilibrium, while governments cannot be assumed to provide sound data; given this instability, some form of safety net has to be in place; domestically, the authority exists to police financial markets, but this is not the case internationally; finally, economic policy is framed in a politicised environment, so that the IMF cannot be expected to follow apolitical rules. As Eichengreen writes: 'I stake out a middle ground between the overly ambitious and politically unrealistic schemes of independent commentators and the excessively timid and ambiguous reports of international bodies and organisations.'[34] That middle ground may be located metaphorically somewhere within the triangle, described by Treasury Secretary Summers as the global 'integration trilemma', whereby the central task of international political economy is defined as the task of reconciling the three goals of greater integration, good public management and national sovereignty.

A common theme in the US debate among economists is that the east Asian crisis came as a bolt from the blue: in the words of Morris Goldstein, the fall of the baht in June 1997 served as a 'wake-up call'.[35] Liberalisation of capital account had provided access for many east Asian countries to global capital markets, while fixing exchange rates to the dollar seemed to ensure long-term stability. Decades of vibrant economic growth attested to sound policies in the past, and the upbeat message about east Asia's performance continued through the early months of the crisis: the World Bank published its yearly *Global Economic Prospects*;[36] and the Organisation for Economic Co-operation and Development (OECD) also brought out a special report, *The World in 2020*, where the 'Big Five' emerging markets – Russia, China, India, Brazil, Indonesia – were forecast as assuming an ever greater weight in the world economy. As late as November 1997, US President Bill Clinton referred to 'a few small glitches on the road'.

It was only with the collapse of the South Korean won that winter, and the sharp deterioration in Indonesia's situation, that the severity of the crisis became evident. Thereafter, the 'international financial community', already cogitating since the Halifax summit of 1995 following the Mexican peso crash of late 1994, returned to their collective pen. A flood of reports ensued:[37] the G-7 finance ministers and central bankers issued a special statement about strengthening international financial institutions (IFIs);[38] the Group of 22 (G-22) – an ad hoc group set up by the United States and including a number of emerging market countries – produced a definitive statement in the form of three studies on strengthening the international financial architecture.[39] The UN Economic and Social Affairs Committee chipped in,[40] as did the Bank of International Settlements. The whole was crowned by a report for the Cologne summit of June 1999 by the G-7 finance ministers. The Asian Development Bank also had its say on the matter.[41] Finally, the Washington-based Institute for International Economics produced two key studies, one more on the causes and cures of the

Asian financial crisis,[42] and the other proposing a 'practical post-Asia agenda' for cautious steps to a new international financial architecture.[43] The Council on Foreign Relations produced the findings of its own task force.[44] Unfortunately, as Peter Kenen wrote, all of this activity demonstrated that 'it has proven easier to draft codes than to find ways of inducing adherence to them'.[45]

The first question which all these studies sought to address was: what were the causes of the Asian crash of 1997–8? There were broadly speaking two interpretations: the internalist argument focused on 'crony capitalism',[46] and the externalist argument focused on the workings of the international financial markets. This distinction between the domestic and international arenas, familiar to the literature of international relations, was accompanied by a propensity to allocate cronyism to the domestic realm and rational capital markets to the international arena. The ultimate cause of the collapse was seen as lying in the close connections established within the states between politics and bank-centred financial systems. The states provided implicit guarantees to banks, encouraging the banks to lend to corporations with good political contacts. As capital controls were eased, foreign creditors lent to the banks and credit exploded, despite multiple warning signals ahead of June 1997. Externally, the inflow of capital to the east Asian countries was stimulated by the near-zero interest rates prevailing in a moribund Japan, and by continued investor pessimism about business prospects in Europe. Consumption and imports boomed, just as volume export growth plummeted. With China's accelerated move into world markets, foreign investors switched their attention to opportunities on the mainland, so that east Asian balance of payments' dependence on short-term capital flows increased. When the Thai 'wake-up call' came, alerted investors withdrew in haste from one currency after another.

While the 'crony capitalism' thesis won broad acceptance, there were nonetheless dissenting voices, arguing that information asymmetries were unavoidable in financial markets between borrowers and lenders, and particularly in the international arena where there was no authority to police markets. As Stiglitz pointed out, 'some of the countries with the weakest financial sectors, the greatest lack of transparency, and the most corrupt political structures were hardly touched by the contagion from East Asia'.[47] If that was the case, then the question could not be evaded as to why global financial markets had failed on such an epic scale. George Soros identified investor infatuation with the prospects in east Asia as the source of unsustainable market conditions,[48] as advanced industrial-country banks lent to hedge funds and engaged in proprietary trading on their own account in the currency markets.[49] Another explanation was that governments provided misleading information, and that this was relayed by 'experts' in the global media talking in closed circuit to each other.[50] Given such chronic mis- or disinformation, the only viable policy principle for market participants was *caveat emptor*.[51] Stiglitz's preferred explanation was that markets were driven by an 'instability of beliefs' to switch from optimism to pessimism. Such a switch in mood created a contagion of chain reactions as investors withdrew from the region. It was not clear why the 'instability of beliefs' should have been manifest over the Thai baht in early June, and not at a different time, with different results.

The second question which all these studies sought to address was: what went wrong in terms of policy responses to the crisis? As Eichengreen has pointed out, the Achilles heel of the international financial system is cross-border interbank funding. In emerging markets, foreign investors tend to assume that their loans are covered by government guarantees. Governments can thus be faced with the choice either of validating such expectations or risking serious disruptions to their payments systems, and perhaps to the financial system as a whole. Their crude choice is either to extend ever bigger bail-outs as one country after another threatens to suspend payments or to allow nature to run its course. This lack of choice in the international financial system was compounded, many of the critics maintained, by policy dilemmas in response to the Asian meltdown or at worst by policy errors.

The main critique directed at the IMF was its insistence that the afflicted countries adopt tight monetary policies, on the grounds that lower interest rates would precipitate a currency collapse, prompting a surge in foreign-currency-denominated debt. But high interest rates condemned highly geared east Asian corporations to bankruptcy as growth ground to a halt, and overvalued exchange rates kept exports languishing.[52] Critics also maintained that the situation was worsened by IMF requests for fiscal tightening – despite the fact that east Asian governments ran tight fiscal policies – so that there would be adequate revenues to finance bank bail-outs. IMF closure of what it considered to be dead banks ignored the fact that the fraction of banking systems in developing countries with dead loans tends to be high, given limited technical, legal and institutional capabilities. The measures also panicked the public, notably in the case of South Korea and Indonesia. Finally, critics argued that the IMF became too deeply engaged in the domestic affairs of states,[53] for which it lacked the necessary expertise. The IMF also intervened to ensure that a balance was struck between a bail-out of investors to limit the damage to confidence in international financial markets and a work-out in the afflicted countries to reconcile the twin requirements of financial viability and political stability.

The third question which these studies sought to address was: what suggestions followed from these critiques for strengthening the 'international financial architecture'? Five critical areas were identified for the working of the international financial system.

First, when and if capital accounts are liberalised, countries become more prone to financial crisis unless market opening is accompanied by adequate supervision and regulation of financial intermediaries. This observation prompted proposals whereby individual states would be justified in closing capital flows in order to offset panics.[54] But capital controls entail a number of penalties, the most obvious of which is that companies seek to keep funds abroad by over-invoicing their shipments into the country, and under-invoicing their exports. Countries are restricted in their access to the huge pool of world savings. If liberalisation is undertaken, the lesson is that the measures should be carefully sequenced to allow strengthening of financial supervision, and for an upgrading of financial practice within the country. A variety of proposals was made also to 'cool the casino', to 'throw sand in the wheels of international finance'.[55] Possibly the best known of these measures is the 'Tobin tax' on foreign exchange transactions. But a Tobin tax is readily avoidable, as currency traders can relabel transactions, or move operations to tax-free jurisdictions. In general, the main lesson on capital controls from the east Asian experience and the subsequent currency upheavals is a modest recognition that macroeconomic policies, capital controls and prudential measures all have a role to play in achieving the widely shared objective of limiting macroeconomic and financial instability.[56]

Second, one key reason for financial crises was identified as exchange rate collapses linked to bad banking, due to under-capitalisation of banks, poor supervision and mismatches between loan maturities and currency exposures.[57] Hence, there was general support for worldwide improvement in regulatory standards but no accord on how to implement them effectively. For instance, the 1988 Basel Capital Accords were designed in part to provide an international standard for assessing risks, but they dated fast as hedge funds developed derivatives and a variety of new instruments to mitigate or to displace the burden of risk. The accords may also have encouraged short-term lending to emerging countries, as the risk weightings are lower for short-term loans. The G-22 therefore recommended that the IMF issue a transparency report along with Article IV assessment of country situations. The requirement for transparency flowed from the circulation of inadequate information. Once the true situation was revealed, investors panicked. But, as has been pointed out, 'In East Asia, much of the important information was available, but it had not been integrated into the assessment of the market.'[58]

Third, flexible exchange rates were identified as preferable to fixed or pegged exchange rates, because they provide greater autonomy for the government in managing an open economy. But there was no clear consensus on exchange rate regimes, other than that they should be re-thought. The hardline argument in favour of flexible exchange rates held that it was the external counterpart to good housekeeping: flexible rates are one aspect of a broader self-help policy, the keys to which are access to substantial international liquidity through the accumulation of foreign exchange reserves and ready access to loans on the international markets.[59] But no country is exempt from contagion, so these externally oriented policies have to be supplemented by measures to improve the functioning of domestic markets. Others were clearly sceptical that emerging market governments could effectively implement such a sophisticated policy, particularly in view of the gyrations in the foreign exchange markets between the main currencies. Their preference may go to the 'joint management of exchange rates' by the governments of the major industrialised countries, as a step to bringing economic policies more in line.[60] That would require strengthening the G-7 system, in order to determine the rates between the currencies. UK Chancellor of the Exchequer Gordon Brown put his oar in with a proposal for a new permanent Standing Committee for Global Financial Regulation bringing together the IMF, the World Bank, the Basel Committee and other regulatory groups. [61]

Fourth, there was a plethora of proposals regarding the IMF's role. One is to abolish it, as each time it bails out creditors after a currency run, they rush back to lend even more.[62] A more moderate proposal was for the IMF to focus more on debt restructuring or standard setting.[63] But as Eichengreen points out, it is still required to act as a brake against meltdown. Clinton came up with the opportunistic idea of creating a contingency fund, 'anchored in the IMF', implying that at each disaster a new 'contingency fund' be placed on call. A further idea was for the IMF to lend only to those countries that signed up to tough loan conditions.[64] But this would create the equivalent of a junk-bond market for defaulters, attractive to those eager to live in exciting times.

Fifth, there was also a plethora of suggestions for regulating the global market for credit. One of the main novelties of the 1990s crises was the multiplication of private credit and debt lines, as state debt became less significant. Steps had been taken by the Group of Ten (G-10) in 1996 to allow for more collective organisation of sovereign liquidity crises. The foundations had been laid by the Brady Plan to deal with the debt overhangs from the 1980s Latin American crises, and to 'bail in the private sector'. But incentives and threats were not sufficient to make individual institutions develop a sense of collective responsibility, so that further appetisers were advanced. One idea was to create an international bankruptcy court, with powers similar to those embodied in US legislation, enabling it to impose a stay on payments and enable the debtor to continue to borrow pending judgement.[65] Even more attention-catching proposals were those for a world financial regulator,[66] a world central bank, or an international authority to insure investors against debt defaults.[67] More modestly, Martin Goldstein argues for actions discouraging private sector borrowers from mismatching their currency liabilities and assets.[68]

The debate about the east Asian crisis, its causes, consequences and suggestions, may be simply summarised: the distinction between the domestic and international arenas was maintained, but it was not clear why some and not other crony-ridden countries were affected in different ways and at different times; why the 'instability of beliefs' should have been manifest over the Thai baht in early June, and not at a different time, with different results; or whether governments should or could simultaneously guarantee their banking systems and end capital controls. There was a widely shared assumption that the IMF committed policy errors and displayed ignorance about the specific features of the east Asian economies. The suggestions flowing from this analysis were necessarily modest: most significant was the key insight that a diverse world could not have rigid rules and regulations applied uniformly.[69]

The implication was that one challenge of global governance was to set broad parameters of policy to allow for diverse policy capabilities around the world. It follows that there was no panacea or magic wand to be waved, but rather diverse conditions of transparency, financial systems and corporate governance,[70] and different regimes for exchange rates, depending on circumstances. Barry Eichengreen concluded that the slow and painful efforts at extending international standards to areas beyond the strictly monetary amounted to 'a very significant development affecting the structure and stability of the international business system'.[71] Not least, the crop of reform proposals served as a reminder that it was relatively easier to advance a proposal to reform institutions than to analyse the politics of international finance. To this we shall now turn.

What has not been written

The conclusion about what has/has not been written about emerges clearly from the matrix. The US-centred debate among economists falls within the neo-liberal and social democrat perspectives, and covers only partial aspects of our four elements. Let us follow the middle ground between the liberal and social democrat perspectives down the elements on the vertical axis, and start with the state system. We can then briefly point out the possibilities for a much wider research agenda regarding reform of the international financial architecture, by making explicit the varied assumptions ventilated in the debate, and thereby to do them justice.

The first conclusion to draw is of a pervasive neo-liberal optimism about the beneficial workings of international organisations and regimes, combined with a social democrat twinge of anxiety that global capitalism may not be readily tamed. The US-centred debate among economists abounds in critiques of IMF policies on interest rates, taxation and the trade-offs between bail-out and work-outs, and makes suggestions – mostly inconclusive – to the effect that policy reforms and moves to capital liberalisation should be carefully sequenced; that transparency is desirable, but not a panacea; that flexible exchange rate regimes are nonetheless vulnerable to contagion; that the IMF's role should be reconsidered; and that perhaps something should be done to regulate global credit. While a plethora of eye-catching proposals was advanced to create a new crop of agencies, more serious people suggested improvements in the functioning of the existing set of institutions. This moderation derives from a sensitivity, notable in Eichengreen, that government failures abound in economic policy, that the fragmented state system ensures that there is no single authority to police financial markets, and that economic policy is framed in a politicised environment, so that the IMF cannot be expected to follow apolitical rules.

The second conclusion is that the debate clearly labels the east Asian states as 'crony capitalists' and cronyism as a major explanation of the meltdown. This is surprising, since prior to June 1997 the east Asian governments had been held up as exemplars of state developmentalism, with an excellent track record in terms of economic performance. Perhaps it is less surprising in view of the US preference for a clear separation between the domains of public power and the private sphere: the crony thesis clearly suggests that failure to separate public policy from private gain can have serious implications for government legitimacy, financial stability and corporate profitability. On the other hand, both neo-liberal and social democrat perspectives accept that government intervention in national markets is the result of negotiated compromises among key participants in an ongoing policy process. Indeed, cronyism in this perspective is not a peculiarity of east Asia, but is the norm of all states. As Jagdish Bhagwati has pointed out with regard to US elites, 'a dense network of like-minded luminaries among the powerful institutions – Wall Street, the Treasury Department, the State Department, the IMF, and the World Bank most prominent among them', have hi-jacked the argument in favour of free trade markets and applied it to promote free capital mobility everywhere.[72]

What was being criticised in east Asia presumably, then, was that Asian norms of governance, previously predicated on narrow insider elites (crony capitalists, for the abusive), should provide better, more reliable information faster. They should practise transparency in decision-making, and develop greater accountability as their economies became more interdependent with the rest of the world. If, on the other hand, the source of the problem lay in the BosWash (Boston–Washington) elites, then the very talk of governance, transparency, accountability was the export of the world's rulers to the barbarian tribes on the periphery of empire.

The third conclusion is that the US-centred debate among economists isolates global financial market failure as a major cause of the Asian meltdown. Growing domestic–external imbalances have accompanied the opening of trade and capital accounts. Because financial markets are imperfect, at any moment an 'instability of beliefs' can switch market moods abruptly between optimism and pessimism. Co-operation between states in international regimes is vital, but not foolproof, as the east Asian crisis indicates. Suggestions for action to avoid such events in the future are allocated to governments or to international organisations. One source of embarrassment is that if global markets are capable of failure on such a grand scale, by what right are they judge and jury over the lives of millions of people? Malaysian Prime Minister Mahathir Mohamed's answer in August 1998 was that world markets do not have the right; states have the right to impose, or to raise, capital controls regardless of what world financial markets' reactions might be. Another source of embarrassment is that the incentives for developing country governments in the future to follow Western demands on countries seeking access to global markets are not strengthened when the IMF is lampooned for the advice it gave in the east Asian crisis.

Beyond that, the US-centred debate leaves great voids in the matrix whether in terms of causes, critiques or recommendations about the east Asian crisis. Let us briefly review some of the gaps by looking, for instance, at three of our elements and tracing them across the perspectives, to see what different angles they highlight.

In terms of the state system, let us start with the classical liberal perspective. The world's political fragmentation is a problem in two ways: it complicates the functioning of international payments, and makes it less likely that all governments agree on what constitutes good policy. There will therefore be international frictions which international organisations can help to treat, but responsibility for the good functioning of the system falls to the states at the top of the world hierarchy. Hence, a classical liberal study would definitely incorporate a careful analysis of US and Japanese global and domestic financial policy contributions to the east Asia meltdown. By contrast, a neo-liberal perspective would place more emphasis on the absence of an overarching financial market regime throughout the region. The neo-liberal position postulates that the fragmented state system requires inter-state co-operation in international institutions and regimes. The way world markets operate will reflect how well or poorly these international regimes operate. This position is duplicated in the social democrat perspective, with more emphasis placed on the interplay through regimes and markets of domestic structures and preferences: in the east Asia case, for instance, a careful analysis of Japanese financial market reform would show that the failure to reform was one major contributing factor to the flow of Japanese funds into Indonesian rupiahs at the height of the Indonesian boom in early 1997. There would also be an emphasis on highly active 'non-governmental organisations' to promote labour standards, to protect the environment, or to promote local cultures against the new imperialism of the Western media. These, too, played a significant part in the east Asian crash, but barely received a mention in the debate.

The prophets of apocalypse, by contrast, see the world system as driven by an economic process detached from its political roots. Rootless multinational corporations, cosmopolitan financial forces, and elites in Anglo-Saxon countries are the winners. The east Asian crash would be an ideal case study to test these hypotheses; after all, multinational corporations had flooded into east

Asian countries in preceding decades. What did they, or did they not, contribute to the Asian meltdown? Was the fast money 'cosmopolitan', or was it mainly local money rushing for the exits? and were those old enemies of Hitler's and Stalin's orphans, the 'Anglo-Saxons', benefiting by the crash? Definitely, with the voices of apocalypse loud indeed in the EU (Forrester), in the United States (Buchanan), in Japan (Ishihara), and indeed in Saudi Arabia as has become evident since the 11 September 2001 dual attack on the symbols of 'Anglo-Saxon' power – here are the sources of reaction to liberalisation, anticipated by Polanyi. Finally, the realist position would start from the observation that the world financial system is unipolar, that the euro and the yen are eventual challengers, and that therefore the Asian crash is worth studying to identify how this struggle was played out there. US Treasury opposition to Japanese proposals from early 1997 on were a central feature of the drama, and was highlighted in the discussions among international political economists. Its absence was notable in the US-centred debate among economists.

Turning to the state as a unit, the US debate among economists and public officials treats politics as a ghost, with an occasional walk-on part, operating as a sort of deus ex machina to enliven proceedings.[73] Only 'cronyism' is isolated as a major contributing factor to meltdown in Bhagwati's broadside, cited above, serving as a reminder that classical liberals are quite prepared to apply the same term to the Western powers. Classical liberals maintain that sound policy starts at home, and sound policy for the world starts in the domestic environment of the lead state. But classical liberals can live easily with political and institutional diversity. Indeed, they argue that specialisations beneficial to international trade arise from the different institutional constructs reached over time by polities, negotiating their insertion into world markets both domestically and internationally. The neo-liberal takes a more affirmative stance, arguing that market imperfections, under restrictive conditions, can be corrected by judicious government intervention in the public interest. Governments of course pursue many different objectives, some of them classifiable in terms of efficiency and others in terms of order, justice and equity. If a state pursues efficiency, then it might liberalise capital movements completely, and draw on world savings to accelerate growth. Under these conditions, it follows that forgoing the benefits of liberalisation on capital account is an expensive way of exercising discretion. If, by contrast, the state's policy may be stylised as a mixture of efficiency and justice, where efficiency refers to measures regarding capital account liberalisation, and justice refers to alteration of prevailing government norms, say to more democracy, the optimal policy to achieve both objectives may require a complex sequencing of measures, which interact one on another.

This situation was descriptive of Indonesia: the rupiah plunged in autumn 1996, when President Suharto's wife died, recording the financial markets' concerns about how the president would manage his succession. In the US debate among economists there was barely mention of this simple point: many east Asian states were undergoing a process of more or less fundamental challenges – political, legal, corporate, financial – to prevailing governance norms before, during and after the east Asian crash. On a broader canvas, this constituted a major oversight: since the 1970s there had not only been global financial market contagions, but also contagions of democratisation and contagions of 'state withdrawal' from the market. Even more blatant, the neo-liberal position on the imperfection of markets is compatible with the position of political economists who argue that different capitalisms have developed as countries have worked out their own distinct political compromises between participants in national markets. If markets were recognised as imperfect, why was there not a much sharper accent in the US debate among economists placed upon the incongruity of global public policy demands for imposing uniform rules on a non-uniform world, as illustrated through the policy preferences of the IMF, the US Treasury or Goldman Sachs?

Finally, let us briefly point out the gaping void in the analysis – the lack of mention of the role of corporations in the east Asian crash. Corporations are a key institutional pillar of modern capitalism, but they barely get a mention. They invested heavily in east Asia prior to the crash; it is recognised that from 1993 onwards the multinationals have been attracted to China, now in competition with east Asian countries as a platform of production for Western markets. Was the Asian meltdown a 'bolt from the blue' for the multinational corporations? No doubt the picture is varied; in any event, many corporations did not waste much time buying up east Asian state assets at knock-down prices. In this sense they were beneficiaries from the outcome of the financial crash. Was this because they were opportunistic, or were there more powerful forces at work, related for instance to the incorporation of local suppliers into multinational global production and marketing networks? Multinationals, of course, feature in the apocalyptic world vision, as does the theme of an undifferentiated global process, the retreat of the state and US power. Are these themes at play in the east Asian crash, or is the timing of the contagion and the choice of countries related to the continued importance of the differentiation between domestic and external environments, a rearrangement of state structures rather than a retreat of the state, and the competition between the business communities of the region?

Where does this leave us with regard to the question: what is/is not written? What is written is from the viewpoint of evolutionists, working within the entrails of the international financial system. There are two categories of evolutionaries: neo-liberals and social democrats, both in some ways linked to a realist perspective. What has not, or has hardly been written about in the ongoing debate about reform of the international financial architecture is the rest. The radical positions are taken up by the classical liberals, few in number but important because of the light they shed on the practice of power in the world political economy. Radical positions from a very different perspective are also occupied by the prophets of apocalypse, baying from the streets surrounding the glass palaces of the international organisations. The realist arguments about power clashes, conducted through states or among corporations, are few. An international political economy approach would have to cover this much wider canvas in order to assess the east Asian crisis, and have its elements weighed in the balance. It would also focus on the complex links between the state system, the domestic structures and performances of states and the workings of world markets, understood as operating in and around political constructs. Above all, there is the salient void of the role of multinational corporations in the Asian crash to be filled. Susan Strange, were she still here, would chide us for that.

Notes

1. See Barry Eichengreen, *Globalizing Capital: A History of the International Monetary System* (New Jersey: Princeton University Press, 1998); Eric Helleiner, *States and the Re-emergence of Global Finance: From Bretton Woods to the 1990s* (New York: Cornell University Press, 1994).
2. Joseph Stiglitz, 'The Role of International Financial Institutions in the Current Global Economy', address to the Chicago Council on Foreign Relations, 1998, at http//www.worldbank.org/html/extrdr/extme/jssp022798.htm.
3. Larry Summers, *Financial Times*, 15 December 1999.
4. Karl Polanyi, *The Great Transformation* (Boston, MA: Beacon Press, 1944).
5. See Bertrand de Jouvenel, *Sovereignty: An Inquiry into the Political Good* (Chicago: University of Chicago Press, 1957).
6. Jonathan Story, *The Frontiers of Fortune: Predicting Capital Prospects and Casualties in the Markets of the Future* (London: Financial Times/Prentice Hall, 1999).
7. See, for example, Joseph S. Nye, *Bound to Lead: The Changing Nature of American Power* (New York: Basic Books, 1991).
8. The point is discussed at length in Henry R. Nau, *The Myth of America's Decline: Leading the World Economy into the 1990s* (New York: Oxford University Press, 1990).
9. See Laurence Whitehead, *The International Dimensions of Democratization: Europe and the Americas* (New York: Oxford University Press, 1996).
10. See Robert Wade, *Governing the Market: Economic Theory and the Role of Government in East Asian Industrialisation* (Princeton: Princeton University Press, 1990).
11. World Bank, *The East Asian Miracle: Economic Growth and Public Policy* (Washington, DC: World Bank, 1993), pp. 4–5.

12. See Lowell Bryan and Diana Farrell, *The Market Unbound: Unleashing Global Capitalism* (New York: John Wiley, 1996).

13. See C. K. Prahalad and Y. L. Doz, *The Multinational Mission: Balancing Local Demands and Global Vision* (New York: Free Press, 1987).

14. See D. K. Fieldhouse, *The West and the Third World, Trade, Colonialism, Dependence and Development* (Oxford: Blackwell, 1999).

15. See David Henderson, *The Changing Fortunes of Economic Liberalism: Yesterday, Today and Tomorrow* (London: Institute of Economic Affairs, 1998); R. Sally, *Classical Liberalism and International Economic Order* (London: Routledge, 1998).

16. See Inge Kaul, Isabelle Gruberg and Marc A. Stern (eds.), *Global Public Goods: International Co-operation in the 21st Century* (Oxford: Oxford University Press, 1999).

17. See Paul Hirst and Grahame Thompson, *Globalisation in Question* (Cambridge: Polity Press, 1996).

18. See Michel Albert, *Capitalism against Capitalism* (London: Whurr, 1993); S. Berger and E. Dore (eds.), *National Diversity and Global Capitalism* (Ithaca: Cornell University Press, 1996); Peter Hall, *Governing the Economy: The Politics of State Intervention in Britain and France* (New York: Oxford University Press, 1986); R. Whitely, 'Internationalization and varieties of capitalism: the limited effects of cross-national co-ordination of economic activities on the nature of business systems', *Review of International Political Economy*, vol. 5, no. 3, 1997, pp. 445–81.

19. See Gary Burtless, Robert Z. Lawrence, Robert E. Litan and Robert J. Shapiro, *Globaphobia: Confronting Fears about Open Trade* (Washington, DC: Brookings Institution, and New York: Twentieth Century Fund, 1998); Dani Rodrick, *Has Globalisation Gone Too Far?* (Washington, DC: Institute for International Economics, 1997).

20. See John Ruggie, 'At Home Abroad, Abroad at Home: International Liberalization and Domestic Stability in the New World Economy', *Millenium: Journal of International Studies*, vol. 24, no. 3, 1995, pp. 507–26.

21. See S. Krasner, *International Regimes* (Ithaca: Cornell University Press, 1983).

22. See Whitely, 'Internationalizaton and Varieties of Capitalism'.

23. See Hirst and Thompson, *Globalisation in Question*.

24. See Kenichi Ohmae, *The Borderless World* (New York: HarperCollins, 1990); *The End of the Nation State* (London: HarperCollins, 1995).

25. See Susan Strange, *The Retreat of the State: The Diffusion of Power in the World Economy* (Cambridge: Cambridge University Press, 1998).

26. See Louis Pauly, *Who Elected the Bankers?: Surveillance and Control in the World Economy* (Ithaca: Cornell University Press, 1997).

27. See Wiliam Greider, *One World: Ready or Not: The Manic Logic of Global Capitalism* (New York: Simon & Schuster, 1996).

28. See John Gray, *False Dawn: the Delusions of Modern Capitalism* (New York: New Press, 1998).

29. See Viviane Forrester, *L'horreur économique* (Paris: Fayard, 1996).

30. See Hans-Peter Martin and Harald Schumann, *The Global Trap* (London: Zed, 1997).

31. See Peter Gowan, *The Global Gamble: Washington's Faustian Bid for World Dominance* (London: Verso, 1999).

32. See Philip G. Cerny, *The Changing Architecture of Politics: Structure, Agency, and the Future of the State* (London: Sage, 1990); François Chesnais, *La Mondialisation Financière: Genèse, Coût et Enjeux* (Paris: Syros, 1996); Eric Helleiner, 'Explaining the globalization of financial markets: bringing the state back in', *Review of International Political Economy*, vol. 2, no. 2, 1995, pp. 315–41; Susan Strange, *Casino Capitalism* (Oxford: Basil Blackwell, 1986); *The Retreat of the State*.

33. See Susan Strange, *States and Markets: An Introduction to International Political Economy* (London: Pinter, 1988).

34. See Eichengreen, *Globalizing Capital*, p. 4.

35. Morris Goldstein, *The Asian Financial Crisis: Causes, Cures, and Systemic Implications* (Washington, DC: Institute for International Economics, 1998).

36. World Bank, *Global Economic Prospects* (Washington, DC: World Bank, 1997).

37. IMF, *International Capital Markets* (Washington DC: IMF, 1998); *World Economic Outlook* (Washington, DC: IMF, May 1998).

38. Group of 7, 'Declaration of G-7 Finance Ministers and Central Bank Governors', G-7, 1998, at http//www.imf.org/external/np/g7/103098dc.htm.

39. Group of 22, *Report of the Working Group on International Financial Crises* (Washington, DC: G-22, 1998); *Report of the Working Group on Strengthening Financial Systems* (Washington, DC: G-22, 1998); *Report of the Working Group on Transparency and Accountability* (Washington, DC: G-22, 1998).

40. United Nations, Executive Committee on Economic and Social Affairs, *Towards a New International Financial Architecture* (Santiago: Economic Commission for Latin America and the Caribbean, 1999).

41. Asian Development Bank, *Asian Development Outlook* (Manila: Asian Development Bank, 1999).

42. See Goldstein, *Asian Financial Crisis*.

43. See Barry Eichengreen, *Toward a New International Financial Architecture: A Practical Post-Asia Agenda* (Washington DC: Institute for International Economics, 1999).

44. 'The Future of the International Financial Architecture: A Report', *Foreign Affairs*, vol. 78, no. 6 (November/December, 1999).

45. Peter B. Kenen, 'The New International Financial Architecture: Reconstruction, Renovation, or Minor Repair?', *International Journal of Finance and Economics*, vol. 5 (2000), pp. 1–14.

46. See Henry Kaufman, 'Preventing the next global financial crisis', *Washington Post*, 28 January 1998.

47. Stiglitz, 'The Role of International Financial Institutions'.

48. George Soros, *The Crisis of Global Capitalism: Open Society Endangered* (London: Little, Blown, 1998).

49. See Patrick Artus and Michele Debonneuil, 'Crises, recherches de rendement et comportement financiers: l'interaction des mécanismes microéconomiques et macroéconomiques', Conseil d'Analyse Economique, Architecture financière internationale, Documentation Francaise, 1999; P. Garber, 'Derivatives in International

Capital Flows', NBER Working paper 6623 (Cambridge, MA: National Bureau of Economic Research, 1998).

50. See David Rothkopf, 'The Disinformation Ages', *Foreign Policy*, Spring 1999.
51. See Laura D'Andrea Tyson, 'The Global Meltdown: What to do next', *Business Week*, 26 October 1998.
52. See Jeffrey Sachs, 'Fixing the IMF remedy', *The Banker*, February 1998.
53. See Martin Feldstein, 'Refocusing the IMF', *Foreign Affairs*, vol. 77, no. 2 (March/April 1998).
54. See Paul Krugman, 'Saving Asia: It's Time to Get Radical', *Fortune*, 7 September 1998.
55. See Barry Eichengreen, J. Tobin and C. Wyplosz, 'Two Cases for Sand in the Wheels of International Finance', *The Economic Journal*, vol. 105 (1995), pp. 162–72; James Tobin, 'A proposal for international monetary reform', *Eastern Economic Journal*, vol. 4 (1978), pp. 153–9.
56. IMF, *Country Experiences with the Use and Liberalisation of Capital Controls* (Washington, DC: IMF, January 2000).
57. See Zanny Minton Beddoes, 'The International Financial System', *Foreign Policy*, Fall 1999.
58. See Joe Stiglitz, 'Redefining the role of the state: What should it do? How Should it do it? And How should these decisions be made?' presented on the Tenth Anniversary of MITI Research Institute (Tokyo, Japan), 17 March 1998.
59. See Martin Feldstein, 'Self-Protection for Emerging Market Economies', NBER Working Paper Series, January 1999, at http://www.nber.Org/papers/w6907.
60. See Fred Bergsten, Olivier Davanne and Pierre Jacquet, 'Pour une Gestion Conjointe de la Fléxibilité des Changes', Conseil d'Analyse Économique, Architecture Financière Internationale, La documentation Française, 1999.
61. See Gordon Brown, 'And impose new codes of conduct', *Wall Street Journal*, 6 October 1998.
62. See Simon Wriston Schulz, 'Who Needs the IMF?' *Wall Street Journal*, 3 February 1998.
63. See Martin Wolf, 'The Last Resort', *Financial Times*, 23 September 1998.
64. See Charles Calomiris, 'The IMF's Imprudent Role as a Lender of Last resort', *Cato Journal*, vol. 17 (1998), pp. 275–95.
65. See Sachs, 'Fixing the IMF remedy'.
66. See Kaufman, 'Preventing the next global financial crisis'.
67. See George Soros, 'Avoiding a Breakdown: Asia's Crisis Demands a Re-think of International Regulation', *Financial Times*, 31 December 1997.
68. Martin Goldstein, 'An Evaluation of Proposals to Reform the International Financial Architecture', paper prepared for NBER Conference on Management of Currency Crises, Monterey, California, 28–31 March 2001.
69. This is the prime argument behind the excellent collection of Keynesian contributions to a special number, edited by Irma Adelman, of *World Development*, vol. 28, no. 6 (2000).
70. See Joseph E. Stiglitz and Shahid Yusuf (eds.), *Rethinking the East Asia Miracle* (Washington, DC: World Bank, and New York: Oxford University Press, 2001).

71. Barry Eichengreen, 'Strengthening the International Financial Architecture: Open Issues, Asian Concerns', prepared for the IMF/KIEP Conference on Recovery from the Asian Crisis, Seoul, 18–19 May 2001.
72. See Jagdish Bhagwati, 'The Capital Myth: The Difference Between Trade in Widgets and Dollars', *Foreign Affairs*, vol. 77, no. 3 (May–June 1998).
73. An exception to this is Gregory Noble and John Ravenhill, *The Asian Financial Crisis and the Architecture of Global Finance* (Cambridge: Cambridge University Press, 2000).

2 Costs and benefits of financial globalisation: concepts, evidence and implications

JOHN WILLIAMSON

In order to have a rational discussion of what should be done to redesign the international financial architecture, it seems natural to start by making sure that we all agree on the basic analytical framework, on what we mean by financial globalisation and what we judge the qualitative nature of its costs and benefits to be. That is what I shall take as my terms of reference in this chapter.

The term 'financial globalisation' is generally taken to mean the integration of capital markets across countries, and, specifically, the belief that this now encompasses most of the world. It does not include monetary globalisation, meaning the global use of a single currency. In fact, outside Europe, there has until recently been almost no sign of monetary integration. It remains to be seen whether the current flurry of interest in dollarisation will translate into the beginning of a widespread movement to curtail the number of currencies.

But for the moment it is the bond market rather than the money market that is unified, in the sense that agents in one political jurisdiction have become willing to hold an unlimited proportion of their portfolio in securities issued in a different country. Similarly, borrowers have become willing to see an unlimited proportion of the securities they issue held by the residents of a different political jurisdiction. Such unification is possible whatever the exchange rate regime, although there is currently a lively debate as to whether capital market integration does not imply going to one or other of the extreme exchange rate regimes (either dollarisation or free floating, the so-called 'two corners' view). My own view is that the theorem of the 'impossible trinity' – the impossibility of having simultaneously a fixed exchange rate, an independent monetary policy and free capital mobility – can perfectly well be resolved by seeking an interior solution rather than going to one or other of the corners, but it seems that this is a minority view.[1]

It is of course an exaggeration to imply that all countries are now plugged into a single global capital market. In fact, if one were to weight countries by population rather than by gross domestic product (GDP), we would still be far from a global capital market. But of course the implicit weighting is by GDP, or perhaps by the size of capital markets, and in that sense globalisation has already come a long way. To the extent that the basis of globalisation is technological advance, in particular in transport and communications, rather than political choice, one has to doubt whether globalisation could be rolled back very far, and indeed countries may not have a lot of choice about how fast they are drawn into the global financial market. But one of the important topics that has been hotly debated in academic circles is whether countries have an effective choice about the speed with which they liberalise their capital accounts. To the extent that they do, there are important policy issues to be discussed. And fundamental to making a rational choice is an understanding about both the benefits and the costs of participating in the global capital market.

The present chapter starts by reviewing the arguments, mainly developed along neo-classical lines, for capital account liberalisation. It then examines the costs of opening capital accounts and integrating with international financial markets, particularly against empirical evidence that has emerged from the recent literature on financial crises in emerging market economies. The claimed benefits and costs of free capital mobility are briefly evaluated by drawing upon extant cross-national studies on the correlation between capital market liberalisation and economic growth. On the basis of the cost-benefit analysis of financial globalisation, the chapter discusses the possible strategies for capital account liberalisation and policy responses to increased global financial integration at national and international levels.

Benefits and costs of financial globalisation

The classic benefit of international capital mobility (the benefit that is formalised in neo-classical analysis) is the ability to divorce the level of investment within a country from the level of national savings. Countries with relatively large investment opportunities at the world rate of interest relative to their national savings can borrow from abroad, while high-savings countries (relative to investment opportunities) can lend. Both parties expect to gain, just as in other voluntary economic transactions. Note that achieving these gains is inherently dependent on current account imbalances, with a deficit in the borrowing country and a surplus in the lending country, offset subsequently by opposite imbalances as the debt comes to be serviced.

The simplest neo-classical analysis assumes that technology is the same everywhere, so that the countries with relatively large investment opportunities are necessarily those with a low stock of capital relative to labour. Capital flows from capital-rich to capital-poor countries, in the process enhancing world output and increasing welfare in both the capital-exporting countries (which get a higher rate of return on their investment than they otherwise would) and in the capital-importing countries (which see their output increase by at least the amount of the debt-service obligation, and by more when the flow of capital is more than marginal).

A case can be made that such intertemporal transactions ought to offer substantial welfare gains in the coming decades, even larger than those depicted by the simplest neo-classical model. The industrial countries face the problem of an ageing population, but at present they have unusually large cohorts in the pre-retirement, high-savings phase of the life cycle. Their populations are also fairly stagnant or even declining in total size, implying limited investment needs. One would therefore expect them to have both an ability to save more than they invest and a motivation for investing the surplus in emerging markets, so as to earn debt service in the future as the proportion of the retired population increases, and thereby be able to finance spending in excess of the income generated at home. At the same time, a large part of the developing world should be at the stage where its largest age cohorts are entering the working population and countries have developed the basic human and institutional infrastructure needed to permit catch-up growth (i.e. have qualified as emerging markets), and thus will be able to absorb large volumes of capital in productive investment with a high rate of return.

The pattern of capital flows suggested by this demographic–development potential modification of neo-classical analysis is from the industrialised countries to the more advanced of the developing countries – the emerging markets – and such a pattern of international capital flows did indeed prevail during the 1990s, until the Asian crisis. Since then there has been a reversal, with the United States, which was already a capital importer, increasing its borrowing to a point where it outweighs the net lending of the other developed countries, while east Asia, the part of the developing world that would seem to best match the description of a natural capital importer offered above, has become a capital-exporting region. One hopes that this situation is a temporary aberration due to east Asia's need to rebuild its liquidity position following the crisis, rather than a permanent shift in the pattern of capital flows. It should be an important objective of policy to secure the resumption of flows from capital-rich countries to those best able to make good use of capital, though 'new economy' aficionados would doubtless claim that the latter include the United States.

There is a second and perhaps comparably important source of welfare gain from international capital movements: risk diversification. Because risks are less correlated between than within countries, an investor can expect to be exposed to less risk to achieve a given expected rate of return (or to achieve a higher rate of return for the same level of risk) by holding an internationally diversified portfolio. This factor is of particular potential significance to residents of small un-diversified economies, whose wealth is otherwise highly dependent on the fortunes of the country's main product. Note that this source of welfare gain does not necessarily depend on current account imbalances at the time when the investment occurs: it is in principle possible that investment flows in opposite directions would exactly offset one another, but this would still enable both parties to gain *ex ante* from the transactions.

One thinks of portfolio investment as being motivated by risk diversification, but two important recent papers of Peter Henry conclude that it also has major effects in terms of stimulating investment.[2] On the basis of an empirical examination of twelve cases where countries liberalised international access to their equity markets in the early 1990s, he shows that on average they experienced abnormal increases in stock prices approaching 30 per cent in total over a period of some eight months leading up to the liberalisation. One would expect this reduction in the cost of capital to stimulate investment, and he finds that this indeed happened. On average the countries experienced a temporary investment boom, of about three years' duration, during which private investment increased by some 22 percentage points more than would have been expected otherwise. This is an interesting contrast to the traditional macroeconomic literature, which has concluded that capital inflows other than foreign direct investment (FDI) tend, like aid, to be split between consumption and investment in much the same proportions as domestic income. (A possible resolution of this paradox is that the empirical studies underlying the traditional result were dominated by inflows of bank capital rather than portfolio equity.)

The third distinct source of potential welfare gain from international capital movements arises when the flow takes the form of FDI. Because FDI brings with it access to intellectual property rights, it typically results in additional benefits to the host country. (The chance to exploit intellectual property rights in an extra market also enables the investors to benefit from FDI.) A particular case involves FDI in the financial services industry, which has often been associated with the introduction of new practices and an increase in competition. Note that while FDI can in principle be financed internally, in practice it usually involves external financing, and is therefore normally (though not inevitably) associated with current account imbalances. The empirical evidence suggests that FDI inflows are typically translated entirely into increased investment: indeed, that investment normally increases by more than the FDI inflow, implying that FDI crowds in domestic investment.

In a neo-classical world, capital mobility would bring gains in the efficiency of allocation of capital without any offsetting costs. In fact most economists are convinced that there are several important costs, the most obvious of which is that foreign borrowing exposes countries to an increased risk of financial crisis. If one asks which of the neo-classical assumptions fail in a way that permits such crises to develop, it is the information structure on the basis of which

Table 2. *Identifying the victims of the crisis.*

Negative growth in 1998		Positive growth in 1998	
(expressed as a percentage of GDP)			
Hong Kong	− 5.1	Bangladesh	5.7
Indonesia	− 13.7	China	7.8
Korea	− 5.5	India	5.8
Malaysia	− 6.2	Myanmar	4.0
Philippines	− 0.5	Pakistan	5.4
Thailand	− 8.0	Singapore	1.5
		Sri Lanka	5.3
		Taiwan	4.8
		Vietnam	4.0

Source: Asian Development Outlook 1999 (Manila: Asian Development Bank).

lending decisions are made. Rather than each investor deciding individually his or her expectations on the basis of their estimate of the fundamentals, investors make their decisions on the basis of what others are expected to do, resulting in herd behaviour.

It is hardly necessary to make the case in detail that financial crises are extremely costly to the countries that experience them: it is sufficient to cite recent events in east Asia. One reason that these costs are so high is a phenomenon to which little attention is paid, namely 'redlining' (something that never happens in a neo-classical model). That is, developing countries in crisis find themselves completely unable to borrow voluntarily from international capital markets, on any terms. Nothing similar happens to developed countries, which may have to pay higher interest rates, or to borrow in foreign currency, but which are still able to borrow. This is one of the few ways in which there appears to be a systematic difference between developing and developed countries.[3] Another such difference, and another explanation for why the costs of crises are so high in these countries, is that developing countries are unable to borrow in their own currency (sometimes referred to as 'original sin'). This means that a currency collapse undermines the net worth of agents that have borrowed abroad, to a point where it can threaten large-scale bankruptcies, as we saw in several east Asian countries.

The role of an open capital account in fomenting the east Asian crisis is sometimes denied.[4] Since the proximate cause of the crisis was a capital flow reversal, and it is difficult to have a reversal in a capital flow without a preceding inflow, this seems a priori implausible. My own approach to the issue has been to ask what distinguishes those Asian countries that fell victim to the crisis from those that did not (see Table 2): factors that have been mentioned include a lack of transparency, the receipt of explicit or implicit guarantees by financial intermediaries, weak macroeconomic fundamentals, non-floating exchange rate regimes, overvaluation and a history of recent domestic financial liberalisation, as well as an open capital account.[5] It is certainly not true that transparency was better in the non-crisis countries (defined as those with positive growth rates in 1998); on the contrary, it was somewhat less problematic in the crisis countries. And it is surely not the quality of bank supervision, which is notoriously bad in several of the non-crisis countries, such as Bangladesh, and is again probably somewhat better on average in the crisis countries. Indeed, one of the crisis countries, namely Hong Kong,[6] is famous for the excellence of its bank supervision. Nor is it the extent to which banks enjoy implicit guarantees, which is at least as great in south Asia as further east. And it is most assuredly not the strength of such traditional macroeconomic fundamentals as the fiscal position, the level of saving, the rate of inflation and growth. Neither is it the exchange rate regime, which involved a loose form of dollar pegging in most of the countries in the table, and was certainly not noticeably more flexible in several of the non-crisis countries. Nor have most observers detected much evidence of overvaluation in the crisis countries, with the exception of Thailand. The extent of financial liberalisation is a more promising candidate, although Singapore is highly liberal domestically, and the south Asian countries also undertook a significant measure of domestic liberalisation in the 1990s.

A far better means of discrimination between the two groups is provided by whether or not they had liberalised the capital account of the balance of payments. All the crisis countries had essentially opened themselves to uncontrolled inflows of short-term funds, and allowed foreign borrowing of their domestic currency such as occurred in Thailand. None of the non-crisis countries had opened their capital accounts, except Singapore, and even Singapore still retained control over foreign borrowing in Singapore dollars, which minimised foreign speculation against its currency.

There is also a certain amount of more formal evidence that associates an open capital account with the likelihood of crisis. The most relevant study to date appears to be that of Demirgüç-Kunt and Detregiache,[7] who examine whether a crisis is more likely in a country with an open capital account by including in a regression that seeks to explain the probability of a banking crisis a dummy variable for the existence of capital controls interacted with the ratio of M2 to international reserves. The sign on the ratio of M2 to international reserves alone was positive, but the interacted variable produced a negative sign of approximately the same magnitude. The authors conclude that a high ratio of bank deposits to foreign exchange reserves increases the risk of a banking crisis occurring when, but only when, the capital account is open.

A second cost of capital mobility would seem to me to be important but receives surprisingly little attention in public discussion.[8] This is the erosion of the tax base. Although I am not aware of any statistical comparisons of the tax yield on assets held abroad versus those invested at home, there is no doubt that tax evasion is a significant motivation for foreign investment.[9] Unlike risk diversification, the gain to the investor comes in this instance at a cost to society. It would in principle be possible to close the tax loopholes, by tax information sharing agreements and withholding of a part of interest to be paid abroad in the absence of proof that the income is being reported to the authorities of the investor's home country, but it seems to be remarkably difficult to get international agreement on even mild steps in this direction.[10]

Since those who own capital tend to be relatively well off, the consequence is a more unequal income distribution. Dennis Quinn presents evidence that capital account liberalisation is associated with greater inequality.[11] Allied with the presumption (from the Stolper-Samuelson theorem) that the wages of low-skilled workers in high-income countries are reduced by international trade, there is at least some reason to support the fear that globalisation has adverse distributional effects in some countries, especially the richer ones.[12]

Growing income inequality, associated with capital account liberalisation and global market integration, may prove deleterious to long-term economic growth. There is some evidence in recent formal analyses of the political economy of growth that income inequality and economic growth are inversely related.[13] These analyses have assumed that the distribution of resources affects growth mainly through fiscal and political channels. In societies with income inequality and thus with many poor agents, the majority of poor voters favour high taxation, which discourages investment and impedes growth. Perhaps more important, countries with more unequal income distributions tend to be more politically unstable, and sociopolitical instability in turn reduces the incentives to save and invest and therefore reduces economic growth.

Capital mobility and economic growth: an evaluation

Several authors have sought to ask whether one can find evidence that an open capital account increases a country's income. In their study of the political economy of capital controls in twenty OECD countries in the period between 1950 and 1989, Alesina, Grilli and Milesi-Ferretti fail to detect any negative impact of capital controls on economic growth.[14] More direct and robust evidence that rejects the hypothesis that an open capital account accelerates growth comes from Dani Rodrik's influential study.[15] For a cross-section of almost one hundred countries, he finds no correlation between open capital accounts and long-term economic performance once the other determinants of growth are controlled for. On the basis of the econometric data of Rodrik but carrying his analysis one step further, Joseph Stiglitz contends that capital market liberalisation has produced instability, in the form of sudden capital reversals and financial crises, which has adverse effects on economic growth.[16]

Dennis Quinn's evidence to the contrary is widely cited.[17] On the basis of a mixed panel of sixty-four developed and developing countries, his multivariate regression analysis shows a positive and statistically significant association between international financial openness and long-run economic growth. This empirical result, Quinn asserts, lends primary support to the neo-classical argument that liberalisation increases the efficiency of investment in capital and labour. An important recent paper by Klein and Olivei finds a strong effect of open capital accounts on financial depth in a cross-section of countries over the period 1986 to 1995.[18] Countries that liberalised their capital accounts over some or all of this period had a greater increase in financial depth and enjoyed faster economic growth than countries that maintained capital account restrictions.

Are these findings in conflict, or is it possible to reconcile them? There is in fact an important difference in the specification of capital account openness between the three studies that found no impact versus that of the Quinn and the Klein and Olivei studies that did. The first three studies use a variable which measures whether the capital account was open or closed,[19] whereas Quinn and Klein and Olivei sought to construct a measure of the *degree* to which the capital account was open (both using data from the IMF's *Exchange Arrangements and Exchange Restrictions* annual report). Now most countries liberalised FDI relatively early on, and most also liberalised long-term before short-term capital. As already argued, we have strong reasons for believing that liberalisation of FDI, portfolio equity and other long-term capital should be beneficial for growth; it is what is usually the last stage – of opening up to unlimited flows of short-term money – that is problematic. Thus many of the observations of Quinn, and of Klein and Olivei, were presumably drawn from episodes where there is a strong probability of benefits of greater liberalisation being positive, so it is not surprising that they find a positive effect. In contrast, the test of Rodrik and Stiglitz is whether complete liberalisation is beneficial, and they find no evidence that it is. These findings are consistent with the view that opening to long-term capital flows is helpful while exposure to short-term capital mobility is harmful.

Furthermore, there is also a major difference with regard to the sample of countries: a large panel of exclusively developing countries in the studies of Rodrik and Stiglitz, in contrast to a mixed panel of developed and developing countries in the cases of Quinn and of Klein and Olivei. Given this difference, Quinn's positive correlation could be due to the inclusion of developed countries in the sample, which generally have more open capital accounts. Indeed, as Klein and Olivei demonstrate in their analysis, the full-sample results concerning the positive effect of capital account liberalisation on financial depth and economic growth are mainly driven by the highly industrialised countries contained in the cross-section; the sub-sample regression results, involving Latin

American countries which tend to have higher levels of international financial openness than many other developing countries, present no evidence that liberalisation has significant impact on financial sector development and overall economic performance. In his study, Quinn also hints that the positive correlation might not hold in developing countries, particularly when one compares east Asian industrialising economies, which achieved more rapid economic growth under more closed foreign exchange regimes, with their Latin American counterparts.[20]

If this judgement is correct, it may not be surprising that the Rodrik and Stiglitz studies, using the same sample of largely developing countries, do not detect any benefit from international financial openness. It could be that capital account liberalisation has harmful as well as benign effects and that the former just outweighs the latter.[21] Their empirical analyses fail to find a relationship between capital account liberalisation and growth, probably because they have excluded many industrial countries that are not only relatively financially open but also enjoy better long-run economic performance. This point, in and of itself, raises an important question: why open capital accounts may not provide the same benefits to developing countries as they often do to industrial nations. One plausible answer to that question, as emphasised in several empirical studies, is that developing countries need a constellation of economic, legal and social institutions that are normally present in industrial countries, in order to minimise the costs associated with capital account liberalisation and to translate international financial openness into greater economic growth.[22]

That is my best judgement of the balance of advantage. (It is no more than a judgement; the most one can claim is that it is not only plausible, but also consistent with such evidence as we have.) Even if one accepts it as true at the moment, it may not remain true in the future, for financial development is continually eroding the ability to make controls work.[23] We probably ought to worry not so much about whether open capital accounts are beneficial, or have been beneficial in the past, as about how to increase the probability that they will bring net benefits in the future.

Coping with financial globalisation: national policy responses

Prior to the east Asian crisis, official opinions (perhaps especially in Washington) seemed incapable of entertaining the thought that faster financial globalisation might not necessarily be better. Each year's new record in private sector capital inflows was trumpeted as another triumph. Virtually no one opposed the IMF's ambition to amend its Articles so as to give it formal authority to supervise the capital controls of its member countries, with a strong presumption that these should be phased out rapidly. Those of us who dissented from this enthusiasm found ourselves almost isolated, except from those who are hostile to markets in general, a group whose company we did not find reassuring.

Matters changed profoundly after the east Asian crisis. The steam went out of the IMF's drive to change its Articles, and even those who continued to advocate this step were also careful to emphasise the importance of correct sequencing of liberalisation and to recognise a possible role for Chilean-style capital inflow controls. Jagdish Bhagwati suddenly emerged as a vehement and eloquent critic of capital account liberalisation.[24] The official world has launched a multi-pronged initiative to reform the international financial architecture. All of a sudden the academic world has found itself with a new agenda to discuss.

Perhaps an appropriate place to start to discuss this new agenda is with an exploration of the possible policy options and strategies that national governments in developing and emerging market economies can adopt to deal with accelerating financial globalisation.[25] While some of these policy issues may seem obvious and were indeed discussed widely in the 1980s, they are worth recapitulating here, particularly with regard to the experiences accrued from recent financial crises in east Asia and elsewhere.

One important policy lesson that has emerged from the Asian currency and financial crises is that policy makers ought to be cautious about opening capital accounts. As noted in the previous sections, it was the hasty liberalisation of capital accounts, specifically short-term capital flows, which subjected many east Asian economies to sudden reversals of foreign funds and exposed them to international financial instabilities. This does not mean that governments should freeze all international financial liberalisation, since long-term capital inflows are beneficial to economic growth, but it does suggest that developing countries that have capital controls should avoid a sudden rush for external financial liberalisation and eschew dogmatic commitments to capital account convertibility.

For many countries, however, financial closure may not be feasible. Despite its real and potential costs, the process of global financial integration is surely intensifying and seems to be irreversible for several plausible reasons. Domestic financial reforms, which have been well under way even in those countries with capital account restrictions, may make it difficult for governments to control the trans-border activities of banks and other financial institutions. Equally, thanks to advances in information and communications technologies, international capital flows are most likely to continue to expand irrespective of government policy. As a result, any attempt to maintain comprehensive capital controls may become administratively onerous. The fundamental issue thus is not whether to liberalise but how best to maximise the benefits of free capital mobility and to cope with financial globalisation. To do so, recent experiences with financial crises have demonstrated, entails well-advised liberalisation strategies and appropriate domestic policy responses.

As argued in the earlier sequencing literature, capital account convertibility should be preceded by the establishment of a liberalised, well-supervised, domestic financial system.[26] The Asian financial crisis appears to have confirmed this conventional wisdom. A part of the blame for the crisis can legitimately be attributed to the coincidence of premature capital account opening with domestic financial weaknesses which derived, among other things, from lax supervision and weak regulation, imprudent debt profiles, non-market practices of credit allocation, and inadequately capitalised financial institutions. Moreover, wrongly sequenced capital decontrols were partly to blame for the accumulation of structural weaknesses in the financial sector of many crisis-stricken economies. In South Korea and Thailand, for instance, granting financial institutions greater access to external short-term funds before liberalising the longer-term components of capital accounts aggravated problems in domestic financial systems and contributed directly to the outbreak of the crisis.

All this points to the importance of removing distorted incentives, strengthening the domestic financial sector and establishing an adequate and effective system of prudential supervision and regulation *before* liberalising capital accounts. For countries that contemplate some capital decontrols or find themselves drawn into the process of global financial integration, the proper order in which the various parts of capital accounts are liberalised is equally important. If the foregoing cost-benefit analysis of capital account liberalisation has any value, it would suggest that liberalisation of long-term capital flows such as FDI should precede the removal of restrictions on offshore bank borrowings, specifically short-term loans. As alluded to above, long-term capital not only has important positive effects on economic growth but also is less footloose and more likely to remain in host countries, even in a financial panic.

Even countries that have already liberalised their capital accounts in a wrong sequence, such as those in east Asia, can adopt some measures to ease the situation, and their policy should focus on deterring excessive inflows of short-term funds. The most promising way of doing this appears to be that pioneered by Chile and Colombia, of imposing an unremunerated reserve requirement against all loans from abroad (perhaps supplemented by a minimum holding period on equity capital). If this reserve has to be deposited for a set period, such as one year, then this provides not only an overall deterrent to capital inflows but an incentive to increase the maturity of loans as well. There have been some doubts about whether this mechanism served to reduce the size of the unwanted inflows into Chile,[27] but no one has denied that it induced a significant lengthening in the maturity of loans, which also helps to make the country less vulnerable to crisis. Although there were leakages and the authorities had to make a series of modifications in the regulations in order to maintain the effectiveness of the mechanism, Chilean experience shows that it is administratively feasible. Such a policy could advantageously be combined with adoption of the sort of restrictions on foreign borrowing of the national currency imposed by Singapore.

Another much discussed way of controlling unwarranted capital inflows is the Tobin tax. This would consist of a small tax on all foreign exchange transactions. There would doubtless be administrative difficulties in getting all the countries with actual or potential foreign exchange markets to agree to impose such a tax, but the more fundamental issue is whether such a tax would help to stabilise the markets. It is far-fetched to suppose that in a crisis such as that which overtook east Asia in late 1997 investors would have been deterred from withdrawing their funds by the prospect of paying a tax of 0.5 per cent or less, so the only issue is whether the prospect of paying such a tax at the time of entry would have deterred the build-up of short-term debt in the first place. What one can surely say is that one would get more mileage out of a tax that discriminated between money that was going in and that which was going out, as the Chilean system does, than out of a Tobin tax which is imposed equally on stabilising and destabilising flows.

Some economists have looked to strong prudential regulation of the financial system placing limitations on short-term cross-border exposure as a better way of resisting short-term inflows. External capital inflows, however, do not all take place through the financial sector. In Indonesia, for instance, the bulk of the external borrowing was undertaken by the corporate sector, particularly by exporters who believed that their export activity gave them a natural hedge against devaluation. It is difficult to envisage substitutes for border controls as a way of imposing effective discipline on the exposure of the corporate sector. Some of the most pernicious practices, such as the insertion of bullet repayment clauses subject to the discretion of the lender (a widespread practice in South Korea's external borrowing), might be declared illegal and thereby rendered unenforceable. One may also be able to impose a tax surcharge on interest income incurred on obligations denominated in a foreign currency, or on short-term obligations denominated in foreign currencies, although there is a danger of that penalising normal trade credit. But it seems to be the case that the simplest way of avoiding the danger of an excessive accumulation of short-term foreign debt is to maintain controls at the border.

The role of international institutions

Important as they are, domestic policy responses alone are insufficient to tackle problems of capital account liberalisation and increased financial globalisation.

While national governments can adopt appropriate strategies to defend themselves, hopes for easing the various strains generated by capital mobility and for reforming the global financial architecture rest with the international policy community. The Asian crisis prompted a flurry of proposals on the role of international institutions in reducing global financial instability and transforming the international economic landscape. Regardless of their merits, these proposals, which involve such ambitious institutions as a world financial authority, an international bankruptcy court[28] and a global debt insurance corporation, are unlikely to materialise in the near future.[29] Meaningful discussions over the role of international institutions should start with more modest and achievable measures, which to my mind fall under the following three areas.[30]

In the first place, international institutions, particularly the IMF, should encourage a cautious approach towards financial liberalisation. In view of the severity of recent currency and financial crises, the IMF has backed away from its general advocacy of rapid capital decontrol in favour of a more carefully sequenced approach.[31] The key question now is whether international institutions should go further and actively encourage controls when capital inflows are excessive. The logic of focusing on inflows is that the accumulation of a large stock of short-term debt obligations was central in making many Asian countries vulnerable to crisis, and that it is much easier to limit the stock that enters than to curtail what wants to flee in the midst of a crisis. Although many of us would not want to see a regression to old-fashioned administrative prohibitions, the key issue is whether there is any role for price-related measures to limit capital inflows in inappropriate forms and excessive quantities. As discussed earlier, the precedent is Chilean-style taxes, which have been intended both to restrict the total size of the capital inflows and to increase the maturity of such debts as Chile contracted. Despite some doubts being raised over their effectiveness, Chilean-style taxes have proved to be a useful instrument to reduce excessive capital inflows. The IMF should actively promote the use of such an instrument, particularly among those emerging economies that have fragile domestic financial sectors and weak prudential frameworks.

Furthermore, international institutions should encourage reforms in the lending practices of those who supply capital to emerging market countries, an important issue that has so far received little attention in the global debate on the new financial architecture. If one believes, as I do, that frequent crises in emerging market economies are primarily due to the preference of the creditors for lending in the forms (short-term loans denominated in their own currencies) that are ill-suited to the needs of the borrowers, and that contribute to a boom–bust pattern of lending, then this ought to be at the core of international efforts to reform the global financial regime. Yet so far the efforts have been largely restricted to investigating how to alter the requirements for risk weights on bank loans embodied in the Basel capital adequacy rules. International institutions ought to be more ambitious, with the objective of encouraging managers of institutional investment companies to take a longer-term view and shifting the burden of risk to the lenders.

More specifically, global intergovernmental forums, such as the Basel Committee on Banking Supervision, and G-7 financial regulators should avoid weighting schemes that provide incentives for short-maturity cross-border flows or for interbank lending. In particular, they should consider imposing lower capital charges (risk weights) for banks that are willing to lend in local currencies, thus effectively placing much of the exchange risk on the lenders (who will, it must be understood, expect higher average returns to compensate). Another form that might discourage too much short-term lending is granting the IMF the right to approve a standstill on amortisation payments when a country is in crisis. Such a right would reflect the reality that a country can only hope to exit from a crisis quickly once debts have been reconfigured to a profile that the market believes the country can meet, but confining the standstill to amortisation payments would hit short-term debts the hardest, and therefore encourage a lengthening of maturities.

Finally, one may expect capital account crises precipitated by widespread contagion similar to those of recent years to be the predominant form of crises in the future, at least for the emerging market economies. The main outstanding issue is how international institutions can help to mitigate the effects of contagion. The IMF has made some progress on this front by establishing in April 1999 a facility called the Contingency Credit Line (CCL), which was supposed to help to prevent contagion. This has been intended to provide semi-automatic access to credit to contagion-hit countries that have good macro policies, maintain good relations with their private creditors, and are willing to comply with minimally acceptable international standards and codes in banking supervision, accounting practices and corporate governance.[32]

So far, however, no country has applied for a CCL. Two reasons have been developed to explain this failure to use the facility. One is that the financial terms are too demanding, with a commitment fee payable when the application for coverage is approved and with the same interest rate as that on the Supplemental Reserve Facility (SRF – which is to be the main instrument for lending to countries in crisis that have not pre-qualified for the CCL) payable when money is drawn. But the interest rate was reduced and the commitment fee abolished in 2001, and there are still no takers. A second reason is the ambiguous signal that application for a CCL would send to the markets. These may see an application as signifying weakness (a need to establish a line of defence) rather than strength. Reinforcing that concern is the certainty that if the IMF subsequently felt obliged to disqualify a country, that would send it into crisis. If this is the true explanation, a workable CCL will require replacement of the provision that countries apply for the CCL by one that they are automatically granted access to the facility in case of need if they satisfy certain standards, without ever going through the process of applying and being approved.

Conclusion

Financial globalisation can bring with it both benefits and costs. While opening an emerging market to foreign financial flows is expected to enhance its welfare in the form of improved economic efficiency and risk diversification, there is an accumulation of evidence that financial integration heightens the prospects of currency crises and contributes to income inequality. These costs have been particularly acute in developing and emerging market economies, where the necessary institutional structures that can help to mitigate problems of capital mobility are weak or non-existent. This chapter suggests that optimal policy is neither to rush for capital account liberalisation nor to freeze all activity in that direction. For many emerging markets that have found themselves increasingly drawn into the process of global financial integration, the crucial question is how they can deal with that process in a way that maximises the net benefits.

National experiences with recent currency and financial crises suggest that emerging market governments should strengthen their domestic financial systems before freeing capital flows, avoid precipitate capital account liberalisation and adopt price-oriented measures to limit excessive capital inflows. To tackle the growing frequency and severity of financial crises, national responses should be accompanied by international initiatives and efforts. Grandiose schemes are unlikely to resolve the immediate threats to the functioning of the international financial order. The more practical measures discussed in this chapter to strengthen the role of international institutions in helping to control capital inflows, reform lending practices and prevent financial contagion constitute an agenda that is more achievable.

Notes

The author acknowledges helpful comments from Geoffrey Underhill and a number of participants in the conference on Global Financial Disorder and Policies for a New Financial Architecture in the Millennium at the University of Amsterdam on 3 February 2000.
1. The basic idea of an interior solution is that the incompatibility be resolved by having an intermediate exchange rate regime that leaves the country with some

flexibility to direct its monetary policy to domestic economic management, but also expects it to direct its monetary policy to exchange rate management to some degree or under some circumstances, with capital mobility circumscribed (e.g. by Chilean-style controls) but not eliminated. See John Williamson, *Exchange Rate Regimes for Emerging Markets: Reviving the Intermediate Option* (Washington, DC: Institute for International Economics, 2000).

2. My view has recently been endorsed by Jeffrey Frankel in his presentation at an IMF Institute seminar on 7 August 2000, reported in *IMF Survey*, 28 August 2000.

3. Peter Blair Henry, 'Stock Market Liberalization, Economic Reform, and Emerging Market Equity Prices', *Journal of Finance*, vol. 50, no. 2 (2000), pp. 529–64; 'Do Stock Market Liberalisations Cause Investment Booms?' *Journal of Financial Economics*, vol. 58, nos. 1–2 (2000), pp. 301–34

4. I recently mused that the only developing country that would seem likely to be exempt from redlining was Singapore, and perhaps Hong Kong. The IMF reclassified these as Advanced Countries shortly before this chapter was written, as is appropriate given their per capita incomes and institutional development.

5. For example, Hubert Neiss, then the Director of the IMF's Asia and Pacific Department, was quoted as having told Reuters on 19 January 2000 that 'The crisis countries did not get into a crisis because they were integrated with international capital markets. They got into a crisis because of long-standing structural problems.' No one doubts that they had structural problems (what country doesn't, and didn't they have them throughout the quarter century of the miracle?), but that proves nothing. Indeed, as pointed out in the text, it is difficult to identify dimensions in which their structural problems were worse than those of countries that did not have crises, whereas they were clearly more exposed to capital flows.

6. See John Williamson, 'External Debt Management and the East Asian Crisis', in A. Vasudevan (ed.), *External Debt Management: Issues, Lessons and Preventive Measures* (Mumbai: Reserve Bank of India, 1999), available at www.iie.com/jwilliamson.htm.

7. Hong Kong is sometimes classified as a non-crisis country because its exchange rate did not collapse, but I treat the criterion for a crisis as a decline in GDP, as certainly happened in Hong Kong.

8. Asli Demirgüç-Kunt and Enrica Detregiache, *Banking Crises Around the World: Are There Any Common Threads?* (Washington, DC: Development Economics Department, World Bank, 1997). See also Irma Adelman and Erinc Yeldan, 'The Minimal Conditions for a Financial Crisis: A Multiregional Intertemporal CGE model of the Asian Crisis', *World Development*, vol. 28, no. 6 (2000), pp. 1087–100; Marco Rossi, 'Financial Fragility and Economic Performance in Developing Economies: Do Capital Controls, Prudential Regulation and Supervision Matter?' IMF Working Paper WP99/66 (Washington, DC: IMF, 1999).

9. After I wrote this, a survey on 'Globalisation and Tax', dealing with these very issues and expressing similar concerns, appeared in the 29 January 2000 issue of *The Economist*.

10. I am thinking here of personal acquisition of foreign financial assets rather than FDI. Dennis Quinn finds no evidence that the corporate tax yield is

lowered by capital account liberalization: 'The Correlates of Change in International Financial Regulation', *American Political Science Review*, vol. 91, no. 3 (1997), pp. 531–51.

11. International co-operation on this issue and potential obstacles thereto are discussed at length by Dani Rodrik and Tanguy van Ypersele, in 'Capital Mobility, Distributive Conflict and International Tax Co-ordination', Working Paper 7150 (Cambridge: National Bureau of Economic Research, 1999).

12. Quinn, 'The Correlates of Change'.

13. There is some evidence which links economic globalisation with widening income inequality, at least within rich nations. See, for instance, Paul Krugman and Anthony J. Venables, 'Globalisation and the Inequality of Nations', *The Quarterly Journal of Economics*, vol. 110, issue 4 (1995), pp. 857–80; Jeffrey G. Williamson, 'Globalisation and Inequality: Then and Now', Working Paper 5491 (Cambridge, MA: National Bureau of Economic Research, 1996).

14. See Alberto Alesina and Roberto Perotti, 'Income Distribution, Political Instability, and Investment', Working Paper 4637 (Cambridge, MA: National Bureau of Economic Research, 1993); 'The Political Economy of Growth: A Critical Survey of the Recent Literature', *The World Bank Economic Review*, vol. 8, no. 3 (1994), pp. 351–71; Alberto Alesina and Dani Rodrik, 'Distributive Politics and Economic Growth', *The Quarterly Journal of Economics*, vol. 109, no. 2 (1994), pp. 465–90.

15. Alberto Alesina, Vittorio Grilli and Gian Maria Milesi-Ferretti, 'The Political Economy of Capital Controls', in L. Leiderman and A. Razin (eds.), *Capital Mobility: The Impact on Consumption and Growth* (Cambridge: Cambridge University Press, 1994), pp. 289–328. Using a different sample and a different specification, however, Rossi finds that the presence of controls on capital inflows is associated with significantly slower growth, in 'Financial Fragility and Economic Performance in Developing Economies'.

16. Dani Rodrik, *Who Needs Capital Account Convertibility?* in Princeton Essays in International Finance 207 (Princeton: International Finance Section, Department of Economics, Princeton University, 1998), pp. 55–65.

17. Joseph E. Stiglitz, 'Capital Market Liberalisation, Economic Growth, and Instability', *World Development*, vol. 28, no. 6 (2000), pp. 1075–86.

18. Quinn, 'The Correlates of Change'.

19. Michael Klein and Giovanni Olivei, 'Capital Account Liberalisation, Financial Depth, and Economic Growth', Working Paper 7384 (Cambridge, MA: National Bureau of Economic Research, 1999).

20. Rodrik took the proportion of years in which the capital account was free of restrictions, but the test was whether the capital account was completely free of restrictions.

21. Quinn, 'The Correlates of Change', p. 532.

22. Rodrik, 'Who Needs Capital Account Convertability?'

23. See Asli Demirgüç-Kunt and Enrica Detragiache, 'Financial Liberalisation and Financial Fragility', IMF Working Paper WP/98/83 (Washington, DC: IMF, 1998); Dani Rodrik, *Making Openness Work: The New Global Economy and the Developing Countries* (Washington, DC: The Overseas Development Council, 1999).

24. For country-specific instances of this point see the International Monetary Fund, *Country Experiences with the Use and Liberalisation of Capital Controls* (Washington, DC: IMF, 2000).

25. Jagdish N. Bhagwati, 'The Capital Myth', *Foreign Affairs*, vol. 77, no. 3 (1998), pp. 7–12.

26. The following discussion draws on John Williamson, 'Implications of the East Asian Crisis for Debt Management', in A. Vasudevan (ed.), *External Debt Management: Issues, Lessons, and Preventive Measures* (Mumbai: Reserve Bank of India, 1999), pp. 127–48; 'Development of the Financial System in Post-Crisis Asia', ADB Institute Working Paper 8 (Tokyo: Asian Development Bank Institute, 2000). See also Martin Feldstein, 'Self-protection for Emerging Market Economies', NBER Working Paper no. 6907, Cambridge, MA: National Bureau for Economic Research, 1999.

27. The classical works on liberalisation sequence include Sebastian Edwards, *The Order of Liberalisation of the External Sector in Developing Countries*, (Princeton: Princeton Essays in International Finance No. 156 International Finance Section, Department of Economics, Princeton University, 1984); Ronald I. McKinnon, 'The Order of Economic Liberalisation: Lessons from Chile and Argentina', in Karl Brunner and Allen Meltzer (eds.), *Economic Policy in a Changing World* (Amsterdam: North-Holland, 1982); *The Order of Economic Liberalisation: Financial Control in the Transition to a Market Economy* (Baltimore: Johns Hopkins University Press, 1991).

28. For a discussion which tends to qualify the effectiveness of Chile's controls on capital inflows see Sebastian Edwards, 'Interest Rates, Contagion and Capital Controls', Working Paper 7801 (Cambridge, MA: National Bureau of Economic Research, 2000). For a counterargument, see John Williamson, *Exchange-Rate Regimes for Emerging Markets: Reviving the Intermediate Option* (Washington, DC: Institute for International Economics, 2000), pp. 37–45.

29. Just before this volume went to press, Anne Krueger, the newly appointed First Deputy Managing Director of the IMF, proposed an international workout mechanism for sovereign debt restructuring, which bore some resemblance to the rules and procedures of a domestic bankruptcy court. While an important development in itself within the context of ongoing efforts to reform the current international financial architecture, the mechanism would not be implemented any time soon, as Krueger herself conceded, even if the IMF were able to garner necessary political support. For details of the proposal, see Anne Krueger, 'International Financial Architecture for 2002: A New Approach to Sovereign Debt Restructuring', available at http://www.imf.org/external/np/speeches/2001/112601.htm.

30. For comprehensive discussions on these proposals and on their respective merits and demerits see Barry Eichengreen, *Toward a New International Financial Architecture: A Practical Post-Asia Agenda* (Washington, DC: Institute for International Economics, 1999), esp. ch. 6; Morris Goldstein, 'Strengthening the International Financial Architecture: Where do We Stand?' Working Paper 00–08 (Washington, DC: Institute for International Economics, 2000); Kenneth Rogoff, 'International Institutions for Reducing Global Financial Instability', *Journal of Economic Perspectives*, vol. 13, no. 4 (1999), pp. 21–42.

31. The following account draws on John Williamson, 'Modernizing the International Financial Architecture: Big Outstanding Issues' (Washington, DC: Institute for International Economics, 2000).

32. IMF, *Reforming the International Financial Architecture – Progress through 2000* (Washington, DC: IMF, 2001). See also Daniel Citrin and Stanley Fischer, 'Strengthening the International Financial System: Key Issues', *World Development*, vol. 28, no. 6 (2000), pp. 1133–42.

33. Goldstein, 'Strengthening the International Financial Architecture'.

3　Capital controls: the neglected option

BENJAMIN J. COHEN

Why don't emerging-market economies make more use of capital controls? Not long ago, in the wake of Asia's great financial crisis, limitations on capital mobility appeared about to make a comeback. At the intellectual level, scholars began to accord new respectability to the old case for controls as an instrument of monetary governance. At a more practical level, one country – Malaysia – imposed comprehensive restraints and, with seeming success, survived to tell the tale. As I wrote soon after the crisis broke: 'The tide . . . is starting to turn. Once scorned as a relic of the past, limits on capital mobility could soon become the wave of the future.'[1] Yet in reality governments in the newly industrialising economies still hesitate to raise or restore impediments to the free flow of capital. Controls remain the neglected option. The question is: why?

Elsewhere, I have suggested that the explanation has much to do with the prominent role of the United States, the still dominant power in international finance.[2] Washington, both directly and through the IMF, has brought its considerable power to bear to resist any significant revival of controls. Reflection suggests, however, that international politics is at best only part of the story; *domestic* politics too must be involved, in a mutually reinforcing interaction with the pressure of outside forces. The purpose of this chapter is to highlight the critical domestic side of the story. My focus is on the thirty or so newly industrialising countries, mostly located in east Asia and Latin America, that are commonly referred to as the 'emerging markets'.[3]

I begin in section one with a quick look back at the transformation of the global financial environment that gradually occurred in recent decades – an epochal change that has made it increasingly difficult for governments everywhere to manage monetary affairs within their own sovereign territories. Capital controls represent one possible response to the growing challenge that global financial markets pose for national monetary governance. The pros and cons of capital controls are evaluated in section two, highlighting the tidal shift that has occurred at the level of scholarly discourse. The analytical case for controls, it is now widely acknowledged, is actually a good deal stronger than conventionally supposed. Reasons for the continued opposition of the United States are briefly summarised in section three.

Section four then takes up the domestic side of the story, stressing the key role of powerful societal interests that, having benefited from liberalisation in the past, now share Washington's preference for keeping financial markets open in the future. In effect, a powerful transnational coalition would seem to be at work to ensure that capital restraints remain the neglected option. In section five I conclude by offering some brief thoughts on what, in practical terms, might be done to mobilise greater political support for controls as a legitimate tool of monetary governance.

The new geography of money[4]

That the global financial environment has been greatly transformed in recent decades is undeniable. The full significance of that change for monetary governance, however, has only lately begun to be widely appreciated. Prior to the Asian crisis in 1997–8, policy makers were only starting to learn how to cope with the rising challenge to their authority.

The postwar resurrection of global finance has been truly phenomenal. Half a century ago, after the ravages of the Great Depression and the Second World War, financial markets everywhere – with the notable exception of the United States – were generally weak, insular and strictly controlled, reduced from their previously central role in international economic relations to offer little more than a negligible amount of trade financing. Starting in the 1950s, however, deregulation and liberalisation began to combine with technological and institutional innovation to breach many of the barriers separating national currencies and monetary systems. In a cumulative process driven by the pressures of domestic and international competition, the range of market opportunities has gradually widened for borrowers and investors alike. The result has been a remarkable growth of capital mobility across political frontiers, reflected in a scale of financial flows unequalled since the glory days of the nineteenth-century gold standard.

Even more phenomenal have been the implications of these changes for monetary governance and the long-standing convention of national monetary sovereignty. With the deepening integration of financial markets, strict dividing lines between separate national monies have become less and less distinct. No longer are economic actors restricted to a single currency – their own home money – as they go about their daily business. Cross-border circulation of currencies, which was once quite common prior to the emergence of the modern state system, has dramatically re-emerged, with competition between national monies gradually accelerating. This is what I have referred to elsewhere as the new geography of money – the evolving configuration of currency space.[5] The functional domain of each money no longer corresponds precisely with the formal jurisdiction of its issuing authority. Currencies instead have become increasingly *deterritorialised*, their circulation determined not by law or politics but rather by the dynamics of supply and demand.

Currency deterritorialisation poses a new and critical challenge to governments, which have long relied upon the privileges derived from a formal monetary monopoly to promote their conception of state interest. These privileges include, in particular, the powers of seigniorage and macroeconomic management. No longer can governments exert the same degree of control over the use of their monies, either by their own citizens or others. Instead, policy makers have been driven to compete, inside and across borders, for the allegiance of market agents – in effect, to sustain or cultivate market share for their own brand of currency. Monopoly has yielded to something more like oligopoly, and monetary governance has been reduced to little more than a choice among marketing strategies designed to shape and manage demand.

Broadly speaking, four strategies are possible, depending on two key considerations – first, whether policy is defensive or offensive, aiming either to preserve or promote market share, and second, whether policy is pursued unilaterally or collusively. The four strategies are:

1. *Market leadership*: an aggressive unilateralist policy intended to maximise use of the national currency, analogous to predatory price leadership in an oligopoly.
2. *Market alliance*: a collusive policy of sharing monetary sovereignty in a monetary union of some kind, analogous to a tacit or explicit cartel.
3. *Market preservation*: a status-quo policy intended to defend, rather than augment, a previously acquired market position.
4. *Market followership*: an acquiescent policy of subordinating monetary sovereignty to a stronger foreign currency via some form of firm exchange rate rule (e.g., a currency board), analogous to passive price followership in an oligopoly. In extremis, followership may entail full replacement of the national currency by the stronger foreign currency (official dollarisation).

Of these four options, the first, market leadership, is generally available only to governments with the most widely circulated monies, such as America's dollar or Germany's mark (now replaced by the euro). Other countries, with less competitive currencies, must select from among the remaining three strategies. The basic question is plain. Should policy makers do what they can to sustain national monetary sovereignty (market preservation)? Or, alternatively, should they countenance delegating some or all of that authority either to a monetary union (market alliance) or to a dominant foreign power (market followership)?

A former president of the Argentine central bank put the point bluntly: 'Should a [country] produce its own money, or should it buy it from a more efficient producer?'[6] For most countries today, the answer is equally plain. Most appear resolved, at least for now, to continue producing their own money – to keep the national currency alive, no matter how uncompetitive it may be. A sovereign money is still seen in most parts of the world as a natural extension of the principle of *political* sovereignty.

How can a national currency be kept alive? Market share can be defended by tactics of either persuasion or coercion. Most governments seek to sustain demand by buttressing their money's reputation, above all by publicly committing themselves to credible policies of 'sound' monetary management. The idea is to preserve market confidence in the value and usability of the nation's brand of currency – the 'confidence game', as Paul Krugman has ironically dubbed it.[7] But demand can also be managed by using the formal powers of the state to coerce rather than persuade. In fact, states regulate monetary use all the time. One way is by such means as legal-tender laws (specifying what currency private creditors must accept in payment of a debt) and public receivability provisions (specifying what currency the government itself will accept in payment of taxes or other public obligations). Another way may be by restraining the movement of funds into or out of the country – in a word, capital controls. Limitations on capital mobility are a logical corollary of any strategy of market preservation.

In practice, of course, the trend in recent decades has been all the other way, reflecting what has come to be known as the 'Washington consensus' – a triumphalist 'neo-liberal' economics emphasising the virtues of privatisation, deregulation and liberalisation wherever possible. The Washington consensus has been widely promoted by the US government together with the Washington-based IMF and World Bank. First the more advanced economies of Europe and Japan, then many emerging market economies, undertook to dismantle as many of their existing controls as possible. Restraints on capital mobility were frowned upon as a relic of an older, more *dirigiste* mentality – wrongheaded if not downright anachronistic. By the 1980s, financial liberalisation had become the goal of almost every self-respecting industrial or middle-income country. By the 1990s, the tide was clearly moving towards the consecration of free capital mobility as a universal norm. Perhaps the high-water mark was reached in early 1997 when the Interim Committee of the IMF approved a plan to begin preparing a new amendment to the Fund's charter to make the promotion of capital account liberalisation a specific IMF objective and responsibility.[8]

But then came Asia's financial crisis, which forced a fundamental reconsideration of the wisdom of financial liberalisation. Governments in east Asia which previously had taken pride in the competitiveness of their currencies suddenly found themselves unable to preserve user loyalty. Strategies that once seemed adequate to sustain market share now had to be re-evaluated in the light of a massive 'flight to quality' by mobile capital. Inevitably, policy makers were drawn to take a new look at the old case for capital controls. Observers could hardly fail to note that China, which had never abandoned its vast panoply of financial restraints, was able to avoid much of the distress afflicting its more liberalised neighbours. Nor could the actions of Malaysia be ignored, once its comprehensive control programme was announced in September 1998. As one source commented at the time, 'capital curbs are an idea whose time, in the minds of many Asian government officials, has come back'.[9] Like it or not, an approach once dismissed as obsolete – a leftover of a more interventionist era – was now back on the policy agenda.

The case for controls

Capital controls are controversial. Critics oppose them as inefficient and unworkable. Advocates justify them as a tonic for stricken economies. For decades the burden of proof was on those who would foolhardily try to block the seemingly irresistible tide of financial globalisation. With the crisis in Asia, however, came a new intellectual respectability for limits of some kind on the cross-border mobility of capital. Both theory and history suggest that the burden of proof has now shifted to those who would defend the conventional wisdom rather than those who attack it.[10]

Pros and cons

The traditional case against capital controls is simple. It is the case for free markets, based on an analogy with standard theoretical arguments for free trade in goods and services. Commercial liberalisation is assumed to be a mutual-gain phenomenon, so why not financial liberalisation too? Like trade based on comparative advantage, capital mobility is assumed to lead to a more productive employment of investment resources, as well as to increased opportunities for effective risk management and welfare-improving inter-temporal consumption smoothing. We are all presumably better off as a result.[11] In the words of Federal Reserve Chairman Alan Greenspan, an authoritative representative of the conventional wisdom:

The accelerating expansion of global finance . . . enhances cross-border trade in goods and services, facilitates cross-border portfolio investment strategies, enhances the lower-cost financing of real capital formation on a world-wide basis, and, hence, leads to an expansion of international trade and rising standards of living.[12]

All these gains, conversely, would be threatened by controls, which it is assumed would almost certainly create economic distortions and inhibit socially desirable risk taking. Worse, given the inexorable advance of financial technology across the globe, restrictions in the end might not even prove to be effective. Again in Alan Greenspan's words: 'We cannot turn back the clock on technology – and we should not try to do so.'[13] Any government that still preferred controls was, in effect, simply living in the past.

Against these arguments, which have long dominated thinking in policy circles, two broad lines of dissent may be found in the scholarly literature. One approach focuses on the assumptions necessary to support the conventional wisdom, which are as demanding for trade in financial assets as they are for trade in goods and services. Strictly speaking, as a matter of theoretical reasoning, we can be certain that free capital flows will optimise welfare only in an idealised world of pure competition and perfect foresight. In reality, economies are rife with distortions (such as asymmetries in the availability of information) that prevent attainment of 'first-best' equilibrium. As Richard Cooper has written:

It has long been established that capital mobility in the presence of significant distortions . . . will result in a misallocation of the world's capital and, indeed can even worsen the economic well-being of the capital-importing country.[14]

A plausible case for controls, therefore, may be made on standard 'second-best' grounds. Judicious introduction of another distortion in the form of capital restrictions could actually turn out to raise rather than lower economic welfare on a net basis. For every possible form of market failure, there is in principle a corresponding form of optimal intervention.

The logic of this kind of argument is not disputed. An omniscient government dealing with one clear distortion could undoubtedly improve welfare with some form of capital-market restriction. What is disputed is the value of such logic in the real world of multiple distortions and imperfect policy making. As Michael Dooley has noted in an oft-cited survey of the relevant literature, the issue is not theoretical but empirical.[15] The assumptions necessary to support an argument based on second-best considerations are no less 'heroic' than those underlying the more conventional laissez-faire view.

The second line of dissent, much more relevant to today's circumstances, looks not to marginal economic distortions but rather to the very nature of financial markets. Even in the absence of other considerations, financial markets tend to be especially prone to frequent crisis and flux. At issue here are the interdependencies of expectations inherent in the buying and selling of claims, which unavoidably lead to both herd behaviour and multiple equilibria. Financial markets are notoriously vulnerable to self-fulfilling speculative 'bubbles' and attacks. They also have a disturbing tendency to react with unpredictable lags to changing fundamentals – and then to overreact, rapidly and often arbitrarily.

The resulting flows of funds, which may be massive, can be highly disruptive to national economies owing to their amplified impact on real economic variables. Hence here too a logical case may be made for judicious intervention by state authorities, in this case to limit the excessive instabilities and contagion effects endemic to the everyday operation of financial markets. Representative are the words of a former governor of the Bank of Mexico:

> Recent experiences of market instability in the new global, electronically linked markets ... have made the potential costs of massive speculative flows difficult to ignore or underestimate ... The assumed gains from free capital mobility will have to be balanced against the very real risks such mobility poses. Some form of regulation or control ... seems necessary to protect emerging-market economies from the devastating financial crises caused by massive capital movements.[16]

Admittedly the value of this sort of argument too may be open to challenge on empirical grounds – but least so in the midst of a global emergency, when the disadvantages of unconstrained mobility are so obvious for everyone to see. In fact, recent research demonstrates that financial liberalisation is almost always associated, sooner or later, with serious systemic crisis.[17] It is precisely the explosion of these costs that was decisive in shifting the terms of discourse on capital controls. Increasingly the question is now posed: why should freedom of capital movement be given absolute priority over all other considerations of policy? Why, in effect, should governments tie one hand behind their back as they seek to shape and manage demand for their currency?

Perhaps most influential in shifting the discourse was a widely quoted article by the prominent trade economist Jagdish Bhagwati, which first appeared in May 1998.[18] Although other economists had been making the case for controls for some time,[19] Bhagwati's celebrity succeeded in bringing the issue to a new level of public awareness. After Asia's painful experience, Bhagwati asked, could anyone remain persuaded by the 'myth' of capital mobility's benign beneficence? In his words:

> It has become apparent that crises attendant on capital mobility cannot be ignored ... When a crisis hits, the downside of free capital mobility arises ... Thus, any nation contemplating the embrace of free capital mobility must reckon with these costs and also consider the probability of running into a crisis. The gains from economic efficiency that would flow from free capital mobility, in a hypothetical crisis-free world, must be set against this loss if a wise decision is to be made.[20]

In a similar vein, shortly afterwards, Krugman decried the failure of more conventional strategies of market preservation, which he labelled Plan A. 'It is time to think seriously about Plan B', he contended, meaning controls. 'There is a virtual consensus among economists that exchange controls work badly. But when you face the kind of disaster now occurring in Asia, the question has to be: badly compared to what?'[21] Likewise, within months, the financier George Soros was writing that 'some form of capital controls may...be preferable to instability even if it would not constitute good policy in an ideal world'.[22] By autumn 1998 the intellectual momentum had clearly shifted towards some manner of reappraisal of the conventional wisdom. As Bhagwati concluded: 'Despite the...assumption that the ideal world is indeed one of free capital flows...the weight of evidence and the force of logic point in the opposite direction, toward restraints on capital flows. It is time to shift the burden of proof from those who oppose to those who favour liberated capital.'[23]

.

Back to the future?

Reappraisal of the conventional wisdom could also be justified on historical grounds. Many people fail to remember that the original design of the IMF did not actually call for free capital mobility. Quite the contrary, in fact. Reflecting an abhorrence for the sort of 'hot-money' flows that had so destabilised monetary relations in the 1920s and 1930s, the charter drafted at Bretton Woods made explicit allowance for the preservation of capital controls. Virtually everyone involved in the negotiations agreed with the influential League of Nations study, *International Currency Experience*, that some form of protection was needed against the risk of 'mass movements of nervous flight capital'.[24] The option of controls, therefore, was explicitly reserved to the discretion of individual states, provided only that such restraints might not be intended to restrict international commerce.[25] The idea was to afford governments sufficient autonomy to promote stability and prosperity at home without endangering the broader structure of multilateral trade and payments that was being laboriously constructed abroad. It was a deliberate compromise between the imperatives of domestic interventionism and international liberalism – the compromise of 'embedded liberalism', as political scientist John Ruggie later called it.[26]

Pivotal in promoting that compromise was none other than John Maynard Keynes, universally respected as the greatest economist of his day and intellectual leader of the British delegation at Bretton Woods. For Keynes, nothing was more damaging than the free movement of speculative capital, which he viewed as 'the major cause of instability...[Without] security against a repetition of this...the whereabouts of "the better 'ole" will shift with the speed of the magic carpet. Loose funds may sweep round the world disorganising all steady business. Nothing is more certain than that the movement of capital funds must be regulated.'[27] Keynes carefully distinguished between genuinely productive investment flows and footloose 'floating funds'. The former, he concurred, were vital to 'developing the world's resources' and should be encouraged. It was only the latter that should be controlled, preferably as a 'permanent feature of the post-war system'.[28] Following Bretton Woods, Keynes expressed satisfaction that his objectives in this regard had been achieved:

Not merely as a feature of the transition, but as a permanent arrangement, the plan accords to every member Government the explicit right to control all capital movements. What used to be heresy is now endorsed as orthodox.[29]

As we know, though, that achievement did not last. Over the course of the next half century, as the phoenix of global finance rose from the ashes, Keynes's strictures were largely forgotten. With the Washington consensus now increasingly dominant, what had been endorsed as orthodox once again became heresy – until the Asian crisis. Despite determined resistance from neo-liberal economists,[30] the tide has now decisively turned. Even the IMF has changed its tune, dropping active discussion of a new amendment to promote financial liberalisation and talking instead of the possible efficacy of financial restraints[31] – a tentative step back to the future envisaged by Keynes and others when the Fund was first created. Plainly, the pressure of events has conspired with a reawakened sense of history to cast the case for capital controls in a new light. Limitations on capital mobility, as a result, have gained new legitimacy as an instrument of monetary governance.

The role of the United States

Yet for all their new-found legitimacy, capital controls remain the neglected option. Can we understand why? Elsewhere, reviewing possible explanations, I have highlighted the key role of the United States, which continues as it has throughout most of the postwar period to dominate management of the international financial architecture.[32] Though somewhat eclipsed in the 1970s and 1980s, America's monetary hegemony was decisively reaffirmed by the long economic expansion of the 1990s – a record of success that stood in sharp contrast to lingering unemployment in Europe, stagnation in Japan and repeated crises elsewhere. Not for nothing do the French now call the United States the world's only hyperpower (*hyperpuissance*). Few governments today are inclined overtly to defy Washington's wishes on monetary and financial issues – and Washington has made no secret of its firm opposition to any significant reversal of financial liberalisation in emerging markets.

In fact, emerging market economies have been openly pressured to keep on playing the confidence game. Influence has been brought to bear both directly and through the policy conditionality imposed on hardest-hit countries by the IMF, which was once described to me by a high US Treasury official as 'a convenient conduit for US influence'.[33] Typical was the advice of the US Council of Economic Advisers following the 1997–8 crisis. For countries facing the prospect of volatile capital flows, the Council suggested, 'the need [is] to strengthen their domestic financial systems and adopt appropriate macroeconomic policies' – not a resort to capital controls.[34] On the contrary, the Council warned, 'many considerations argue against the use of capital controls'.[35] Similarly, Joseph Stiglitz, the World Bank's recently retired chief economist, has vividly described the close collaboration between the Treasury and the Fund that was instrumental in enforcing neo-liberal orthodoxy after the crisis broke.[36] We know that countries such as South Korea, which was willing to play the game by Washington's rules, were rewarded with generous financial assistance and other forms of support. Conversely, when Indonesia's newly elected president, Abdurrahman Wahid, briefly flirted with the idea of controls during a period of renewed currency pressure in June 2000, he was firmly discouraged by the IMF's Managing Director, who insisted that Indonesia must adhere strictly to the Fund's policy prescriptions.[37] We also know that Malaysia came in for much opprobrium after its rash break with the Washington consensus in 1998. In such an atmosphere, is it any wonder that most policy makers might hesitate to follow in Kuala Lumpur's footsteps?

Undoubtedly, one reason for Washington's determined opposition lay in ideological conviction. Most of the officials recently in charge of US policy, including Treasury Secretary Robert Rubin and his successor Lawrence Summers, were trained in neo-liberal economics and firmly persuaded of its essential merit; and the same can be said as well of their replacements following the presidential election of 2000. But that was hardly the only reason. Intellectual bias can explain only a predisposition towards some set of policies. It is unlikely to dominate hard-nosed political calculation. In practice, two other considerations clearly took precedence.

First was a concern for systemic stability, which obviously seemed jeopardised by the Asian crisis and its subsequent spread to Russia, Brazil and elsewhere. Not only did lending markets around the world threaten to seize up, risking a global credit crunch. There was also the possibility of crashing stock markets, worldwide depression and resurgent protectionism in international trade. Nightmare scenarios were a dime a dozen once the crisis started. As the dominant architect of the prevailing monetary structure, the United States is presumably also one of its principal beneficiaries. In that context America's leaders had every reason to seek to suppress any challenge to the status quo.

Second was domestic politics within the United States, which also favoured preservation of the status quo. Few American constituencies would be directly benefited by restraints on capital mobility in emerging markets. Many, however, could see their interests hurt, including especially major financial institutions and investors. Such powerful market actors are not the kind to keep their preferences under a bushel; nor are their elected representatives apt to be entirely insensitive to their pleas for support. This is not to suggest that Washington is merely the tool of an exploitative capitalist class. The world is rarely as simple as that. But it does imply a common interest in opposing controls. As political scientist Robert Wade has commented, in polemical but compelling terms:

> The United States has a powerful interest in maintaining and expanding the free world-wide movement of capital . . . Moreover, Wall Street banks and brokerage firms want to expand their sales by doing business in emerging markets . . . [Hence] there is a powerful confluence of interests between Wall Street and multinational corporations in favour of open capital accounts world-wide. In response, the US Treasury has been leading a campaign . . . to promote capital liberalisation.[38]

Elsewhere, Wade calls this the 'Wall Street–Treasury complex'.[39] Such a formidable coalition of forces is undoubtedly difficult to resist.

Domestic politics

Resistance, however, is not impossible – neither in principle nor in practice. Legally, there is nothing to prevent a sovereign government from limiting capital flows if it so chooses; politically, few emerging market countries are so supine as to knuckle under to the first whiff of pressure from Washington. Restraints on capital mobility, to repeat, are a logical corollary of a currency strategy of market preservation. Hence something else must be involved as well to explain why policy makers continue to hesitate to make more use of controls, effectively tying one hand behind their back even as they strive to maintain market share for their money. Reason suggests that the 'something else' is most likely to be found at home, in each country's own domestic politics and political institutions.

Significantly, formal analysis of the domestic politics of capital controls suggests that, if anything, governments should be biased *in favour of* restraints rather than hesitant.[40] In addition to their role in limiting the risk or damage of currency crises, controls can be highly useful to policy makers for both revenue and redistributive purposes. On the one hand, controls make it easier for governments to exploit the power of seigniorage, otherwise known as the 'inflation tax'. Seigniorage represents the capacity that a monetary monopoly gives policy makers to augment public expenditures at will. Resources can be extracted from the private sector via inflationary money creation. On the other hand, controls can be used to shift the tax burden towards capital owners by closing off opportunities for tax avoidance. The hesitancy of governments to make more use of capital restraints certainly cannot be attributed to a lack of plausible motivations.

Rather, one must look to the motivations of other domestic actors with a capacity to influence official policy. Such actors are not difficult to find. Numerous studies have analysed the politics of the wave of financial liberalisation that swept emerging market economies in the 1980s and 1990s.[41] All point to the key role played by powerful societal interests in helping to persuade policy makers to reduce or eliminate past restraints on capital mobility. Critical constituencies benefited measurably from the opening of a new range of market opportunities. These included, in particular, big tradable-goods producers, banks and other financial services firms, and large private asset holders. Exporters and importers, as well as domestic banks, gained improved access to loanable funds and lower borrowing costs; the owners and managers of financial wealth were freed to seek out more profitable investments or to develop new strategies for portfolio diversification. All these benefits, plainly, would be curtailed or lost if controls were now to be reimposed. It stands to reason, therefore, that these same constituencies would now do everything possible to ensure that governments sustain their commitment to the Washington consensus. These too are actors who are unlikely to keep their preferences under a bushel.

Details differ from country to country, of course, depending on the specific characteristics of each state's economic structure and political institutions. In Mexico, for instance, it was the banking industry that was most prominent in lobbying for liberalisation, acting in a de facto coalition with like-minded officials in the federal bureaucracy – what Sylvia Maxfield has called Mexico's 'bankers' alliance'.[42] According to Maxfield, the bankers' alliance was able to succeed as it did because of several key characteristics of the country's institutional structure. These included a relatively autonomous central bank, a finance ministry able to exercise hegemony over other state economic policy-making agencies, and a high degree of conglomeration between private industrial and financial enterprises. In countries like South Korea and Taiwan, by contrast, it was the industrial sector that was most directly involved – especially big manufacturers who, as they shifted towards more capital-intensive activities, sought to attain easier access to large-scale external financing.[43] Again, institutional factors, including in particular the relative strength of the central bank and allied agencies within the structure of government, were decisive in determining how much influence such sectoral interests could exercise over policy outcomes. And in yet other economies, such as Indonesia, it was large asset holders who were among the most influential, aided no doubt by close political (and even familial) ties to governmental authorities.[44]

Whatever the details, however, the broad implication is clear. Governments have been under pressure from not one but *two* directions. Opposition to controls comes not just from the United States and the IMF, on the outside, but also, undoubtedly, from key elements of the private sector at home, determined to preserve the benefits and privileges derived from liberalised financial markets.

Interacting with the 'Wall Street–Treasury complex', in other words, is a comparably influential bank–industry–wealth-holder complex – in effect, a powerful transnational coalition that works in a mutually reinforcing fashion to bar any retreat from the Washington consensus. External pressure from the United States is amplified internally by the natural desire of influential societal actors to defend acquired privileges. In turn, the impact of those same domestic actors is strengthened and legitimised by the backing of the world's acknowledged monetary hegemon.

No evidence exists, of course, to suggest that this sort of coalition, which is informal at best, is in any way the result of deliberate design. No conspiracy is needed to explain a pattern of co-operation when there is so evident a confluence of interests. Premeditated or not, however, the coalition has certainly proved its effectiveness in constraining the actions of governments that might otherwise have been more partial to a revival of controls. Even the rashest of policy makers are bound to hesitate when faced by such a united front of opposition.

Conclusion

The Asian crisis provided one of those rare watershed moments when conventional wisdom could be seriously challenged. With the apparent failure of more orthodox strategies of market preservation – the confidence game – the time seemed ripe for a revival of capital controls as a legitimate tool of monetary governance. Yet governments in emerging markets still hesitate, despite the persuasiveness of both theoretical argument and historical precedent. That they do still hesitate is testament to the combined power of the United States and determined domestic interests, acting in tandem to preserve existing commitments to the Washington consensus.

In that case, what is to be done? Capital controls need not remain the neglected option. In practical terms, the critical issue is one of feasibility: how to fight fire with fire. Against foes of controls, whether at home or abroad, it is necessary to build an even more forceful coalition of proponents. The aim must be to mobilise political constituencies everywhere with an interest in restoring the compromise of embedded liberalism written into the Fund charter at Bretton Woods – to free governments to use the hand presently tied behind their back. To be effective, such a coalition could not rely on emerging market governments alone. Quite obviously, it would also have to draw in sympathetic and influential elements in the United States or elsewhere that until now have maintained a relatively low profile on the issue.

Potential allies are there. One source of support might be found in the World Bank, which has delicately suggested that 'The benefits of capital account liberalisation and increased capital flows have to be weighed against the likeli-hood of crisis and its costs.'[45] Stiglitz, while still at the Bank, was certainly well known for his opposition to Treasury views on capital controls. Other support might be found among the leadership of such elite organisations as America's Council on Foreign Relations, which recently published a task force report highly favourable to certain kinds of capital controls.[46] If elements like these could be recruited to the cause, governments might finally hesitate no longer.

Notes

1. Benjamin J. Cohen, 'Taming the Phoenix: Monetary Governance after the Crisis', in Gregory W. Noble and John Ravenhill (eds.), *The Asian Financial Crisis and the Architecture of Global Finance* (New York: Cambridge University Press), pp. 192–3. This paper was first prepared for a conference on the Asian financial crisis held in Melbourne, Australia, in December 1998.
2. Benjamin J. Cohen, 'Capital Controls: Why Do Governments Hesitate?' in Leslie Elliott Armijo (ed.), *Debating the Global Financial Architecture* (Albany, NY: SUNY Press, 2002).
3. See, for example, Michael Mussa, Paul Masson, Alexander Swoboda, Esteban Jadresic, Paolo Mauro and Andrew Berg, *Exchange Rate Regimes in an Increasingly Integrated World Economy* (Washington, DC: International Monetary Fund, 2000), p. 13. These countries are distinguished from the much larger number of poorer developing countries in sub-Saharan Africa and elsewhere, many with inconvertible currencies, that have long maintained significant restraints on capital flows.
4. The discussion in this section, which is necessarily condensed, is based on arguments presented at greater length in Benjamin J. Cohen, *The Geography of Money* (Ithaca, NY: Cornell University Press, 1998).
5. *Ibid.*
6. Pedro Pou, 'Is Globalisation Really to Blame?' in Jane Sneddon Little and Giovanni P. Olivei (eds.), *Rethinking the International Monetary System* (Boston, MA: Federal Reserve Bank of Boston, 1999), p. 244.
7. Paul Krugman, 'The Confidence Game', *The New Republic*, 5 October 1998, pp. 23–5; *The Return of Depression Economics* (New York: Norton, 1999).
8. Interim Committee Communiqué, 28 April 1997, para. 7. Under the plan, two Arti-cles were to be amended – Article I, where 'orderly liberalisation of capital' would be added to the list of the Fund's formal purposes; and Article VIII, which would give the Fund the same jurisdiction over the capital account of its members as it already enjoys over the current account. The language would also have *required* countries to commit themselves to capital liberalisation as a goal.
9. Robert Wade and Frank Veneroso, 'The Gathering Support for Capital Controls', *Challenge*, vol. 41, no. 6 (1998), p. 23.
10. The earliest example I can find of this change of tone was a column by *Financial Times* commentator Martin Wolf in early March 1998. Ordinarily a firm champion

of free markets, Wolf reluctantly concluded: 'After the crisis, the question can no longer be whether these flows should be regulated in some way. It can only be how.' Ten months later, at the annual World Economic Forum in Davos, Switzerland – always a useful means for tracking authoritative public- and private-sector opinion – it was clear from most remarks that absolutely unrestricted capital mobility was no longer much in favour. See, for example, *The New York Times*, 29 January 1999, p. C1.

11. Maurice Obstfeld and Kenneth Rogoff provide elegant theoretical arguments to demonstrate the potential for gains from inter-temporal trade through a free international market for securities, in *Foundations of International Finance* (Cambridge, MA: MIT Press, 1996).

12. Alan Greenspan, 'The Globalization of Finance', *Cato Journal*, vol. 17, no. 3 (Winter 1998), p. 246.

13. *Ibid.*, p. 249.

14. Richard N. Cooper, 'Should Capital Controls be Banished?' *Brookings Papers on Economic Activity*, no. 1 (1999), p. 105. See also Barry Eichengreen, Michael Mussa and a Staff Team, *Capital Account Liberalisation: Theoretical and Practical Aspects* (Washington, DC: International Monetary Fund, 1998); Alejandro López-Mejía, 'Large Capital Flows: A Survey of the Causes, Consequences, and Policy Responses', Working Paper WP/99/17 (Washington, DC: International Monetary Fund, 1999).

15. Michael P. Dooley, 'A Survey of Literature on Controls over International Capital Transactions', *International Monetary Fund Staff Papers*, vol. 43, no. 4 (1996), pp. 639–87.

16. Ariel Buira, *An Alternative Approach to Financial Crises* (Princeton, NJ: International Finance Section, 1999), pp. 8–10.

17. John Williamson and Molly Mahar, *A Survey of Financial Liberalisation* (Princeton, NJ: International Finance Section, 1998).

18. Jagdish Bhagwati, 'The Capital Myth', *Foreign Affairs*, vol. 77, no. 3 (1998), pp. 7–12.

19. See, for example, Ilene Grabel, 'Financial Markets, the State, and Economic Development: Controversies within Theory and Policy', *International Papers in Political Economy*, vol. 3, no. 1 (1996); 'Marketing the Third World: The Contradictions of Portfolio Investment in the Global Economy', *World Development*, vol. 24 (1996), pp. 1761–76.

20. Bhagwati, 'The Capital Myth', pp. 8–9.

21. Paul Krugman, 'Saving Asia: It's Time to Get Radical', *Fortune Magazine*, vol. 138, no. 5 (1998), p. 78. See also Paul Krugman, *The Return of Depression Economics* (New York: Norton, 1999), ch. 9.

22. George Soros, *The Crisis of Global Capitalism* (New York: Public Affairs, 1998), pp. 192–3.

23. Bhagwati, 'The Capital Myth', p. 12.

24. Ragnar Nurkse, *International Currency Experience: Lessons from the Inter-War Period* (Geneva: League of Nations, 1944), p. 188.

25. See Article VI, sections 1 and 3 of the Articles of Agreement of the International Monetary Fund.

26. John G. Ruggie, 'International Regimes, Transactions, and Change: Embedded Liberalism in the Postwar Economic Order', in Stephen D. Krasner (ed.), *International Regimes* (Ithaca, NY: Cornell University Press, 1983).

27. 'Post-War Currency Policy', a British Treasury memorandum dated September 1941, reprinted in *The Collected Writings of John Maynard Keynes*, ed. Donald Moggridge, XXV (Cambridge: Cambridge University Press, 1980), p. 31.

28. 'Plan for an International Currency (or Clearing) Union', January 1942, reprinted in *The Collected Writings*, pp. 129–30.

29. As quoted in Louis W. Pauly, *Who Elected the Bankers? Surveillance and Control in the World Economy* (Ithaca, NY: Cornell University Press, 1997), p. 94. For more on Keynes's views and how they relate to the contemporary scene, see John Cassidy, 'The New World Disorder', *The New Yorker*, 26 October 1998, pp. 198–207; and Jonathan Kirshner, 'Keynes, Capital Mobility and the Crisis of Embedded Liberalism', *Review of International Political Economy*, vol. 6, no. 3 (1999), pp. 313–37.

30. See, for example, Sebastian Edwards, 'How Effective are Capital Controls?' *Journal of Economic Perspectives*, vol. 13, no. 4 (1999), pp. 65–84; 'International Capital Flows and Emerging Markets: Amending the Rules of the Game?' in Little and Olivei, pp. 137–57; Günther G. Schulze, *The Political Economy of Capital Controls* (New York: Cambridge University Press, 2000).

31. See, for example, Charles Adams, Donald J. Mathieson, Garry Schinasi and Bankim Chadha, *International Capital Markets: Developments, Prospects, and Key Policy Issues* (Washington, DC: International Monetary Fund, 1998), p. 79; Charles Adams, Donald J. Mathieson and Garry Schinasi, *International Capital Markets: Developments, Prospects, and Key Policy Issues* (Washington, DC: IMF, 1999), pp. 92, 101; Akira Ariyoshi, Karl Habermeier, Bernard Laurens, Inci Otker-Robe, Jorge Iván Canales-Kriljenko and Andrei Kirilenko, *Country Experiences with the Use and Liberalisation of Capital Controls* (Washington, DC: IMF, 2000); Eichengreen *et al.*, *Capital Account Liberalisation*, pp. 2–3, 29; Mussa *et al.*, pp. 30–1. The Fund's annual report for 1999 reports that its Board of Executive Directors took up the issue of capital controls at a meeting in March 1999, when several directors were said to argue that, in a crisis, limitations on capital flows 'could play a useful role' (IMF, *Annual Report* 1999, p. 47).

32. Cohen, 'Capital Controls: Why Do Governments Hesitate?'

33. As quoted in Benjamin J. Cohen, *In Whose Interest? International Banking and American Foreign Policy* (New Haven, CT: Yale University Press, 1986), p. 229.

34. Council of Economic Advisers, *Annual Report* (Washington, DC: US Government Printing Office, 2000), p. 226.

35. Council of Economic Advisers, *Annual Report* (Washington, DC: US Government Printing Office, 1999), p. 281.

36. Joseph Stiglitz, 'The Insider: What I Learned at the World Economic Crisis', *The New Republic*, 17 and 24 April 2000, pp. 56–60.

37. *New York Times*, 6 June 2000, p. C4.

38. Robert Wade, 'The Coming Fight Over Capital Controls', *Foreign Policy*, vol. 113 (1998–99), pp. 45–7.

39. Robert Wade, 'National Power, Coercive Liberalism and "Global" Finance', in Robert Art and Robert Jervis (eds.), *International Politics: Enduring Concepts and Contemporary Issues* (Ithaca, NY: Cornell University Press, 1999).

40. See, for example, Alberto Alesina, Vittorio Grilli and Gian Maria Milesi-Ferretti, 'The Political Economy of Capital Controls', in Leonardo Leiderman and Assaf Razin (eds.), *Capital Mobility: The Impact on Consumption, Investment and Growth* (New York: Cambridge University Press, 1994), ch. 11; Günther G. Schulze, *The Political Economy of Capital Controls* (New York: Cambridge University Press, 2000).

41. Among the most influential of these studies were Stephan Haggard, Chung H. Lee and Sylvia Maxfield (eds.), *The Politics of Finance in Developing Countries* (Ithaca, NY: Cornell University Press, 1993); Michael Loriaux, Meredith Woo-Cumings, Kent E. Calder, Sylvia Maxfield and Sofia A. Pérez, *Capital Ungoverned: Liberalising Finance in Interventionist States* (Ithaca, NY: Cornell University Press, 1997); Sylvia Maxfield, *Governing Capital: International Finance and Mexican Politics* (Ithaca, NY: Cornell University Press, 1990); Louis W. Pauly, *Opening Financial Markets: Banking Politics on the Pacific Rim* (Ithaca, NY: Cornell University Press, 1988).

42. Sylvia Maxfield, 'Bankers' Alliances and Economic Policy Patterns: Evidence from Mexico and Brazil', *Comparative Political Studies*, vol. 23, no. 4 (1991), pp. 419–58.

43. Stephan Haggard and Sylvia Maxfield, 'The Political Economy of Capital Account Liberalisation', in Helmut Reisen and Bernhard Fischer (eds.), *Financial Opening: Policy Issues and Experiences in Developing Countries* (Paris: Organization for Economic Co-operation and Development, 1993), pp. 65–91; 'Political Explanations of Financial Policy in Developing Countries', in Haggard *et al.*, *The Politics of Finance*, ch. 10; Meredith Woo-Cumings, 'Slouching Toward the Market: The Politics of Liberalisation in South Korea', in Loriaux, *Capital Ungoverned*, ch. 3.

44. Stephan Haggard and Sylvia Maxfield, 'The Political Economy of Financial Internationalization in the Developing World', in Robert O. Keohane and Helen V. Milner (eds.), *Internationalisation and Domestic Politics* (New York: Cambridge University Press, 1996), ch. 9.

45. World Bank, *Global Economic Prospects and the Developing Countries, 1998/99: Beyond Financial Crisis* (Washington, DC: International Bank for Reconstruction and Development, 1999), p. xxi.

46. Council on Foreign Relations, *Safeguarding Prosperity in a Global Financial System: The Future International Financial Architecture*, Report of an Independent Task Force (New York: Council on Foreign Relations, 1999).

4 Global structures and political imperatives: in search of normative underpinnings for international financial order

GEOFFREY R. D. UNDERHILL AND XIAOKE ZHANG

For ordinary people, firms and governments of the affected countries and regions, the financial crises in east Asia, Russia and Latin America were major events of enormous economic and political consequence. The fallout manifested itself in soaring interest rates, repressed investment activities and outright recession. In connection with these economic woes, unemployment rose to an unprecedented high and the income of a wide range of social groups declined sharply, leading to increased social instability and political unrest. In the crisis-stricken economies, political leaders struggled to balance strong external pressures from international financial institutions (IFIs), creditor countries and market agents for neo-liberal reforms with vigorous demands from domestic constituents for protection against growing international financial volatility.

These developments, despite national and regional diversity, have a common background: the process of global financial integration. This process has increasingly entangled once essentially closed and discreet national markets, greatly enhancing movements of capital across national frontiers. It is widely perceived to have generated increased strains in domestic sociopolitical and policy-making processes and intensified the conflicts between the dictates of financial globalisation and national policy imperatives. These tensions have raised serious doubts over the sustainability of economic growth in an environment of untamed capital movements, calling into question the legitimacy of the prevailing market order in the global system. Building on earlier work on the political economy of international finance, this chapter seeks to interpret, in three different but interrelated arguments, the constraints of global capital mobility and their consequences for democratic governance. These arguments in turn have important implications for the norms which underpin the reform of global financial architecture.

First, the process of global financial integration and opening of domestic economic space have constrained in important ways (though not eliminated) the autonomy of national governments in managing their macroeconomic variables, deploying social welfare policies and making strategic choices about the character of their respective societies. While state autonomy has been constrained, citizens of democracies continue to hold their political leaders to account for policy changes that they are less able to influence. The national responsibility of democratic governments for the socioeconomic security of their population has not diminished. If anything, that responsibility has become greater as the transnationalisation of financial structures has subjected domestic groups to growing economic crises. Although the problem is asymmetrically distributed across economies in the global system, the increasing inability of national policy makers to address the consequences of globalisation has dented the credibility of governments elected through democratic processes. This has given rise to the deepening tension between democratic governance and financial openness and accentuated what Susan Strange called the 'clash between the legitimacy of the liberal economy and the legitimacy of the liberal polity'.[1] The problem is all the greater to the extent that global financial integration has correlated to growing inequalities across most societies.[2]

Second, while considerably curtailing the policy capacity of states, integration with global financial structures has strengthened the position of private market actors over public authority. Powerful private actors come to dominate the formulation of national economic policies which, in their attempts to extract benefits from global integration, tend increasingly to serve the interests of market agents. This has crucially changed the notions of public interests that underpin the operation of financial systems and has posed a fundamental problem of democratic accountability. The accountability problem becomes more acute in the transnational domain. The original Bretton Woods agreement was designed to mitigate this problem and placed financial management in the hands of domestic and international public institutions. The ongoing process of global monetary and financial integration since the 1970s, however, has weakened this system of public control over capital flows and transactions.[3] In the absence of strong public authority over private market power, the global financial order is becoming less compatible with the imperatives of domestic political legitimacy. The frequency of financial crisis will only enhance this problem.

Thirdly, given that states have been constrained in their ability to make fundamental choices concerning key areas of policy and forms of governance, they have been less able to defend their specific development patterns and the underlying values, norms and institutions. The transnational integration of financial markets has generated growing pressures for convergence of national economic models, a convergence towards the Anglo-Saxon style of capitalism.[4] As particular economic models and financial systems are embedded in distinctive national development experiences and thereby show historical stickiness, pressures for convergence are bound to generate serious tensions in domestic political arenas. This is especially true if the process of convergence destabilises the institutions that underpin the accumulated economic successes and democratic mandates of elected governments. Where financial integration unleashes forces that undermine domestic arrangements and the resulting tensions threaten socioeconomic stability, the legitimacy of capitalist development and a market-based society as such may come into question. The speed of transformation is of considerable significance under the circumstances. One may safely assume that the legitimacy of reform and restructuring can be enhanced if social and economic structures have adequate time to adjust. Legitimacy is not about perfection, but about pleasing enough of the people enough of the time.

An adequate understanding of the above-mentioned tensions is indispensable to the efforts to tackle financial instability in the international system and to build a new global financial architecture. Without such an understanding, policy reactions at both national and international levels are likely to be ill-advised and ineffective. The most serious challenge for the global political economy lies in containing the potentially destabilising impact of increased capital mobility and in making the international financial order more compatible with the imperatives of domestic economic and political developments. Unless the tensions associated with accelerated financial integration are addressed in an effective and timely manner, they may deepen the frustration of citizens, add support to anti-democratic movements and lead (in a worst case scenario) to a sudden and costly reversal of global integration processes.

Capital mobility, state policy capacity and political legitimacy

It has been widely recognised that capital mobility is a prominent feature of the global economic order.[5] As capital mobility has increased, it has limited the ability of governments to make independent macroeconomic decisions concerning fiscal, monetary and exchange rate policies. In an environment of high capital mobility, governments might pursue autonomous macroeconomic strategies relative to domestic imperatives only if they are willing to give up some degree of exchange rate stability. Even this is uncertain for the more vulnerable economies. Conversely, an independent exchange rate target may be maintained only at the cost of reduced control over monetary policy. Attempts by governments to affect national economic performance by following monetary policies diverging from international trends can lead to balance-of-payments disequilibrium, speculative attacks and exchange rate volatility.[6] All this only too clearly shows the logic of what Benjamin Cohen labels 'the unholy trinity' – the intrinsic incompatibility of currency stability, capital mobility and national policy autonomy.[7]

Although all are affected, financial integration in particular draws in those national political economies reliant on external funds. If these states wish to benefit from foreign capital, they must provide a policy framework that is sufficiently attractive. They thus have incentives to maintain fixed or heavily managed exchange rate regimes, with a view to increasing market confidence in the credibility of their economic policy.[8] Seeking currency stability also reflects the desire of governments to establish reputations for price stability, because inflationary expectations may lead market players to behave in ways that harm the real economy. As a result, there has been a tendency for policy to converge towards an agenda set by financial markets, with governments focusing more and more on exchange rate and monetary stability rather than other policy goals.[9] Fiscal policy is therefore likely to bear the brunt of the resulting anti-inflationary effects. The prospects of rising inflationary pressures and currency instability associated with deficit financing are powerful disincentives against government attempts to run generous public spending programmes and counter-cyclical budget deficits.

The constraints of rising capital mobility on monetary and exchange rate policies and their knock-on effects on fiscal policy lead Philip Cerny to claim that financial integration has undercut the capacity of national states to provide redistributive public goods, including those associated with the social welfare state.[10] While some formal analyses have produced inconsistent results on this front,[11] broad evidence that emerges from important empirical case studies seems to confirm the validity of the claim. In many OECD countries, independent exchange rate policy has lost its role, and rising deficits and debts has circumscribed the fiscal policy options of welfare states. Growing financial integration has amplified the risk of speculative panic and has increasingly held national economic policies hostage to financial market sentiment. This has created strong pressures for cutbacks in public service spending and for the reversal of welfare policies traditionally associated with social democracy.[12]

While financial globalisation has made it difficult for governments to sustain social welfare policies, the same structural forces have often augmented political demands for enhanced social insurance and welfare spending. Global financial market integration has subjected domestic groups to increasing market risks and dislocations and heightened feelings of economic insecurity among broad segments of society.[13] Furthermore, although financial integration tends to benefit mobile asset holders and enhances their ability to hedge against market volatility, it generally leads to welfare losses of internationally immobile factors of production, such as domestically oriented firms, labour and agriculture. This, together with reduced government intervention in market activities, has contributed to growing income inequality among different social groups within countries.[14]

The welfare costs of financial integration may strengthen political incentives for governments to mitigate market dislocations by redistributing risks and wealth. As made clear in the above analysis, however, increased capital mobility also imposes costs to fiscal laxity associated with open-ended social programmes. While developed countries generally have not reduced the overall weight of welfare spending in the economy, large and rising public deficits have raised serious doubts about the sustainability of such spending.[15] Significantly, most have introduced reforms aimed at cutting benefit entitlements and thus controlling the *growth* of social budgets. The fact that governments have been unable to raise taxes to match their spending suggests that they may have difficulty maintaining a solid tax base in the context of financial integration, as it allows business and finance to move with ease across borders and renders an important source of tax revenues precarious.[16] This possibility of arbitrage amongst regulatory and tax regimes points to difficulties governments experience in deploying redistributive taxation and welfare programmes.

That states are increasingly caught between transnational financial constraints and growing domestic demands poses serious and difficult questions for democratic politics. The fundamental problem is that the concepts and practice of modern democracy are deeply rooted in states as self-contained units. This notion guides essential socioeconomic choices concerning wealth generation and distribution. Democratic choices are thus largely understood with reference to the internal dynamics and structures of nation states. The capacity to implement policies deemed necessary to ensure their political legitimacy in a democratic context is assumed.[17] Citizens hold their leaders to account for crucial socioeconomic decisions and expect governments to take care of their welfare. The expectation became stronger as financial globalisation subjected a wide range of social groups to market dislocations, as noted earlier, and as democracy spread and consolidated in developed and developing countries.

The traditional concept of democracy has therefore been rendered problematic by the fundamental mismatch between the national dominion of democratic politics and the global scope of markets which limit the competence and effectiveness of national political authorities.[18] To varying degrees depending on their place in the hierarchy of states, governments are losing the capacity to control changes within their borders and to pursue effectively macroeconomic policies in line with the imperatives of domestic political legitimacy. The tension can lead to voter apathy or otherwise shake public confidence in the democratic form of governance. Governments in most advanced industrial countries have begun to lose credibility with the majority of the population as they experience increasing difficulty acting in the interests and on the desires of their citizens.[19] The problem is most acute in recently democratised but fundamentally weak political economies. In many developing countries, the accentuation of already intolerable economic and social inequalities under the impact of financial globalisation has led to dangerous pressures on emerging democratic governance and perhaps a retreat of democracy.[20]

Financial integration, private power and democratic accountability

The process of global financial integration, while considerably curtailing the policy autonomy of states, has bolstered the position of private market actors in governance at both national and transnational levels. The result is that powerful private interests have increased their dominance of national economic policy making, whereby state policies tend to promote market-led adjustment policies. In turn, this has changed the notions of the public interest that underpin the operation of the financial order, altered policy parameters and objectives in issue-areas of crucial public responsibility, and posed a fundamental problem of democratic accountability.[21]

Few elements of national economic governance are more important to the public interest than the design and function of a financial system. The connotations of the public interest or the public good in relation to the financial domain are much wider than merely inflation control and systemic stability; they are intimately related to and have broad implications for distributional outcomes, for institutions and modes of governance, and for the issue of accountability in democratic political systems. The elaboration of the public interest and normative principles behind it with regard to a particular financial order affect who can *and should* benefit from that order. Moreover, the institutional mechanisms through which financial resources are allocated both reflect and shape the basic characteristics of the wider political economy. Finally, the changing balance of public authority versus private market power in the process of financial and regulatory policy making influences in fundamental ways not only the stability of the financial system but also the nature of the civic democratic order.

A well-functioning and stable financial system in a democratic context rests on the practical notion that the diverse interests of private individuals and entities cannot adequately be provided for without clear definition of collective interests. A satisfactory balance of public and particularistic interests which is appropriate to the imperatives of national economic and political development is vital to the successful and legitimate functioning of a market economy. Historical experience demonstrates that if financial sector regulatory processes are unduly dominated by profit-seeking private interests, we risk not only financial crises, but severe problems of democratic accountability as well. While the argument that the financial system is exclusively a public prerogative does not carry much weight today, there is little basis for the claim that the system should reside exclusively in the private domain of the market. Admittedly, financial transactions in the market-based economies are largely private, but the way in which the financial system operates as a whole makes it part of that essential infrastructure in any political economy, of such overwhelming value to the operation of markets, to the political needs of states and to the wellbeing of civil society that it must be firmly placed at the heart of the public domain.[22]

The financial system is thus too important to be left in private hands and, if history is any guide, the public interest would be better served by binding the financial Prometheus with a view to publicly controlled monetary governance. Historical lessons obviously remained fresh in the memory of the architects of the postwar economic order when they convened at the Bretton Woods conference in 1944. The agreements sought to resolve the tension between pursuit of private gain and the realisation of public policy goals in a democratic system definitively in favour of public control of the monetary and financial order. The aim of the Bretton Woods architects was to 'drive the usurious money lenders from the temple of international finance'.[23] Private financial markets were to be at the service of national economic development and public policy objectives, in order to ensure that financial instability would never again undermine the political legitimacy of emerging democratic countries.

Much has changed since Bretton Woods, however. Since then, regulatory change, corporate innovation and the altered environment within which competition takes place has transformed the postwar financial system from a global order segmented on nationally regulated lines, with tight controls on the short-term movements of capital, to a more market-oriented and globally integrated system characterised by a high degree of capital mobility.[24] Global financial structures have emerged as a result of the integration of financial markets and the activities of financial institutions across borders, which have in turn been attributable in large measure to the liberalisation of financial systems and of capital flows by governments since the 1970s.[25] These developments represent a distinct change in the normative consensus achieved at Bretton Woods, undermining the public management of private financial markets and capital movements.

With the process of financial globalisation has come a change in the balance of power between public authority and private market interests and the accompanying transformation in the notion of 'public interest' that defines the financial order. First, the increased transnational integration of financial markets has clearly enhanced the ability of internationally mobile capital to move with greater ease across national borders into different business ventures. Private financiers and multinational firms can credibly threaten to (and indeed do) exit national economies in which economic policies and business practices are not closely tailored to their desires, with implications for the levels of market activity and employment in national financial and non-financial sectors. Most governments have responded to these pressures with policies which reinforce the market-driven financial order. Financial globalisation thus gives private market actors a stronger voice within the political system to promote their own preferences. Governments often take account of these concerns at the expense of broader public interests, unless they wish to risk serious dislocation between their policy options and the flows of the wider international economy.

Furthermore, financial integration and innovation has rendered public agencies and their longstanding policies increasingly ill-suited to the crucial functions of corporate and systemic risk management, central to any concept of the public interest in financial governance. The principal result has been the emergence of 'market-based' approaches to supervision, where private firms are responsible for risk management through complex mathematical models implemented under the approval of supervisory agencies.[26] Crucial information and expertise for the process remains the proprietary domain of firms which supervisors admit they cannot match. In a highly competitive environment state agencies also seek to improve market opportunities for national players by granting them greater freedom in product innovation and business expansion. This relative disarmament of public authorities has implied that private market interests increasingly define supervisory criteria, and that the crucial aspect of public policy – the safety and stability of the financial system – is dominated by the preferences of those private market makers who stand to benefit from it most.

Equally important, regulatory agencies (for example, central banks) have close and relatively exclusive relationships with financial firms and their associations. While statutorily independent from politicians and other state institutions, these agencies are more responsive to the demands of private financiers, their main domestic political constituencies from whom they draw their legitimacy, and work in close communion with private financial firms to fulfil their supervisory functions. The views and interests of their constituencies are crucial to a consideration of the competitiveness of national firms operating in the transnational marketplace. The close ties of private and public are also reinforced by common professional norms, the specialised and technical nature of expertise in the financial sector, and the use of secrecy to maintain public confidence in the financial system itself. Symbiotic relations and shared world-views, which are developed in the narrow confines of public–private interactions, provide private interests with the opportunity to capture policy-making and regulatory processes in the financial domain and to influence the nature of monetary and financial governance. Clear definition of the public interest distinct from the particularistic claims of private market actors in relation to the financial system has thus become increasingly difficult.[27]

The growing dominance of the financial system by narrow private interests can lead to problems of democratic accountability. Autonomous public agencies, which design and implement financial policy in close consultation with private financiers, lie largely (though not necessarily completely) outside the direct oversight of governments and domestic political processes. The guardians responsible for making the rules of the financial market and governing the monetary and financial order are thus separated off from the traditional means of democratic accountability and control. Changes in financial and regulatory policies, perceived as necessary to enhance the efficiency of financial markets, are made in the closed policy-making processes that are monopolised by private and public financiers but exclude broad public participation. The difficulties which these policy changes would present for the realisation of important policy commitments of democratic regimes are often neglected. The legitimacy deficit which private market preferences for macroeconomic policies may pose for democratically elected governments needs to be better considered.

The problems of democratic accountability and legitimacy become more acute in the transnational arena. Increasingly, the policy process and substantive decisions associated with global financial markets, which affect domestic economic performance, are escaping the control of national governments. As the lines of authority over monetary and financial governance are unclear in the absence of sovereign jurisdiction, there has been a poorly defined sense of the public interest in the international domain. On the other hand, with their control over knowledge and expertise and with their ever-expanding scope of business, powerful private interests have become the key actors in transnational policy processes and are in a strong position to set the agenda for financial sector policies. Private institutional investors have attempted to shape the investment environment in emerging market economies by pressing these economies to adopt policy frameworks favourable to their interests.[28] This pressure is often reinforced by 'advice' from IFIs, especially the IMF, often at the moment when emerging market economies are most vulnerable to external pressures, such as during the Asian crisis. Governments, particularly in developing countries, have found it increasingly difficult to deviate from the policy preferences of international financial markets, no matter how important particular policies may be for resolving their individual problems of economic development and sociopolitical stability.

As national authorities are constrained in their ability to shape global financial transactions, they have sought to co-operate with their overseas equivalents in order to increase the effectiveness of policies and fulfil their respective legal mandates. Co-operation in an international system of competing state jurisdictions has nonetheless posed serious challenges to democratic politics. The international co-operative regimes governing banking at the Basel Committee and securities markets at the International Organisation of Securities Commissions (IOSCO), for instance, are characterised not only by exclusion and narrowness of policy deliberations but also by virtual separation from any accountable political process.[29] The problem of the weak accountability structures of international regimes is further exacerbated by their frequent recourse to self-regulation. As a result, the transnational financial structure is increasingly regulated not by states but by de facto private regimes centred on the financial markets.[30] Lacking a global governance mechanism to discipline self-interested behaviour, these regimes have actually become instruments of private economic interests rather than of the public good.[31]

This less than democratic policy process shaping and governing international financial markets would matter little were it not for the high stakes for states and their societies. It has been argued above that decisions concerning the financial order are fundamental not only to the way in which markets are structured but also to the distribution of relative costs and benefits among both social groups and states in the international system. They also affect the capacity of states to shape their political economies in line with democratic preferences. Finally, the decisions made in relatively unaccountable policy processes are often aimed at increasing the levels of transnationalisation and marketisation of economic policy making, benefiting private market interests at the expense of the wellbeing of the general public and frustrating national policy processes.

The frustration diminishes the chance that these decisions will be regarded as politically legitimate. Legitimacy for governmental policy choices is dependent on such democratic institutions and processes as political parties, regular elections and policy-making accountability. Where national policy makers cede regulatory autonomy to private market forces without seeking the consent of their citizens and where they participate in international regimes whose policy agenda is beyond their effective capacity to control, there are serious questions to be raised about the accountability of national decision-making entities themselves.

Global market structures versus domestic political imperatives

If the fundamental choices of states in key areas of policy and forms of governance are constrained, it follows that they have been increasingly unable to defend the norms and institutions that history has, for better or for worse, conferred upon them and with which citizens understandably identify. The accelerated integration of national economies with international financial structures thus makes it difficult for states to sustain alternate models of capitalist development. States remain vulnerable to the aggregate behaviour of global investors who identify their interests with market-oriented policies and are able to pass direct judgement on local business practices. This risk of volatile capital flows constitutes increased pressure for general policy convergence towards the Anglo-Saxon style of capitalism. Yet the process of adaptation is not something which can take place overnight and can in itself prove destabilising.

An obvious source of convergence is regulatory change in financial systems, a process which does not take place in a political vacuum. Indeed, states face constant political pressures for regulatory reform at domestic, intergovernmental and international levels.[32] First, there are external pressures on national regulatory policies to permit more liberal market access for foreign financial institutions in domestic financial sectors. US and European banks and finance companies have been most active in lobbying for deregulation and aggressive in securing diplomatic support for their interests. This sort of pressure was greatly enhanced by the advent of and eventual conclusion of the WTO agreement on the liberalisation of trade in financial services.[33]

External pressures may translate into actual regulatory preferences through interests and coalitions among state and social actors at the domestic level. States may seek to enhance the provision of capital to industrial development and upgrade. Growth and innovation in the financial sector may also be associated with increased growth in the economy as a whole. Such motivation certainly lay behind the 1980s reforms in many European countries and the 1990s liberalisation efforts among the east Asian and Latin American newly industrialised countries (NICs). Government interests in regulatory reform are often accompanied by demands from domestic financial sectors for deregulating restrictive regulatory provisions. This is particularly true of those financial institutions which either find themselves in saturated markets and thus constrained by regulatory policies or have already had overseas operations and have therefore benefited from more liberal regimes.

Finally, as global financial integration proceeds, even the most cautious regulators may find that their domestic firms are involved in some form of overseas activity and international transactions. In this way, national regulatory authorities can find themselves drawn into such international co-operative institutions for the regulation of financial markets as the Basel Committee and the IOSCO. By containing some of the risks for transnational firms and promoting the norms governing financial market operations, these co-operative institutions have played a role in facilitating the liberalisation of financial regulatory policies. In these international co-operative arrangements, the dominant political economies of Europe and North America, particularly the United States, have considerable pull, and their preferences are far more likely to prevail than those of smaller and developing countries.[34]

The result of these pressures and the associated regulatory changes has been a steady transnational integration of the global financial system and a blurring of the traditional distinctions between banking and securities markets. Equally important, the process of financial system convergence has led to the acceptance and promotion of the market-oriented norms and practices that emphasise competition, national treatment of foreign firms, internationally acceptable accounting standards, and liquidity and transparency in financial markets. Once these regulatory changes have begun to affect the nature of financial systems beyond the borders of the dominant states, drawing most market economies into the web of financial interdependence, there have emerged pressures on a wide range of governments to undertake similar programmes of regulatory reforms. If these pressures can be sustained, one would expect national financial systems increasingly to resemble each other over time.

While regulatory reforms have precipitated generalised changes in financial systems, the greatest pressures in favour of the convergence of national economic systems and development models come from the impact of global financial structures on state policy capacity and on the patterns of corporate governance and behaviour. As illustrated in the first section, the transnational integration of financial markets has severely limited the ability of states to finance their independent policy preferences and to pursue macroeconomic and social policies in line with domestic imperatives. State policies become increasingly aimed at ensuring that national markets are attractive to investors and that domestic financial institutions remain competitive and relatively free of regulatory restrictions. Though the degree of change has varied considerably from state to state, the result has been more market-based and liberal systems of economic regulation, and corresponding pressures on social policies of welfare states.

Changes in corporate governance and practices, induced by global integration, also constitute pressure for the convergence of national economic development models. Corporate governance and behaviour, as an integral part of any political economy, is closely linked to the type of financial system and to the relationships between the financial sector, producer firms, labour market practices and the state. In other words, differences in financial systems and corporate governance are central to what makes different models of capitalism different, and are part of the sociopolitical compromises which have characterised a particular political economy over time. Changes in the financial system may unravel these relationships to yield transformations in corporate governance, new (global) links between finance and industry, altered ties between labour and the employers, and thus a possible change in the distinguishing features of economic development models themselves.

The literature has made a basic distinction between capital-market-based and bank-based financial systems and related mechanisms of corporate governance.[35] Financial globalisation appears to have created pressures for the convergence of national systems of corporate governance towards the capital market model. Even where the bank-based model seems to be well entrenched in national political economies in Europe or Asia, the liberalisation and integration of financial markets have represented a fundamental change in the system of finance and corporate control and offered incentives that may lead to its transformation. Once restrictive regulations and state capital controls are removed, banks can use their dominance of their financial systems to initiate significant change, either taking exit options or pressing their governments to reform in a liberal direction. Furthermore, as capital markets and the securitisation of banking businesses develop, financial assets are seen more and more for their tradable value than for their role in long-term corporate finance. The profitability of financial institutions will become increasingly tied to global securities markets, and long-term intermediated lending declines as a vehicle for investment finance. The financial system and corporate governance nexus that lay at the heart of social democratic or developmental state institutions in postwar Europe and Asia may over time wither from within, as corporate managers adjust their behaviour and strategies to focus on shareholder value in global securities markets under the condition of intensified competition.

The practices promoted by key international organisations also play a role in facilitating the convergence towards the capital market model. In the aftermath of the Asian financial crisis, there were strong pressures from multilateral institutions for the promotion of capital markets, the reform of closed bank–industry ties and the removal of state intervention as an integral part of their rescue packages. The crisis greatly increased the constraints which individual states experienced on their macroeconomic and indeed micro-policy-making autonomy. As the need for capital, debt rescheduling and the re-establishment of currency stability increased, so dependence on the global financial system is directly enhanced. International organisations are now more than ever involved at such micro-level policy issues as local corporate practices, banking supervision and accounting standards. One does not wish to imply that all or even most of this intrusion into domestic autonomy is necessarily negative, but it does represent important pressures for convergence among national structures of corporate governance.

If this convergence process is unduly rapid or unsuccessful, it can add to pressures which call into question the legitimacy of national political economies, democratic or not. So a major difficulty is the cumulative nature of the pressures described in the first three sections of this chapter. Even if the end result of the convergence process turns out to be positive, the pressures of transition may be worrying. Yet there is little in ongoing global integration which offers comfort that the end result will represent a positive development. Let us remind ourselves that many 'repressed' financial systems in Europe and Asia proved themselves historically as policy instruments of tremendous efficiency and growth. The record of the global (and most national) economy since the advent of the financial integration process in the late 1970s has fallen short relative to the period of national control of money and finance following the Second World War.[36] Even the national economy most successful at promoting and adapting to global financial integration, that of the United States, only recently emerged in the 1990s as an outstanding success in terms of growth, yet has seen dramatic growth in inequalities at the same time. It is difficult to argue that the liberalisation of financial systems and the global integration it inspires correlate to a long-term improvement in the trend of leading economic indicators.

It should be noted that the convergence process is likely to be incomplete and patchy across a wide range of countries. Financial structures, corporate practices and economic systems remain embedded in the fabric of local societies, nationally defined for the most part at the moment. Local constituencies will resist and may be successful in a number of ways. Differences among national forms of capitalism would exist to some degree as each local economy continues to refract the constraints of financial globalisation in its own way and as there may still be room for preservation of distinctive national policies and structures.[37] The process of convergence is thus a long one and is never likely to attain the homogenisation expected by neo-classical economists.

Thus it is not part of our argument that the individuality and distinctiveness of national states and economic development patterns have been wholly subverted. It is our argument, however, that the forces for real and significant convergence, associated with global financial integration, are there to be observed and that these forces have led to growing tensions in domestic sociopolitical processes and have created dilemmas at the centre of democratic governance. Most critically, policy convergence towards neo-liberal practices has consequences for the patterns of gains and losses among actors in the market and society in general. More market-oriented policies will lead to intensified competition among individual firms and favour multinational firms and mobile asset holders over domestically based enterprises and internationally immobile factors of production. This will result in considerable social and industrial restructuring, which some may well argue is beneficial in an aggregate and long-term sense, but involves important short-term costs for the more vulnerable market players. As their control over socioeconomic policies dwindles vis-à-vis market forces, states are less able to alleviate the restructuring pains and to direct structural adjustment in line with domestic priorities.

Further, the process of convergence, which has disturbing effects on the patterns of welfare gains and losses among various societal groups, has posed a serious challenge to the existing mechanisms for income distribution. Complex political and institutional systems have emerged over time to manage distributional conflicts with varying degrees of success in different historical epochs and national settings. The contemporary instability of continuous adjustment to global market pressures, however, risks displacing these systems too rapidly for them to survive. Labour–capital bargains in corporatist arrangements or employment-for-life in Japan, for instance, are being challenged as regulatory changes and increased capital mobility have enabled firms to seek an escape from their more costly provisions. To the extent that these systems have contributed to sociopolitical stability and the legitimacy of national governments, constant adjustment to liberal market pressures and structures can systematically sap governments of their political credibility and undermine the established patterns of accountability in democratic societies.

Thus the challenge to democratic governance lies in the ongoing transformations of norms and institutions that underpin national economic development models. These changes and the increasingly disembedded financial systems and corporate and labour market practices of political economies can weaken intricate compromises and arrangements closely linked to the legitimacy of prevailing regimes. Where the desire of governments to adopt independent economic strategies emerges from internal democratic processes – such as the desire to maintain and enhance an elaborate welfare state with the corporate tax burdens, labour market compromises and the high wage levels which that implies – the effects of market liberalisation and transnationalisation can have a clear impact on the democratic legitimacy of governments. As emerging market economies are forced to accept constant restructuring, which may destabilise the very domestic arrangements that have underpinned the accumulated successes and legitimacy of governments, this is likely to threaten the nascent, and often fragile, democratisation process in these economies.

Conclusion

This chapter has aimed at exploring the consequences of global financial integration for the maintenance of a democratic civic order and for the legitimate functioning of an international financial architecture and order. Three different but interrelated arguments have been developed in this regard. First, the tension between what national policy makers are required to do in a democratic context and what they can actually do in the face of global financial constraints has affected public confidence in the democratic form of governance. Second, financial globalisation has strengthened the position of private actors, rendered regulators and supervisors more dependent on private market interests and contributed to the emergence of closed policy networks. These changes have increasingly aligned financial policy and regulatory processes to the preferences of powerful market players, crucially altered the notion of the public interest in relation to the financial domain and posed a fundamental problem of democratic accountability. Third, the convergence of financial systems, corporate governance patterns and development models towards neo-liberal practices, propelled by the liberalisation and transnationalisation of financial markets, threatens to destabilise the complex sociopolitical arrangements that underpin the contrasting forms of capitalist development and to undermine the established basis of democratic credibility associated with these forms. As mentioned earlier, these problems are cumulative.

These issues focus our attention on the key question of political legitimacy and democratic accountability as the real bottom line when it comes to the normative constructs of international financial architecture. If the erosion of state policy capacity, the dominance of private market interests and the convergence of national economic development models conflict excessively with the imperatives of national economic security, the mandates of democratically elected governments and the requirements of domestic political stability, then the process of global financial integration and the architecture/policies which underpin it may be called into question or indeed unravel. This was certainly the case subsequent to the crisis of 1929 and the rapid disintegration of the international economic system, followed by a descent into political ugliness in a number of societies and eventual war. It is thus essential that the integration of financial markets and the reform of global financial architecture should proceed cautiously so as to maintain the legitimacy of the market order in the international system. Without such legitimacy, citizens' frustrations with democratic governance will deepen, extreme political movements intensify and global markets and institutions retreat.[38]

So the arguments in this chapter have considerable implications for the debate over the future of global financial architecture. Legitimacy, and resolving the tensions between national and global instances, should be much higher profile concerns than currently is the case.[39] One possible solution could involve the development of administrative capacity and political resources at regional and global levels or the process of what has become known as 'cosmopolitan democracy'. The emphasis would be on the strengthening of the accountability of regional institutions like the EU along with developing accountability and administrative capacity of IFIs. By pooling sovereignty, attenuating the raw exercise of state and private corporate power and developing co-operative institutional arrangements for economic governance,[40] 'cosmopolitan democracy' can attenuate some of the legitimacy deficit at the same time as it helps individual states to confront the tensions created by financial globalisation.[41] Not only is this easier said than done, but it would certainly run into the fierce opposition of transnational corporate interests, which most enjoy the freedoms and profits of global markets. Equally important, co-operative governance and the required abrogation of national prerogatives may be the most difficult hurdle (especially for the strong) in the development of (democratic) institutions of accountability at regional and global levels. These difficulties, however, do not diminish the potential advantages of the successful operation of cosmopolitan democracy, at the same time as current efforts at reforming global financial architecture fail to address the problems identified in this chapter. In the end, as at Bretton Woods, some resolution of the sociopolitical tensions and legitimacy problems associated with financial integration on the domestic front is needed, as are legitimate forms of global financial governance.

Notes

Research for this chapter was generously funded by Phase Two of the Global Economic Institutions research programme of the Economic and Social Research Council of the United Kingdom, 'International Regulatory Institutions and Global Securities Markets', grant no. L120251029.

1. Susan Strange, 'Wake up Krasner! The World has Changed', *Review of International Political Economy*, vol. 1, no. 2 (1994), p. 216.
2. See James K. Galbraith and Lu Jiaqing, 'Financial Instability and Economic Inequality: Consequences of Ungoverned Globalisation', in James K. Galbraith and Maureen Berner (eds.), *Inequality and Industrial Change: A Global View* (New York: Cambridge University Press, 2001); Jeffrey G. Williamson, 'Globalisation and Inequality Then and Now', Working Paper 5491 (Cambridge, MA: National Bureau of Economic Research, 1996).
3. See Eric Helleiner, 'From Bretton Woods to Global Finance: A World Turned Upside Down', in Richard Stubbs and Geoffrey Underhill (eds.), *Political Economy and the Changing Global Order* (London: Macmillan, 1994), pp. 163–75; David T. Llewellyn, 'The Role of International Banking', in Loukas Tsoukalis (ed.), *The Political Economy of International Money* (London: Sage, 1985), pp. 203–32.
4. Susan Strange, 'The Future of Global Capitalism; or Will Divergence Persist Forever?' in Colin Crouch and Wolfgang Streeck (eds.), *The Political Economy of Modern Capitalism* (London: Sage, 1997), pp. 183–91.
5. See Barry Eichengreen and Albert Fishlow, 'Contending with Capital Flows: What is Different about the 1990s?' in Miles Kahler (ed.), *Capital Flows and Financial Crises* (Ithaca: Cornell University Press, 1998), pp. 23–68; IMF, *International Capital Markets, Part I: Exchange Rate Management and International Capital Flows* (Washington, DC: IMF, 1993), pp. 1–7.
6. See David M. Andrews, 'Capital Mobility and State Autonomy', *International Studies Quarterly*, vol. 38, no. 3 (1994), pp. 194–7; Michael Webb, 'International Economic Structures, Government Interests, and International Co-ordination of Macroeconomic Adjustment Policies', *International Organisation*, vol. 45, no. 3 (1991), pp. 318–19.
7. Benjamin J. Cohen, 'The Triad and the Unholy Trinity: Lessons for the Pacific Region', in Richard Higgot, Richard Leaver and John Ravenhill (eds.), *Pacific Economic Relations in the 1990s* (St Leonards: Allen & Unwin, 1993), pp. 133–58.
8. See Fritz W. Scharf, *Crisis and Choice in European Social Democracy* (Ithaca: Cornell University Press, 1991), esp. ch. 2.
9. See Philip G. Cerny, 'International Finance and the Erosion of State Policy Capacity', in Philip Gummet (ed.), *Globalisation and Public Policy* (Cheltenham: Edward Elgar, 1996), pp. 83–104.
10. Philip Cerny, 'Globalisation and the Changing Logic of Collective Action', *International Organisation*, vol. 49, no. 4 (1995), pp. 611–12; 'International Finance and the Erosion of State Policy Capacity', pp. 96–7.

94   Geoffrey R. D. Underhill and Xiaoke Zhang

11. Prominent examples of econometric studies that lend support to the claim are Dani
    Rodrik, 'Trade, Social Insurance, and the Limits of Globalisation', Working Paper
    5905 (Cambridge, MA: National Bureau of Economic Research, 1997) and *Has
    Globalisation Gone Too Far?* (Washington, DC: Institute for International Eco-
    nomics, 1997), ch. 4. The claim tends to be contested by, among others, Geoffrey
    Garrett, 'Globalisation and National Autonomy', in Ngaire Woods (ed.), *The Polit-
    ical Economy of Globalisation* (London: Macmillan, 2000), pp. 107–46.
12. See, for example, Jonathan W. Moses, 'Abdication from National Policy Autonomy:
    What's Left to Leave', *Politics and Society*, vol. 22, no. 2 (1994), pp. 125–48; 'The
    Fiscal Constraints on Social Democracy', *Nordic Journal of Political Economy*,
    vol. 22 (1995), pp. 49–68; Martin Rhodes, 'Subversive Liberalism: Market Integra-
    tion, Globalisation and West European Welfare States', in William Coleman and
    Geoffrey Underhill (eds.), *Regionalism and Global Economic Integration* (London:
    Routledge, 1998), pp. 99–121.
13. See Pierre-Richard Agénor and Joshua Aizenman, 'Volatility and the Welfare
    Costs of Financial Market Integration', Working Paper 6782 (Cambridge, MA:
    National Bureau of Economic Research, 1998); Mansoor Dailami, 'Financial Open-
    ness, Democracy and Redistributive Policy', Policy Research Working Paper 2372
    (Washington, DC: World Bank, 2000).
14. There is considerable literature that establishes the impact of economic and financial
    globalisation on the widening gap of wealth and income within both developed
    and developing countries. See, for example, Andrew Hurrell and Ngaire Woods
    (eds.), *Inequality, Globalisation, and World Politics* (Oxford: Oxford University
    Press, 1999); Dennis Quinn, 'The Correlates of Change in International Financial
    Regulation', *American Political Science Review*, vol. 91, no. 3 (1997), pp. 531–51;
    Jeffrey G. Williamson, 'Globalisation and Inequality Then and Now'.
15. See Garrett, 'Globalisation and National Autonomy', pp. 123–5.
16. See the chapter by John Williamson in this volume; Rodrik, *Has Globalisation Gone
    Too Far?* ch. 4; Dani Rodrik and Tanguy van Ypersele, 'Capital Mobility, Distribu-
    tive Conflict and International Tax Co-ordination', Working Paper 7150 (Cam-
    bridge, MA: National Bureau of Economic Research, 1999); Sven Steinmo, 'The
    End of Redistribution? International Pressures and Domestic Tax Policy Choices',
    Challenge, vol. 37, no. 6 (November 1994), pp. 9–17. The general claim that finan-
    cial integration reduces the redistributive role of corporate taxation is qualified by
    Garrett's econometric analysis, which shows that the effects of integration on capital
    taxation are contingent on the partisan balance of power. See Garrett, 'Globalisation
    and National Autonomy', pp. 130–6.
17. See Coleman and Underhill, 'Introduction', in Coleman and Underhill, *Region-
    alism and Global Economic Integration*, pp. 5–11; David Held, 'Democracy, the
    Nation State and the Global System', in David Held (ed.), *Political Theory Today*
    (Cambridge: Polity Press, 1991), pp. 197–235; *Democracy and the Global Order*
    (Cambridge: Polity Press, 1995), pp. 3–23.
18. Held, *Democracy and the Global Order*, pp. 127–34. See also David Held and
    Anthony McGrew, 'Globalisation and the Liberal Democratic State', *Government
    and Opposition*, vol. 28, no. 2 (1993), pp. 268–71.

19. See Susan J. Pharr, Robert D. Putnam and Russell J. Dalton, 'A Quarter-Century of Declining Confidence', *Journal of Democracy*, vol. 11, no. 2 (2000), pp. 19–23.

20. Terry Lynn Karl, 'Economic Inequality and Democratic Instability', *Journal of Democracy*, vol. 11, no. 1 (2000), pp. 149–56. We certainly realise that the relationship between financial globalisation and democracy is necessarily complicated and defies simple and linear depiction. For a more nuanced treatment, see Sylvia Maxfield, 'Understanding the Political Implications of Financial Internationalisation in Emerging Market Countries', *World Development*, vol. 26, no. 7 (1998), pp. 1201–19.

21. We are not attempting to argue that the proper functioning of markets is contrary to the public interest. It was Adam Smith's contention that the individual pursuit of private gain can (under specified conditions) serve an important public purpose. Our argument is that we should be concerned not only with whether markets function efficiently, but also with the overall legitimacy of the *outcome* of market mechanisms as a system of governance, including distributional issues. This implies a broader definition of the public interest than is typically assumed in economic analysis, and this definition is heavily conditioned by democracy. We argue that democratic forms of government will tend to propel the market system towards this broader definition, and thus we argue that it is imperative that democratic governments must prevent the requirements of market efficiency from becoming an alibi for private interests assuming the mantle of the public good in the name of the freedom of enterprise. Our thanks to Claude Serfati (Université de Versailles/St. Quentin-en-Yvelines), for drawing attention to this issue.

22. For a more detailed discussion on the notion of the pubic domain and corresponding interpretations of the public interest in relation to the financial order, see Geoffrey Underhill, 'The Public Good versus Private Interests in the Global Financial and Monetary System', *International Comparative and Corporate Law Journal*, vol. 2, no. 3 (2000), pp. 335–59.

23. Henry Morgenthau, US Treasury Secretary (1944), as quoted in Richard Gardner, *Sterling–Dollar Diplomacy in Current Perspective* (New York: Columbia University Press, 1981), p. 76.

24. See Benjamin J. Cohen, *The Geography of Money* (Ithaca: Cornell University Press, 1999); Eric Helleiner, *States and the Reemergence of Global Finance: From Bretton Woods to the 1990s* (Ithaca: Cornell University Press, 1994).

25. The domestic and international factors that prompted financial policy changes are not dealt with here. Relevant discussions of these factors include John B. Goodman and Louis W. Pauly, 'The Obsolescence of Capital Controls? Economic Management in an Age of Global Markets', *World Politics*, vol. 46, no. 1 (1993), pp. 50–82; Helleiner, *States and the Reemergence of Global Finance*; Geoffrey Underhill, 'Markets Beyond Politics? The State and the Internationalisation of Financial Markets', *European Journal of Political Research*, vol. 19, nos. 2 and 3 (1991), pp. 173–96.

26. Market-based supervisory methods in the banking sector are still uncharted territory (awaiting the implementation of the new Basel Committee on Banking Supervision's capital adequacy standards – see Basel Committee on Banking Supervision, *The New Basle Capital Accord*, consultative document, Bank for International Settlements,

January 2001) and there are questions which may be raised concerning the appropriateness of these methods. Avinash Persaud of State Street Bank (London), has argued ('Sending the Herd off the Cliff Edge: the Disturbing Interaction between Herding and Market-sensitive Risk Management Practices', 1st prize, Jacques de la Rosière essay competition, Institute for International Finance, Washington, published in E-Risk Erisks.com, Dec. 2000) that the use of market-sensitive risk management models may yield good risk management practices for individual firms, but may yield herd behaviour in aggregate and thus enhance the probability of systemic risk. It can be argued that the same problem applies to market-based supervisory methods employing these same models: what is good for individual firms in prudential terms may in aggregate prove problematic. Our acknowledgements on this point go to Jean-Pierre Patat, Director-General, Banque de France, presentation to the conference 'From Naples to Genoa: a New World of Finance and Development', Treasury Ministry, Rome, 31 May–1 June 2001. Similar questions concerning new supervisory techniques are raised in Underhill, 'The Public Good versus Private Interests'.

27. For more detailed discussions of these issues see Geoffrey Underhill, 'Keeping Governments out of Politics', *Review of International Studies*, vol. 21, no. 3 (1995), pp. 251–78; 'Private Markets and Public Responsibility', in Underhill (ed.), *The New World Order in International Finance* (London: Macmillan, 1997), pp. 17–49.

28. See Maxfield, 'Understanding the Political Implications of Financial Internationalisation'; Tony Porter, 'The Transnational Agenda for Financial Regulation in Developing Countries', in Leslie Elliott Armijo (ed.), *Financial Globalisation and Democracy in Emerging Markets* (London: Macmillan, 1999), pp. 106–8.

29. See Underhill, 'Keeping Governments out of Politics'; 'Private Markets and Public Responsibility'.

30. See Cerny, 'International Finance and the Erosion of State Policy Capacity', pp. 96, 99; Porter, 'The Transnational Agenda for Financial Regulation'.

31. Thomas Oatley and Robert Nabors document how the Basel Accord was created to respond to the rent-seeking demands of private financial firms in leading industrial nations, in 'Redistributive Co-operation: Market Failure, Wealth Transfers, and the Basle Accord', *International Organisation*, vol. 52, no. 1 (1998), pp. 35–54.

32. This point is argued more systematically in Geoffrey Underhill, 'Transnational Financial Markets and National Economic Development Models: Global Structures versus Domestic Imperatives', in *Économies et Sociétés*, Série 'Monnaie', ME, n° 1–2, 9–10/1999, pp. 43–50.

33. See Wendy Dobson and Pierre Jaquet, *Financial Services Liberalisation in the WTO* (Washington, DC: Institute for International Economics, 1998).

34. See Porter, 'The Transnational Agenda for Financial Regulation'.

35. These two models are primarily distinguished by the relative importance of capital markets in corporate development, the nature of bank–industry relations and the extent of government intervention in financial systems. A classical discussion of these differences can be found in John Zysman, *Governments, Markets, and Growth: Financial Systems and the Politics of Industrial Change* (Ithaca: Cornell University Press, 1983), pp. 69–75; see also Underhill, 'Transnational Financial Markets'.

36. See, for instance, Nicholas F. R. Crafts and Terence C. Mills, 'Europe's Golden Age: An Econometric Investigation of Changing Trend Rates of Growth', Discussion Paper No. 1087 (London: Centre for Economic Policy Research, 1995).

37. See Geoffrey Garrett, 'Capital Mobility, Trade, and the Domestic Politics of Economic Policy', *International Organisation*, vol. 49, no. 4 (1995), pp. 675–87; Louis Pauly, 'National Financial Structures, Capital Mobility, and International Economic Rules', *Policy Sciences*, vol. 27, no. 4 (1994), pp. 343–63.

38. See Louis Pauly, 'Capital Mobility, State Autonomy and Political Legitimacy', *Journal of International Affairs*, vol. 48, no. 2 (1995), pp. 369–88; *Who Elected the Bankers? Surveillance and Control in the World Economy* (Ithaca: Cornell University Press, 1997), esp. ch. 7; Susan Strange, *Mad Money* (Manchester: Manchester University Press, 1998).

39. The recent endorsement by IMF First Deputy Managing Director Ann Krueger of an international debt workout mechanism resembling domestic bankruptcy proceedings will hopefully prove a step in this direction, though implementation is still a long way off; see address by Ann Krueger, 'International Financial Architecture for 2002: a New Approach to Sovereign Debt Restructuring', National Economists' Club Annual Dinner, 26 November 2001, available at www.imf.org/external/np/speeches/2001/112601.htm. See also discussion in Kumar and Miller in this volume.

40. See chapter 17 by Kumar and Miller in this volume.

41. 'Cosmopolitan democracy' as a regional and global solution to the democratic deficit caused by economic globalisation is elaborated in James Bohman, 'International Regimes and Democratic Governance: Political Equality and Influence in Global Institutions', *International Affairs*, vol. 75, no. 3 (1999), pp. 499–513; Held, *Democracy and the Global Order*, pp. 267–82. On accountability, see Robert O. Keohane, 'Democracy, Accountability, and Global Governance', paper for conference on Globalization and Governance, University of California Institute on Global Conflict and Co-operation, La Jolla, CA, 23–4 March 2001.

Part II

Globalisation, financial crises and national experiences

5 Crisis consequences: lessons from Thailand

PASUK PHONGPAICHIT AND CHRIS BAKER

The failure to manage the Asian crisis, to understand the mistakes and to institute reforms with any meaning for crisis-vulnerable countries, restates the importance of local, national and regional responses to financial globalisation.

The crisis which began when Thailand floated its currency on 2 July 1997 became a regional crisis and then a global crisis. The focus of subsequent analysis has, quite rightly, been on the international implications of the event. Thailand became a side-show in a much larger global drama. Yet the course of the crisis in the affected countries contains important lessons. Developing countries whose GDPs represent a minute fraction of the world economy are especially vulnerable to financial volatility. The discussion of reform in the international financial system petered out in 1999 once the crisis was contained in eastern Europe and Latin America. Proposals that the international financial institutions should have a duty to control volatility had already been struck off the agenda before this time. While the dangers of capital account liberalisation without appropriate monetary and regulatory policies are now well understood and thus unlikely to be repeated, the underlying vulnerability to volatility remains.

The lessons from the Thai case are obscured because early interpretations of the Thai crisis were highly ideological, and because the IMF has been intent on claiming credit for successful crisis management. In 1999, Michel Camdessus, the then Managing Director of the IMF, announced that Thailand has 'graduated from the IMF University *summa cum laude* ... graduation means victory ... the job is done'. A year later he emerged from retirement to claim that 'the IMF response to the Asian crisis has been an outstanding success',[1]

This chapter sets out some lessons from the Thai experience of the 1997–9 crisis. It does not cover the importance of avoiding the policy failures which Thailand committed in the course of capital account liberalisation. This topic is well covered elsewhere. Instead, this chapter focuses on the lessons which can be learned about what happens once a financial crisis has struck. To set the scene we first give a brief account of the event.

The Thai crisis

Over the forty years before 1997, the Thai economy grew at an average of 7.7 per cent a year, and the rate never fell below 4 per cent. The Thai economy had long been oriented to trade, and throughout the second half of the twentieth century was relatively open in the context of the time. The growth strategy was export-led, starting with agricultural exports and transiting to industry and services (tourism) over the 1980s. Foreign investment was small as a proportion of total investment, but had two important functions: it brought in technology, and it often set the direction for domestic investment. The state provided a business-friendly environment, and protected a domestic banking cartel which served as the engine of capital accumulation for domestic firms.

After 1986, the economy accelerated as a result of the relocation of manufacturing from Japan. A sixth of the labour force was transferred out of agriculture within five years. The speed and scale of this boom created scarcities, particularly of skilled manpower and infrastructure. By the early 1990s this cycle was already into a downturn.

Over 1991–3 Thailand liberalised its capital account. This move was strongly encouraged by international financial institutions, but also promoted by local technocrats and businessmen, who believed that the domestic financial cartel was a bottleneck on growth. Liberalisation led to an immediate financial boom. Local entrepreneurs suddenly had access to capital at a fraction of the cost they had been accustomed to pay. International financial firms, starved of good profit rates in the advanced economies, were in love with 'emerging markets' and especially with developing Asia.

The government failed to control the resulting flood, either by imposing closer regulation on banks, or by floating the currency.[2] The economy quickly became distorted. The real value of the currency rose, wages increased, export competitiveness fell and the balance of trade deteriorated. The flood of investment had nowhere to go as the economy was already into a cyclical downturn and the overvalued currency discouraged investment in export-producing sectors. Much of the capital inflow went into poor-quality investments in non-tradable sectors – real estate, financial services and some import-substituting industries such as petrochemicals. By 1996, private foreign debt had risen to over 40 per cent of GDP, with a high proportion contracted short-term. The current account deficit exceeded 8 per cent of GDP. In late 1996, these signals induced speculators to attack the currency, leading to the float in July 1997.

The IMF interpreted the Thai problem as 'a current account-problem-led crisis combined with a fixed exchange rate'.[3] In other words, the IMF did not diagnose a capital account crisis. This phrase did not enter its vocabulary until a year later. Accordingly, the IMF applied the same formula used to treat current account crises in Latin America over the previous two decades caused by government overspending. The IMF solution was a deflationary package of budget cuts and tight money.

The IMF was totally deaf to local criticism that this was an inappropriate solution in the Thai case. More strikingly, it was also deaf to criticism from international financial firms. Several noted that there seemed nothing in the package which addressed the problems of the private sector's high foreign debt. They also observed that the value of support for the reserves (US$17.2 billion) was only a third of the amount raised in the 1994 Mexican crisis, and possibly inadequate for the task. In addition, the IMF forced the Thai government to reveal its forward positions in the foreign exchange market, and disclose the amount lent to finance firms, before the IMF support package was announced. All together, these moves prompted an immediate, panicky capital flight.

In the year following the float, private capital outflows, net of foreign direct investment (FDI), were equivalent to 18.5 per cent of GDP. Outflows of this scale acquired their own momentum. Four years after the float the leakage was still running at close to 10 per cent of GDP (see Figure 1).

Under the impact of this capital flight and the IMF's deflationary medicine, the economy spiralled downwards. One year later, GDP was shrinking at an annualised rate of 13 per cent. Over two million people – one-in seven of the non-agricultural workforce – lost their jobs. Real wages for the remainder declined by around 15 per cent. Thousands of companies went out of operation.

Figure 1. *Thailand's capital account, 1985–2001.*

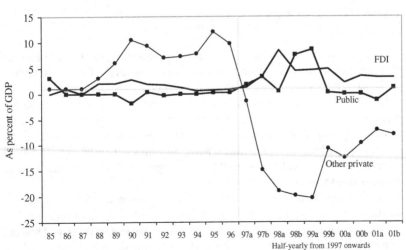

According to the IMF, its own package would stimulate exports, maintain a positive capital inflow and deliver GDP growth in 1998. None of this came about. However, the economy began to stabilise in mid-1998 through different logic. The vicious decline in demand caused imports to plummet to almost half their former level, delivering a positive current account balance. At the same time, FDI flowed in to buy up distressed companies at bargain prices. Government was able to use the external account surplus to strengthen the currency. In addition, the Thai government rebelled against the IMF fiscal policy in mid-1998, and secured Japanese funds under the Miyazawa scheme to implement a fiscal stimulus. The downward spiral levelled out over the first half of 1999. At this turning point, in terms of GDP per capita and several other indicators, the economy had been driven backwards by around five to seven years.[4]

In late 1999, GDP began to grow on the traditional basis of rising exports. But the economy was still crippled, largely because the financial system had seized up (see below) and many domestic firms had ceased operation. The moderate recovery which began in late 1999 was very uneven. Growth came largely from fiscal stimulus and from exports in a few sectors such as electronic, electrical and automotive goods which were dominated by multinationals and had high import content. The domestic economy wallowed. In 2000, when the Miyazawa funds ran out and international trade cycled downwards, the recovery petered out. Low agricultural prices and low consumer confidence held down domestic demand. The collapse of the financial system retarded business activity. Burdened by a socialised portion of the financial debt, the government lacked the resources to contrive domestic recovery.

Controlling capital flight

The major risk in a capital account crisis is unchecked capital flight. It ensures that currency depreciation overshoots any reasonable level – the baht bottomed in January 1998 at 56.9 baht to the dollar, around 40 per cent of its pre-float value. It drains away liquidity. Combined with the depreciation, it wrecks the balance sheets and cash-flow positions of financial intermediaries. It raises domestic costs and reduces demand. The result is a very rapid contraction of the economy which, beyond a critical point, becomes self-sustaining. The flight of foreign capital localises the problem of corporate debt and makes it much more difficult to unwind.

Debtors and creditors were jointly and equally responsible for the incautious lending which created the crisis. Some foreign lenders were explicitly guilty of moral hazard. An international banker stated: 'We lent so much to Thailand at that time because we always believed the government would bail us out.'[5] In

Table 3. Thailand: half-yearly GDP changes (constant prices), 1997–2001.

Sectors	1997		1998		1999		2000		2001	
	Q1/2	Q3/4	Q1/2	Q3/4	Q1/2	Q3/4	Q1/2	Q3/4	Q1/2	Q3/4
			(per cent year-on-year real change)							
Agriculture	−0.8	−0.6	−4.9	1.8	4.9	−0.2	6.0	3.7	1.2	1.8
Manufacturing	5.4	0.7	**−10.7**	**−9.0**	6.5	15.6	9.4	3.4	1.5	1.7
Construction	**−26.5**	**−24.9**	**−36.4**	**−40.0**	**−12.1**	**−1.5**	**−2.7**	**−15.4**	**−10.4**	4.7
Commerce	−0.7	−0.7	**−10.8**	**−11.1**	3.5	5.7	5.8	5.1	3.5	1.7
Finance and real estate	−2.0	**−10.9**	**−13.1**	**−26.1**	**−24.8**	**−7.8**	0.2	−2.4	1.7	2.4
Services	4.9	5.3	4.1	6.6	4.7	3.6	3.5	3.5	1.4	2.1
Total GDP	0.2	−2.9	**−10.5**	**−10.6**	1.6	7.3	6.4	2.9	1.8	1.9
Private consumption expenditure	2.9	**−5.5**	**−11.8**	**−11.3**	−1.0	9.9	7.0	2.9	3.9	3.0
Government expenditure	0.1	**−5.4**	**−5.8**	13.0	9.1	−1.4	2.9	2.3	4.5	−0.3
Capital formation	**−13.4**	**−27.2**	**−44.6**	**−44.1**	**−10.6**	4.9	10.5	0.8	0.5	1.1
Export of goods and services	1.1	13.3	13.6	3.5	1.3	16.7	19.8	15.7	−1.5	−6.6
Import of goods and services	−9.7	**−12.9**	**−27.1**	**−15.7**	3.8	16.7	34.5	21.3	−5.3	−11.1

Note: Numbers in bold show periods of steepest decline.
Source: National Economic and Social Development Board.

late 1997, the IMF pressured the Thai government to guarantee the debts of the Thai financial institutions which were closed down. Both South Korea and Malaysia avoided panicky capital flight. Malaysia imposed currency controls. South Korea bargained with the IMF and the United States to negotiate a standstill agreement with the main creditors among international banks. Thailand and Indonesia offered no such resistance. Both Malaysia and South Korea had prior experience of financial crises; South Korea in particular had suffered two major recessions in the recent past.[6] Both countries were more sensitive to the risk of severe capital flight. In Thailand the issue was scarcely discussed until the flight had begun. Both South Korea and Malaysia had the political will to bargain with the capital markets. Thailand and Indonesia did not.

In its early analyses of the Thai crisis, nowhere did the IMF acknowledge the risk of severe capital flight. In the Latin American current account crises which formed the Fund's mental model for the Thai case, there might be some initial leakage while the currency was readjusting, but the IMF's presence and its stringent package would rapidly restore the confidence of the international financial markets. High interest rates would be enough to deter capital flight. The initial Thai package in August 1997 stated that a tight monetary policy would 'prevent capital flight', and the IMF initially projected a positive balance on Thailand's capital account in 1998. But international creditors interpreted the high interest rates as a signal of certain deterioration, and hence an incentive to get out quickly.

Since 1997, some economists have pointed out that modern capital account crises require different treatment. Akyüz and Cornford note that modern crises are characterised by 'a sharp increase in capital inflows followed by an equally sharp reversal', and relate this directly to the increase in private lending to developing countries and the 'manifest herd-like behaviour' of the international finance markets.[7] Miller and Zhang point out that collectively it may be in the best interests of international creditors to refrain from capital flight which will undermine the host economy, but individually each creditor will find it logical to withdraw funds as rapidly as possible.[8] Both sets of authors advocate some institutional mechanism to forestall capital flight. Akyüz and Cornford discuss developing the IMF as an international lender of last resort. Miller and Zhang suggest that countries swamped by private debt should be treated analogously to bankrupt companies – through standstill agreements and debt workouts. Akyüz and Cornford also point out that if 'lenders and investors knew in advance that they might be locked in, should a financial panic develop', it would deter careless lending practices and help eliminate moral hazard.

Proposals for reform of the international financial system discussed during 1998–9 included involving private international creditors in crisis management. But the issue was not resolved before enthusiasm for reform faded. At the conference on this project, international financiers welcomed the principle of greater private involvement, but fiercely resisted any formal framework. They argued that each crisis differs, and hence flexibility is required. In essence they want the freedom to make a choice.

The failure to resolve this issue at the international level returns the responsibility to the national government. Akyüz and Cornford argue strongly that countries must retain the right to defend themselves against the threat of capital account volatility. The Thai experience in the 1997–9 crisis emphasises the importance of some form of moratorium, capital controls or standstill agreement to forestall capital panic.

Avoiding financial seizure

The Thai crisis was significantly worsened by an ambitious attempt to transform the country's financial system. This attempt stemmed from American policy makers' sense of their international mission.

Although the crisis management was handled by the IMF, US policy makers were directly involved, especially the then Treasury Secretary, Robert Rubin, and his deputy, Larry Summers. The handling directly reflected the aims of American economic diplomacy in Asia. The IMF's actions seem to have been guided by three graded priorities. The first was to preserve the stability of the international financial system, which of course is the IMF's reason for being. The second was to impose economic, legal and political changes in the crisis countries. The third was to bring about a recovery.

The importance of the second priority was set out in a series of speeches which Larry Summers made over the first year of the crisis.[9] In summary, these speeches made the following main points. First, as the 'world's only economic superpower', the United States has both the ability and the duty to shape the global economy. Second, market liberalisation is beneficial both to the United States and to the liberalised economies. The benefit to the liberalised economies arises from the usual gains attributed to free trade, and from the replacement of backward local firms by superior international firms. Third, the Asian crisis arose from 'crony capitalism', which has to be dismantled in the interests of the mass of the people in the crisis countries. Fourth, interventions to reshape local economies often provoke resistance because of the threat to 'vested interests' and because of concerns about sovereignty. Such interventions are much more palatable if they are mediated through international organisations. Fifth, financial crises offer unique opportunities to enforce change because the forces of opposition are in disarray. Summers liked to repeat that one of the two characters in the Chinese for 'crisis' meant 'opportunity', and he titled one of his speeches of this era (March 1998) 'Opportunities Out of Crises: Lessons from Asia'. Summers noted that the United States had pressured the IMF to expand the conditions attached to its crisis loans to cover a much wider range of issues, including: 'sweeping liberalisation of the domestic economy', 'radical financial sector reform', 'foreign competition and participation', and 'reforms to reduce trade barriers and unproductive expenditures, promote core labour standards and mitigate the social costs of economic adjustments'.

Accordingly, the second Letter of Intent between Thailand and the IMF in November 1997 set out an ambitious programme of restructuring. The financial sector would be totally overhauled through new legislation and foreign participation. The public sector would be overhauled by privatisation, with the initial sell-offs 'by mid 1998'. A week after this Letter was published, the American Chamber of Commerce in Bangkok called for removal of all remaining barriers to foreign participation in the economy.

The Thai government had been committed to restructuring the financial system since the early 1990s. Both technocrats and businessmen recognised that the banking cartel was no longer justifiable. However, they also understood that the banking system was the heart of the Thai capital market. Stock trading was still in its infancy and the bond market non-existent. Thai technocrats envisioned an evolutionary change, achieved by gradually exposing the Thai banks to foreign participation. The offshore banking facility established in 1993 was the first stage of this scheme. Subsequent steps were laid out in a financial restructuring plan in 1995. Five new foreign banking licences were being issued when the crisis struck. Certainly there was some opposition to these plans from the established banks. But the direction of change was broadly agreed.

The analysis of the crisis articulated by Summers and echoed by the international press legitimated a destroy-and-replace approach to institutional change, in place of the evolutionary path envisaged by Thai policy makers.

Destruction was appealing in the circumstances. Most Thai financial firms had been rendered both illiquid and technically bankrupt once three things happened at once: their foreign liabilities escalated in value as the baht fell; their cash flow deteriorated as the economy spiralled down; their capital base shrank as foreign creditors withdrew funds. Government initially proposed to manage this problem by closing down the firms beyond hope of rescue and dividing their good and bad assets between a good bank and bad bank. However, it soon abandoned this model because of the technical difficulties of deciding which assets were good and which bad. Financial firms were simply closed down and the assets put up for auction. Real-sector clients immediately found their savings and their credit lines frozen. All debtor firms faced penal rates of interest under the IMF's monetary policy. Government then imposed Basel rules for credit provisioning. Following the three problems already mentioned, these rules set near-impossible tasks for bank recapitalisation.

At the same time, government threw the bad debt problem back at the commercial banks, set up a structure for debt negotiation and incentivised the banks with offers of capital subventions. This plan failed completely because the weight of bad debts was simply too large. The depreciation of the currency (from around 25 baht to the dollar to around 40) had increased the baht value of foreign debts, and added around 15 per cent to the total debt incidence. The rapid capital flight meant that most of the problem was localised. Over 2 trillion baht flowed out of the country, effectively transferring debts from foreign lenders to local financial intermediaries. Out of the remaining corporate debt of 6.5 trillion baht, all but 0.8 trillion was owed to local financial institutions. In effect, both local debtors and local creditors had been decapitalised. With the economy stopped dead, there was little prospect for debt workouts.

Both creditors and debtors rebelled. Led by a steel magnate who advocated the Three Don'ts – don't pay interest, don't negotiate, don't run away – debtors stopped repayments. Some justified this as 'a scheme to counter the threat of extinction' and, since repayments were simply fuelling the capital drain, 'the corporate equivalent of Mahathir-style currency controls'.[10] In the old system of personalised relations between bankers and clients, default was unthinkable because of social sanctions. Within a very short space of time, the social base of this trust was destroyed. In early 1999, a banker fumed, 'Over the past three months, Thai businessmen suddenly and joyfully have discovered that there are no legal sanctions and they can get away with it.'[11] Banks began scaling back their loan portfolios, as 'Under the current circumstances, downsizing is not unusual as our priority is survival.'[12] The credit system seized up.

Non-performing loans rose to around one half of the total. Debt restructuring proceeded slowly. The IMF urged the government to pass better bankruptcy laws, but even these proved ineffective, partly because the process was slow, but also because debtors and creditors saw little point in fighting over nothing.

The IMF's model seemed to assume that the financial system could be restructured rapidly through shock therapy. Around this time there was a lot of talk about the Schumpeterian 'creative destruction' at the heart of American-style free market capitalism. Summers explicitly stated: 'The American financial sector is the largest – and most successful – financial sector in the world. It goes without saying that we believe countries will only enjoy the benefits of a truly global market if our firms are given greater access to their markets.'[13]

But American financial capital showed little interest in bricks-and-mortar banking. The foreign banks which bought into collapsed Thai institutions were either Singaporean or north European with a colonial heritage. American finance, in the form of Goldman Sachs and GE Finance, showed interest only in bottom-fishing – buying and selling distressed assets.

In short, the IMF's enthusiasm for enforcing financial restructuring in the teeth of the crisis was driven by opportunism and ignorance. It showed no appreciation of the role which commercial banking had played in the Thai economy in the past. It simply stigmatised all past practice as 'cronyism', legitimating the total destruction of the institutions responsible. It took no account of the realities of attempting such restructuring at a time when both creditors and debtors had been decapitalised. It ignored the cultural and institutional difficulties of making a transition. As a result the attempt at rapid restructuring deepened the crisis by seizing up the credit system, delayed recovery and posed long-term problems through the decline of trust.

By mid-1998, analysis of the crisis moved away from micro explanations about cronyism, bad banking practice and Asian models of capitalism, and began to focus on macro policy and the sequencing of capital account liberalisation. Studies appeared which showed that Thailand's pre-crisis banking system had been efficient relative to the requirements and sophistication of the overall economy.[14] Thai policy makers stepped back from the prospect of a wholesale internationalisation of the banking system (as happened in some Latin American crises). Even some enthusiasts for restructuring admitted that the banking system had played a major part in previous growth, and that restructuring would need time.[15] But by this time, the system was already seized.

The importance of region

Crises re-emphasise the importance of regional links. Because the Mexican crisis was an embarrassment to the recently signed North American Free Trade Agreement (NAFTA), the US government mobilised co-operation from American firms to substantiate the official bail-out. When asked why the funding applied to the Thai IMF package was only a third of the Mexican package, Larry Summers replied: 'Thailand is not on our border.' Thailand was the origin of the Asian crisis, but not the priority for international policy makers. South Korea and Indonesia were more important for economic and political reasons respectively. The spread of the contagion to Russia and Latin America soon captured the US policy makers' main attention. When Robert Rubin visited Bangkok in June 1998, his message to Thailand's finance minister was: you're on your own. In private he was prepared to admit that the IMF's initial package had failed, and that global political–economic realities meant that Thailand would now have to find its own way out of the crisis.

From the start, Thai leaders sought a regional approach to managing the crisis. In early 1997, there was a flurry of attempts by central bankers in southeast Asia to strengthen co-operation to resist currency speculation. In the final weeks before Thailand had to float the baht, Thai ministers and central bankers visited Asian capitals, trying to raise funding, but without success. After the

Thai government opened talks with the IMF, Japan took over the responsibility of raising the package funding within Asia. As Eisuke Sakakibara, the Japanese deputy finance minister, explained, 'we thought it was a good opportunity for Asian countries to recognise that the Asian currency crisis was our own problem, and that we could strengthen regional co-operation within Asia'.[16] This effort led directly to more ambitious plans to create an Asian Monetary Fund (AMF). Summers, according to Sakakibara, interpreted this scheme as 'a challenge from Japan to US hegemony in Asia', and killed it during September 1997.

Over the next year, there was a vigorous debate within Japan over the country's proper response to the Asian crisis. One party argued that all Japan's resources should be devoted to its own domestic problem. Others dissented on the grounds of Japan's long-term interests in the Asian region. Eventually the balance tipped in favour of the pro-region side. Japanese firms had reaped high profit rates from their south-east Asian operations in the pre-crisis era. Faced with the choice between abandoning these ventures or recapitalising them and acquiring full control, many took the latter option. Japanese firms and policy makers were concerned about American firms achieving greater penetration in a region which they liked to consider their own backyard. They were also concerned about the Americans' aggressive advocacy of a pure free-market model in countries where Japan had patiently been preaching its own guided approach to catch-up development over the past quarter-century. Sakakibara saw the crisis as an opportunity to expand the usage of the·yen as an international currency.

The widespread criticism of the IMF in the last quarter of 1998 and the faltering of discussion on reform of the international financial system created the opportunity for Japan to reassert its role in managing the crisis. In September, Japan announced the US$30 billion Miyazawa scheme for promoting recovery in crisis-hit Asia. The United States immediately threatened to launch its own rival version. But Japan convinced the United States to accept a token participation by the World Bank in Miyazawa scheme projects. The Thai finance minister welcomed the Miyazawa scheme as 'exactly what we need', and was the first to attend Tokyo to discuss details.

On a broader level, the crisis sparked a revived interest in regional economic co-operation. Before the crisis, plans to create an ASEAN (Association of South East Asian Nations) free trade area (AFTA) had moved slowly, and co-operation on finance had never been discussed. After the killing of the AMF proposal, several Asian countries discussed the idea of pooling reserves to strengthen resistance against currency speculation and crisis. Since such pooling only made sense if it involved the region's countries with big reserves (Japan, China, South Korea), this debate gave rise to a new informal grouping dubbed 'ASEAN+3'. At the annual meeting of the Asian Development Bank (ADB) held in Thailand in December 2000, this grouping announced a plan for a network of bilateral currency swaps. The United States again responded antagonistically by warning against the dangers of such a scheme, and threatening to withhold any additional US contributions to ADB capitalisation. But the United States was mollified when the IMF was involved in the scheme to provide technical surveillance. Several bilateral swap arrangements were signed over the next two years. Japanese officials argued that the swap network would eventually evolve into an Asian Monetary Fund.

ASEAN also reacted to the crisis by resolving to accelerate plans to create a free trade area. This resolve crumbled in practice. But in 2000, several countries in the region began to discuss schemes for bilateral and multilateral free trade schemes. By late 2001, at least ten such schemes were under negotiation, while ASEAN and China announced the intention to create a joint free trade area 'within ten years'.[17] Any serious progress towards regional integration in Asia faces large problems. Within south-east Asia, moves towards trade integration are hampered because countries are often mutually competitive. The smaller nations of south-east Asia are nervous of Japanese domination. The region's major countries – Japan, China, South Korea – are divided by historical enmities. In the past, Japan's aspirations for greater regional leadership have always been compromised by the political economy of its relationship with the United States. Recently, the economic rise of China has turned this into a more complex triangle of forces.

Despite these difficulties, the crisis has delivered a clear message about the importance of regional co-operation. The comparative success of the Mexican bail-out was predicated on regional politics. The American assertion of leadership in managing the Asian crisis was both a restatement of its status as 'the world's only economic superpower', and an opportunistic attempt to reassert influence in a region where America had lost ground since the withdrawals of 1975. The initial American-dominated analysis of the crisis and proposed solution reflected a highly ideological view of Asian economies. The evident failure of this solution raised doubts about the consequences of allowing the United States to assume such a leadership role. Regional co-operation became important as a strategy for achieving greater independence or bargaining power to resist damaging forms of intervention.

The defence of national policy

Financial crises create opportunities for international capital to supplant local capital. But short-term gains may provoke political reactions with long-term consequences.

In the Cold War era, strengthening local capitalisms was a key part of US political strategy. But the rationale for such support dissolved with the collapse of the Eastern bloc. Almost overnight, local capitalisms ceased to be bases of political alliance, and became instead sources of economic competition. The result has been attempts to institutionalise the advantages of advanced capital through international organisations, while dismantling the support provided for local capital by national states.

In late 1997, the IMF demanded that the Thai government remove many forms of protection for local business. Foreign chambers of commerce in Bangkok, and the international press, cheered this agenda. As noted above, the financial system which had served as the engine of capital accumulation for domestic firms was partly dismantled, and partly seized up.[18] In parallel, there was a step-change in the degree of foreign ownership. In the two years after the July 1997 float, more foreign direct investment flowed into Thailand than over the ten years of the previous boom – a boom often attributed to foreign investment. Almost none of this inflow went into new investments. Almost all was buying up cheap assets – especially in finance, export manufacturing and retail.[19]

These rapid transfers created a political reaction. This was complex. The political forces favouring globalisation were undermined, while those opposing them were substantially strengthened.

Over the 1990s, the Democrat Party had become identified as the party which best represented those groups whose interests were tied up with Thailand's modern urban economy, namely big business and the urban middle class. But these groups were in a minority in a society where around half the population was employed in agriculture, and most businesses were small-scale family firms. By simple electoral arithmetic, parties which rose on provincial support dominated the parliament and cabinet in the mid-1990s. From early 1997, the deterioration of the economy provoked an urban fear that these provincial-based parties had neither the skills nor interest to manage and protect the modern urban economy. IMF criticism of the government, and the steep slide which began in August, turned this fear into panic. The urban press and business leaders called for the government to resign. White-collar workers staged demonstrations in the financial district and outside Government House. In late 1997, this urban political upsurge forced the government to resign and be replaced by a cabinet headed by the Democrat Party.

The Democrat leaders set out to appear as the 'good pupils' of the IMF. Although they used this relationship to bargain with the IMF, from the domestic perspective they were identified with the IMF and its policies of liberalisation and shock-therapy restructuring. In the face of local opposition to legal changes and other restructuring measures, the Democrats argued that resistance would result in Thailand being abandoned by the financial markets and reduced to a status similar to its neighbours, Burma and Cambodia. The consequences would be 'like triggering an atom bomb' or falling into a 'bottomless pit'. Co-operation with the IMF would bring recovery through the 'return of international confidence' and a reversal of the capital outflows. From the beginning, this turning point was estimated as six months away. The relentless capital drain over three years undermined the credibility of this argument.

Opposition grew. A group of businessmen branded the IMF programme as 'neo-colonial' and 'imperialist', and attempted to build a nationalist platform of resistance. This was perceived as a self-interested strategy by heavy debtors to evade bankruptcy legislation, and failed to gain any mass support. However, over 1998–2000, a more diffuse nationalist reaction came together.

In December 1997, the king delivered a speech calling on villages to become more self-sufficient and self-reliant in order to bear the social impact of the crisis. Initially this message was interpreted literally as advice on village-level strategy. But over time the rhetoric was invested with a much broader meaning. 'Sufficiency' and 'self-reliance' were reinterpreted not as moves towards local autarky, but as self-strengthening in order to negotiate more effectively with the forces of globalisation. The largest commercial bank put a quotation about self-sufficiency from the king's speech on the cover of its annual report. The mainstream economic think-tank, TDRI, devoted its flagship annual conference in 1999 to the 'Sufficiency Economy', redefined as 'moderation and due consideration in all modes of conduct, as well as the need for sufficient protection from internal and external shocks' in order to 'cope appropriately with critical challenges arising from extensive and rapid socioeconomic, environmental and cultural changes occurring as a result of globalisation'. The usually neo-classical TDRI suffused this strategy with cultural values inherent in Buddhism and the face-to-face society of the nation's rural past.[20]

This proto-nationalist dissidence developed two key bases of political support – small businessmen and farmers. Both groups were only remotely connected to the modern, externally oriented economy, and could not perceive the importance of efforts devoted to its revival. Yet both suffered inordinately from the economic crisis. Small businesses were especially vulnerable to the collapse of the credit system and decline of consumer demand.[21] Farmers initially prospered as crop prices rose in 1997–8 with the baht depreciation, but then suffered as worldwide prices fell, opportunities for off-farm income shrank and disemployed migrants were thrown back on the rural economy. From early 1998, there were waves of rural protest demanding debt relief, price support for various crops and better access to land.

In late 1998 a new political party was launched to crystallise these sources of dissidence. The party's leader, Thaksin Shinawatra, emphasised his difference from the Democrats with the remark, 'I wouldn't solve this crisis just from a commercial banker's point of view.'[22] The party's name – Thai Rak Thai (Thais love Thais) – espoused a soft nationalism. The party's platform specifically targeted small businesses, with promises of credit, and farmers, with promises of a debt moratorium and marketing assistance. The party's propaganda echoed the rhetoric of sufficiency and self-reliance. As elections approached in late 2000, the electorate was for the first time ever treated to a policy debate. Thai Rak Thai (and other parties competing for the provincial vote) promised to make significant withdrawals from the trends of globalisation and liberalisation, including relaxation of financial restructuring, proactive support for local business through directed credit and industrial policy, and schemes to help the rural mass. In January 2001, Thai Rak Thai won a landslide victory at the polls.[23] Thaksin subsequently absorbed two provincial parties, and allied with two others to create an overwhelming majority in parliament (370 out of 500). His government pumped money into the countryside to stimulate demand, while extending schemes to resuscitate domestic entrepreneurs.

Conclusion

Although the crisis can be blamed on Thailand's mismanagement of liberalisation in the early 1990s, the impact was much worse than it should have been. A country with one of the best growth records in the developing world saw its economy driven backwards by up to seven years. The aftermath will be painful because of high public debt, extensive damage to the entrepreneurial class, seizure in the credit system and an upsurge in ideological and oppositional politics. Why did the crisis have such an impact? What are the key lessons?

First, modern capital account crises must be acknowledged for what they are, and panicky capital flight must be understood as the mechanism which inflicts severe results. The IMF interpreted the Thai problem as a current account crisis of the pre-liberalisation era. It has only partially admitted fault and revised its interpretation. Reforms in the international financial system have stopped short of equipping the IMF (or any other institution) with the ability to manage such events. While avoidance of crisis is obviously the preferred strategy, the enthusiasm of international financial firms for making profits out of the volatility of financial markets through increasingly sophisticated techniques makes it unlikely that such crises will never recur. Countries which fall into crisis must therefore place a priority on constraining panic capital flight. Ideally this should be through a negotiated and mediated process. But as the international financiers and the G-7 resist institutionalising such a system, countries must be prepared to react unilaterally if necessary. The much-vaunted dangers of a debt moratorium are more acceptable than the consequences of major capital flight.

Second, countries must be prepared to resist plans for financial restructuring through shock therapy in the midst of crisis. The US policy establishment has arrogated responsibility for restructuring local economies on a global scale. The manifesto of this project – open markets and good governance – is the modern version of the civilising mission of the colonial era. The fulfilment of this mission, its proponents believe, is opposed by 'elites', 'vested interests' or 'crony capitalists'. Periods of crisis and dislocation, when these opposing forces are in disarray, provide opportunities to fulfil the mission. The oppressed mass of 'the poor' will benefit, and their silent support legitimates interventions which undercut governments. Hence crises packages are divided between overcoming a crisis and taking advantage of it. These two aims conflict.

The proposition that Thailand's poorly regulated, over-protected bank-based financial system was rendered inadequate by financial liberalisation was absolutely correct. But the attempt to restructure it rapidly in the teeth of a crisis was dangerous. The IMF saw no need to understand how Thailand's financial systems had functioned before. The past was demonised as 'cronyism'. The 'destroy-and-replace' strategy assumed away the time required to build institutions and change legal cultures.

Third, the crisis has re-emphasised the significance of regional groupings within the context of globalisation. The failed results of plans pushed by the IMF and US policy establishment resulted from an ignorant and ideological view of Asia, and a lack of sympathy for those affected by the policy outcomes. The contrast with the attention paid to the crises in Latin America and eastern Europe highlights the importance of region. This regional bias might not arise if the governing structure of the international financial institutions were to become more democratic, but this is unlikely to happen. Hence regional grouping and regional strategies are important. This is evident in Europe, where regional and sub-regional institutions have helped to defend social provisions and local financial cultures. In Asia, achieving such regional grouping is problematic because of political tensions. But the imperatives to overcome these tensions increase as globalisation advances.

Fourth, financial crises accentuate the vulnerability of local capitalisms to global competition, and bring this issue into the forefront of political debate. The local accommodation with the pressures of globalisation is negotiated through the political system. Pro-globalisation advocates characterise the political contest as 'reform' or 'governance' against vested interests. Reality is more subtle. As Robert Cox has observed, one of the consequences of the rising power of globalised finance is that 'power within the state becomes more concentrated in those agencies in closest touch with global finance', especially finance ministries and central banks, while ministries which service domestic clients (commerce, agriculture, industry) are downgraded.[24] More broadly, government as a whole is focused on negotiating the accommodation with global finance. In a crisis this focus can be near-complete. But in a country such as Thailand, the political constituency which perceives that its interests are directly bound up with financial globalisation is a fraction of the whole. This constituency extends no farther than modern business and an urban middle class with aspirations of belonging to the advanced world. The economic fate of the mass of small businesses and the majority agrarian population may in fact rise and fall with the cycles of the open economy, but these social forces imagine themselves as remote from globalisation. In a crisis, they feel they suffer for mistakes committed by others. In a democracy, this backlash finds expression through the ballot box. The dissidence is not specifically anti-globalisation, but seeks to preserve and mobilise the national state in order to protect domestic interests and further domestic social goals.

Notes

1. Interview by *Foreign Policy*, reproduced in *The Nation* (Bangkok), 24 September 2000.
2. The transition to a floating exchange rate was debated intermittently from 1993 onwards. A conservative faction in the central bank favoured the dollar peg on the grounds that it had made Thailand attractive to trade partners and investors in the past.
3. Stanley Fischer in *The Nation*, 5 March 1999.
4. Pasuk Phongpaichit and Chris Baker, *Thailand's Crisis* (Chiang Mai: Silkworm Books, 2000), ch. 3.
5. Said at the 'What Is to Be Done?' conference, Amsterdam, February 2000.
6. H.-J. Chang and C. G. Yoo, 'Triumph of the rentiers?' *Challenge*, January/February 2000.
7. Yilmaz Akyüz and Andrew Cornford, 'Capital flows to developing countries and the reform of the international financial system', UNCTAD discussion papers no. 143, 1999.
8. Marcus Miller and Lei Zhang, 'Sovereign liquidity crises: the strategic case for a payments standstill', *Economic Journal*, 110 (January 2000).
9. 'Remarks before the IMF', 9 March 1998, US Treasury RR-2286; 'Opportunities out of crises: lessons from Asia', 19 March 1998, US Treasury RR-2309; 'The new economy and the global economy. Remarks at the Chemical Manufacturers' Association', 9 November 1998, US Treasury RR-2808; 'Reflections on managing global integration', speech at Annual Meeting of the Association of Government Economists, New York City, 4 January 1999, US Treasury RR-2877; 'Remarks to Senate Foreign Relations Subcommittee on international economic policy and export/trade promotion', 27 January 1999, US Treasury RR-2916; 'Roots of the Asian crises and the road to a stronger global financial system', 25 April 1999, US Treasury RR-3102.
10. Suthep Kittikulsingh, 'Non-performing loans (NPLs): the borrower's viewpoint', *TDRI Quarterly Review*, vol. 14, no. 4 (December 1999), pp. 24, 28.
11. *The Nation*, 6 March 1999.
12. Chatri Sophonpanich, chairman of Bangkok Bank, *Bangkok Post*, 28 November 1998.

13. *The Nation*, 16 August 1997.
14. For example, Lukas Menkhoff, 'Bad banking in Thailand? An empirical analysis of macro indicators', *Journal of Development Studies*, vol. 36, no. 5 (1999).
15. For instance, the economist Ammar Siamwalla admitted that bank lending was fundamental to 'a system which worked for 40 years' and had delivered Thailand high growth. See *The Nation*, 4 March 1999.
16. Eisuke Sakakibara, 'Thai crisis played part in AMF idea', *Yomiuri Shimbun*, 26 November 1999.
17. Saori N. Katada, 'Japan and Asian Monetary Regionalization: Cultivating a New Regional Leadership after the Asian Financial Crisis', *Geopolitics*, vol. 6 (2001); Ramkishen S. Rajan, 'Safeguarding Against Capital Account Crises: Unilateral, Regional and Multilateral Options for east Asia', in G. de Brouwer (ed.), *Regional Financial Arrangements in east Asia* (London: Routledge, 2002).
18. Of the ninety-one finance companies which existed before the crisis (and were key to financing small and medium industries), only two are expected to survive. Of the thirteen commercial banks, two have been closed, five have been sold to international banks and two others are in the process of being sold. The four remaining are the biggest, but three of them have sold 49 per cent shares to foreign investors.
19. Pasuk Phongpaichit and Baker, *Thailand's Crisis*, ch. 9.
20. Thailand Development Research Institute, *Ekkasan prakop kan sammana wichakan pracham pi 2542 setthakit pho phiang* (Papers from the 1999 annual seminar on the sufficiency economy), 18–19 December 1999, Jomthien.
21. Labour force data show that the steepest declines in employment were among small and medium firms. NESDB, *Indicators*, vol. 2, no. 4 (October 1998), p. 12.
22. *Far Eastern Economic Review*, 17 June 1999, p. 25.
23. Pasuk Phongpaichit and Chris Baker, *Thailand: Economy and Politics*, 2nd edn (Kuala Lumpur: Oxford University Press, 2002), ch. 12.
24. Robert W. Cox, 'Political economy and world order: problems of power and knowledge at the turn of the millennium', in Richard Stubbs and Geoffrey R. D. Underhill (eds.), *Political Economy and the Changing Global Order* (Don Mills, Ontario: Oxford University Press Canada, 2000).

6 The politics of financial reform: recapitalising Indonesia's banks

RICHARD ROBISON

Before Asia's financial crisis there was general agreement within the broad neo-liberal camp that deregulation, not least in the financial sector, was the key ingredient of effective market reform. Western governments, their aid agencies and international financial institutions, notably the IMF and the World Bank, enthusiastically pressed for the opening of capital markets and the removal of state control and ownership in domestic financial and banking sectors. But the crisis was to change all that, setting in train a bitter debate over whether these reforms had, ironically, been at the heart of the crisis.

For hardline neo-classical economists within the IMF and elements of the economic press, the crisis was confirmation that economies built around systems of state-managed markets were not sustainable in the long term. For these hardliners, the Asian economies that collapsed in 1997 fell under the weight of their own inherent inefficiency and dysfunction. The crisis was a reminder that deregulation had not gone far enough and that economies must embrace the natural efficiencies of the market.[1]

Others within the neo-liberal camp were, however, to propose that the roots of the crisis were to be explained in terms of panic and speculation in open global financial markets and an ensuing rush for the exits when confidence collapsed.[2] Such interpretations led naturally to policy prescriptions centring on reform in global financial architecture rather than a reconstruction of domestic economic and political regimes. In particular, the introduction of various controls over capital accounts and the orderly management of capital flows were considered to be essential steps. The creation of viable market economies was de-linked from the radical opening of international capital markets that had been advocated by the IMF and other neo-classical reformers within the so-called Washington consensus.[3]

Such an interpretation was attractive to those institutional and/or 'statist' political economists who had long argued, albeit from often diverging positions, that successful and powerful national economic engines could be driven by strategic industry plans and under the leadership of the state.[4] For these, the crisis was no indictment of the state-led regimes of north-east Asia. It was, instead, an instance of viable and healthy 'high debt' economic models made vulnerable by hasty and imprudent deregulation of global and domestic capital markets at the insistence of neo-liberal reformers operating out of Washington and New York.[5]

Asia's economic crisis had also come as a severe shock to many in the neo-classical camp and in the business world, where the notion of an inexorably evolving and almost inevitable 'Asian century' was increasingly accepted. The undeniable success of Asia's industrial juggernauts had been reconciled with a theory of markets in which specific forms of state intervention were redefined as market-facilitating.[6] Neo-classical economists had, particularly in the case of Indonesia, been among the staunchest supporters of the state through its economic technocracy and predicted strong and continuing growth.[7] Clearly, the crisis appeared to cut much of the ground from under their feet. An explanation that focused on global financial markets rather than domestic economic regimes suited their agendas.

At one level there appeared much to recommend the proposition that the origins of the crisis were not to be found within the economies of the region. After all, economic growth had proceeded for decades in the economies now prostrated by the crisis and within regimes elsewhere where corruption, crony-ism and internal problems had prevailed. International investors had continued to come, convinced that the rewards outweighed the clear risks.

But there is another way of looking at the problem. It may be argued that volatile capital markets and their flows of short-term bank credit and speculative financial investments had made it possible for profoundly flawed and crisis-ridden domestic economic and political regimes to persist. For decades, banking systems and corporations burdened with debt had been saved by the flood of easy credit in the international system and propped up by government bail-out and political protection. Global financial crisis and capital flight, in this view, laid bare the over-borrowed and over-invested corporate moguls of these weak and predatory systems. As a leading national newspaper observed in the case of Indonesia, the crisis '... exposed the rotten core of the self-serving system Soeharto had built and protected with an iron fist'.[8]

In this view, the significance of the crisis is that it ruptured the mutually beneficial relationship between mobile and speculative global capital markets and predatory domestic economic regimes, revealing structural and political tensions and fractures previously papered over by continuing inflows of loans. Most importantly, it undermined the political capacity of the state in Thailand and South Korea, but particularly in Indonesia, to continue guaranteeing the system of monopolies, subsidies, bail-outs and protection within which banks and corporations had survived and flourished. What mattered was not so much the currency crisis itself but the depth and severity of the economic, corporate and political disintegration set in train. At one level, then, the question is why not all economies hit by the currency crisis suffered the same traumatic consequences as Indonesia, Thailand and South Korea. Policy responses must focus on factors that made some domestic regimes so vulnerable to swings in global markets. In any case, the issue is primarily a political one. Just as volatile global financial markets made possible the rapid expansion of unconstrained and predatory domestic financial regimes, the panic and speculation of 1997 meant that these could no longer operate in the old ways. They became part of a larger political struggle.

All this leads to a second question. How are financial and economic regimes changed? Much of the discussion about reform, whether in global or domestic markets, assumes a highly voluntarist process of technical fixes and policy choices made on grounds of greater functional efficiency. But even at the global level, all the talk of financial market reform has come to little. The will to change just is not there. An open architecture suits the capital markets, the equity funds and international banks. Within domestic regimes, too, attempts at structural reform have also floundered. In some cases this has been the result of political opposition to reform by powerful state–business alliances. In other cases, reforms have simply been appropriated to form the basis of shifts from state capitalism to systems of predatory capitalism and money politics that serve the interests of private, politically connected conglomerates.

This is because reform and resistance is not primarily about efficiency but about power and its allocation and about the fate of entrenched political and social coalitions. Grappling with the problems of corporate banking debt and insolvency strikes at the heart of entrenched systems of power and interest. What is critical about the crisis is the extent to which it has weakened those prevailing coalitions and strengthened the reformers, opening the door to change. Restructuring these regimes is no technical matter of policy fixes – of separating the 'natural' market from the intervention of politics and vested interest or of better leadership and cleverer policies.[9] No less than any other, the neo-liberal agenda is embedded in coalitions of interest and power, and its success relies upon a political victory. Along with a range of other broad coalitions, neo-liberals and their allies are engaged in a bitter struggle to determine the new financial and banking systems in a range of Asian economies.

Nowhere is this process of collapse and political struggle more clearly defined than in Indonesia. It is in the context of the Indonesian case that this chapter will track the origins of institutional collapse in the banking and financial sector and the processes by which it is being reformed. Here, the crisis was to prove most devastating and pervasive, the downward spiral of the rupiah quickly translating into the collapse of Indonesia's largest corporate groups and the immobilisation of its banking system. The reasons for this unravelling of corporate and financial institutions, I propose, are to be found in the rise of coalitions of corporate and political oligarchies and their expropriation of economic deregulation in the 1980s. With the power of the state harnessed directly to such predatory forms of private interest, an unconstrained bout of investment and borrowing resulted, facilitated by the new global financial markets as bank debt replaced oil revenue as the engine of economic and corporate growth. It was the corrupt and inefficient banking system that precipitated Indonesia's unravelling in the wake of the currency crisis. Operating as a mechanism to channel money into the financially questionable schemes of corporate conglomerates and politico-business families, it had played a critical role in ensuring the vulnerability of the Indonesian economy. It was a process in which foreign creditors and bankers were an integral element. However, such a system proved difficult to reform in the wake of the crisis, despite universal agreement about its culpability. This was no problem to be solved by a simple policy fix. The question of banking recapitalisation was to be at the very heart of the political struggle to dismantle the grand alliance of bureaucratic power and corporate interest.

The roots of the problem

The origins of the banking crisis in Indonesia and the levels of corporate debt that are making it so difficult to resolve lie in the circumstances of economic dereg-ulation following the collapse of oil prices in the 1980s. In that decade, liberal reformers welcomed unprecedented programmes of deregulation in banking, finance, trade and investment. Strategic public sector monopolies were opened to private investors. The reforms were to usher in an era of spectacular growth of private business conglomerates. Whereas in 1980 the private sector accounted for only 51 per cent of total investment, it grew to 65 per cent in 1990.[10] Just before the crisis it had reached around 75 per cent. However, this was not a flow-ering of business within liberal markets defined by formal systems of regulation based in law. State capitalism had not been ended but merely appropriated by powerful private interests and harnessed to them.

In the deregulation of the Indonesian economy in the 1980s and 1990s, pub-lic monopoly was to become private monopoly. Powerful political gatekeepers (by far the most important of which was President Soeharto himself) now allocated the licences, credit and contracts that allowed rapidly expanding corporate conglomerates to move into lucrative new areas of public utili-ties, petrochemicals, road and port construction, television broadcasting and telecommunications.[11] In the process, the formerly dominant state managers were pushed aside in a series of bitter disputes over the allocation of trade monopolies, licences and state contracts.[12] What emerged was an economic and political regime in which the state had become the possession of a powerful coalition of private interests able totally to overwhelm any collective constraints upon its activities.

The effect of this was a private corporate sector that was to become grossly over-extended and vulnerable to the increasing volatility of global financial markets. Opportunities for quick profits based on monopoly market positions and easy credit overrode calculations about market saturation and declining competitiveness. In the petrochemical industry, foreign investors and lenders rushed into partnership with well-connected licence holders able to guarantee protection from foreign competition and to secure subsidised inputs from the state oil company, Pertamina and the state electricity company, PLN, as well as assured downstream markets.[13] Despite the growing over-supply of electricity, private investors now streaming into the power generation industry were able to secure remarkably favourable contracts from PLN. These were written in US dollars and at levels higher than PLN was permitted to charge to consumers.[14]

As a consequence, Indonesia's private sector conglomerates experienced a period of rapid economic growth, not only in the newly deregulated sectors but in new resource industries such as pulp and paper manufacture and plantations. The new private sector projects were increasingly financed by foreign loans. It was calculated by one source in 1991 that so-called mega-projects potentially involved US$70 billion in foreign loans.[15] The prospect for a massive debt crisis was recognised by Indonesia's economic technocrats, who were faced with the task of reining back the domestic money supply, curtailing overseas loans and imposing systems for prudential supervision of banks. In a series of financial shocks in 1991, Finance Minister Sumarlin severely reduced the liquidity of state banks and sent interest rates to levels of 50 per cent and above. A ten-person team (Team 39 or COLT) was established to regulate foreign loans, resulting in the postponement of four projects worth US$9.8 billion. These included the giant Chandra Asri petrochemical project and others owned by large conglomerates and the Soeharto family.[16]

In the end, however, the technocrats were unable to contain the conglomerates and the powerful politico-business families. While several large companies went to the wall during the period of tight money and high interest rates, powerful companies soon circumvented attempts to control borrowing. Although the tight money policy precipitated a flight of Chinese capital to Hong Kong and Singapore,[17] survival did not necessarily mean leaving Indonesia. The owners of the giant Chandra Asri petrochemical project, for example, simply sidestepped the restrictions by reorganising their investment through Hong Kong subsidiaries. Through a consortium of state and foreign banks the owners of Chandra Asri and their foreign partners raised over US$700 million in loans.[18]

But the rise of the conglomerates also created new levels of demand for credit domestically. Such demands were to change dramatically the structure of Indonesia's financial institutions. Traditionally acting as 'agents of development' for strategic government investment projects, state banks were now to be harnessed to the growing investment needs of the conglomerates. At the same time, the new demand for credit was to transform what had been a small private banking sector, effectively removing regulatory constraints.

The state banks

Indonesia's state banks had been traditionally the instruments of national economic strategies, providing funds for priority state investments in upstream industries. In the 1980s, the role of state banks as 'agents of development' was increasingly subordinated to the needs of the emerging private sector corporate conglomerates. Large investments by these groups in petrochemicals and power generation, forestry and plantation development relied heavily on state bank loans and injections of capital from state pension funds. In particular, the growing Soeharto family interests were to draw on state bank loans as they expanded their cartels and monopolies in such areas as clove trading and in the import and manufacture of automobiles.[19]

Increasingly, state banks were to operate as the financiers of the new corporate oligarchies. It was common knowledge that powerful officials and power holders decided the allocation of loans to well-connected business figures. Funds were often allocated without collateral and on the basis of inflated and unsubstantiated cost projections, freeing credit for speculative use.[20] It was also known that state banks had a growing bad debt problem. As early as 1993, Kwik Kian Gie (a prominent critic of the conglomerates and later economics minister in the Wahid government) had claimed in a local newspaper that bad debts in the state system stood at Rp. 10 trillion or around 7 per cent of all debt.[21] A document anonymously issued in 1993, probably from within the Ministry of Finance or Bank Indonesia, identified Indonesia's largest conglomerates as the holders of the largest non-performing loans (NPLs). It claimed that the state industrial bank, Bapindo, had bad or doubtful debts at levels of 28 per cent of total outstanding loans.[22]

When Bapindo was left with a US$650 million loss after the collapse of a chemical project headed by Eddy Tansil, a business partner of Hutomo Putera Mandala (Tommy Soeharto), a further window into the whole relationship between state banks and private corporate moguls was opened. Not only was this loan issued on the basis of letters from powerful officials, it was issued on the basis of grossly overstated asset values. In fact, there was little evidence that the loans were used for the purpose intended or that repaying debt to state banks was taken as a serious proposition.[23] Despite apparently widespread efforts to clean up the state banks in the wake of the scandal, the bad debt problem remained. In 1995, the World Bank reported that state bank 'classified assets' (loans classified as 'substandard', 'doubtful' or 'loss') stood at 18.6 per cent.[24]

The private banks

The entry of private banks into the banking system in the 1980s was only to exacerbate the situation. New banking laws in 1983 and 1988 removed controls on loan and deposit rates at state banks and eliminated restrictions on the entry of new private banks.[25] State-owned corporations could now deposit up to 50 per cent of their funds in private banks. New banks could be established with a minimum paid-up capital of as little as Rp. 10 billion – around US$8 million at prevailing exchange rates.[26] These moves not only increased the amount of credit available, they saw the number of banks increase from 111 to 240 between 1988 and 1994.[27] Holding 14 per cent of credit outstanding in 1982, private banks were to surpass state banks in 1994 to hold over 48 per cent of credit outstanding and 53 per cent of bank funds.[28]

For the most part, private banks were established as mechanisms for mobilising cheap finance for the larger corporate groups of which they were part. In a situation where there was no separation of lender and borrower, intra-group lending by banks was restricted to 50 per cent of total equity capital. Only 20 per cent of total equity capital could be lent to any single borrower. Attempts to impose legal lending limits were generally ignored. When audits of private banks were concluded in 1999, it was revealed that inter-group lending was often in excess of 70–80 per cent of all private bank lending. When taken over by the Indonesian Bank Restructuring Agency (IBRA), three of the largest private banks, BDNI, BUN and Modern were revealed to have 85 per cent, 70 per cent and 100 per cent respectively of all loans channelled to related business groups.[29]

In such circumstances it is not surprising that private bank disasters were well under way in the decade before the crisis. Large numbers of private banks found themselves unable to continue because of the weight of bad debts from inter-group loans. These were simply rescued by the injection of public funds channelled mainly through state banks.[30] Bank Indonesia (BI) played a critical role as a broker in assigning ailing private banks to state banks and even to private banks for these rescue programmes.[31] Of numerous private-banking disasters in this period, only one major bank was allowed to collapse, the Soerjadjajas' Bank Summa.[32]

The legacy of this was a private banking sector parts of which were perpetually haemorrhaging under the weight of huge non-performing loans. The state banks, too, were in similar trouble and in constant need of government injection of funds. In November 1992 the government obtained a US$307 million 'financial Sector Development Project Loan' from the World Bank, of which US$300 million was used for capital injections into state banks.[33] When the currency crisis struck, the Indonesian state could no longer continue to bail out insolvent banks and corporations. Insolvency and debt came to mean something real, especially when highly mobile global capital withdrew and foreign creditors began to demand their pound of flesh.

The crisis and the banks

Of all the banking crises in Asia, it is clear that Indonesia's has been the most protracted and difficult. Relative to the size of its economy, the costs of re-capitalisation and the levels of bad debt are the largest in the region. Standard and Poor's have estimated non-performing loans in Indonesia's banking system reached between 75 per cent and 85 per cent of total loans by the end of 1999. Costs of recapitalisation are estimated at US$87 billion or around 82 per cent of GDP. This compares with Thailand's 35 per cent, South Korea's 29 per cent and Malaysia's 22 per cent.[34] It is no surprise that the IMF included the re-form and recapitalisation of Indonesia's banking system as one of its priorities in the agreements it concluded with the Indonesian government as part of its US$42 billion rescue package. In the sixteen Letters of Intent (LOI) and/or Memorandums of Economic and Financial Policies (MEFP) signed between October 1997 and September 2000, the Indonesian government agreed to the creation of a new Central Bank Law and the establishment of IBRA. The latter would preside over the closure of weak banks and the recapitalisation of those considered able to meet strict operating criteria.[35]

As IBRA moved to centre stage it became clear that the closure of weak banks and the capitalisation of potentially viable ones was only the beginning of the problem. Indonesia's debt crisis was somewhat different from the others in that it was a crisis of private sector debt in which private corporate inter-ests directly borrowed from international banks. By the time of the Asian eco-nomic crisis the World Bank estimated Indonesia's private sector external debt at US$72 billion, with repayments of US$20.8 billion due by the end of 1997.[36] Other estimates were gloomier. Analysts at Indosuez estimated the corporate sector debt at US$140 billion, of which US$83 billion was undeclared off-shore borrowing. According to de Koning, economist at ABN/AMRO Bank in Jakarta, total repayment of private sector debt and interest in 1998 would be US$59.8 billion.[37] Even at an exchange rate of Rp. 5,000/US$, Soesastro and Basri estimate that about 50 per cent of all listed companies have a dollar debt to asset ratio of around 50 per cent.[38]

The fact that the largest debtors were also usually the bank owners themselves meant that IBRA was drawn into protracted and bitter conflict with powerful corporate and political interests as it attempted to force debtors to hand over assets and funds to cover the costs of recapitalisation. The problem of bank recapitalisation could not be separated from that of debt rescheduling in the private sector. At stake was the very survival of Indonesia's largest corporate moguls and the system of predatory power that bound them to political gatekeepers within the state apparatus. At one level, then, the struggle was over who would fund recapitalisation. Would the government, now in serious fiscal difficulty, once again bail out the conglomerates? A second problem was the larger question of structural reform. Even if it could be recapitalised successfully, would Indonesia's banking system simply continue to operate in the old way or would it be subject to a new and rigorous regulatory regime? Here, the reformers would come into conflict with powerful interests embedded in the state apparatus and with the new political entrepreneurs emerging in the post-authoritarian era.

The struggle to recapitalise banks and restructure debt

As Indonesia's private corporate sector began to renege on its debts, domestic banks were soon paralysed by a surge in non-performing loans. Established in January 1998, IBRA began the task of restructuring in the teeth of determined opposition. Initial attempts to close banks had been strenuously resisted by the Soehartos and other major corporate figures. However, by mid-1999, sixty-six of the 160 private banks that had existed in July 1997 had been closed and a further twelve had been taken over by the state and recapitalised.[39] Decisions about which banks to close and which to recapitalise were not merely technical considerations enforced in law. They were subject to protracted negotiation and public dispute. In the process, many of the rescued banks clearly had few prospects for survival and did not meet capital adequacy ratio (CAR) criteria.[40]

Exactly why the government and the IMF decided to rescue the banks themselves rather than just guaranteeing depositors is unclear. Nor is it entirely clear why many of the bank owners were interested in hanging on to them, given that they were primarily mechanisms for raising cheap funds for corporate expansion rather than commercial ventures in themselves. In the event, recapitalisation has proven to be a real problem. Large numbers of chronically weak banks remained within the system with little prospect of meeting the 8 per cent CAR levels required by 2001. As late as December 2000, it became clear that it was becoming increasingly difficult to make further closures, a development confirmed by Finance Minister Prijadi Prapto Suhardjo.[41] Nor, by mid-2000, had the recapitalisation programmes restored the flow of credit from domestic banks. With poor asset levels and few creditworthy customers, domestic credit stagnated. While some recapitalised banks were now doing well, this was not on the basis of an expansion of lending. Although deposit rates had climbed, outstanding credit levels had declined. This was due largely to the massive transfer of NPLs to IBRA, but it was also because banks were still wary of high default rates on loans and were unwilling to test their CAR levels by large lending programmes. Banks preferred to invest in Bank Indonesia SBI promissory notes.[42]

Recapitalisation had effectively meant that the government became the owner of over 70 per cent of the country's banks along with their bad debts. This was funded with the issue of over Rp. 650 trillion (US$84 billion) in bonds, placing an enormous fiscal burden on the government. It was critical not only that the government sell the banks and get the credit system moving but that it should recover the costs it had incurred in the bond issue. Achieving these aims was to prove elusive. It was clear that most of the bank owners – the big conglomerates – had decided to dig in and refuse to repay debt. They proved unwilling to surrender assets and hand over control of their enterprises. Their plan was to resist restructuring of debt and to force the government to bail out the banks. In the long term, a crucial question was who would pay the bill for recapitalisation? Would it prove simply to be an exercise in which the Indonesian government carried the cost of the crisis for the old conglomerates?

Despite their efforts to avoid debt restructuring and surrendering assets, there is no doubt that the conglomerates were hit hard by the crisis. Powerful business figures like Liem Sioe Liong, Sjamsul Nursalim, Prajogo Pangestu, Bob Hasan and the Soeharto family lost control of a range of important corporate icons in the debt restructuring exercises that followed the crisis. In the Master Settlement and Acquisition Agreements (MSAA) signed between IBRA and its largest creditors, the latter were forced to hand over assets valued at Rp. 112 trillion to cover their debt to IBRA banks. Yet, by mid-2000, it was clear that the conglomerates once again had the upper hand. Beset by increasing fiscal pressures and desperate to draw capital back into Indonesia, the government had little choice but to carry much of the costs of recapitalisation and negotiate generous debt settlements with the conglomerates. Realisation of assets was expected to be as little as 20–30 per cent. How then, did the conglomerates survive and begin to dictate the terms of their re-entry into the Indonesian economy?

They were rescued initially by the decision to inject over Rp.146 trillion (US$11 billion) in liquidity funds by Bank Indonesia intended to guarantee deposits and meet inter-bank loan commitments. A subsequent investigation by the Supreme Audit Agency (BPK) revealed that some Rp. 80.25 trillion of these funds were allocated to banks that had violated BI's own guidelines on CAR and legal lending limits.[43] Not only were the troubled banks able to access government largesse virtually unconditionally, they were able to use these funds for a range of other purposes, including new overseas investment, currency speculation and debt servicing on other companies. In June 2000, BPK and the State Comptroller of Finance and Development (BPKP) reported that Rp. 62.6 trillion of Bank Indonesia Liquidity Funds (BLBI) had been diverted for unauthorised purposes.[44]

When it came to negotiating the transfer of assets to IBRA, the conglomerates had the upper hand to the extent that it was difficult to penetrate the opaque financial statements to discover the real value of assets. It soon became clear that the government faced a huge shortfall. For example, to cover a debt of Rp. 47.7 trillion, the Salim group surrendered assets of Rp. 53 trillion in September 1998, subsequently valued at Rp. 20 trillion, representing an effective loss of Rp. 30 trillion for the government.[45] This was a pattern repeated across the spectrum of IBRA debtors. At the same time they were stalling debt negotiations with IBRA and foreign creditors, the conglomerates were able to insulate their highly profitable enterprises in forestry, pulp and paper, and agriculture. These provided strong cash flows for more strategic debt repayments and for new investment.

Nor did the domestic debt problems halt the strategic investments of Indonesian conglomerates overseas. The activities of Liem Sioe Liong's Salim group are instructive and represent a broader pattern. Its food manufacturer, Indofood, turned a Rp. 1.2 trillion foreign exchange loss in 1998 into a Rp. 209 billion gain in 1999, enabling the group to repay a US$400 million debt without having to spin off the Bogasari flour mills as earlier planned.[46] Overseas, cash rich with the US$1.8 billion sale of its Hagermeyer group, Liem was able to buy new foreign assets, including a US$700 million stake in the Philippine Long Distance Phone Company and a 40 per cent stake in Indofood. The latter deal enabled Liem to keep a grip on Indofood, shift the controlling stake overseas and generate funds to repay foreign creditors.[47]

Perhaps the major advantage enjoyed by the conglomerates has been the weakness and corruption of Indonesia's judicial institutions. In a series of startling acquittals in both the Bankruptcy Court and the Supreme Court, high profile business figures walked away from bankruptcy proceedings and criminal charges. It was an arena in which political influence and money were at a premium. Economics Coordinating Minister, Kwik Kian Gie, was to complain of ' "dark forces" who buy favours'.[48] So unsuccessful were both IBRA and foreign creditors in the courts that it was soon recognised that debt had to be resolved through negotiation.

But it was the increasing fiscal pressure brought to bear on the government by the recapitalisation exercise that was to be decisive. To cover the costs of recapitalisation the government had issued bonds to the value of US$54 billion and provided a further US$28.5 billion to BLBI. Interest on these bonds in 1999/2000 was Rp. 34 billion, rising to Rp. 77 trillion in 2001.[49] Dispersal of the assets held by IBRA now became a matter of urgency. IBRA's asset disposal rate languished at 2.5 per cent in early 2000, compared with rates of 38 per cent in South Korea, 40 per cent in Malaysia and 78 per cent in Thailand.[50] Of deep concern was the reluctance of foreign investors to buy up Indonesian assets as they had done in South Korea and Thailand. This dilemma threw the spotlight on the government's attitude to the way in which IBRA should treat the major conglomerates and politico-business families.

As we have seen, conglomerates continued to resist demands to hand over cash and assets, dragging protracted disputes through the courts and insulating high-quality assets. It had become clear that the original MSAA had grossly overvalued assets transferred to the government and now potentially involved huge losses for IBRA. The appointment of Cacuk Sudarijanto as head of IBRA in January 2000 was seen as a signal that the government intended to increase the pace of recapitalisation and the recouping and sale of assets. Several property seizures were made and legal action was taken or planned against the owners of forty-eight commercial banks for alleged misuse of some Rp. 144.5 trillion (US$17 billion) of BLBI. Among these were Marimutu Sinivasan, the head of the textile giant, Texmaco, the head of the giant Gajah Tunggal conglomerate, Sjamsul Nursalim, and a range of Soeharto family members and associates, including Hashim Djojohadikusumo, Bob Hasan and Barito Pacific chairman Prajogo Pangestu.[51]

Tough action against the conglomerates and the Soeharto family was not only driven by the necessity of shoring up looming budget shortfalls. There was widespread popular demand for prosecution of those business interests involved in misuse of the BLBI and for cancellation of the MSAA. Former Economics Coordinating Minister Kwik Kian Gie launched a strong attack on the government, accusing it of collusion with unscrupulous tycoons and failing to take legal action against corporate criminals. Under no circumstances, he argued, should they be allowed to buy back their old assets.[52]

However, the government also faced the reality that if investment were to flow back into Indonesia and the banking and corporate sectors put back on track, the conglomerates were the key factors. From this perspective, the government was under pressure to drop its prosecutions, to compromise on debt restructuring and to allow conglomerates to buy back their assets. The choice appeared to be one between justice and money. As Hong Goei Siauw of Nomura Securities observed, in the present situation no one would want to outlay US$2.5–3 billion to buy IBRA assets when they knew the condition of these assets and Indonesia's circumstances. The re-entry of high profile conglomerates would act as a magnet to foreign investors.[53]

In the end, to speed up the debt restructuring and assets sale process, IBRA and the government accepted that they had to negotiate discounts to large debtors, and be prepared to offer discounts in the sale of assets. This approach certainly accelerated debt restructuring. Contentious restructuring deals were negotiated with Chandra Asri (effectively bailing out Marubeni, the large Japanese trading group), Texmaco and other high profile conglomerates. The provision of a US$96 million credit facility to the financially besieged industrial company Texmaco and the assumption of Rp. 19 trillion of its debts by IBRA in March 2000 appeared to be a repeat of the indiscriminate allocation of state funds so disastrously undertaken by BI in 1997 and 1998. Like many of the recipients of BLBI just a year earlier, Texmaco was a company that appeared to be hopelessly insolvent and without prospects of recovery. So puzzling was the rescue that the journal *Tempo* asked whether Tommy Soeharto might not now ask for credit to revive the Timor car project or Prajogo might not seek government assistance to re-enter Chandra Asri.[54]

Liem and other tycoons were reported to be negotiating to buy back into their businesses.[55] President Wahid announced that he had asked prosecutors to delay legal proceedings against Sinivasan, Prajogo and Nursalim.[56] But the strategy was also a dangerous one politically, raising claims of collusion and fears of a revival of the old predatory relations within the Wahid government.

For the IMF and the World Bank, the situation was contradictory. While supporting the need for speed in restructuring, they also expressed their concern at the opaque nature of the negotiations between the government and the debtors and at the generous terms given to companies with poor quality assets. They warned of future burdens on the public purse as the government shouldered the burden of debt restructuring.[57] Within parliament, resistance to the perceived bail-outs grew. Legislators blocked the planned divestment of IBRA assets in Bank Central Asia (BCA) and Bank Niaga. Such resistance was driven by the fear that assets were being sold off cheaply. More precisely, it was the prospect that assets would go cheaply to foreign investors or return to the conglomerates at a discount that propelled nationalist sentiment in the parliament.[58]

Recapitalisation, asset seizures and sales had failed to transform Indonesia's banking system. Despite the sale of BCA to US interests in 2002, foreign investors refused to come into the industry. Most important, recapitalisation aimed at little more than recreating those same structures that had existed before. There was no attempt to separate borrowers from lenders, the very problem that had given rise to huge intra-group lending before. Neither was there any evidence that effective supervision could be put in place.

In the struggle to determine the recapitalisation and debt rescheduling, the contestants were caught in the structural pressures to rekindle economic resurgence. Although now subjected to public scrutiny, seizure of assets and closure of their banks, the conglomerates' ultimate strength lies in their economic indispensability. Without substantial interest from foreign investors, there is little muscle behind neo-liberal demands for transparency and disclosure in corporate restructuring. While coalitions of nationalists and populists earlier demanded the expropriation of conglomerates and the distribution of their wealth, in the end the proposition that co-operatives or indigenous business might lead an economic revival was never a serious one. Essentially, reformists of all persuasions had been unable to mobilise powerful and cohesive coalitions behind their agenda.

The politics of reform: tackling the state apparatus

While reformers struggled to force a restructuring of the old conglomerates and political families, they also faced difficulties in addressing the other side of the equation: bringing the state institutions and its corps of officials to heel. After all, it was not the conglomerates per se that were the problem, it was the system of predatory relations in which they were embedded. Here, the new reformers confronted the deeply entrenched strategic gatekeeping institutions described earlier and the extensive interests vested in them. Prominent among these was BI, and now, of course, perhaps the most potentially glittering prize of all, IBRA. But reformers also confronted the problem of a compliant and corrupt judiciary. Little progress could be made in either banking or corporate reform while these remained the creatures of powerful corporate interests.

President Wahid's government inherited a corps of judges widely regarded as the instruments of the grand alliance of state power, political oligarchy and corporate wealth. They operated within a 'black state', outside the rule of law, where the real business of power and politics took place.[59] As a *Jakarta Post* editorial noted, 'subordination of the judiciary (under Soeharto) paved the way for total control by the state of every aspect of public life in Indonesia'.[60] Wahid also inherited, in the view of Tim Lindsey, a new set of commercial and competition laws designed in haste after the fall of Soeharto to be easily manipulated in favour of entrenched commercial interests in the less predictable environment of democratic Indonesia.[61]

With legal actions filed by the Attorney General and IBRA against a range of non-co-operating borrowers and those not complying with MSAA agreements, the government's capacity to retrieve the massive outlay of funds in the bank rescue lay with the courts. Yet, without an effective judiciary, reformers were to find their agenda seriously undermined. IBRA has met with constant frustration in its attempts to pursue unco-operative debtors through the bankruptcy courts. Most important, though, the failure of the Attorney General and the courts to prosecute successfully any of the major figures of the old regime, with the exceptions of Bob Hasan and Tommy Soeharto (who has finally been imprisoned after a substantial time on the run), signals that the state simply does not have the capacity to enforce rule of law. Although the Wahid government appeared to make a breakthrough with the replacement of 70 per cent of the judges sitting in the Jakarta courts in July 2000, including a number of Commercial Court judges, and with new appointments to the Supreme Court also in train, it is yet to be seen whether these new faces signal the end of judicial corruption or just a switch to new political masters.

Within the banking system itself, reform of BI was to be a priority for the IMF. Bank Indonesia had always been a central instrument in the allocation of state resources under Soeharto. Ostensibly responsible for the supervision of banks, BI had allowed widespread disregard of the rules governing legal lending limits (LLLs) and capital adequacy ratios. Responsible for allocation of special liquidity loans, it presided over their distribution to the Soeharto family and its cronies, often for highly dubious projects. It was once characterised by economist Anwar Nasution, later to become deputy governor under the Wahid presidency, as a 'den of thieves'.[62]

The IMF pressed ahead with reform. Under the provisions of the new central banking law introduced in May 1999, the Governor of the Bank was to be independent of the government and would no longer sit in the cabinet. BI's function in channelling subsidised liquidity loans to individual borrowers was abolished and its authority to supervise banks was transferred to a new independent institution to be established by the end of 2002.[63] Both IBRA and BI were subjected to audits and several high-profile former officials were arrested on corruption charges. Yet, even these seemingly decisive moves proved inconclusive. Transfer of authority over banking supervision simply shifted the same potential problem from one government agency to another. In any case, as McLeod has noted, the regulatory authority over banks was watered down substantially with the lowering of CAR and LLL requirements.[64] Whoever presided over bank regulation now had reduced powers. Perhaps the most important observation that might be made about structural changes to the banking system is the failure to reconsider the rules that had allowed banks in Indonesia to be owned directly by larger corporate entities. As elements in larger corporate groupings their function as cash cows was a natural outcome in the larger predatory environment.

Less than a year after the new banking bill had been introduced both President Wahid and the parliament began backtracking on the issue of its independence. In a bizarre series of skirmishes, BI governor Sjahril Sabirin was arrested on corruption charges linked with the Bank Bali scandal, but was released from house arrest six months later to resume his place in the Bank. A mass resignation of five of the Bank's deputy governors in November 2000, intended to set in train the resignation of the entire Board of Governors, backfired. Several refused to go and parliament refused to step in to force the issue. At a time of great difficulty Bank Indonesia is the centre of a stand-off. In the meantime, amendments to the banking bill were being debated in parliament. Such amendments included measures to force BI to report regularly to parliament and giving the parliament the right to nominate the Board of Governors.[65]

In this complex struggle, several issues are at stake. As IBRA assumed the assets of an ever widening circle of banks and corporations, it became, together with Bank Indonesia, a prize target for contending factions intent on building their war chests for the 2004 elections and for constructing political coalitions in the meantime. The Bank Bali scandal in 1999 was an early indication of these dynamics. Over US$80 million in funds allocated by IBRA and Bank Indonesia for recapitalisation found its way into the election campaign funds of Golkar, the state political party, indicating that neither IBRA nor BI could expect an easy escape from political control.[66]

On the other hand, it is widely recognised within reformist circles that Bank Indonesia and its officials need cleaning out as a precondition for real reform.[67] In the wake of the BLBI scandals, many critics felt that autonomy given to the governor by the 1999 banking laws merely sealed off from scrutiny the very individuals that had been at the heart of BI's problems for so long. A purge was considered a necessary prerequisite for reform. Bank autonomy does not guarantee a bank free of corruption. But it does place the advantage in any negotiations with the bank.

The broader struggle

In the end, the key to the outcome rests within a broader struggle for power. Although the IMF is able to force reforms upon a government that is fiscally beleaguered, the neo-liberal agenda has not been successful in assembling a broad and powerful political coalition. While it enjoyed a brief and important conjuncture of interest with other reformers who saw the IMF as a useful mechanism for dismantling the old Soeharto interests, there are few within the broader Indonesian reform movement who are attracted by the idea of open markets and economic rationalist prescriptions. At the same time, the reformers who have been propelled into office have been able to make inroads into the power of conglomerates and the old political families not imaginable under Soeharto. Although they were able initially to work on the basis of common agendas with populist forces on the basis of their drive against corruption and arbitrary authority, they proved increasingly isolated under Wahid.

Constructing a broader reformist coalition that is politically cohesive and ideologically coherent has proved difficult. This is not, as neo-modernisation theorists have argued, because of the non-existence or weakness of a bourgeoisie or a secular, rational middle class. Rather, sheltered from the underlying xenophobia of populism and reliant on monopolies and privileged economic access and protection from global competition, these forces have flourished under regimes of economic nationalism and predatory capitalism, preferring to build relationships with political gatekeepers than fight for market reforms or rule of law. While the accession of Megawati Sukarnoputri to the presidency appears to have solved many of the worries about the disintegrating state that emerged under Wahid, she confronts the task of mobilising parliament and even her own party behind the reformist agenda. Yet it is increasingly clear that support for neo-liberal market or institutional reforms among the contending coalitions in Indonesia's fledgling democracy is ambiguous. In the competition to build party alliances and strong bases of popular votes, securing control of strategic gatekeeping institutions, rather than their abolition, is important. Extra-budgetary funds will continue to remain attractive sources of discretionary money. As late as July 2000, ministries and agencies reported the existence of off-budget funds of around Rp. 7.7 trillion (US$860 million),[68] while a state (BPKP) audit reported about Rp. 2 trillion in non-budgetary funds allocated to Bulog, the State Logistics Agency,[69] still in existence, with disbursements going to businesses controlled by the Soeharto family and former Bulog chief, Bustanil Arifin.[70]

Rather than mobilising behind the neo-liberal agenda, it is a system of money politics that will best suit Indonesia's bourgeoisie for whom the imposition of rules, regulations, disclosure and an effective tax system are more of a threat than the crisis ever was. As in the case of Thailand, a system of parties and parliament animated by money offers real advantages.[71]

Global financial architecture again

There are two main ways of envisaging how the problem of rapid meltdown exposed by the Asian economic crisis might be avoided in future. One is by reining in the capacity of global financial markets to move with such volatility by looking again at the question of capital accounts and other methods of reporting and control. As in the case of China, countries like Indonesia could presumably be sealed off by closed capital accounts with their creaking banks and financial institutions intact. Or, domestic financial architecture might be reformed so that assaults by global speculators or waves of panic will not find such a fragile and vulnerable house of cards.

These very questions assume that a technical choice is possible in what is really a political problem. In the end, the decision will be forged in conflicts and accommodations involving global bankers and financiers, contending state and private interests and state power. In the case of Indonesia, for example, it is doubtful whether Indonesian Chinese investors would be interested in locating large sums in a country so politically volatile where their exit was cut off by a closed or restricted capital account. Similarly, international investors would require greater certainty in domestic markets if their exit were to be impeded.

The alternative is for a return to a situation much the same as before if old corporate interests in the region recover and global investors begin once again to think that the risks might be worth the huge rewards so long as political stability and order are re-established.

The critical question is to what extent the crisis has shifted the weight of power. Has it strengthened the hands of reformist technocrats and given international investors more leverage to impose new systems of rules and processes in management and governance? Has it enabled reformist parties based upon clear agendas to replace the machines of power and patronage that dominated the parliaments and state apparatus of the pre-crisis era?

Notes

1. Michel Camdessus, 'Asia Will Survive with Realistic Economic Policies', Parts I and II, *Jakarta Post*, 8, 9 December 1997; *The Economist*, 7 March 1998, pp. 6–22.
2. See Jeffrey Sachs, 'The IMF and the Asian Flu', *The American Prospect*, March–April 1998.
3. Jagdish Bhagwati, cited in Robert Wade, 'The Asian Debt and Development Crisis of 1997–? Causes and Consequences', *World Development*, vol. 26, no. 8 (1998), p. 1546.
4. The statist works are exemplified in Alice H. Amsden, *Asia's Next Giant: South Korea and Late Industrialisation* (New York: Oxford University Press 1989); Stephan Haggard, *Pathways from the Periphery: The Politics of Growth in Newly Industrialising Countries* (Ithaca: Cornell University Press, 1990); Chalmers Johnson, *MITI and the Japanese Miracle: The Growth of Industrial Policy, 1925–1975* (Stanford: Stanford University Press, 1982); Robert Wade, *Governing the Market: Economic Theory and Government in East Asian Industrialisation* (Princeton: Princeton University Press, 1990).
5. Represented, for instance, by Robert Wade and F. Veneroso, 'The Asian Crisis: The High Debt Model Versus the Wall Street–Treasury–IMF Complex', *New Left Review*, vol. 228, no. 1 (1998), pp. 24–33.
6. See World Bank, *The East Asian Miracle: Economic Growth and Public Policy* (Oxford: Oxford University Press, 1993).
7. For good discussions see Hal Hill, *The Indonesian Economy Since 1966: Asia's Emerging Giant* (Cambridge: Cambridge University Press, 1996); Steven Radelat and J. Sachs, 'Asia's Re-emergence', *Foreign Affairs*, vol. 76, no. 6 (1997), pp. 44–59.
8. *Jakarta Post*, 31 December 1998, p. 4.
9. See, for example, Hal Hill, 'Indonesia: the Strange and Sudden Death of a Tiger Economy', *Oxford Development Studies*, vol. 28, no. 2 (2000), pp. 117–39; 'Indonesia to Keep on Muddling Through in the next few Years', *Jakarta Post*, 21 December 2000, Special Supplement.

10. See A. Bhattacharya and M. Pangestu, 'Indonesia: Development and Transformation Since 1965 and the Role of Public Policy', paper prepared for the World Bank Workshop on the Role of Government and East Asian Success, East West Centre, November 1992, p. 7.

11. These are detailed in Richard Robison, 'Politics and Markets in Indonesia's Post-Oil Era', in Garry Rodan, Kevin Hewison and Richard Robison (eds.), *The Political Economy of Southeast Asia: An Introduction* (Melbourne: Oxford University Press, 1997), pp. 29–63.

12. *Jakarta Post*, 17 and 18 January and 12 October 1992; *Gatra*, 7 August 1992; *Prospek*, 22 June 1992.

13. See Robison, 'Politics and Markets', pp. 54–5.

14. *Ibid.*, p. 40; *Forum Keadilan*, 29 December 1997; World Bank, *Indonesia: Improving Efficiency and Equity – Changes in the Public Sector's Role* (Jakarta: Country Department III, East Asia and Pacific Region, 4 June, 1995) p. 71.

15. As reported in *Tempo*, 27 July 1991.

16. See *Kompas*, 14 October 1991; *Far Eastern Economic Review*, 19 September 1991, pp. 80–1, and 24 October 1991, pp. 70–1.

17. *Business Indonesia*, 3 August 1991, p. 1; *Tempo*, 17 August 1991, p. 86.

18. *Tempo*, 24 August 1991, p. 91, and 20 June 1992, p. 94; *Warta Ekonomi*, 29 April 1991, pp. 30–9.

19. For example, Bank Indonesia loaned Tommy Soeharto US$345 million to establish his infamous clove monopoly. Bank Bumi Daya provided a US$550 million loan to timber tycoon Prajogo Pangestu for his Chandra Asri petrochemical project. A US$600 million guarantee was provided by a consortium of state and private banks for Tommy Soeharto's national car project.

20. Kwik Kian Gie, 'A Tale of a Conglomerate', *Economic and Business Review Indonesia*, 5 June 1993, pp. 26–7, and 12 June 1993, pp. 26–7; *Tempo*, 9 March 1991, pp. 86–90.

21. *Kompas*, 4 May and 24 June 1993.

22. Richard Robison, 'Organising the Transition: Indonesian Politics in 1993/94', in Ross H. McLeod (ed.), *Indonesia Assessment 1994: Finance as a Key Sector in Indonesia's Development* (Singapore: ISEAS, 1994), pp. 65–8; *Tempo*, 19 and 26 February, 5 and 12 March and 2 April, 1994.

23. *Tempo*, 26 February 1994, pp. 21–30.

24. World Bank, *Indonesia*, p. 19.

25. Andrew Rosser, 'Creating Markets: The Politics of Economic Liberalisation in Indonesia Since the Mid-1980s', unpublished Ph.D. thesis, Murdoch University, 1999, p. 99; *Kompas*, 28 October 1988.

26. See, Djisman S. Simandjuntak, 'Survey of Recent Developments', *BIES*, vol. 25, no. 1 (April 1989), pp. 21–4.

27. See Rosser, 'Creating Markets', p. 100.

28. See Econit Advisory Group, *Dampak Kelangkaan Semu Pupuk Urea Terhadap Impor Beras dan Kesejahteraan Petani Tahun* (Jakarta: 1996), pp. 4–7; World Bank, *Indonesia*, p. 17.

29. *Jakarta Post*, 22 August 1998.

30. Bank Yama (belonging to Soeharto's daughter, Siti Hardiyanti Rukmana – Tutut) along with Bank Continental and Bank Pacific (owned by members of the Sutowo family) were rescued with help from Bank Indonesia and Bank Negara Indonesia in 1995, and creditors were paid out of state funds. Sixty per cent of Bank Industri, belonging to Soeharto's brother-in-law, Hashim Djojohadikusumo, was taken over by the state bank, Bank Rakyat, Indonesia when it got into difficulties in 1990. See *Infobank*, February 1997, p. 21; Rosser, 'Creating Markets', p. 122. Private business interests rescued the Soeharto-associated Bank Duta in 1992 when it encountered heavy losses from illegal foreign exchange speculation. No formal charges against the bank were ever laid. See Adam Schwarz, *A Nation in Waiting* (St Leonards: Allen & Unwin 1994), pp. 112, 128, 141.
31. *Gatra*, 26 April 1997, p. 30.
32. See Schwarz, *A Nation in Waiting*, pp. 150–1.
33. See Anwar Nasution, 'The Years of Living Dangerously: The Impacts of Financial Sector Policy Reforms and Increasing Private Sector Indebtedness in Indonesia, 1983–1992', *The Indonesian Quarterly*, vol. 20, no. 4 (1992), p. 151.
34. *Asian Wall Street Journal*, 11–12 June 1999, p. 3.
35. See Government of Indonesia, *Letters of Intent and Memoranda of Economic and Financial Policies Addressed to the International Monetary Fund* (1997, 1998, 1999, 2000) (http://www.imf.org/external/NP/LOI).
36. See World Bank, *Indonesia in Crisis: A Macroeconomic Update* (Washington, DC: World Bank, 1998).
37. Hadi Soesastro and M. Chatib Basri, 'Survey of Recent Developments', *Bulletin of Indonesian Economic Development*, vol. 34, no. 1, (April 1998), p. 37.
38. *Ibid.*, p. 38.
39. World Bank, *Indonesia: From Crisis to Opportunity* (Washington, DC: World Bank, 1999), Table 2.1.
40. *Asian Wall Street Journal*, 4 March 1999, p. 1; 15 March 1999, p. 1; *Jakarta Post*, 1 March 1999, p. 1; 11 December 1999, p. 1.
41. *Asiawise*, 8 December 2000.
42. *Jakarta Post*, 16 October 2000, p. 10; 18 October 2000, p. 12.
43. *Jakarta Post*, 20 January 2000, p. 1; *Forum Keadilan*, 12 March 2000, pp. 12–13.
44. *Kontan Online*, 3 July 2000.
45. *Tempo*, 11 June 2000, p. 130.
46. *Asian Wall Street Journal*, 25–26 February 2000, p. 1.
47. *Warta Ekonomi* online: 14 January 1999; *Forum Keadilan*, 11 January 1999, p. 61; *Tempo*, 16 July 2000, pp. 103, 104; *Asian Wall Street Journal*, 23 June 1999, pp. 1, 4.
48. *Kompas Online*, 6 March 2000; *Tempo*, 26 March 2000, pp. 102, 103.
49. The *Jakarta Post.com*, 1 July 2000.
50. *Jakarta Post*, 21 June 2000, p. 8.
51. *Jakarta Post*, 5 July 2000, p. 1; 24 October 2000, p. 3.
52. *Jakarta Post*, 16 September 2000, p. 1.
53. *Tempo* online, 27 August 2000.
54. *Tempo*, 26 March 2000, pp. 98, 99.

55. *Asian Wall Street Journal*, 13 January 2000, pp. 1, 10.
56. *Jakarta Post*, 20 October 2000, p. 1.
57. *Jakarta Post*, 7 October 2000, p. 1.
58. *Jakarta Post*, 6 October 2000, p. 1.
59. See Tim Lindsey, 'Black Letter, Black Market and Bad Faith: Corruption and the Failure of Law Reform', in Chris Manning and Peter van Diermen (eds.), *Indonesia in Transition: Social Aspects of Reformasi and Crisis* (Singapore: Institute of Southeast Asian Studies 2000), p. 288.
60. *Jakarta Post*, 22 November 1999, p. 4.
61. Lindsey, 'Black Letter', p. 283.
62. *Jakarta Post*, 26 June 2000, p. 10.
63. Ross McLeod, 'Crisis-Driven Changes to the Banking Law and Regulations', *Bulletin of Indonesian Economic Studies*, vol. 35, no. 2 (1999), pp. 148, 149.
64. *Ibid.*, pp. 150–2.
65. *Straits Times*, 20 December 2000.
66. *Jakarta Post*, 5 November 1999, p. 12.
67. *Jakarta Post*, 13 June 2000, p. 1; 26 June 2000, p. 10; 5 August 2000, pp. 1, 4.
68. See Government of Indonesia, *Letters of Intent*, 31 July 2000, p. 8.
69. Bulog controlled the import and distribution of basic commodities such as rice and sugar.
70. *Jakarta Post*, 13 June 2000, p. 9; 20 July 2000, p. 4. A bizarre scandal involving President Wahid's masseur, Suwondo, and Bulog deputy chairman, Saupan, in the appropriation of Rp. 35 billion from Bulog, drew attention to the difficulties involved in eliminating this factor.
71. This point is discussed at length in Benedict Anderson, 'Murder and Progress in Modern Siam', *New Left Review*, no. 181 (1990), pp. 33–48.

7 South Korea and the Asian crisis: the impact of the democratic deficit and OECD accession

STEPHEN L. HARRIS

The purpose of this chapter is to explore the consequences for South Korea of both its democratic deficit and its accession to membership of the Organisation for Economic Co-operation and Development (OECD) in late 1996. It is argued that the interaction of weak governance and imprudent liberalisation was a material contributor to the financial crisis that occurred in late 1997.

This chapter attempts to put governance at the centre of the policy quandary faced by this important Asian country. Thus this analysis of the events leading up to the 1997 financial calamity will go beyond the calculus of economists. That calculus portrays such concepts as 'crony capitalism', imbalances in the trade account, exchange rate disequilibria, moral hazard, the herd instinct in the market and systemic contagion as the major causes of the country's financial problems.[1] It is argued in this chapter that these factors were manifestations of the shortcomings in the country's governance structures.

The chapter will show that 'authoritarian capitalism' in South Korea – its hybridity – was not compatible with the state's desire for the economy to engage as a fully competitive participant in international finance and commerce. Korean society generally, and the business and political elites in particular, did not share the important values of democratic capitalism. Indeed, there was a 'democratic deficit' because of the absence of purposeful beliefs in business values such as transparency, legitimate oversight, a strong sense of ethical (honest) conduct and fairness, a statutory responsibility of corporate directors for governance and accountability to shareholders, and ultimately the absence of legitimate democratic political accountability in the conduct of private and public transactions. The absence of these important democratic governance values created incentives in the South Korean economy that would not work satisfactorily and indeed were inconsistent with practices elsewhere in the industrialised community.

This chapter will also show that both the South Koreans and the other industrial democracies should be held jointly responsible for the unfortunate events in autumn 1997. First, the public policy wishes of the political and bureaucratic elites within the South Korean state were incompatible with the precepts of the neo-liberal capitalist paradigm (essentially removing obstacles to international trade and to domestic competition) that were pursued, more or less, by most OECD members. The value of the prospective tangible and intangible benefits that could accrue to the elites as a consequence of OECD membership was greater than the value of the interests of South Korean civil society and of good public policy.

Second, this democratic deficit was heightened by the government's continuous intrusiveness in the private sector. This intrusiveness gave rise to moral hazard that had the effect of short-circuiting the development of a strong set of democratic values enumerated above. This was also an obstacle to the development of the necessary skills that would be consistent with the set of values needed for a safe and sound financial system. Thus, in the absence of a willingness to change the governance paradigm (from bureaucratic authoritarianism to the rule of democratic law), it was not surprising that South Korea eventually found itself in a financial mess.[2]

Third, beginning in 1993 the commercial and political interests of the United States resulted in intense pressure on the South Korean authorities to liberalise the economy generally and specifically to open its financial markets to the same degree as that in the other industrialised democracies.

Fourth, this apparent coercion was an important factor in the evolution of South Korea's financial problems because, as will be argued later on, the secretariat staff of the OECD and its member countries, as well as the other international agencies – particularly the IMF and the Bank for International Settlements (BIS)[3] – were aware of the financial fragility of the country. Policy advice, particularly from the Fund, was not timely with respect to the governance issue.[4] Even the governance shortcomings – particularly the dreadful plight of South Korea's financial oversight apparatus – were evident in 1992 and documented as early as February 1994, but not acted upon by the influential international agencies.

Fifth, implicit in the analysis in this chapter is that the evolution of the crisis was exacerbated by the fact that regulators in the industrial democracies, while aware of the general shortcomings in South Korean governance, did not send up caution flags to their indigenous financial services industries. Indeed, banks in the industrial democracies continued to be important sources of loanable funds to both the South Korean banks and the chaebols (conglomerates). This served to intensify the resulting financial crisis.

It is not the purpose of this chapter to go into the details of the financial crisis. It is sufficient to note that less than one year after its accession to OECD membership, South Korea was struck by the Asian financial debacle that had started in Thailand in mid-1997.[5] When South Korea's reserves of foreign exchange were depleted by autumn 1997 the government had no choice but to appeal to the IMF for assistance. The crisis was foreshadowed by the bankruptcy of Hanbo Steel in January 1997 and the subsequent problems in the Sammi, Jinro and Kia groups – as well as in many others.[6] When the crisis struck the chaebols were heavily indebted to the banks and non-bank institutions. This indebtedness was a consequence of the immature character of South Korean debt and equity markets and the government's industrial policy that directed the banks to provide financing to the conglomerates. The concentration of chaebols' debt was an inordinate burden for the banks to carry when the conglomerates had trouble servicing their liabilities.

The remainder of the chapter will proceed as follows: the next section will outline some of the salient features of the 'hybridity' pursued by South Korea over the past forty years or so. This historical review is necessary in order to explain how the values of business, government and civil society evolved over this period and the role of the state in the economy, involvement that hindered the process of socialisation into democratic capitalism. Section three will describe and analyse the process of accession to the OECD. Section four will document the acknowledgements, inconsistencies and contradictions of the financial sector problems in South Korea. And the final section will provide some policy lessons and recommendations.

South Korean hybridity: a stylised review of its economics and politics

The period since the early 1960s has been one of intense social and economic change in South Korea. The country moved from a war-torn agrarian society to one of the world's most powerful economies. This economic development, particularly between the 1960s and mid-1980s, was not accompanied by a comparable degree of political and social development typical of democratic capitalist states. Indeed, Park-Chung Hee, the architect of modern industrial South Korea, brought with him from Japan the model of development that had been so successful in that country in the post-Second World War period.

This Japanese development model, accompanied by an authoritarian dictatorship, resulted in rapid industrialisation as the state fashioned a partnership with business that gave rise to the powerful chaebols. The chaebols became important financial benefactors to the ruling regimes/party.[7] On the other hand, civil society and the development of a comprehensive social safety net were largely left out of this bipolar arrangement during South Korea's postwar development. This is not to say that civil society did not benefit in economic terms from this 'Asian miracle', but the social and political development of the society did not advance nearly to the same extent. Pressure for a corporatist societal compromise, such as evolved in Japan, did not materialise through the industrialisation period, although there had been a short-lived experiment with tripartism in the midst of the financial crisis. Thus it was this limiting by the state of democratic participation in the early economic transformation of Korea that served to set the stage for the kind of financial crisis experienced in 1997.

The success of South Korea's industrialisation in the period beginning in the 1960s through to the early 1990s was not based on ideas of openness embedded in liberalism, but on an inward-looking model rooted in mercantilism and mirroring the export-led economic development policies of Japan. The neo-mercantilist commercial policy pursued by South Korea was designed to ensure the nation state's autonomy – to build an autarkic society. Thus South Korea imposed import restrictions on most manufactured products – particularly labour-intensive consumer goods – and severely restricted the use of offshore services – particularly financial services. The South Korean state provided significant financial support to the emerging manufacturing industry by ensuring that it had easy access to 'cheap' finance.[8] The state was also a key actor in promoting South Korean manufactured exports to complement its import restrictions. Later on – in the late 1970s and early 1980s – South Korean industrial strategy shifted emphasis on to heavy industries including steel, chemicals and passenger vehicles. The same neo-mercantilist tendencies that worked so successfully in the consumer goods area was also used in this latter area.

The intrusiveness of the state in the financial sector of the South Korean economy, beginning in the 1960s, was the primary source of the 1997 crisis in South Korean finance. The state used its power to direct the banks to make 'policy loans' to the strategic sectors of the economy. Moreover, the state appointed the presidents, chairpersons and directors of the banks, even after the banks were privatised in the 1980s. This created a dependency relationship between the elites in the public and financial sectors – and the finance elites were not tempted to violate that relationship. Because of this state intrusiveness, the risks undertaken by the banks were underwritten by the state, and the financial welfare of the 'corporate' sector became socialised. All of these measures gave life to moral hazard in South Korea.

The moral hazard problem also worked to undermine the internal governance in the financial institutions and minimised the development of risk analysis skills within the state, within the institutions themselves and within the oversight authorities. There was effectively no oversight and direction to the financial sector except the industrial policy directives emanating from the Ministry of Finance and Economy.[9] '... although the banks realised that large borrowers such as the chaebols were on the verge of default, they could not even dare declare them as failing firms for fear of repercussions throughout the whole economy.'[10] The oversight authorities were under similar constraints.[11] The South Korean authorities estimated that the banks had 29 trillion won of non-performing loans in September 1997 (about 6 to 7 per cent of all loans outstanding).[12]

Thus for much of its economic history, South Korea was subjected to 'authoritarian capitalist' development – its hybridity – in the absence of the enduring
values, attitudes, behaviours and traditions that oil the wheels of a smoothly
functioning democratic system. The official institutions were equally impo-
tent. Indeed, the complexity of the authoritarian capitalist system that was
evolving in South Korea was 'out of balance with the low professionalism
of the political elite and the routinisation of administrative decision-making
and implementation'.[13] A more flexible but rational process was required for
a rapidly advancing economic system that was gradually being integrated into
the international political economy. Because of the extensive government regulations, with licences and subsidies provided by the government, and the state
also controlling credit allocation, any potential reforms could not take hold until state intrusiveness in the economy was considerably reduced and the policy
capacity of the bureaucracy was strengthened.

The transition to democracy in South Korea began in 1987 in the face of the
widespread popular protests, defection of the middle class from the authoritarian
regime and the more general advancing illegitimacy of the Chun Doo Hwan
government.[14] Indeed, the problem with attempting to implement reforms in
such an environment is that the mere passing of laws does not ensure that civil
society can change its practices and traditions in a short period in order to
comply with a reformed economic regime. Moreover, the complexity of the
economic system was exacerbated by the 'decreasing management capabilities
of the government'.[15] Civil society must be socialised to the new order – a
process that takes time. South Korean society was not prepared for the shift to
the neo-liberal policies even by 1993, when the Kim Young Sam administration
was elected.[16] As will be shown, the system was on a path to financial collapse.

South Korea and the OECD

The seed of the idea that South Korea should seek membership of the OECD was
sown in the aftermath of the 1988 Olympic Games, held in Seoul. State elites
were particularly vigorous in spuriously linking the international accolades for
South Korea's organisational performance at the Games with the country's right
to join the other industrial powers in the OECD.[17] There was little recognition
within the state at the time, however, that there was no functioning market to
speak of in South Korea. Some in the state administration saw OECD membership, in addition to being an important political achievement for South Korea,
as a way to exert pressure on the state and the chaebols to restructure and to
reform authoritative practices and to pursue international standards.[18] Many
of the private and quasi-private think-tanks opposed the OECD accession plan

Table 4. *Main elements of the 1993 South Korean financial reform blueprint.*

1. A phased deregulation of interest rates.
2. The introduction of market principles for the conduct of monetary policy.
3. The encouragement of the development of a money market by eliminating restrictions on the issuance of short-term financial instruments.
4. An easing of the restrictions on foreign exchange transactions.
5. Allowing the international value of the won to fluctuate in response to the ebb and flow of payments.
6. The liberalisation of the capital account including restrictions on overseas borrowing – particularly at the short-end of the yield curve.

because they knew full well that South Korea did not have in place the structural, democratic and institutional prerequisites to meet OECD requirements.[19] By 1993, some senior advisers to President Kim Young Sam were also opposed, for the same reasons, and urged a gradual implementation of neo-liberal reforms.[20]

In the 1980s there had been a number of aborted attempts at financial liberalisation, but the resulting instability gave rise, on four separate occasions, to the reimposition of interest rate controls. It was not until the regime of Kim Young Sam, beginning in 1993, that serious reforms were considered – not only in finance, but also in the economy more generally. Following the emergence of South Korea's trade surplus in the late 1980s, and under pressure from the United States,[21] the government issued a blueprint for financial liberalisation and market opening in 1993 (see Table 4). The IMF and the World Bank were instrumental in giving advice to the Ministry of Finance in the fashioning of the blueprint.[22] However, it is generally understood in South Korea that the impetus for reform came from the US Treasury, which had been under pressure from its own financial services industry to obtain access to the South Korean market.[23]

Given the extent of financial deregulation that was proposed in the blueprint, it was remarkable that it did not contain any serious proposals for the strengthening of the financial oversight regime. At the time, oversight was the responsibility of the Bank of Korea (the central bank). Indeed, there was surprise in Seoul that the IMF was not more forceful in using its influence to persuade the South Korean authorities to strengthen the financial regulatory regime.[24]

This blueprint set the stage for the first appearance by a delegation from South Korea before the OECD Committee on Financial Markets (CFM). This meeting occurred in February 1994, at which time the South Korean authorities were seeking observership status on the Committee. Such status was seen as a precursor to formal membership of the Organisation. This meeting had been preceded by an OECD Secretariat mission to Seoul to examine the state of affairs in the South Korean financial services industry and markets. The main concern of the mission, in considering South Korea's request, was the extent to which

Table 5. *Issues raised by the OECD Committee on Financial Markets (CFM)*
in its First Discussion Paper on South Korea.

1. When policy loans would be discontinued.
2. Whether the bad loan problem could be resolved without jeopardising the basic precepts of the blueprint.
3. Whether the deregulation of interest rates could be speeded up from the gradualist approach in the blueprint.
4. Timing of the elimination of restrictions on foreign bank entry.
5. Timing of foreign access to the South Korean bond, money and equity markets.

the country was on its way to meeting the OECD liberalisation codes. In that regard the OECD was concerned about the degree of financial market openness and the obstacles to trade in financial services. This concern for liberalisation was not closely linked to the adequacy of the oversight system, although some anxiety about its inadequacy was expressed rather late in the accession process and was a crucial miscalculation.

In preparation for the meeting of the CFM, the Secretariat prepared a short descriptive background note on the South Korean financial system and raised some issues for discussion between the Committee and the South Korean delegation. Importantly, the background paper pointed out that banks' non-performing loans at the end of June 1993 stood at around 2.7 trillion won (US$3.4 billion) – around 2.2 per cent of loans outstanding. It was clearly noted in the Secretariat's document that unofficial estimates by independent bank analysts had indicated that the actual figure might be much higher, with bad assets close to 11 trillion won.[25] Moreover, the situation on the reporting quality and accuracy had not improved by September 1997, when the Ministry of Finance and Economy could not provide an IMF mission with an accurate measure of the banks' non-performing loans (NPLs).[26] It was well known that the NPLs were systematically understated in South Korea, mainly because there were no firm and strong criteria for placing loans in this category and for valuing loan collateral.[27]

The discussion between the CFM and the South Korean delegation focused on the government's plans for further financial sector liberalisation. In the prepared discussion paper the absence of specific questions to the South Koreans about the quality of financial oversight and of risk assessment with financial institutions was conspicuous. Also noticeable by their absence were questions about the governance role of boards of directors and internal institutional governance structures more generally, and about the plans to strengthen risk and project assessment capacity in view of the poor credit performance of the banks' loan portfolios.

What is interesting about the issues highlighted in Table 5 is that they did not take account of the important linkages between a programme of financial liberalisation, macroeconomic stability and strong regulatory oversight. This omission was particularly negligent, given the experience of the Nordic countries not many years earlier when many banks went belly up in the face of imprudent lending following the deregulation of their financial systems – a predicament exacerbated by inappropriate macroeconomic policy.[28] In the years between 1995 and 1997, in the midst of South Korean financial sector liberalisation, the banks' loan-to-deposit ratio rose to between 150 and 170 per cent.[29] This was a clear signal that problems were on the horizon. Indeed, this was a repeat of patterns in the Nordic countries.

Unfortunately for the South Koreans, their performance at this first meeting with the CFM was dreadful. While the blueprint reflected the extent of the official bureaucracy's thinking on financial sector reform, the delegation from Seoul was unable to deal satisfactorily with issues raised by the CFM's questions. The Committee was particularly exercised about the prospects for progress in following the path set out in the blueprint; and, moreover, South Korea did not seem to be on track for meeting the minimum requirements of the OECD Codes. The message was clear to the South Koreans – they would have to do more and at a faster pace if they were to be successful in achieving the observer status so desperately sought by the political elite. Moreover, there was no evidence that the South Koreans 'were being met where they were at'. That is to say, there was no apparent understanding by the OECD of the South Korean culture, the reasons for the values held in finance and commerce, the character of their governance practices and how and why the South Korean economy had thrived over the course of the preceding period of some thirty-five years.

In November 1994 the South Koreans appeared again before the OECD Committee on Financial Markets to review the 'progress' that had been achieved since their last encounter. Many of the issues raised with the South Korean delegation were the same as those covered in the first meeting.[30] This review had been preceded by yet another mission from the Secretariat to Seoul to help South Korean officials prepare for their second appearance. The OECD Secretariat's officials complained that 'the Koreans don't get it'.[31] It was unfortunate that the Secretariat focused solely on the economic issues rather than attempting to integrate the commercial concerns with the weakness in South Korea's governance regimes. Some of the actors in Seoul were critical of the quality and 'seriousness' of the work of the OECD missions. In a number of instances these concerns were communicated directly to the Organisation.[32]

Some of the issues raised at this second meeting concerned governance issues – or issues of how the state could reform itself and become less intrusive in matters related to finance and financial markets. The Committee's approach was asymmetrical. It sought a less intrusive government or smaller state when what was really needed was a larger state to deal with the risks inherent in the policy prescriptions of the blueprint and the CFM and the effects of globalisation more generally. It appeared as though the CFM members wanted to deconstruct the structures of South Korean commerce without being assured that the South Korean economic infrastructure was prepared for the neo-liberal conception of a market economy.

In addition, there was a policy capacity problem in South Korea, which escaped not only all of the experts involved in dissecting South Korean policies and providing advice on how to reform the economic system but also World Bank officials when it graduated South Korea from the ranks of developing countries.[33] The academic training of the South Korean bureaucracy and of members of the research institutes in the public and private sectors was robust – reflecting human capital that had been accumulated in the course of graduate studies. However, this so-called 'policy cadre' was unable to formulate polices that would have permitted a smooth entry of South Korea into the community of democratic capitalist countries. The OECD Secretariat did not recognise this important weakness, and encouraged South Korea to pursue policies that would eventually be harmful to South Korean enterprises and South Korean civil society. Unfortunately, neither did the CFM take sufficient account of the official governance weaknesses in South Korea.

However, the OECD was not the only international organisation overwhelmed by the calculus of economists. The IMF Article IV consultation with South Korea, which occurred in June 1995, some six months after South Korea's appearance before the CFM, argued that the medium-term policy challenge for South Korean financial policy makers was to deregulate the country's highly interventionist system. In particular, IMF officials suggested that the government should implement its plan for financial liberalisation and external account opening.[34] There was no apparent appreciation in the Fund's analysis of the policy capacity and governance problems in South Korea's financial sector – and there was no hint of the problems that South Korea would face only twenty-four months later.[35]

Table 6 shows how important the state was in the operations of the financial system. It further suggests that the absence of a market-based financial system in Korea would probably have resulted in a paucity of human capital to oversee the operations of a safe and sound market-based system. In the event, the CFM was not completely satisfied with the progress South Korea had made over the year 1994 in getting on track for meeting the OECD Liberalisation Codes. However, there was sufficient suggestion in the delegation's comments to indicate that the Committee was beginning to hear what it wanted. With that in mind the South Koreans were granted observer status on the Committee.

It is unfortunate that the bureaucrats representing the South Korean government were so concerned about realising the wishes of their political superiors (observership and eventually membership in the OECD) that they could not see the folly in their words and deeds. Their objective function had little to do with ensuring that policies were in place to advance social welfare but was solely to

Table 6. *Issues raised by the CFM in its Second Discussion Paper on South Korea.*

1. The time-line for abolishing policy loans in the banking system.
2. The impact of 'window guidance' by the central bank and the scope for market setting of the banks' prime lending rate.
3. Whether gradual deregulation of deposit rates would pose a threat to the deposit base of the banks compared with a quick elimination of interest rate controls.
4. The future role of the government in the approval process for the introduction of new financial products.
5. The time-line for commercial bank privatisation and foreign bank-branch entry.
6. The considerations to be taken into account in approving foreign bank-branch licences.
7. The reason for the prohibition of foreign bank subsidiaries.
8. Policy towards improving commercial bank governance.
9. The timing of the government's easing its intrusion in the stock market through its Stock Market Stabilisation Fund and Guarantee Stock Fund.
10. The reason for maintaining restrictions on international capital flows.

ensure that the annual South Korean government promotion and salary review cycle would be kind to them.[36] This apparent one-dimensional perspective of the South Korean bureaucracy exacerbated the rent-seeking activities of most of the other domestic and international cast of players who had an interest in the trajectory of South Korean reform.

At the OECD Ministerial Meeting in May 1995 the Secretariat was told to complete the South Korean membership accession process as soon as the country was *ready* to take on membership responsibilities.[37] *Ready* meant that South Korea should satisfy the OECD Liberalisation Codes and thus be prepared to participate as a full partner in trade relations with other OECD members by abolishing its barriers to trade in goods and services. *Ready* did not mean that South Korea should have the appropriate democratic governance structures in place. The OECD was not troubled by the one-dimensional nature of the South Korean commitment. Indeed, South Korea could not both comply with the OECD Codes (which on accession would be legal commitments of the South Korean state) and assure its civil society and the international financial community that there would be no undue risks associated with a more open South Korean economic system.

The OECD community was not concerned about the adequacy of democratic governance structures as they related to the conduct of business. All this is not to say that South Korea was not a democratic society, but it was the case that South Korea was unable to conduct its business activities according to the standards of the democracies of the OECD community. South Korea was moving in the right direction, but it was a long way from meeting the standards of a safe and sound financial and business system and to participate as a responsible member of the global economic community. It is interesting to note that South Korea would not give up its status as a developing country in the WTO.

By the time South Korea again appeared before the CFM, in February 1996, many constraints on a market-based financial system had been eliminated or would soon be abolished. Thus the issues reviewed on this occasion related to the operation of financial markets, the implementation of a market-based monetary policy, the timetable for a fully floating exchange rate regime and allowing South Korean firms to borrow from foreign banks. At this late stage in the accession process the Committee made specific inquiries into prudential regulation and depositor protection. The Committee wanted to know to what extent the South Korean authorities had addressed these issues.[38] While still concerned about the 'bad loan' problem in the commercial banks,[39] the CFM appeared pleased with the efforts that had been made by the South Korean authorities in modernising its domestic financial system. It was particularly satisfied with the accelerated pace of financial reform and liberalisation that had taken place in the period since the first meeting between the CFM and South Korean officials in February 1994.[40]

Having commended the South Koreans for the progress made thus far, the CFM made a number of additional demands on the authorities before it would conclude that South Korea had met the requirements for OECD membership.[41] In the first place, South Korea was required to eliminate remaining controls on financial prices and credit allocation, expand the opportunities for long-term foreign borrowing by South Korean enterprises, and set a firm schedule for the removal of all restrictions on international capital flows and foreign exchange transactions. Many of these requirements appeared odd, given the fact that continental European countries had only recently fully liberalised their systems, and that many countries, including Canada and the United States and those in the European Union, had asset allocation ratios shrouded under the veil of safety and soundness.

Furthermore, the Committee 'welcomed' South Korea's intention to upgrade its prudential oversight regime. This was the only significant comment by the CFM regarding official supervision of the financial system. It was an implicit acknowledgement that the existing regime was inadequate for an economy wishing to participate in global financial markets. It is unfortunate that the same detailed recommendations that were demanded on the liberalisation front were not sought from the South Koreans for strengthening the oversight regime, particularly given the global systemic risks that were on the horizon. Finally, the CFM wanted the South Koreans to promote the internationalisation of their domestic markets by further broadening access to them by foreign investors, mainly under pressure from the US government acting in the interests of US financial institutions.

At this point the South Koreans knew that they were getting close to satisfying the CFM.[42] The 'shows' that they had put on for the CFM had got progressively better. The bureaucrats in Seoul did not want to take a chance in not telling the Committee what it wanted to hear. So the bureaucrats did just that. The

Table 7. *Issues raised by the CFM in its Third Discussion Paper on South Korea.*

1. A clear timetable for post-accession liberalisation of long-term capital flows – including long-term foreign borrowing by South Korean enterprises.
2. A clear commitment to abolishing ceilings on non-resident ownership of South Korean equities.
3. A more rapid liberalisation of foreign participation in the corporate bond market.
4. An early liberalisation of foreign entry into the investment advisory and investment trust (collective investment) businesses.
5. Full national treatment for foreign banks and securities firms.

concessions offered by the bureaucratic authorities were questionable from a public welfare perspective.[43]

The South Korean government promised to allow, by the end of 1996, small and medium enterprises (SMEs), domestic enterprises with 50 per cent foreign ownership and companies involved in infrastructure development to borrow long-term funds offshore; and all commercial enterprises would also be permitted to borrow long-term in foreign markets by the end of 1997. In the meantime, the South Koreans indicated that complete capital decontrols were likely to lead to a substantial inflow of volatile short-term capital which would interfere with the objective of macroeconomic stability. The South Korean authorities proposed that full liberalisation should occur when the domestic–international interest rate differential narrowed to 2 per cent. At this point the South Koreans were aware that domestic banks were active in the international interbank market, borrowing short and lending long,[44] and that the demands of the CFM were expected to exacerbate an already problematic situation. Nevertheless, this explicit point was not made by the South Korean delegation in its response to the CFM.

On the question of prudential oversight the South Korean authorities noted that they had been monitoring the classification of performing and non-performing loans and the large exposures of banks. Also, the banks were now required to make their financial statements public. Subsequent investigation made it clear that the regulatory authorities were unable to account for all of the non-performing bank loans when the crisis became a matter of public record. Moreover, there was no effort at this juncture to introduce generally accepted accounting principles so that financial statements would be meaningful to the offshore institutions that were engaged in transactions with South Korean institutions. CFM members knew full well that their own institutions were probably engaging in imprudent behaviour by lending short-term money, in the interbank market, to their South Korean counterparts.

Despite the concessions made by the South Koreans, the CFM was still not satisfied. At its meeting in June 1996 the earlier demands were reinforced (see Table 7).[45] The South Korean authorities, desperate to achieve their objective of OECD membership, acquiesced in all of the demands of the Committee. That is to say, they agreed that at the end of 1999 virtually all of the restrictions that had been identified would be removed. However, complete liberalisation of capital flows would have to wait until the 2 per cent domestic–international interest rate differential, noted earlier, was reached. With these assurances the Committee felt it had done its job and indicated that South Korea had met the requirements for OECD membership in the area of the CFM's responsibility.

The foregoing empirical analysis underscores that the South Korean financial system was not ready for the kind of liberalisation that was being demanded of it by the other industrial democracies. Indeed, the South Koreans knew that their financial system was in trouble well into the accession process.[46] The tip of the iceberg was the magnitude of banks' non-performing loans noted earlier. The CFM did not undertake the appropriate due diligence on problem loan resolution and regulatory oversight. Moreover, the conduct of commerce in South Korea was not subject to the same transparency and ethics as in most of the other industrial countries. Finally, responsibility for the subsequent fiasco must rest with both the South Koreans and the industrial democracies.

Financial sector reform: the substantive problem acknowledged

About a month after South Korean accession to OECD membership on 12 December 1996,[47] President Kim Young Sam announced plans to appoint a presidential commission whose mandate would be to prepare a 'comprehensive plan for the reform of the financial sector'.[48] The motivation for the appointment of the presidential commission and the study of financial sector reform was 'Korea's recent entry into the OECD and the opening of financial markets'.[49]

The commission began its work on 22 January 1997. In its *First Report*, published in spring 1997, the South Korean confession about the inadequacy of its financial regulatory oversight regime appeared. This was just a few months before the Asian financial crisis reached South Korea and about four years after both the OECD formally began examining its financial system and the *Blueprint for Reform* was adopted.[50] This confession largely acknowledged the weaknesses in the South Korean financial system which were identified earlier in this paper. The core strategy pursued by the commission to tackle these weaknesses focused on further deregulation of the domestic financial market, institutional innovations designed to make regulatory authorities more independent, realignment of accounting practices with international standards, and more reliable and speedy dissemination of information on the financial position of banks.[51]

This was all well and good, but unfortunately neither the South Koreans nor the OECD itself *had* followed the advice that was contained in the Organisation's *Report on Regulatory Reform*:

reform efforts are likely to be more usefully directed toward enhancing fundamental functions of the financial system, such as: improving internal governance of financial institutions; improving efficiency and competition within financial markets; enhancing market discipline; upgrading the accounting, legal and payments system, and other infrastructure needed to ensure that financial transactions can be carried out efficiently and risks effectively managed and monitored. *It is particularly important in this context to make necessary reforms to establish adequate prudential oversight before and as reforms are being undertaken.*[52]

A similar point was made in the South Korean academic literature:

reorganisation of [the] domestic financial system, especially of the banking system should precede implementation of liberalisation policy of the financial market, foreign exchange and capital market. That is, safeguards of liberalisation such as enhancement of the banking systems to the level of those of the advanced industrial countries and institutions ... should have been implemented before the liberalisation policy measures were taken. But the Kim government rushed to policy change toward liberalisation of the foreign exchange and capital market without preparing proper [safeguard] measures.[53]

The OECD subsequently echoed this confession by the South Korean authorities – this time not the CFM, but the Economic Development Review Committee (EDRC). In its annual review of South Korea it offered no support for the conclusions of the CFM in its examinations of South Korea leading up to accession:

The pattern of deregulation that was pursued in Korea may well have added to the fragility of the system. In general, the commercial banks continued to face obligations to act in accordance with government policy, and did not develop the autonomy needed in a market economy. Deregulation was co-ordinated with a concept to upgrade supervision. There was no consistent policy aimed at transforming institutions, especially banks, into independent profit seeking entities. Owing to a continuing lack of consensus as to whether deregulation, institutional and regulatory reform, and the opening of the financial system to foreign participation were in the national interest, deregulation was slow and measures were often contradictory. Furthermore, in liberalising external borrowing non-financial entities were allowed to borrow short-term, even though long-term borrowing was still restricted. In fact the peculiar mix of partial deregulation and continued rigidities left Korea rather susceptible to pressures in the 1990s which reached a culmination in 1997.[54]

So here we have both the South Korean authorities and one arm of the OECD condemning practices in the financial services industry. What was the dynamic which permitted the CFM, supposedly under the guidance of the Secretariat, to collaborate in providing the OECD with a recommendation that South Korea did or would satisfy the membership accession criteria? The character of the analysis undertaken by the Secretariat, coincident with its missions to Seoul, leading up to the various meetings among officials and the CFM, was faulty. It was faulty from the perspective of its incoherence. The analysis and discussion were focused on specific constraints in the system and not on a vision of a competitive, efficient and safe and sound financial system. Part of the reason for this disjointed attack on the South Korean financial system by the CFM was the fact that its members were technocrats and not conceptual thinkers about good comprehensive public policy. Each country's technocrats on the Committee thought that regulatory and business practices in their respective countries was the 'first best'. This forced the South Koreans continuously to come back to the Committee with micro-liberalisation proposals that were unrelated to one another, despite the fact that the overarching framework of the *Blueprint* was in the background. Virtually all of the discussions were focused on the details and thus the 'big picture' was out of focus.

Most of the staff of the Secretariat charged with analysing the South Korean situation were also micro-tacticians and thus did not get a proper view of the 'big picture'. For the most part, practices in the US market were used as the benchmark for the Secretariat's analysis. An equally important constraint on this analysis was the influence of the permanent US delegation to the OECD. Little in the way of analysis prepared by the Secretariat on the South Korean accession process was disseminated to the CFM without prior approval of the permanent US delegation or the US representative on the Committee.[55] The bottom line for the US authorities was unfettered access to the South Korean market for its financial services industry.[56]

The United States was able to impose its wishes on the Secretariat because the US authorities effectively held a veto over the Organisation's budget, and moreover were not satisfied with the work of the Financial Affairs Division specifically and the Directorate for Fiscal, Financial and Enterprise Affairs more generally.[57] (It will be recalled that the United States was the impetus in the first instance for the development of the 1993 *Blueprint*.) So the objective function of the international bureaucrats was to preserve their budget allocation in a time of severe financial restraint in the Organisation. As such they worked at the behest of the US authorities.

Conclusions: policy lessons and recommendations

So what can we say about where we have been and where we are going? First, it seems clear that the societal paradigm pursued by the South Koreans, to use Thomas Kuhn's terminology, was and is very different from that pursued by the other industrial democracies. The members of the OECD, and its Secretariat, did not recognise that difference. Second, in proposing to the South Koreans the neo-liberal path for its financial services industry and for its commerce more generally, the OECD recommendations – as well as those from the other international organisations – did not distinguish adequately between what was important and what was unimportant in achieving the desired goal. A safe and sound financial system was not clearly on the policy agenda. Third, the OECD did not take account of the South Korean culture in proposing policy choices. It was neo-liberalism whether or not it clashed with South Korean sensibilities. The lingering negative effects on policy of the 'hybridity' that so characterised South Korea's authoritarian capitalism was disregarded. The democratic deficit was neglected. Fourth, the objectives of most of the actors in this drama – the political and bureaucratic elites, the Secretariat of the OECD, the countries that participated in prescribing the reforms, and the other international agencies – were related not to the welfare of South Korean civil society, but to their own welfare. Rent-seeking was ubiquitous.

Fifth, prescriptions for a smaller South Korean state were misguided. A smaller state was needed in some domains, but a larger state was clearly needed in others. Symmetry in policy prescriptions was necessary – but was not prescribed. Sixth, regulators in the industrial democracies were negligent in not raising caution flags for their indigenous financial services industries about their activities in South Korea. Signals regarding credit and market risk were not functioning adequately. Such market failures clearly call for state intrusiveness. When will regulators realise that they cannot regulate for one or two failures without there being significant systemic implications? Seventh, international bureaucrats, particularly those at the OECD (and probably at the IMF), must recognise that what they prescribe matters a lot. Their policy prescription cannot be seen as simply putting theory into practice – particularly economic theory. Policy prescriptions must be contextual. They must take account of the conjunctural and societal considerations if they are to be successful. Policy linkages can only be ignored with perilous costs. These policy linkages relate not only to regulatory, structural and economic policies, but also to policies of governance.

So what can be done to avoid a repeat of these events in another venue? What should be done to bring countries in transition smoothly into the community of democratic capitalist states? How can structural reform assist civil societies through reform and not burden them unnecessarily with the costs of reform?

To begin with, structural reform prescription should not be left solely in the domain of economists. What is efficient in economic terms may not be efficient in political terms. And most of us know that much of what governments do is inefficient. In such circumstances the economists' paradigm – its analytical richness – must be supplemented by the body of knowledge from the other social sciences. Thus teams of so-called 'experts' from the international organisations – when on missions to emerging market countries and countries in transition to democratic capitalism – should comprise 'experts' from all of the social science fields: for example, political scientists, sociologists, anthropologists and psychologists. Societal change, which is what the bottom line of the South Korean accession to the OECD was all about, is not a one-dimensional economic game. This was even more evident in the reforms proposed to the east Asian countries in the aftermath of financial crisis. How many times does the price of bread have to be increased before economists will conclude that such action inhibits the success of future change? A psychologist or sociologist would probably answer not even once – and that other solutions should be looked for. Furthermore, it is not obvious from the most recent published scholarly work in the area of improving the financial architecture that the questions of governance and societal values have been adequately addressed.[58] Unfortunately, ideas from economics continue to be pre-eminent. There is a lot of room for interdisciplinarity.

Furthermore, it is important to get the sequencing of policy change right. The OECD seemed to avoid all of the literature on policy sequencing, including the advice of some in its own Secretariat. Getting the sequencing right cannot be done without the interdisciplinary team – of the sort noted above. Finally, policies of gradualism in matters of societal change are more likely to be successful than policies of 'cold turkey'. Perhaps 'cold turkey' prescriptions will work on problems that are purely economic, but they will not work when the changes needed are more profound. Gradualism combined with appropriate policy sequencing will have a higher probability of a successful outcome than otherwise would be the case. The landscape is littered with the failures. South Korea did not follow a scheme of gradualism, but one of autonomous change – the choices made in the course of discussions with the OECD were random. A policy of the 'show must go on' is unworkable. The South Koreans know that now – but do others? Certainly the Chinese authorities should be cautious in formulating liberalisation policies and not fall into the same trap.

Notes

The author is grateful to Ms Tamara Guttman, First Secretary, and Ms Myung Joo Ok, Political-Economic Officer, both at the Canadian embassy in Seoul, and to Mr Guntae Lee, Economic Counsellor at the Korean embassy in Ottawa, for their assistance in arranging confidential meetings with key actors in Seoul from academia, the research institutes and major government agencies during the period 27 September–5 October 1999. The author also thanks Dr Lisa Harris for constructive comments on an early draft. Earlier versions of this chapter were presented at a University of Amsterdam conference in January 2000, the ISA Annual Conference in Los Angeles, March 2000, and the annual meetings of the Canadian Political Science Association, Quebec, July 2000.

1. See Wang Sik Kim, 'Foreign Exchange Crisis: Causes and Process', prepared for the International Studies Association Meeting in Washington, February 1999, p. 1.
2. Sung-Sup Rhee, 'Bureaucratic Authoritarianism', mimeo, Soongsil University, 22 January 1999, p. 2.
3. The BIS had been regularly publishing the indebtedness of Korea.
4. Based on confidential interviews.
5. It is interesting to note that both Mexico and the Czech Republic experienced a severe crisis not long after becoming members of the OECD. This pattern of events certainly calls into question the 'due diligence' of the OECD (as well as the other major international institutions) and the benign neglect of the fragile situation in these emerging market countries by the regulators in the industrial democracies.
6. See Jang-Hee Yoo, *Real Success, Financial Fall: A Reassessment of the Korean Dynamism* (Seoul: Ewha Womans University Press, 1999), p. 106.
7. Based on confidential interviews.
8. There have been a number of suggestions that the chaebols themselves influenced interest rate policy. See Sung-Sup Rhee, 'Bureaucratic Authoritarianism', p. 3. Also confirmed in confidential interviews.
9. See Jang-Hee Yoo, *Real Success, Financial Fall*, p. 103.
10. *Ibid.*
11. Based on confidential interviews.
12. Korean Ministry of Finance, 'Financial Market Stabilization Package', mimeo, 26 November 1997.
13. Wolfgang Merkel, 'The Consolidation of Post-autocratic Regimes: A multilevel Analysis', in Chung-in Moon and Jongryn Mo (eds.), *Democratization and Globalization in Korea* (Seoul: Yonsei University Press, 1999), p. 50.
14. Chung-in Moon and Jongryn Mo, 'Introduction', in Moon and Mo, *Democratization and Globalization*, p. 12.
15. Wang Sik Kim, 'Foreign Exchange Crisis: Causes and Process,' p. 3.
16. *Ibid.*, p. 5.
17. Based on confidential interviews.
18. Based on confidential interviews.
19. Based on confidential interviews.
20. Based on confidential interviews.
21. See Stephan Haggard and Sylvia Maxfield, 'The Political Economy of Financial Internationalization in the Developing World', in Benjamin J. Cohen and Charles Lipson (eds.), *Issues and Agents in International Political Economy* (Cambridge, MA: MIT Press, 1999). Also confirmed in confidential interviews.
22. Based on confidential interviews.
23. Based on confidential interviews.
24. Based on confidential interviews.
25. OECD, 'Financial Market Reforms in Korea: Issues for Discussion Between the Enlarged Bureau of the Committee on Financial Markets and Korean Officials', mimeo, 20 January 1994.
26. Based on confidential interviews.

27. Jang-Yung Lee, 'Korean Currency Crisis', in *Crisis in Asia: Differences and Similarities* (Seoul: Institute of Economic Research, Seoul National University and Korea Institute of Finance, 1999), p. 180.
28. See Charles Goodhart, Phillip Hartman, David Llewellyn, Lillian Rojas-Suarez and Steven Weisbrod, *Financial Regulation: Why, How and Where Now?* (London: Routledge, 1998), pp. 17–33; Stephen Harris and Charles Pigott, 'Regulatory Reform in the Financial Services Industry', in *OECD Report on Regulatory Reform: Volume 1, Sectoral Studies* (Paris: OECD, 1997), pp. 69–114.
29. Jang-Yung Lee, 'Korean Currency Crisis', p. 181.
30. OECD, 'Financial Market Reforms in Korea: Issues for Discussion Between the Enlarged Bureau of the Committee on Financial Markets and Korean Officials, November 7, 1994', mimeo, 21 September 1994.
31. Based on confidential interviews.
32. Based on confidential interviews.
33. Based on confidential interviews.
34. Based on confidential interviews.
35. Based on confidential interviews.
36. Conclusions based on confidential interviews.
37. OECD, 'Issues for Discussion Between the Committee on Financial Markets and Korean Officials, February 26, 1995', mimeo, 26 January 1995, p. 1.
38. *Ibid.*, p. 5.
39. By the fall of 1997 the South Koreans were still not well placed to tell the IMF what the definitive situation was with respect to the bad loan problem. Based on confidential interviews in Seoul.
40. OECD Committee on Financial Markets, 'Report to the Council on Korean Accession to OECD Membership', mimeo 1996.
41. *Ibid.*, pp. 6–7.
42. The following account draws on OECD Committee on Financial Markets, 'Report to the Council on Korean Accession to OECD Membership', pp. 8–16.
43. *Ibid.*, p. 17.
44. Based on confidential interviews.
45. OECD Committee on Financial Markets, 'Report to the Council on Korean Accession to OECD Membership', pp. 19–21.
46. Based on confidential interviews.
47. OECD, Statement by the Secretary-General on the Republic of Korea, Paris, 10 January 1997.
48. South Korea: The Presidential Commission for Financial Reform, 'Preface', *Financial Reform in Korea: The First Report* (April 1997).
49. *Ibid.*, p. 2.
50. *Ibid.*, pp. 2–3.
51. *Ibid.*, pp. 6, 13, 15, 19, 30, 33, 44; South Korea: The Presidential Commission for Financial Reform, *Financial Reform in Korea: The Second Report* (June 1997), p. 3.
52. Stephen L. Harris and Charles A. Pigott, 'Regulatory Reform in the Financial Services Industry', in OECD, *OECD Report on Regulatory Reform, Volume 1*, p. 92, emphasis added.

53. Wang Sik Kim, 'Foreign Exchange Crisis', p. 7.
54. OECD, Economics Department, Economic Development Review Committee, '1997–1998 Annual Review – Korea', mimeo 19 June 1998, pp. 39, 41.
55. Based on confidential discussions.
56. Based on confidential discussions.
57. Based on confidential discussions.
58. See Council on Foreign Relations, *Safeguarding Prosperity in a Global Financial System: The Future International Financial Architecture* (Washington, DC: Institute for International Economics, 1999); and Barry Eichengreen, *Toward A New International Financial Architecture: A Practical Post-Asia Agenda* (Washington, DC: Institution for International Economics, 1999).

8 Currency crises in Russia and other transition economies

VLADIMIR POPOV

Recent currency crises have affected not only east Asian countries but transition economies as well. The Russian crisis of August 1998 was perhaps the most spectacular example. It was preceded by a series of currency crises in Bulgaria and Romania in 1996 and in Ukraine and Belarus in 1997–8, and was followed by similar crises in Kyrghyzstan and Georgia in late 1998 and in Kazakhstan in early 1999. Did these crises result from financial contagion that spread across the global economy? Or were they caused by national institutional factors similar to those in east Asia? This chapter argues that neither of the above explanations are completely true. It proposes a third explanation: currency crises in transition economies resulted primarily from domestic policy mistakes, but of a different nature from those in east Asia.

The argument will be developed in the following five sections. The first section will critically review the prevailing approaches to examining the Russian currency crisis, and evaluate their respective explanatory values. On the basis of the theoretical review, the chapter will proceed to a detailed discussion of the macroeconomic background and causes of the August 1998 crisis in Russia in the second section. The third section will extend the argument to a broader analysis of currency and financial crises in other transition economies. The penultimate section will explore the sociopolitical factors that underlay the mismanagement of exchange rate policy. The final section will summarise the empirical findings and present major policy lessons, particularly for the reform of the international financial architecture.

Prevailing explanations of the Russian crisis

There are several prevailing (and not mutually exclusive) explanations of the August 1998 currency crisis in Russia. One stresses the unfortunate coincidence of events (the Asian crisis, a drop in oil prices, political instability, etc.). Yevgeny Yasin, the minister without portfolio in the former Kirienko government and a respected academic economist, contended that the Russian crisis was not just the result of evil forces or incompetence, but was caused by the coincidence of circumstances, most of which were against Russia.[1] Sergey Kirienko himself believed that even in June 1998 Russia would have had a chance to avoid the crisis if the Duma had accepted tax increases suggested by the government.[2] Anders Åslund takes a similar view, arguing that the Duma, by rejecting the government package of sensible policies, pushed the country 'over the brink into a financial abyss'.[3]

Another explanation is that the crisis was caused by budgetary problems – persistent deficits and mounting government debts, or 'the GKO (short-term government bonds) pyramid'. It does not surprise anybody that former high-ranking central bank officials take this view. 'No doubt, the current financial crisis is mostly of budgetary and debt origin', argues Sergey Alexashenko, the then deputy chairman of the Central Bank of Russia (CBR).[4] According to this view, it is the government, not the CBR, that should be blamed, as the latter was able to stick firmly to the restrictive monetary policy without being supported by the government, which continued to pursue a loose fiscal policy. In response, former government officials claim that they were fully aware of the problem, but were not able to force the parliament to accept the necessary tough measures to improve tax collection. Hence the scapegoat was again the red–brown parliament, which, as everyone seems to know, was strongly opposed to policy reform.

Popular Western accounts of the Russian crisis focus on the crony and criminal nature of Russian capitalism. The government is accused of acting on the interests of 'oligarchs' – heads of large financial–industrial groups in the Russian economy – that have effectively 'privatised' the state and care only about enriching themselves in the short run. The basic assumption is that everything was so rotten in Russia that it would be unreasonable to expect a successful macroeconomic stabilisation.

It is often argued that funds obtained by the state through domestic and external sources were misused, if not embezzled or stolen, and that the inefficient and corrupt system of public administration cannot ensure any kind of macroeconomic stabilisation, be it exchange-rate-based or money-based. Oligarchs, who are generally described as myopic, are unable to agree on measures to increase tax revenues, stem capital flight and control debt growth. Paul Krugman lamented that IMF and World Bank funds were just wasted, if not stolen, by the short-sighted and selfish oligarchs.[5] Similarly, Åslund believes that the August 1998 crash had its origin in intense competition over the 'evasive rent' that decreased from 15–80 per cent of GDP in 1991–4 to 5–15 per cent in

1995–8.[6] Some even ascribe all Russia's evils to misunderstandings of the nature of money and to the seventy years of bolshevism that virtually abolished money as a legal tender of predictable value.[7]

These explanations have missed several important points. First, although the role of money and credit in the Soviet centrally planned economy (CPE) was limited, the degree of monetisation (measured by the M2/GDP ratio) and creditisation (bank credit outstanding as a percentage of GDP) in the 1980s was much higher than that in the Russian market economy of the 1990s. In a sense the Soviet CPE was much more monetised than the new Russian market economy. Soviet planners, as a matter of fact, were quite prudent in macroeconomic management. From 1947 (Stalin's confiscatory monetary reform) to 1987 (the beginning of macroeconomic mismanagement under Gorbachev), the annual average inflation (open and hidden, i.e. the increase in monetary overhang) was only 3 per cent, lower than inflation rates in most countries during this period. Budget deficits were low or non-existent, government domestic debts minuscule, external debts low, and payment systems as regular as clockwork. The argument about 'the impact of Soviet legacies' thus does not seem to hold much water. These 'Soviet legacies' in macroeconomic management were much better than the record of the Russian government in the 1990s.

Second, there is hardly any doubt that Russian state institutions have weakened in recent years. The weakening of state institutions is the main *long-term* factor that has accounted for the poor performance of the Russian (and Commonwealth of Independent States – CIS) economy, as compared with more rapid growth in China and Vietnam, with strong authoritarian institutions, and in central European countries, with strong democratic institutions. As a matter of fact, recent research that compares twenty-eight transition economies, including China and Vietnam, suggests that it is not the speed of liberalisation but the institutional capacity of the state which is responsible for varying economic performance. This factor has been overlooked by the two dominant schools of transition thought – shock therapists and gradualists.[8]

Nevertheless, while institutional weakness is the single most important *long-term* factor that contributed to the extreme magnitude of the Russian recession, it is not linked directly to the collapse of the rouble. During the early and mid-1990s, the debt levels of the Russian government and Russian companies were very modest by international standards. Even if borrowed funds were embezzled, this could not and did not lead to the debt and currency crises, since the critical point of excessive indebtedness would not have been reached for several years at least. Equally important, there were no major changes with respect to such structural problems as 'cronyism', corruption and institutional weaknesses. Explanations that have emphasised the criminal nature of Russian capitalism thus cannot take us far enough.

Finally, the goal of maintaining an appropriate (not overvalued) exchange rate is perhaps the least politicised issue of government economic policy. Had they made any efforts to keep the rouble low through timely and gradual devaluation, the government and the CBR might not have encountered any opposition either from industrial lobbies or from oligarchs. While macroeconomic stabilisation in Russia did not materialise in 1992–4, because of the lack of consensus among powerful interest groups on how to finance cuts in government expenditure, there is no evidence that political factors worked against the formulation of a low rouble strategy in 1995–8.

Russia's 1998 financial collapse

The August 1998 currency crisis in Russia was perhaps the most drastic of all the crises that occurred in transition economies. In a matter of days the exchange rate that had been stable during the preceding three years lost over 60 per cent of its value – a much sharper decline than the currency depreciation in all Latin American and south-east Asian countries, except Indonesia (see Figures 2 and 3). At the same time, prices increased by nearly 50 per cent in only two months after the crisis, as compared with less than 1 per cent monthly

Figure 2. *Exchange rates in transition economies (national currencies per $1, January 1997 = 100 per cent), 1997–8.*

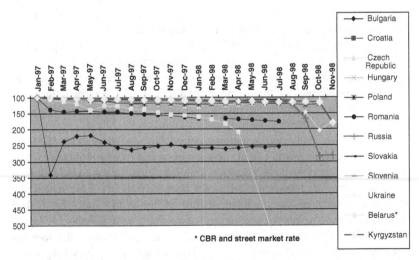

Sources: IMF (*International Financial Statistics*, various issues) and the Central Bank of Russia.

Figure 3. *Exchange rates in south-east Asia (national currencies per $1, Jan.*
1997 = 100 per cent) and in Mexico (Jan. 1994 = 100 per cent), 1997–8.

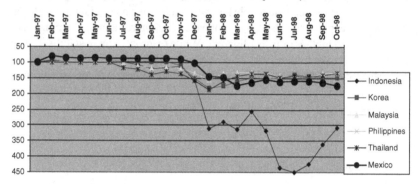

Sources: IMF (*International Financial Statistics*, various issues) and the Central Bank of Russia.

inflation before the crisis.[9] Real output also fell by about 6 per cent in 1998
after registering a small increase of 0.6 per cent in 1997 for the first time since
1989.[10]

Macroeconomic stabilisation of 1995–8

The financial collapse in Russia marked the failure of the macroeconomic stabilisation programme that had been pursued for over three years prior to the
crisis. After experiencing high inflation of several hundred and more per cent
a year during the period immediately following the deregulation of prices on
2 January 1992, Russia finally opted for the programme of exchange-rate-based
stabilisation. After accumulating foreign exchange reserves and managing to
maintain a stable rate for the rouble in the first half of 1995, the CBR introduced a system of the crawling peg in mid-1995 – an exchange rate corridor
with initially pretty narrow boundaries (see Figure 4).

The programme reflected the determination of the government and the CBR
to bring down the growth rate of money supply and to curb inflation. It was
designed to contain the budget deficit within reasonable limits and to find non-
inflationary ways to finance the deficit. On both the fronts the government was
able to keep its promises for three years. It managed to control the budget
deficit, even though this required drastic expenditure cuts as budget revenues
continued to fall, despite all efforts to improve tax collection.[11] It also managed to finance the deficit mostly through borrowings – partly by selling short-
term rouble-denominated treasury bills (which were also purchased by foreign

Figure 4. *Consumer prices, exchange rate of the dollar (Dec. 1994 = 100 per cent) and the ratio of Russian to US prices (percentage, bars), 1994–2000.*

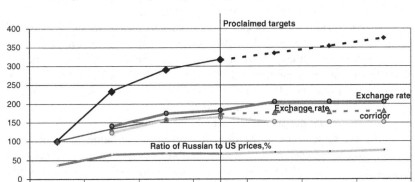

Sources: Narodnoye Khozyaistvo SSSR (National Economy of the USSR); Rossiysky Statistichesky Yezhegodnik (Moscow: Russian Statistical Yearbook, various issues).

investors), partly by borrowing from international financial institutions, Western governments, banks and the Eurobond market. Under the circumstances, the CBR was able to reduce the growth rates of money supply and to bring down inflation.

The weak foundations of macroeconomic stabilisation

Immediately before the crisis, inflation had been running at only 6 per cent a year (July 1997 to July 1998), the rate of output reduction slowed down in 1996, and the country looked forward to economic growth in 1997. The macroeconomic stabilisation, however, was based on a weak foundation of the overvalued exchange rate of the rouble and on the policy of the CBR to keep the real exchange rate intact, that is, to proceed with the devaluation of the nominal rate only in line with the ongoing inflation.

As a result, the 'Dutch disease' emerged in Russia from 1995, when the exchange rate of the rouble approached some 70 per cent of the purchasing power parity (PPP) and stayed at that level until the outbreak of the crisis (see Figure 4). The previously high rates of export growth slowed down substantially (from 20 per cent in 1995 to 8 per cent in 1996 for total exports, and from 25 per cent to 9 per cent for exports to non-CIS states). In 1997 total exports fell for the first time since 1992. Needless to say, it was Russia's already weak export of manufactured goods that was most affected by the appreciation of the real exchange rate. In 1996, among all transition economies, Russia (and Slovenia, by then the richest country that experienced recovery from 1993) had the smallest gap between domestic and international prices.[12]

The decrease in world oil prices in 1997–8 added insult to injury: accelerated export reduction in the first half of 1998, together with rising imports, wiped out virtually completely the trade surplus, which had amounted to US$20 billion in 1996.[13] The current account turned into a deficit in the first half of 1998.[14] Given the need to service the debt and the continuation of capital flight (which is partly captured in the 'errors and omissions' in the balance-of-payments statistics),[15] the current account deficit was the sure recipe for disaster.

Under the circumstances the exchange rate became hardly sustainable in 1998. There also developed a new vulnerability of the rouble to short-term capital flows. Since the GKOs were introduced by the authorities in 1995, foreign purchases of rouble-denominated government treasury bills (including purchases of GKOs through 'grey schemes', i.e. resident intermediaries) quickly increased to nearly one third of the $50 billion market for treasury bills in 1997. From February 1998 the total amount of treasury bills held by non-residents started to exceed the value of the country's foreign exchange reserves – just as the value of dollar-denominated Tesobonos exceeded total reserves in Mexico in June 1994.[16]

Foreign investors also started to withdraw from the Russian stock market. They were estimated to control no less than 10 per cent of the shares traded in the booming stock market whose capitalisation surpassed $100 billion in autumn 1997. From that time to mid-1998 – in just about nine months – the stock prices in dollar terms fell by over 80 per cent to their lowest level since 1994. The CBR's decision to expand slightly the width of the exchange rate band from the beginning of 1998 (see Figure 4) was a cosmetic measure and did not create much room for policy manoeuvre. The CBR had to increase the refinancing rate to 150 per cent in May 1998 to prevent capital from fleeing at a rate of about $0.5 billion a week at a time when foreign exchange reserves were about $15 billion only. Later the refinancing rate was lowered, but yields on government securities remained at a level of nearly 50 per cent in real terms and then again increased to over 100 per cent in August. The central bank and the government, however, stuck to the policy of a strong rouble up to the very last moment, maintaining high interest rates that eliminated the prospects for economic recovery and negotiating a standby package with the IMF. In a sense this was a policy designed to maintain consumption and imports and to avoid export-oriented restructuring. The IMF finally provided the first instalment ($4 billion) of the $20 billion dollar package that went directly to the CBR to replenish vanishing foreign exchange reserves. But the IMF assistance failed to restore investor confidence. Statements by public officials about the stability of the rouble, including those that had been made by Yeltsin shortly before the devaluation, had only the opposite effect, if any.

Figure 5. *Russian government debt as percentage of GDP, 1994–8.*

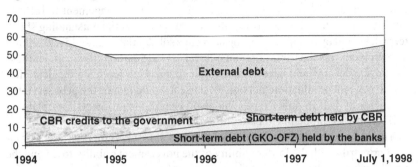

Sources: Institute of Economics of Transition (*The Russian Economy*, various issues); Bank of Finland (*The Monthly Review*, no. 1 1998)); *Narodnoye Khozyaistvo SSSR* (*National Economy of the USSR*); *Rossiysky Statistichesky Yezhegodnik* (Moscow: *Russian Statistical Yearbook*, various issues).

(Mis)managing the August 1998 crisis

Like a number of other economists,[17] I had strongly believed, prior to the crisis, that the rouble was overvalued. I argued that if it was not devalued 'from above' in a timely manner, it was likely to be devalued 'from below' in the form of a currency crisis, with much heavier costs.[18] In a sense, it was not so difficult to predict the crisis, and quite a number of scholars had done so several months before it occurred. Even Jeffrey Sachs, previously a strong advocate of exchange-rate-based stabilisation, spoke out publicly in favour of devaluation in June 1998.[19] What virtually nobody was able to predict was the way in which the Russian government handled the devaluation: it declared a default on its domestic debt and on part of its international debt held by banks and companies. This was by no means necessary, since basically there was no debt crisis, but only the currency crisis, which should have been dealt with only by devaluing the rouble.

As Figure 5 suggests, government debts in Russia did grow in the mid-1990s, but they were not significant as compared with GDP (GDP in dollar terms grew more rapidly due to the real appreciation of the rouble). In absolute terms total government debts had not even reached the threshold of 60 per cent of GDP by mid-1998. Even when the wage and payment arrears of the Russian government were taken into account, the total debts did not increase very much. Government wage arrears right before the crisis had stood at 13 billion roubles, or just 0.5 per cent of annual GDP, whereas total government arrears that were several times higher than just wage arrears were largely offset by tax arrears to the government.

It is true that the GKOs held by non-residents exceeded total foreign exchange reserves in early 1998, which was an obvious policy mismanagement and clearly contributed to the crisis. However, the absolute value of the outstanding short-term debt held by foreigners was by no means substantial – only $15–20 billion. The problem was the trivial amount of reserves ($15 billion). Even under these circumstances it would have been possible to continue servicing the debt after the 50 per cent devaluation, not only because it would reduce the debt servicing payments by half in dollar terms but also because the prospects for obtaining IMF credits would be much better after the devaluation.[20]

The collapse of investor confidence during the first half of 1998 was associated primarily with the low credibility of the government's ability to defend the rouble, whereas the ability of the government to service its debt was not really called into question. The difference between the rates at which the Russian government borrowed abroad in hard currency (returns on Eurobonds were around 15 per cent) and the rates offered to prime borrowers (7 per cent) was much smaller than the gap between returns on rouble-denominated bonds (about 100 per cent in real terms) and Eurobonds (15 per cent). Because the first gap is the indicator of the country risk (i.e. the risk associated with the default by the government of this particular country), and the second one reflects the currency risk (i.e. the risk associated with the devaluation), it is clear that the anticipation of the market at that time was that of devaluation, but not of default.

Unfortunately, crisis mismanagement on the part of the government was not merely related to the default. Shortly after the default, the CBR provoked by its clumsy efforts a run on banks and contributed to a banking crisis. Banks had already been badly hurt by the devaluation, as well as by the default (partly because they held a considerable portion of their assets in short-term government securities and partly because they lost opportunities for external financing after the government imposed a ninety-day moratorium on servicing their external debts). To make matters worse, the CBR introduced a scheme to guarantee personal deposits in commercial banks in early September, which implied losses for depositors, especially for the holders of dollar accounts at private banks.[21] The run on banks contributed to the growing paralysis of the banking system. In September 1998 banks could hardly process any payments, and businesses started to conduct their transactions purely in cash, barter or cash substitutes.

After the crisis

After the August 1998 financial crash, the ailing Russian industry sector experienced a boom, registering high growth rates that had not been seen for nearly half a century. Industrial output had been more or less stable for the three years

1995–7, but started to decline at the very beginning of 1998, and the decline continued until the August 1998 currency crisis. Beginning in September 1998, industrial recovery occurred at a rate of about 1 per cent a month.[22] Industrial output experienced strong growth, not because of, but despite, government policy. Whereas the overvalued rouble had undermined the competitiveness of domestically produced goods before the crisis, after the devaluation domestic producers took advantage of new export opportunities and of the shift in demand from foreign to Russian-made goods.

In fact, the 1998 recession that had occurred before the crisis was artificially caused by the poor policy of keeping the exchange rate at an unreasonably high and unsustainable level. The market corrected the mistake of the government and the central bank that had persisted, with the support of the IMF, in the unsustainable peg, which is what the August 1998 crisis was all about. The different patterns of output decline in Russia (before the currency crisis) and in east Asia (after the financial crisis) provide additional evidence of the different nature of currency and financial crises. In east Asia, where exchange rates were not overvalued, the devaluation, coupled with the depressing effects of the collapse of the previously overextended credit, led to an adverse supply shock. In Russia, by contrast, the devaluation of the previously overvalued currency eliminated demand constraints, restored the previously depressed competitiveness and led to an increase in capacity utilisation rates.[23] Unlike east Asian countries, the Russian economy experienced a boom, not a recession, after the currency crisis.

Exchange rate policy for transition and developing economies

Whereas in Latin American countries currency crises were often caused by the excessive government debt, and in east Asian countries by excessive private debt accumulation, in transition economies recent currency crises resulted largely from the overvaluation of their currencies. One of the basic stylised facts about the exchange rate in transition economies is the substantial appreciation of the real exchange rate following the deregulation of prices and the introduction of convertibility. Among the major east European and former Soviet Union economies only in Slovenia was the real exchange rate relatively stable. In other countries there was generally a prolonged (usually several years) period of the real appreciation of national currencies.

However, real appreciation had slowed down in many of these countries by the mid-1990s and stopped completely in some. Moreover, during 1996–8 eight post-communist countries with previously rapidly appreciating real exchange rates (Bulgaria, Romania, Belarus, Ukraine, Russia, Kyrghyzstan, Georgia and

Kazakhstan) witnessed the collapse of their currencies, as clearly shown in Figure 2. In these countries the devaluation of their currencies was no less significant than that in Asia in 1997–8 (with the exception of Indonesia) and no less significant than that of Mexico in 1994–5. In fact, the depreciation was significant in Bulgaria and Russia and was even sharper in Belarus than that in Indonesia (see Figures 2 and 3).

Unlike Latin American countries, post-communist governments were not considerably indebted. Unlike companies and banks in east Asian countries, those in the former CPEs did not accumulate sizeable debts. Most communist governments before transition had been quite prudent in foreign borrowing. Moreover, external debts of many of the former CPEs were written off on the eve of transition. On the other hand, companies and banks in transition economies (which had not been allowed to borrow under the communist regime) did not have much of a credit history and just started to accumulate foreign debts.[24]

Undervaluation of domestic currencies has been a common economic feature in most developing and transition countries, as they usually need to maintain a trade surplus to finance debt service payments and to tackle capital flight.[25] Unlike those of mature market economies, exchange rates in most poor countries tend to be lower than their PPP rates.[26] In resource-rich countries, however, there is a danger of 'Dutch disease', due to the fact that resource exports are so profitable that they allow these countries to earn a trade surplus even under the overpriced exchange rate. Thus, Middle Eastern countries (mainly oil exporters) are the only major group of states in the developing world that have the exchange rate set close to the PPP rate.

On the other hand, many other developing countries (including those that are rich in resources) pursue the conscious policy of low exchange rates as part of their export-oriented strategy. By creating a downward pressure on their currencies through building up foreign exchange reserves, they are able to limit consumption and imports while stimulating exports, investment and growth. This used to be the development strategy of Japan, South Korea, Taiwan and Singapore some time ago, when those countries were still poor and were catching up with high-income countries. This is currently the strategy adopted by many emerging market economies, especially China, which continues to keep the exchange rate at an extremely low level (five times lower than the PPP rate) and to accumulate foreign exchange reserves at a record pace.

To put it differently, there are generally two major reasons for maintaining relatively low exchange rates. One reason is that the generally lower level of development imposes a burden on the balance of payments in the form of capital flight and debt service payments (non-policy factors). The low exchange rate policy is thus needed to tackle these problems. The other reason relates to the conscious efforts on the part of governments to underprice the exchange rate in order to use it as a instrument of export-oriented growth (policy factor).

The specifics of the exchange rate policy in transition economies are deter-mined, among other factors, by the challenge of macroeconomic stabilisation, which policy makers would have to face in most post-communist countries after the deregulation of prices. Economists and policy makers tend to disagree on what should be the primal exchange rate regime for transition economies. Some emphasise the importance of maintaining the stable nominal exchange rate as a nominal anchor to fight inflation – exchange-rate-based stabilisation.[27] Others claim that real exchange rates should be kept stable (which implies constant devaluations, if inflation is higher than elsewhere) so as to ensure that the actual rate is substantially below the PPP rate in order to stimulate export and growth.

The conventional shock-therapy approach to macroeconomic stabilisation recommends that the pegged exchange rate be used as a nominal anchor when a country pursues an anti-inflationary policy.[28] There is certainly a reason for such an argument: by increasing import competition high exchange rates help to hold down inflation. In fact this was the case in many east European and former Soviet Union countries, including Russia in 1995–8.

As noticed above, however, virtually all transition economies experienced an appreciation of real exchange rates after the start of the transition (see Table 8). This undermined the competitiveness of exporters, worsened the cur-rent account, and forced governments to maintain high interest rates (to slow down capital flight and attract new foreign funds) at a time when exactly the opposite policy action was needed. It now appears that even in those countries that avoided the currency crisis, the real appreciation of the exchange rate has become a major policy concern.

In those transition economies that had currency board arrangements for a longer period (Estonia and Lithuania, which established such arrangements in June 1992 and October 1994 respectively), domestic prices continued to grow despite the stability of the nominal exchange rate. Due to the real appreciation of their currencies, the current account deficit in 1998 increased to over 10 per cent of GDP, and it was totally financed by the inflows of foreign capital. Both these countries managed to escape the Asian crisis and the Russian crisis, but their growth rates in 1998–9 fell significantly and even turned negative.

Overall, the major problem in the region now seems to be the overvaluation of national currencies that hinders economic growth and creates the threat of currency crises. There appears to be a growing recognition of the fact that the exchange rate is far too important to be used only for the purpose of fighting inflation. Most transition economies have currently achieved macroeconomic stability and are preoccupied with economic growth. Exchange rate manage-ment as a weapon to fight inflation can only play a limited role. It is argued that at the end of the day inflation has to be dealt with at its source, that is, high budget deficits, poorly regulated banking systems and ineffective revenue collections.[29]

Table 8. *Ratio of the actual exchange rate to the PPP rate of the dollar for selected economies in transition (range of monthly averages), 1990–9.*

	1990	1991	1992	1993	1994	1995	1996	1997	1998	1999
Slovenia	0.9–1.4	1.0–1.7	1.4–1.6	1.4–1.6	1.3–1.6	1.1–1.3	1.3–1.3	1.4–1.5	1.3–1.5	1.3–1.5
Hungary	1.9–2.4	1.9–2.0	1.7–1.8	1.6–1.8	1.6–1.8	1.5–1.6	1.7–1.8	1.6–1.8	1.7–1.8	1.7–1.8
Poland	2.1–3.9	1.6–1.9	1.8–2.0	1.8–2.0	2.1–2.3	1.8–2.0	1.8–1.8	1.8–2.1	1.8–2.0	1.9–2.1
Czech Republic	2.5–3.8	3.1–3.5	2.7–3.1	2.5–2.6	2.2–2.5	2.0–2.2	1.9–2.0	2.0–2.3	1.8–2.3	1.9–2.3
Slovak Republic	2.9–3.9	3.0–3.6	2.9–3.0	2.6–2.8	2.4–2.7	2.1–2.3	2.1–2.2	2.3–2.4	2.2–2.4	2.3–2.7
Croatia	–	–	–	–	–	–	–	1.7–1.9	1.7–1.9	1.8–2.0
Lithuania	–	–	–	–	2.4–3.2	1.8–2.3	1.7–1.8	1.5–1.6		–
Romania	1.8–2.6	1.6–5.0	2.8–4.2	2.2–3.1	2.1–2.6	2.1–2.5	2.4–2.6	2.0–3.3	1.7–2.0	2.0–2.3
Bulgaria	3.3–5.1	2.9–10.9	3.0–4.7	2.3–2.8	2.3–3.1	1.8–2.2	1.9–2.8	1.7–3.2	1.6–1.8	1.6–1.9
Ukraine	–	–		–	–	1.8–2.5	1.3–1.7	1.3–1.4	1.3–2.1	2.0–2.7
RUSSIA	–	33.0–131.0	10.2–45.7	2.5–8.0	2.4–2.8	1.4–2.4	1.4–1.5	1.4–1.5	1.5–2.8	2.7–2.9

Source: PlanEcon (Washington, DC, various issues).

The policy of keeping the *real* exchange rate stable appears to appeal more to policy makers now, after the currency crises of 1996–8. More important, countries pursuing this kind of policy for quite some time are now doing no worse than others. Zettermeyer and Citrin found that money-based stabilisation has been successful in quite a number of countries (for instance, Albania, Slovenia, Croatia and Macedonia) and there has been no evidence that it is an inferior strategy as compared with the exchange rate peg used to control inflation.[30] With an appropriate monetary policy (at least partial sterilisation of increases in the money supply caused by the rapid build-up of foreign exchange reserves) inflationary pressures may be effectively dealt with, as has been proved by the policy-making experiences of many emerging market economies.

The problem, of course, is that there are political obstacles to the adoption of economically optimal policy. Exchange rate overvaluation occurred in Russia and other transition economies despite the experience of other (mainly Latin American) countries and despite the recognition that such a policy could have ruinous consequences.

Political economy of exchange rate overvaluation

The sociopolitical factors that lead to sub-optimal policies in transition economies seem to be no different from those in other countries. A decade ago studies of the macroeconomics of populism in Latin America raised a similar question and suggested two explanatory variables. The one is sharp asset and income inequalities (as compared with Asian countries), and the other is the sharp division between the primary products export sector controlled by the traditional oligarchy on the one hand, and employers and workers in the industrial and service sectors on the other.[31] It was argued that high-income groups were generally in a strong position to resist taxation, and that this placed a limit on the capacity of Latin American governments to deal with distributive pressures within the context of the growth-oriented export models. In small, open European economies the expansion of the welfare state that facilitated the painless adjustment to the costs of internationalisation was an important political concomitant of liberal trade policies. In east Asian countries the political weight of urban popular groups, which often pressed for redistribution of export revenues in their favour, was counterbalanced by the presence of independent farmers or small export-oriented manufacturing firms. By contrast, Latin American states had much more limited capacity to tax income and assets directly. The export-oriented oligarchy was not willing to share its revenues, but at the same time was not able to resist the pressure for income redistribution because of political isolation.

Due to the legacies of the CPE, transition economies found themselves in a situation somewhat similar to that in Latin American countries. Whatever might be the reasons for the wide-scale redistribution of income in former socialist countries, at the very beginning of transition they experienced a dramatic and quick increase in income inequalities and sectoral inequalities, particularly after the deregulation of prices. Previously, under the authoritarian regime, the government was strong enough to impose the substantial burden of transfers on producers (the government revenues in most former socialist countries were well above 50 per cent of GDP). Weak democratic governments that faced falling budget revenues, however, were not in a position to maintain large-scale subsidies, and had to choose between gradually eliminating the bulk of all subsidies and finding alternative ways of financing these subsidies. These often include, among other things, inflationary financing, the build-up of domestic and foreign debts, and overvalued exchange rates.

The inability of the transition economy government to cut subsidies, which was derived from the era of central planning, was widely observed in the CIS region (where the newly emerged democratic governments were weak). This was the major reason for the macroeconomic instability experienced by these countries – budget deficits, inflation, increased domestic and foreign debts, overvalued exchange rates and the resulting currency crises.

The need to redistribute income in favour of the poorest social groups and weakest enterprises, coupled with the inability of the governments to raise enough taxes for this redistribution activity, is likely to result in a sociopolitical situation very similar to the Latin American macroeconomic populism.[32] Constrained by the tensions between the inability to raise tax receipts and the simultaneous need to maintain redistribution in favour of particular social groups, governments are left basically only with options for the indirect financing of subsidies. These include (1) controls over particular prices, generally for resource goods in order to take away rent of the resource sector and redistribute it to consumers; (2) inflationary financing of the government budget; (3) debt financing of the budget deficit – either domestic or external borrowing; (4) subsidisation through the accumulation of non-payments, barter transactions and monetary substitutes; (5) the overvalued exchange rate.

This last policy option is particularly important to the central concerns of this chapter, and needs more elaboration. The overvalued exchange rate that favours consumers over producers and importers over exporters can lead to increases in consumption at the expense of savings. Consumption increases because of greater demands for imports that are generally financed by external borrowings or foreign exchange reserves. This option obviously provides only a temporary solution, and can lead to the balance-of-payments crisis in the long run. It has been shown that the overvaluation of the exchange rate is detrimental to economic growth in developing countries.[33]

Overvaluation of the exchange rate is usually supported by the governments (that collect their taxes in domestic currencies but service international debts in foreign currencies) and, of course, by importers, whose political influence may exceed that of exporters. Transition economies, Russia in particular, that maintained overvalued exchange rates (and that later, in 1998–9, experienced the currency crises), had a number of severe problems with their macroeconomic management. Although Russian exports are highly concentrated (a few resource commodities account for the bulk of exports and only dozens of companies control the key export sectors), major exporters had not pressed for a lower exchange rate before the 1998 crisis.[34]

This is another reason why exchange-rate-based stabilisation and currency board arrangements are quite risky for transition economies.[35] Opening the possibility for the appreciation of the real exchange rate (and achieving equilibrium only through the balance-of-payments crisis), these arrangements contribute to the continuation of populist policies – redistribution of income from producers to consumers. Using exchange rate management as a weapon to fight inflation has serious limitations.

Different countries in different periods resorted to one or more of the above-mentioned mechanisms of implicit redistribution. In Russia, for instance, the government initially (1992–4) relied on controlling resource prices and inflationary financing. Beginning in 1995, when exchange-rate-based stabilisation was carried out and the rouble reached 70 per cent of its purchasing power parity value (which means that Russian prices, including resource prices, approached 70 per cent of the US prices, indicating the apparent overvaluation of the rouble), the government resorted to debt (domestic and foreign) financing and redistribution via an overvalued exchange rate. But since the 1998 financial crisis, which led to the collapse of the overvalued rate and to the cessation of international and domestic debt financing, the government has had to rely largely on price control (via export taxes and export restrictions) on major tradable goods (oil, gas, metals).

Concluding remarks

Generally, there are two important policy lessons for transition economies. First, they need to avoid the appreciation of the real exchange rate that can lead to currency crises. Second, if they find themselves in a situation of increasing external debts, they should draw early lessons from more complex government debt crises (in Latin American countries in the early 1980s and in 1994–5) and from private sector debt crises (in east Asia in 1997–8), in order to avoid financial crises in the future.

Preventing the appreciation of the real exchange rate

Unlike financial crises in Latin America and East Asia, recent currency crises in transition economies seem to be caused not by the excessive accumulation of debts – private or government – but by the appreciation of the exchange rate. This undermined the competitiveness of the export sector, led to the deterioration of the current account and finally caused the outflow of capital in anticipation of devaluation. Theories that have been developed to explain the trend towards real exchange rate appreciation in transition economies have proved to be of limited applicability. In transition economies, as in other countries, the appreciation of the real exchange rate cannot be indefinite, and is likely to lead to a crisis if it goes too far.

Furthermore, the policy of keeping the exchange rate low through the accumulation of reserves seems to be not only prudent but also conducive to economic growth. For transition economies facing the challenge of export-oriented restructuring, the policy is highly desirable. The inflationary consequences of such a policy, as demonstrated in the policy-making experiences of east Asian countries, can be dealt with through sterilisation operations.

However, no matter how optimal the low exchange rate policy may be from a purely economic point of view, there are important sociopolitical factors that may push the real exchange rate up. An overvalued exchange rate favours consumers over producers and importers over exporters, and can lead to increases in consumption at the expense of savings, as discussed in the previous sections. Such income redistribution in favour of importers and consumers may be an important part of the social pact, as was the case in many Latin American countries in the 1970s and 1980s. Strong governments willing and able to resist such populist pressures are required to break this type of vicious circle.

Exchange-rate-based versus money-based stabilisation

Whereas exchange-rate-based stabilisation may be effective in controlling inflation at the initial stages of transition, there is growing evidence that at later stages it can become an obstacle to economic growth and create the potential for a currency crisis by allowing the real exchange rate to appreciate.

Bringing inflation under control in transition and other emerging market economies with a lot of market imperfections and structural rigidities is in itself a questionable policy. It is true that in countries with a highly inflationary environment chances are high that output growth will be impaired. However, it has been shown that an annual inflation of 40 per cent may be the threshold:

there is no evidence that annual inflation below 40 per cent is ruinous to growth, and there is some evidence that annual inflation below 20 per cent may be even beneficial.[36] It may be argued that the threshold for transition economies is actually higher than for other emerging markets because of numerous structural rigidities. In many countries that have successfully implemented economic reforms, inflation was by no means insignificant. Inflation never fell below 20 per cent a year in the first five years of transition in Poland and Uzbekistan. While inflation was low most of the time in China, there were outbreaks of inflation in 1988–9 and in 1993–5.

It seems that the Russian authorities in this respect went from one extreme (very high inflation during 1992–4) to the other. After the exchange-rate-based stabilisation programme was enacted in 1995, the government pursued the programme with great effort right up to the outbreak of the crisis. In July 1998, year-to-year inflation was brought to its lowest level, 6 per cent – lower than inflation rates in most transition economies. Arguably this low level of inflation imposed unnecessary strains on the economy, causing the avalanche of non-payments and leading to sluggish demand and reduced growth.

Fixed versus flexible exchange rates

Given that most emerging market economies are relatively small and not fully integrated into the world economy, floating exchange rates may provide them with more flexibility and help them to adjust to external shocks. Most developing and transition economies, with the exception of small ones such as Hong Kong, Singapore and perhaps the Baltic states, are large enough to remain partially closed to world market competition and hence to retain some domestic price inflexibility vis-à-vis that of world market prices. Nevertheless, they are not large enough to create an appropriate cushion in the form of strong foreign exchange reserves and to shield themselves completely from the vulnerability associated with international capital flows. Most emerging market economies (with the possible exception of China) do not have enough foreign exchange reserves to withstand intensive speculative attacks on their currencies. Because major international banks and investment and hedge funds operate with large pools of funds that are comparable with or even exceed the value of reserves in most countries, flexible exchange rates remain the only reliable and efficient safety valve that can provide these countries with protection against external shocks.

Countries that maintain fixed exchange rates or currency board arrangements may be forced to abandon their independent monetary policy. They have no choice but to adjust to capital inflows and outflows through real indicators. When the exchange rate is pegged and prices are not completely flexible, changes in the money supply (caused by fluctuations in foreign exchange reserves) may affect output rather than prices. As revealed in the recent experience of transition economies and Argentina, this kind of real sector adjustment is quite costly. To put it in simple terms, under a fixed exchange rate regime neither changes in foreign exchange reserves nor changes in domestic prices in response to money supply fluctuations provide enough room for handling international capital flows.

Capital account opening and the strength of the banking system

As argued earlier, currency crises in transition economies were not triggered by the debt and lending boom. An important lesson to be learned from the east Asian experience concerns 'twin liberalisations' – capital account liberalisation and domestic financial liberalisation. As the debt levels – both public and private – in these economies continued to grow, measures should have been taken to ensure that the safety and soundness of banking institutions was not compromised by the openness of capital accounts.

The credit and banking crisis in Russia was by no means unavoidable and resulted mainly from poor policies (the government's default on its short-term debt and the CBR measures that undermined the credibility of commercial banks). No matter what the sources of the crisis were, it revealed the longstanding and widely discussed weaknesses of the Russian domestic banking system. When the next shock comes as a result of volatile international capital flows, Russian banks may not be able to withstand it unless prudent regulations are improved and a strong and viable banking sector is created. Until source countries and international financial institutions are willing or able to adopt effective measures to regulate short-term capital flows, the continuing policy of pursuing capital account openness may be an invitation to financial crisis.

Notes

1. E. Yasin, 'Defeat or Retreat? (Russian Reforms and Financial Crisis)', report to Economic Club, Moscow, January 1999 (in Russian).
2. See *Expert*, 18 January 1999.
3. Anders Åslund, 'Russia's collapse', *Foreign Affairs*, vol. 78, no. 5 (Sept./Oct. 1999).
4. S. Alexashenko, *The Battle for the Rouble* (in Russian) (Mosow: Alma Mater, 1999).

5. P. Krugman, 'What Happened to Asia?' 1998, at http://web.mit.edu/krugman/www/ DISINTER.html.
6. A. Åslund, 'Why Has Russia's Economic Transformation Been So Arduous?' World Bank's Annual Conference on Development Economics, Washington, DC, 28–30 April 1999.
7. See *The Economist*, 19 December 1998.
8. See V. Popov, 'Economic Outcomes of Transformation: The Impact of Initial Conditions and Economic Policy', *Voprosy Ekonomiky*, no. 7 (1998) (in Russian); 'Institutional Capacity Is More Important than the Speed of Reforms', *Voprosy Ekonomiky*, no. 8 (1998) (in Russian); 'Shock Therapy versus Gradualism: The End of the Debate (Explaining the Magnitude of the Transformational Recession)', *Comparative Economic Studies*, vol. 42, no. 1 (Spring 2000), pp. 1–57.
9. *Narodnoye Khozyaistvo SSSR* (*National Economy of the USSR*); *Rossiysky Statistichesky Yezhegodnik* (Moscow: *Russian Statistical Yearbook*, various issues).
10. *Ibid.*
11. *Transition Report* (London: European Bank for Reconstruction and Development, various years).
12. See V. Popov, 'Inflation During Transition: Is Russia's Case Special?' *Acta Slavica Iaponica*, Tomus XIV, 1996, Sapporo, Japan, pp. 59–75; *A Russian Puzzle. What Makes the Russian Economic Transformation a Special Case?* WIDER research for action 29 (Helsinki: UNU/WIDER 1996); 'Preparing Russian Economy for the World Market Integration', in A. Fernandez Jilberto and Andre Mommen (eds.), *Regionalisation and Globalisation in the Modern World Economy* (London: Routledge, 1998), pp. 86–127.
13. *Narodnoye Khozyaistvo SSSR* (*National Economy of the USSR*); *Rossiysky Statistichesky Yezhegodnik* (Moscow: *Russian Statistical Yearbook*, various issues).
14. *Ibid.*
15. N. Smorodinskaya, 'Capital Flight in Theory and in Practice: The Analysis of the Russian Situation', *Banking Services*, no. 9 (1998) (in Russian), Figure 9.
16. S. Griffith-Jones, *Causes and Lessons of the Mexican Peso Crisis*, WIDER working papers 132 (Helsinki: UNU/WIDER, 1997).
17. See, for instance, A. Illarionov, 'How the Russian Financial Crisis Was Organized', *Voprosy Ekonomiky*, nos. 11, 12 (1998) (in Russian); N. Shmelev, 'The Crisis Inside the Crisis', *Voprosy Ekonomiky*, no. 10 (1998) (in Russian).
18. See papers listed in n. 12. This argument was also developed in newspaper articles. See: 'Growth Strategy', *Segodnya*, 14 March 1996 (in Russian); 'The Currency Crisis Is Possible in Russia', *Finansoviye Izvestiya*, 30 October 1997 (in Russian); 'An Emerging Economy's Unaffordable Luxury', *Financial Times*, 11 December 1997; 'What Exchange Rate of the Rouble Is Needed for Russia?' *Nezavisimaya Gazeta*, 21 May 1998 (in Russian); 'Arithmetic of Devaluation: Why Do We Need a Rate of 12 Roubles per Dollar?' *Nezavisimaya Gazeta*, June 1998, Supplement (in Russian).
19. See *New York Times*, 4 June 1998. The other major proponent of the exchange-rate-based stabilisation and also the former adviser of the Russian government, Anders Åslund, pretty much like the IMF, continued to deny the need to devalue even in July (his article 'Don't Devalue the Rouble', *Moscow Times*, 7 July 1998).

20. This was a sharp contrast to the Mexican situation in the second half of 1994. As in Russia, the value of outstanding short-term government debts exceeded foreign exchange reserves. But unlike Russian GKOs, Mexican Tesobonos were denominated in dollars, not in the national currency. Thus the devaluation of the peso could not and did not reduce the dollar value of the debt.

21. In the state owned Sberbank (Savings Bank) that accounted for 75 per cent of all household deposits, savings were guaranteed by the state. CBR, while extending the guarantees to the personal deposits, at commercial banks, asked the depositors to move them to Sberbank, promising to pay them back only in two months and only in part (dollar deposits, for instance, were supposed to be converted into roubles at a 1 September rate of 9.33 roubles per dollar, whereas the market rate of the dollar was already about twice as high.

22. *Russian Economic Trends*, various issues.

23. For more details on the differences between the currency crises in Latin America, south-east Asia and Russia see M. Montes, and V. Popov, *The Asian Crisis Turns Global* (Singapore: Institute of Southeast Asian Studies, 1999); V. Popov, 'The Currency Crisis in Russia in a Wider Context', *C. D. Howe Institute Commentary*, no. 138 (March 2000) (http://www.cdhowe.org/eng/PUB/frame.html).

24. Popov, 'The Currency Crisis in Russia'.

25. Hölscher makes a similar argument with respect to east European countries drawing on the West German experience with the undervalued mark in the 1950s: J. Hölscher, 'Economic Dynamism in Transition Economies: Lessons from Germany', *Communist Economies and Economic Transformation*, vol. 9, no. 2 (1997), pp. 173–81.

26. Popov, 'The Currency Crisis in Russia'.

27. See P. Bofinger, H. Flassbeck and L. Hoffmann, 'Orthodox Money-Based Stabilization (OMBS) versus Heterodox Exchange Rate-Based Stabilization (HERBS): the Case of Russia, the Ukraine and Kazakhstan', *Economic Systems*, vol. 21, no. 1 (March 1997), pp. 1–33.

28. See Anders Åslund, 'The Case for Radical Reform', *Journal of Democracy*, vol. 5, no. 4 (October 1994); J. Sachs, 'Russia's Struggle with Stabilization: Conceptual Issues and Evidence', a paper prepared for the World Bank's Annual Conference on Development Economics, Washington, DC, 28–9 April 1994; *Why Russia Has Failed to Stabilize*, Working Paper 103 (Stockholm: Stockholm Institute of East European Economics, 1995).

29. See P. Desai, 'Macroeconomic Fragility and Exchange Rate Vulnerability: A Cautionary Record of Transition Economies', *Journal of Comparative Economics*, vol. 26, no. 4 (1998), pp. 621–41.

30. J. Zettermeyer and D. Citrin, *Stabilization: fixed versus flexible exchange rates. Policy experiences and issues in the Baltics, Russian and other countries of the former Soviet Union* (Washington, DC: IMF, 1995).

31. Robert R. Kaufman and Barbara Stallings, in R. Dornbusch and S. Edwards (eds.), 'The Political Economy of Latin American Populism', in *Macroeconomics of Populism in Latin America* (Chicago and London: University of Chicago Press, 1991).

32. See Rudiger Dornbusch and Sebastian Edwards, *The Economic Populism Paradigm*, NBER Working Paper 2986 (Cambridge, MA: National Bureau of Economic Research, 1989).

33. See William Easterly, *The Lost Decades: Explaining Developing Countries' Stagnation 1980–1998* (Washington, DC: World Bank, 1999).

34. Of all Russian 'oligarchs' and main exporters only one (Boris Berezovsky) spoke out openly in favour of devaluation before the August 1998 crisis, whereas the others (Vladimir Potanin, for instance) publicly opposed devaluation until the very last moment.

35. Montes and Popov, *The Asian Crisis Turns Global*.

36. See Michael Bruno, 'Does Inflation Really Lower Growth?' *Finance & Development* (September 1995); Michael Bruno and William Easterly, 'Inflation Crisis and Long-Run Growth', unpublished manuscript, Washington, DC: World Bank (1995); Joseph Stiglitz, *More Instruments and Broader Goals: Moving Toward the Post-Washington Consensus* (Helsinki: UNU/WIDER, 1998).

9   Capital account convertibility and the national interest: has India got it right?

VIJAY JOSHI

One of the striking features of the Asian crisis is that some countries, including India, were largely unaffected by it and the contagion that followed.[1] This chapter argues that capital account controls are critical in explaining India's stability, a conclusion that should reinforce the second thoughts that have begun to emerge as regards the desirability of capital account convertibility (CAC) as an integral element of the redesign of the international financial architecture. Section one of this chapter describes India's capital account controls and their place in the country's payments regime. Section two examines various episodes of balance-of-payments strain in the 1990s and the role played by capital controls in managing them. Section three analyses why India escaped the Asian crisis and contagion and highlights the importance of capital controls in this context. Section four discusses the political economy of India's resistance to the adoption of CAC. Section five considers the desirability of adopting CAC in India in the near future. Section six offers some concluding remarks.

India's payments regime: managed floating and capital controls

India's capital controls operate within the framework of a payments regime, inaugurated in March 1993, that is officially described as a 'market determined unified exchange rate'. The de facto position is different. 'Market determined' should not be understood to mean a clean float. There is active, sometimes heavy, intervention by the Reserve Bank of India (RBI) in the foreign exchange market. In practice, exchange rate management appears to have been guided by the aim of keeping the exchange rate stable vis-à-vis the US dollar, but with occasional bouts of depreciation to correct overvaluation of the real effective exchange rate. In other words, the authorities have certainly had exchange rate targets in mind though the targets have shifted from time to time. As I shall emphasise below, the smooth management of this system has been greatly helped by capital controls.

Capital account controls were imposed in the late 1950s and became comprehensive and draconian in 1973. There was *selective* liberalisation of these controls in the early 1990s when the reform process began.[2] Since then, variations have been relatively minor. Currently, these controls acquire their bite not so much from variations in their intensity as by the limits they set on activity and expectations in the foreign exchange market.[3] The highlights of the system, pertaining to different kinds of capital flow, are given below.[4]

Foreign direct investment

Before 1991, restrictions operated on a case-by-case basis and were so strict that foreign direct investment (FDI) was reduced to a trickle. In the reforms of 1991/2, automatic approval of foreign investment of up to 51 per cent of shareholding was allowed for a wide range of industries. Proposals for a higher percentage of foreign ownership are considered by a Foreign Investment Promotion Board. Since 1996, the list of industries in which FDI is permitted has been further widened, with foreign equity up to 74 per cent allowed in a few. The rules have been made particularly liberal for non-resident Indians (NRIs). In practice, however, the system is more restrictive than it sounds, because there still remain numerous hurdles to jump, erected by state governments if not by the centre. FDI has risen from about $150 million in the 1980s (annual average) to about $2 billion in 1998/99. The latter figure is still very small compared with the inflow into east Asian countries.

Foreign portfolio investment

Before 1991, foreign portfolio investment was not permitted, apart from some trivial exceptions. In 1992, foreign institutional investors (FIIs) such as pension funds and mutual funds were allowed to invest in listed securities in primary and secondary markets in equities and bonds (other than government bonds), subject only to registration with the Securities and Exchange Board of India and ceilings on the percentage of equity or debt held in a single firm. Since 1997, FIIs have also been allowed to invest in primary and secondary markets in government securities and treasury bills. Repatriation of capital, income and capital gains is freely allowed at the market exchange rate. The income tax rate on dividends for offshore FIIs is 20 per cent and the long-term capital gains tax is 10 per cent (the same as for domestic investors), but the tax treatment of short-term capital gains is somewhat less favourable than for domestic investors. In 1992, Indian companies were also allowed to issue equity in overseas capital markets in the form of global depository receipts, subject to close control by the Ministry of Finance. The latter imposed various end-use requirements which have been somewhat liberalised over time.

External commercial borrowing

Offshore borrowing by Indian companies (commercial bank loans, eurobonds, etc.) is under the jurisdiction of the Ministry of Finance, which exercises control on a case-by-case basis. There are controls not only on the amount of each loan but on maturity (short-term loans are strongly disfavoured) and end-use (priority is given to projects in the energy and infrastructure sectors). There is also an overall annual ceiling on approvals for external commercial borrowing.

Bank deposits of non-resident Indians (NRI deposits)

There were conscious efforts in the 1980s to attract non-resident Indian bank deposits by offering both higher interest rates and exchange rate guarantees. These deposits proved to be highly volatile in the crisis of 1991, so the exchange guarantee has been withdrawn and interest rate incentives have been progressively eliminated. The cash and liquidity ratios applicable to these deposits have been harmonised with those of domestic deposits.

Credit operations of resident commercial banks

Banks are not allowed to accept deposits or extend loans denominated in foreign currencies, and there are strict controls on their foreign asset and liability positions. It goes without saying that this is a critical element of the system of capital controls. Some liberalisation has occurred since 1998. Transactions in derivatives (swaps, options, forwards) are now permitted, though on a highly controlled basis. In addition, banks have been permitted to borrow and lend small amounts (up to 15 per cent of Tier I unimpaired capital) in overseas money markets.

Capital outflows

Repatriation is freely permitted for non-resident FIIs and non-resident Indians who have invested in the country under recognised schemes. But capital outflows by residents are strictly prohibited, apart from some minor exceptions. The latter concern the overseas lending facilities given to domestic banks noted above and permission granted to Indian companies (e.g. in the information technology sector) to make foreign acquisitions on a restricted scale.

In sum, India has a comprehensive system of capital controls which has been selectively liberalised in the 1990s. The liberalisation has mainly been focused on direct and portfolio equity inflows. Debt-creating external borrowing is tightly controlled (indeed more tightly controlled than in the 1980s), particularly if it is short-term. Capital outflows by residents continue to be forbidden, apart from some minor exceptions.

Management of India's balance of payments in the 1990s

Despite a partially closed capital account, the Indian authorities were confronted in the 1990s with several difficult challenges that required active management.[5] This is because capital account pressures can make themselves felt in various ways – for example, leads and lags in current account transactions, evasion of capital controls and changes in capital inflows and outflows in the permitted categories (these can be big enough to result in swings in net capital flows that range from negative to significantly positive as a proportion of GDP). In this section I shall review various 'episodes' that have a bearing on the debate regarding the desirability of capital account convertibility.

The payments crisis of 1991

This was an old-fashioned crisis that resulted from weak fundamentals, in particular large fiscal deficits (around 8–10 per cent of GNP) and current account deficits (around 3 per cent of GNP, 45 per cent of exports), throughout the decade of the 1980s.[6] To finance the latter, the government relaxed capital controls and permitted sizeable amounts of external (including short-term) borrowing from commercial sources.[7] The trigger for the crisis was provided by the brief spike in oil prices that followed the Iraqi invasion of Kuwait, combined with an unsettled political situation in India. When the crisis broke, there was a net outflow of non-resident deposits and a cut-off of short-term loans, and for a time India teetered on the edge of default.[8]

This crisis was corrected fairly rapidly (1991/2 and 1992/3) and in an orthodox manner by a combination of devaluation, deflation and borrowing from the IMF. Simultaneously with this stabilisation effort the government embarked on a programme of economic reform.

The surge in capital inflows, 1993–5

In 1993–5 India faced an unfamiliar problem. There was a surge of private capital flows into India as a result of the push factor of lower US interest rates, the 'pull' factor of profit opportunities opened up by the reform process and some bandwagon behaviour. In addition, high domestic interest rates caused by India's fiscal/monetary policy mix created a strong incentive for Indian companies to raise capital abroad. Non-debt-creating private inflows rose from negligible levels to $4 billion in 1993/94 and $5 billion in 1994/95, amounting in total to about 3 per cent of GDP. About a quarter of this was direct foreign investment; the rest was portfolio equity capital.

The policy issue faced by the authorities was how to conduct macroeconomic policy, in particular exchange rate policy, in the face of the capital inflow. The two extreme options available were (a) to float the nominal exchange rate cleanly (i.e. without intervention), and (b) to fix the nominal exchange rate by buying foreign exchange and to allow the money supply to increase, that is, to practise unsterilised intervention. At the level of abstract theory, there is an essential similarity between these two approaches. Both involve an appreciation of the real exchange rate, a worsening of the current account deficit, and an acceptance of market forces in effecting the transfer of capital. But there is also an important difference. In alternative (a) the real appreciation follows from the appreciation of the nominal exchange rate. The effect on trade and current account payments is rapid, with a real transfer of resources. There is no inflationary effect: indeed the deterioration of the trade account will be deflationary. In alternative (b) the real appreciation is brought about by inflation consequent upon money supply expansion; and the transfer is effected slowly as the initial accumulation of reserves is run down.

The Indian authorities decisively rejected alternative (a) in view of the possibly transient nature of the inflow. They feared various consequences of allowing a nominal (and hence real) exchange rate appreciation. First, it could have aborted the export recovery, an outcome that could not be regarded as benign if the inflow turned out to be temporary. Exports, once discouraged, cannot easily revive, being subject to lags and hysteresis effects. Second, it could have created resistance to import liberalisation, an important aspect of the reform process. Third, even if the inflow proved to be reasonably long lasting, it was important that the associated increase in the current account deficit should reflect an increase in investment, not a reduction in saving. The absorption of the foreign inflow into investment was more likely if it took place at a measured pace rather than in a rush. In this context, it is also relevant that the inflow began when investment and industrial growth were below normal. It was hoped that economic recovery would increase the current account deficit and absorb the inflow without inflation and real appreciation.

Thus, while alternative (b), if carried through in its pure form, would have been similar in essential respects to (a), it did have the advantage of delaying the transfer and buying time. The government decided to accept the inflationary risk associated with this alternative but attempted to reduce it by the use of sterilisation policies to break the link between reserve accumulation and monetary expansion.[9] In addition, the opportunity was taken to use the inflow to extend import liberalisation and to improve the debt structure by repaying short-term external debt.

In the event, the authorities were rather successful. There was a welcome strengthening of the reserve position along with an export and industrial boom. Some expected problems did materialise. The money supply grew faster in 1994/5 followed by higher inflation in 1995/6. But the situation remained under control. In retrospect, the outcome may have been even better if there had been fiscal retrenchment, and if some limited exchange rate flexibility (within a band) had been permitted. But overall, the episode showed that a temporary surge in capital inflow can be handled without sacrificing other policy objectives.[10] Of course, the surge that the Indian authorities had to deal with was considerably smaller than that faced by many east Asian countries. But that was itself partly because of the existence of various price and quantity measures to prevent excessive inflows, such as limits on external commercial borrowing, stipulations requiring that the latter should be kept outside the country until they were committed to a specific investment use, and measures to reduce the attractiveness of non-resident deposits.

Volatility, 1995–9

The uniformly upward pressure on the rupee that was evident from 1993 to early 1995 did not continue. The next three years were characterised by significant ups and downs in capital flows. From time to time there was strong downward pressure on the exchange rate, particularly in the following periods: mid-1995–early 1996, following the Mexican crisis; mid-1997–early 1998, in the aftermath of the Asian crisis; and mid-1998–early 1999, following nuclear tests by India and international disapprobation of them. Below, I shall describe each episode and then comment more generally on why India escaped crisis and contagion.

Mid-1995–early 1996

From the middle of 1995 there was downward pressure on the exchange rate as a result of a widening current account deficit that followed a domestic cyclical upturn, coupled with a shrinkage in capital inflows in reaction to the Mexican crisis. The real effective exchange rate had appreciated by about 7 per cent since 1993. The government tried to engineer a moderate depreciation but the effort threatened to get out of hand as speculative pressures took hold and the nominal exchange rate overshot the desired mark. The authorities responded with monetary tightening, which they wanted in any case on anti-inflationary grounds. Additional unsterilised intervention, undertaken to support the exchange rate, added painfully to the tightness of the short-term money market, so that the RBI had to pump in money every now and then to ease the liquidity squeeze. By March 1996, after a depreciation of approximately 10 per cent, the exchange rate stabilised around the level desired by the authorities.

Mid-1997–early 1998

Between August 1997 and February 1998, following the Asian crisis, there was significant and repeated downward pressure in both spot and forward foreign exchange markets. The RBI responded by permitting a moderate depreciation (10 per cent) of the rupee against the dollar, selling dollars both spot (about $2 billion) and forward (about $3 billion), and imposing two tough monetary packages (raising interest rates, raising the cash reserve ratio and reducing refinance limits) in November 1997 and January 1998. The RBI was careful not to squander foreign exchange reserves in large quantities: it relied more on monetary measures and 'announcement effects'.

Mid-1998–early 1999

India's nuclear tests in May 1998 were followed by another bout of intense downward pressure on the rupee, followed in its turn by the Russian default and the Brazilian currency crisis. The authorities responded in a manner very similar to that after the Asian crisis by moderate depreciation, moderate intervention and restrictive monetary policy measures. By early 1999 the rupee had stabilised to move within a narrow range.

Table 9. *Comparison of economic 'fundamentals', India and south-east Asia, 1996.*

	FB/GNP	ΔP/P p.a.	CAB/GNP	CAB/XGS	NPA
			percent		
India	−5.0	9.0	−1.7	−11.7	17.3
Indonesia	−1.0	8.0	−3.5	−13.0	8.8
Malaysia	0.7	3.5	−4.9	−6.4	3.9
Philippines	0.3	8.4	−4.6	−9.9	n.a.
South Korea	0.0	4.9	−4.8	−14.6	4.1
Thailand	0.7	5.8	−8.3	−19.5	7.7

Notation
FB: fiscal balance of the central government
ΔP/P: rate of consumer price inflation
CAB: current account balance
GNP: gross national product
XGS: exports of goods and services
NPA: non-performing assets of commercial banks as a proportion of their total advances
Sources: FB/GNP, NPA: Bank of International Settlements, *Annual Reports* 1997/98 and 1999/2000; ΔP/P: International Monetary Fund, *International Financial Statistics*; CAB/GNP, CAB/XGS: World Bank, *Global Development Finance* 1999.

In the second and third of the above three episodes, the RBI faced a classic policy dilemma. On the one hand, it wished to avoid an exchange rate collapse and this required a restrictive monetary policy. On the other hand, 'real' considerations called for monetary easing, as exports and industrial growth had slowed down substantially in 1996/97. Fiscal expansion had to be ruled out because the fiscal deficit needed to be brought down to ensure long-run sustainability. In the event, the RBI succeeded in its balancing act. In both cases, it achieved a soft landing for the exchange rate. When the exchange rate was stabilised after depreciating modestly, the RBI managed to ease monetary tightness and avoid choking off industrial and export recovery.

Why did India escape crisis and contagion?

It is evident that India got off very lightly in the Asian currency turmoil. Why? One possible explanation is that India had sounder 'fundamentals' than the countries that succumbed. Table 9 compares India with five east Asian crisis countries. The current account deficit is one of the traditional 'fundamentals'. While Thailand had a clearly excessive deficit (about 8 per cent of GNP) in

1996, other east Asian countries had deficits in the region of 4–5 per cent of GNP; by comparison India's deficit was only 1.7 per cent. However, for a large, low-trading country like India, the current account/exports ratio is arguably a better measure of vulnerability than the current account/GNP ratio. On this basis, India looks very similar to the crisis countries. Another traditional 'fundamental' is inflation. On this count, India's performance was again no better than that of the crisis countries. As regards the fiscal balance, possibly the most important 'fundamental', India had a deficit that was manifestly excessive, indeed unsustainable. In 1996, the east Asian countries were roughly in fiscal balance while the fiscal deficit of India's central government was 5 per cent of GNP. India's relative fiscal performance was in reality even worse than Table 9 suggests. This is because India's consolidated fiscal deficit (which incorporates the deficits of the state governments and public sector enterprises) was much higher, around 9 per cent of GNP. With the east Asian countries, however, the consolidated budget position differed little from the position of the central government.[11]

Another non-explanation for India's avoidance of crisis is that India's financial system was 'sounder' than that of the east Asian countries. While it is true that India had initiated financial sector reform in 1991, its financial system was still in poor health. 'Implicit guarantees', which have been much criticised in the east Asian context, were certainly present in India's largely nationalised banking system and 'crony capitalism' was also rife. As Table 9 makes clear, there was also a heavy overhang of non-performing assets (about 17 per cent of total advances), on official figures heavier than in the crisis countries. Of course, it turned out that the east Asian figures understated the magnitude of the bad loans problem but the Indian figures too have a significant downward bias (see below).

Another possible explanation for India's relative success in crisis avoidance relates to exchange rate policy. It has been argued that dollar pegging in the crisis countries lulled their private sectors into complacency about exchange risk and led them to indulge in massive unhedged short-term foreign currency borrowing. How does India compare? I have already alluded to the fact that India's exchange rate was heavily managed. Indeed from March 1993, when the new exchange rate system got going, until mid-1995, the exchange rate barely moved from the level of $1 = Rs 31.37. It would certainly be hard to argue that in this period there was any perceived exchange risk in short-term borrowing. Admittedly, the rupee–dollar rate then depreciated by about 10 per cent but it was stable again from mid-1996 to mid-1997. A comparison with the crisis countries is provided in Table 10.

None of the above countries maintained a rigidly inflexible dollar peg. Indonesia depreciated steadily against the dollar, while South Korea, Malaysia, Philippines and Thailand show a mix of alternating depreciation and

Table 10. *Percentage change in the nominal exchange rate against the US dollar, India and south-east Asia, 1993–6.*

	1993	1994	1995	1996
	annual average			
India	−0.2*	−0.1	−3.4	−9.3
Indonesia	−2.8	−3.5	−4.1	−4.2
Malaysia	−1.1	−2.0	+4.6	−0.5
Philippines	−6.3	+2.6	+2.7	−2.0
South Korea	−2.8	0.0	+4.0	−4.3
Thailand	+0.3	+0.7	+0.9	−1.7

*Beginning March 1993, when the new exchange rate system was instituted.
Source: IMF, *International Financial Statistics.*

Table 11. *(Percentage) standard deviation of the average monthly exchange rate against the dollar from the trend.*

	March 1993–March 1995	March 1993–July 1997
India	0.2	2.9
Indonesia	0.2	0.6
Malaysia	2.5	2.1
Philippines	3.9	3.5
South Korea	1.4	3.8
Thailand	0.6	2.6

Source: IMF, *International Financial Statistics.*

appreciation. On the basis of these figures it is not clear that in the period 1993–5 the incentive to borrow unhedged would have been greater in the crisis countries than in India, with the possible exception of Thailand. All these countries, including India, were on a *loose* dollar peg, though the precise mechanism – band, crawl or managed float – varied.

While Table 10 is informative, it only gives annual figures and hence does not throw light on the short-run predictability of the exchange rate. I have tried to address this issue by regressing the (natural logarithm of the) monthly nominal exchange rate of India and the crisis countries against time (months) and a constant. In each case, the standard error of the residuals from the regression equation (i.e. the standard deviation of monthly exchange rate observations from the trend) provides a measure of predictability – the lower the standard error, the greater the predictability.[12] Table 11 gives this statistic for the relevant countries.

It can be seen that from March 1993 to July 1995, the predictability of India's exchange rate is (joint) highest. If the observational period is extended to July 1997, India's position is fourth highest.[13] This confirms that India was no different from the crisis countries as regards the incentive to undertake unhedged short-term external borrowing.[14]

Deftness of Indian policy makers in the way in which they handled the crisis after it broke could also be offered as an explanation for India's relative success. They did indeed perform a skilful balancing act involving intervention, moderate depreciation and monetary tightening. But they did not do anything in the sphere of conventional macroeconomic policy that was not also tried in the crisis countries. Policy makers in the crisis countries were simply overwhelmed by the avalanche of capital flow reversal.

It is difficult to avoid the conclusion that there were two reasons (themselves not unrelated) for India's favourable outcome: debt management and capital controls. Policy makers made a conscious effort to reduce external debt and improve its structure after the 1991 payments crisis. To this end, much short-term debt was retired and strict controls were imposed on new short-term debt; long-term external commercial borrowing was capped; an attempt was made to attract non-debt flows such as FDI and portfolio equity; and the excessive incentives given to inflows of non-resident deposits (e.g. higher interest rates and exchange rate guarantees) were scrapped. By 1996, these measures had paid off and India's external debt situation had improved significantly compared with 1991. The debt/GNP ratio and debt-service/exports ratio came down from 41 per cent and 35 per cent respectively in March 1991 to 24 per cent and 21 per cent in March 1997. There was a significant shift from debt-creating to non-debt-creating inflows. Short-term debt as a proportion of total debt fell from 10 per cent to 5 per cent. Over the same period foreign exchange reserves increased from $2 billion to $28 billion. The comparison presented in Table 12 is instructive.

India has a low debt/GNP ratio but it is noteworthy that India looks no better than east Asia on the basis of a more relevant ratio, namely non-concessional debt divided by exports of goods and services. Nor does India's debt position look favourable as measured by the conventional debt-service ratio. The critical difference can be seen in the last two columns. India managed to keep short-term debt under control, both in relation to total debt and in relation to foreign exchange reserves. The lesson of the recent crisis, that the structure of external debt matters, is thus emphatically borne out.[15]

The conclusion that I would draw from the above review is that India benefited from eschewing premature CAC, in contrast to many east Asian economies.[16] This cautious approach helped in several respects: it enabled the country to tailor the capital controls in such a way as to achieve a less volatile structure of external debt; it enabled policy makers to perform the high-wire act

Table 12. *Debt indicators, India and south-east Asia, 1996.*

	EDT/GNP	NCEDT/XGS	TDS/XGS	SDT/EDT	SDT/RES
		Percentage			
India*	23.8	103.6	21.2	5.3	27.1
Indonesia	58.3	180.5	36.6	25.0	166.7
Malaysia	42.0	40.4	9.0	27.9	39.7
Philippines	46.5	80.1	13.4	19.9	67.9
South Korea	27.4	82.0	9.4	49.9	192.7
Thailand	51.3	110.9	12.6	41.5	97.4

Notation
EDT: total external debt
GNP: gross national product
NCEDT: total non-concessional external debt
XGS: exports of goods and services
TDS: total debt service on long-term debt *plus* interest payments on short-term debt
SDT: short-term debt
RES: international reserves
*Indian data refer to March 1997.
Sources: World Bank, *Global Development Finance* 1999; Government of India, *Economic Survey*, various years.

of balancing exchange rate and interest rate targets; and during crisis periods, the presence of effective capital controls served to reassure the foreign exchange market. Recent theorising has highlighted the possibility of multiple equilibria in currency markets. India's capital controls enabled policy makers to avoid a 'bad' equilibrium driven by panic, herding and destabilising speculation.

Political economy

I have attributed to capital controls a highly significant role in avoiding currency crisis and contagion. Two issues naturally arise. First, why were India's capital controls effective?[17] And second, why was India, unlike some other countries, able to resist the concerted pressure in favour of thoroughgoing CAC exerted by influential international bodies such as the IMF and by the US Treasury in the early 1990s? It is illuminating to classify the relevant considerations under the following headings: technical issues, ideological principle, evidence and experience, domestic politics and international politics. This classification is used by Benjamin Cohen in explaining why governments do not *adopt* capital controls.[18] I use it here to explain why India did not *abandon* capital controls.

Technical issues

Setting up a complex system of capital controls with associated prohibitions and exemptions is a difficult and administratively cumbersome exercise. India already had comprehensive capital controls and had long experience in operating them. The reform programme of 1991 aimed to ease these controls selectively – a much easier task than instituting a system from scratch. Moreover, the selective easing primarily concerned inflows. This selectivity was not difficult to administer because there is a built-in incentive to report such flows, since the investor would wish to establish legal title to the funds in India. It is also relevant that penalties for evasion by domestic residents were harsh, being governed by the Foreign Exchange Regulation Act which treated violations as a *criminal* offence.

Ideological principle

Full CAC is evidently consonant with a free-market ideology. But this ideology has never been influential in India. The dominant bias in postwar Indian economic policy was in favour of inward-looking socialist planning, with a negative attitude to both trade and foreign investment. When India embarked on liberalisation, it was a top-down affair, led by a few politicians and bureaucrats. Most of the political and administrative elite was at best a reluctant convert. Any sweeping move to CAC would therefore have been a non-starter. Even the reformers' enthusiasm for liberalisation was pragmatic and measured, not extreme. Moreover, they had reason to be suspicious of dependence on external borrowing, as outlined below.

Evidence and experience

For twenty years from the mid-1950s, India's policy was isolationist and protectionist. Some hesitant liberalisation then took place. In the 1980s, external borrowing rose markedly, first from the IMF, later from commercial banks and non-resident Indians, including a significant amount of short-term borrowing. The macroeconomic vulnerability generated by excessive foreign debt (and by excessive fiscal deficits) led to a crisis in 1991. In this crisis, India's credit rating was severely downgraded, the inflow of non-resident deposits dried up and there was a cut-off of short-term foreign credit. This experience undoubtedly contributed to a cautious attitude to CAC, especially to liberalising short-term capital flows. Government reports and documents in the early 1990s are quite explicit about the need to go slow on CAC.

Domestic politics

For various reasons, there was no strong domestic constituency that favoured a radical move to CAC. The obvious potential pro-CAC pressure group would have been the top industrial corporates. But the Indian capital control system had already allowed them to borrow abroad in the 1980s and this access was continued in the 1990s. In addition, the easing of regulations on portfolio equity inflows also enabled them to access external capital. Small industrial companies were not informed enough about world capital markets to lobby strongly for access. Moreover, industrial companies generally were preoccupied with lobbying against liberalisation of trade and direct foreign investment, which was of immediate concern to them. Another pressure group that one might naturally expect to favour CAC, particularly at the short end, is the banking system. But in India the banks were overwhelmingly in the public sector. Both the managers and the workers of these banks were fearful of the foreign competition that would inevitably accompany CAC. By 1997, however, quite a strong lobby was beginning to develop in favour of CAC, particularly in parts of the private non-bank financial sector, and its influence is seen to some extent in the Tarapore Committee Report (see below). Then the Asian crisis supervened and provided an *ex post facto* justification for India's cautious policy stance.

International politics

As is well known, the international financial community was a strong pressure group in favour of CAC. In this context, two points are important. First, the foreign banks were not a major presence in India. So while CAC was a potentially important issue for foreign banks in the future, its immediate importance was not as great as in other countries where these banks already had extensive connections. Second, and more importantly, India is a big country with some international clout. Both in its foreign and economic policy there has been a strong tradition of resistance to being pushed around by the superpowers or by international agencies. The latter in their turn were content that India had at long last adopted a liberalisation and reform programme. They were anxious not to jeopardise the relationship with India by putting undue pressure as regards CAC.

In sum, the highly selective capital account liberalisation that India adopted was made easier by the fact that India had long experience in administering comprehensive exchange control. In addition, India was also fortunate in being 'too big to be bullied' by international agencies and in not having any strong domestic constituency that favoured a dramatic move to CAC.

Should India move to CAC in the near future?

I have argued above that a prime reason for India's avoidance of crisis and contagion in the 1990s was the presence of capital controls. It does not follow that India should continue with capital controls indefinitely. Indeed, a committee set up by the RBI (under the chairmanship of S. S. Tarapore) reported in 1997 and concluded that India should move towards CAC in a phased manner in three years concurrently with achieving certain preconditions, namely fiscal stabilisation, low inflation and a competitive, solvent, well-regulated banking system.[19] I comment below on the CAC debate in the Indian context.[20]

In my judgement, the case for adopting CAC in India in the near future (say five years) is weak. The following points are pertinent.

- Despite substantial trade liberalisation in the 1990s, India still retains relatively high protection. Though quantitative restrictions are due to be phased out by 2001, the average tariff is in the region of 25 per cent. Protection is high enough to produce substantial misallocation of capital if CAC were adopted.
- The optimisation of aggregate saving and investment does not require CAC. India could continue to run current account deficits of appropriate size consistently with controlling capital outflows and influencing the structure of inflows.
- There is a portfolio risk-diversification argument in favour of CAC, but it does not seem a high priority at the present stage of Indian reform.
- The argument that CAC would act as a discipline on policy makers is subject to the criticism that capital market discipline is often inappropriately exercised. This was certainly the experience in the late 1980s when the world capital market allowed India to run high fiscal and current account deficits for several years before the crunch in 1991.
- The argument that capital controls are ineffective has to be taken seriously. Empirical work on India suggests that capital controls have been effective so far. It is probable that Indian capital controls do not prevent a slow seepage

but do inhibit large, sudden, wholesale movements that can create a financial crisis and greatly complicate macroeconomic policy.

• As confirmed in a previous section, capital controls have given Indian policy makers a significant extra degree of freedom in counter-cyclical monetary policy. It is important to observe in this context that (a) counter-cyclical fiscal policy in India faces severe solvency constraints; and (b) the Indian government would (rightly in my judgement) be unwilling to give up exchange rate targeting altogether and adopt fully floating exchange rates.

• Liberalisation of capital outflows could erode the tax base, a highly important consideration in a country where fewer than 10 million people (i.e. one in a hundred) pay income tax.

• Complete CAC would be politically dangerous in a country where sensitivities about 'being run by foreigners' are very strong. Trade liberalisation is a big enough agenda for the near future. If CAC is followed by capital flight in a crisis, an abandonment of CAC, and even of trade liberalisation, is entirely possible in the Indian political context – and the possibility of such an outcome would of course increase the likelihood of capital flight!

• The Tarapore conditions are little closer to achievement than they were in 1997. The fiscal deficit remains very high. Inflation fell after 1997 but money supply growth did not. That suggests that the fall in inflation may have been due to fortuitous reasons such as the run of good monsoons and soft world commodity prices. Indeed, inflation appears to be on the rise again. The cash reserve ratio is not lower than it was when the Committee's report came out, and there has been no improvement in the non-performing assets (NPAs) of the banking system. India does not yet possess an efficient financial sector suitable for a sophisticated modern economy. This important point is elaborated below.

CAC and India's financial sector[21]

Before the reform of 1991, India's financial system was heavily repressed. Ironically, this highly interventionist regime was accompanied by lax regulation and supervision of the banks' financial health. In 1991, non-performing assets of banks were 25 per cent of their advances and half of the banking system had negative net worth.

Many useful changes have now been made, but there is a long way to go. Interest rates have been substantially freed. Government pre-emption of bank deposits has been reduced but remains high: the cash reserve ratio is 9 per cent and the statutory liquidity ratio (which stipulates the proportion of bank deposits that must be invested in government securities) is still 25 per cent. Competition among banks has increased a little as a result of interest rate deregulation and the entry of new private banks. Prudential norms have been tightened and a supervisory system has been set up. Banks have to achieve a capital adequacy ratio of 8 per cent and most of them have done so, mainly through infusion of public capital from the budget. Norms have been put in place as regards income recognition and provisioning.

The critical question is whether the health of the financial sector has improved sufficiently to permit a move to CAC. I remain unconvinced. Achievement of the 8 per cent capital adequacy ratio is a misleading indicator of progress, since it takes no account of the quality of the portfolio. The critical point is that the incidence of NPAs is still very high. The latest official estimate of gross NPAs is about 18 per cent of advances; and ten out of twenty-seven public sector banks have NPAs higher than 20 per cent. Unofficial estimates of NPAs (e.g. by Standard and Poor's, the credit rating agency) are, however, much higher, in the region of 50 per cent. Banks with relatively large NPAs are known to have undertaken rapid expansion of credit and rolled over bad debts, to bring down measured NPAs.

Thus it is not at all clear that asset quality has improved. Debt recovery is inadequate and a substantial proportion of bank credit is still locked up in 'sick industries'. Note also that trends in bank profitability and efficiency do not yet show an improvement in performance. There is little evidence of cost-cutting and the weakest banks remain a serious problem. Various structural problems such as overmanning, militant and regressive trade unionism, and lack of administrative autonomy continue to dog the industry. Some of these problems are directly connected with the public ownership of banks. In theory, publicly owned banks could compete vigorously with one another and with private banks, and the pressures of competition would bring managerial autonomy in its train. In practice, this is far-fetched. Given the inherited advantages of public sector banks in terms of branch coverage and customer base, the competitive threat from private banks is too distant to deter interference by politicians and bureaucrats. However, the government is still stuck with the fetish of 51 per cent public ownership.

It is very doubtful whether the banking sector is as yet strong enough to withstand any serious move to CAC. The Tarapore Committee's 'signposts' for the financial sector (3 per cent cash ratio, 5 per cent gross NPAs, better risk management in banks and other financial institutions, efficient supervisory systems etc.) are very far from being achieved. CAC would put significant pressure on banks as their clients (both borrowers and depositors) take advantage of international markets. It is not difficult to imagine a scenario in which the exit of the best customers leads to a large increase in the riskiness of bank portfolios and an exacerbation of NPA problems. A macroeconomic shock under such conditions could prove to be devastating.[22]

Concluding remarks

Capital controls have played a major role in enabling India to balance exchange rate stability and monetary autonomy in the 1990s and to avoid contagion from the Asian crisis. Although India is in some respects an untypical developing country, its experience is instructive. It shows that it is possible to tailor capital controls in such a way as to run current account deficits financed by stable rather than volatile types of capital inflow; and that capital outflow controls may also have a useful role to play in avoiding a sudden and large-scale contagious exit of capital which can impose major costs on the economy. India's experience thus serves to reinforce the caution that many now feel about incorporating CAC as an integral element of the new international financial architecture. It also suggests that it is feasible to operate capital account controls so as to secure many of the benefits of mobile capital flows while avoiding the costs.

As regards the future, the main argument in favour of CAC for India is that the country may well have a long-term comparative advantage in the export of some financial services, as it does in the export of software. Therefore, at some point, India's financial sector may well need to be exposed to CAC in order to sharpen its efficiency.[23] But the time is not right for such a move. Given the present state of the financial sector, the cold shower of CAC would be freezing rather than bracing. CAC would also increase the potential for macroeconomic crises that could disrupt the country's large and unfinished reform agenda. This agenda embraces fiscal consolidation; deeper liberalisation of trade, finance and factor markets; privatisation; and purposive state action in the infrastructure and social sectors. The immediate priority for India lies in vigorously implementing these reforms rather than in pursuing the goal of capital account convertibility.

Notes

The author is grateful to Shankar Acharya, Kamakshya Trivedi and the editors of this volume for useful comments.
1. India's GNP grew at 6.3 per cent per annum during 1992–7 and 6 per cent in 1998, a year during which many east Asian countries experienced large negative rates of growth. India's industrial sector, however, did experience a slight fall in its growth rate in 1998 (from 6 per cent to 4 per cent).
2. The word 'selective' must be stressed. In the 1980s, capital inflow controls were relaxed in order to finance current account deficits caused by expansionary macro-economic policies. In the 1990s, capital controls on debt-creating inflows were tightened while those on non-debt-creating inflows were liberalised.

3. Note that India achieved formal current account convertibility (IMF Art. VIII) in 1994. Some current account restrictions (that were consistent with Art. VIII) were retained as an aid to working the capital controls system.
4. For analysis and description of India's capital controls system see Karl Habermeier, 'India's experience with the Liberalisation of Capital Flows since 1991', in A. Ariyoshi *et al.*, *Capital Controls: Country Experiences with their Use and Liberalisation*. Occasional Paper no. 190 (Washington, DC: IMF, 2000); Vijay Joshi and I. M. D. Little, *India's Economic Reforms 1991–2001* (Oxford: Clarendon Press, 1996); Y. V. Reddy, 'Operationalising Capital Account Liberalisation: Indian Experience', in *Reserve Bank of India Bulletin*, Bombay (2000). Capital controls prior to the 1991 reforms are discussed in Vijay Joshi and I. M. D. Little, *India – Macroeconomics and Political Economy 1964–1991* (New York: World Bank and Oxford University Press, 1994).
5. India's balance of payments experience in the 1990s is illuminatingly analysed in Shankar Acharya, *Managing External Economic Challenges in the Nineties: Lessons for the Future*, Occasional Papers Number 93, (Central Bank of Sri Lanka, 1999); and Hiranya Mukhopadhyaya, 'Exchange Rate Management and Monetary Measures: RBI's Policy Dilemma in the Context of the Currency Crisis', *Money and Finance*, July-Sept. 1999.
6. See Joshi and Little, *India*.
7. Most of the borrowing was by the government or by enterprises and financial institutions in the public sector. Note that concessional official capital inflows declined in this period.
8. On the eve of the crisis, India's foreign exchange reserves were $2 billion, but short-term debt was $6 billion.
9. The extent of sterilisation was limited by the fiscal cost (particularly in view of the high fiscal deficit and thus the extent of new borrowing by the government) and the shallowness of the debt market.
10. It is an open secret that the IMF advised the Indian government to let the rupee appreciate.
11. Note that India's relative performance on 'fundamentals' looks no different if we take averages for the period 1990–6.
12. This procedure is similar to that followed by P. Alba, A. Bhattacharya, S. Claessens, S. Ghosh and L. Hernandez, 'The role of macroeconomic and financial sector linkages in East Asia's financial crisis' in P. Agénor, M. Miller, D. Vines and A. Weber (eds.), *The Asian Financial Crisis – Causes and Consequences* (Cambridge: Cambridge University Press, 1999). They do not, however, compare India with the crisis countries.
13. Using the standard error of residuals as a measure of predictability assumes that the market's predictions of movements in the nominal exchange rate are captured by a straightforward time trend. (Note that in each regression, the t statistic on the time trend is significant at the 5 per cent level.)
14. Dollar-pegging in the east Asian countries has also been criticised in another respect: when the dollar began to appreciate in 1995, the east Asian currencies followed the dollar and thus lost real competitiveness. On this count, India did follow a

more sensible strategy. Policy makers in India realised that to maintain the dollar peg when the dollar began appreciating during 1995 would result in a sharp real effective overvaluation. From mid-1995, they therefore engineered or acquiesced in moderate depreciations against the dollar. As a result, India's real exchange rate appreciation in the period mid-1995–mid-1997 was much less than that of the crisis countries. However, this does not have a bearing on the critical point that over the period 1993–5, when inflows into India were at their heaviest, the incentive not to hedge short-term borrowing was as much present in India as in the crisis countries.

15. For completeness, another argument that must be addressed is that India escaped the crisis because it was not a major recipient of capital flows. First, India's size is again relevant. It is true that as a proportion of GNP, private capital flows into India over the period 1992–6 were only about 1.5 per cent as against a range in east Asia from 3.2 per cent (South Korea) to 10.3 per cent (Malaysia). But as a proportion of exports, the ratios are 10.3 per cent (India) as against a range in east Asia of 9.7 per cent (South Korea) to 20.2 per cent (Thailand). On the latter measure, India was clearly not a minor recipient. Second, and more importantly, the above ratios mask the composition of capital flows. The main reason for the difference in aggregate flows between India and the crisis countries concerns the volume of *debt-creating (especially short-term) inflows*. These were very large in the crisis countries and small in India. Moreover, this was *intentional*: India's capital controls were operated in a manner designed to keep out such inflows. In addition, India's outflow controls were also helpful in avoiding contagion.

16. Curiously, in 1997, South Korea was in the position of having retained controls on foreign direct investment but having abandoned controls on short-term capital movements!

17. This presumes that India's capital controls *were* effective. The fact that India was able to limit debt-creating inflows surely counts as indirect evidence for this proposition. Econometric studies based on an examination of interest rate differentials between India and foreign markets also suggest that India's capital controls are effective (see P. Haque and M. Montiel, *Capital Mobility in Developing Countries*, IMF Working Paper WP/90/117 (Washington, DC: IMF, 1990), even in the 1990s (see H. Joshi and M. Sagger, 'Excess Returns, Risk-premia and Efficiency of the Foreign Exchange Market', Reserve Bank of India Occasional Papers, vol.19 (June 1998), pp.129–52). On the other hand, there is some evidence of illegal capital outflows, partly through misinvoicing of trade (see M. Rishi and J. Boyce, 'The Hidden Balance of Payments: Capital Flight and Trade Misinvoicing in India 1971–1986', *Economic and Political Weekly* vol. 25, no, 50 (1990), pp. 1645–8; Joshi and Little, *India's Economic Reforms*). I think it is reasonable to conclude from the available evidence that India's capital controls do not stop modest, regular retail outflows by individuals but can prevent sudden, wholesale hot money flows that could precipitate macroeconomic crises.

18. See Benjamin Cohen, 'Capital Controls: Why Do Governments Hesitate?' in Leslie Elliott Armijo (ed.), *Debating the Global Financial Architecture* (Albany, NY: SUNY Press, 2000).

19. See Reserve Bank of India, *Report of the Committee on Capital Account Convertibility (Tarapore Committee 1997)*. The Committee also suggested monitoring four variables, namely the current account deficit, the real effective exchange rate, the ratio of foreign exchange reserves to short-term debt and to domestic currency in circulation, and the strength of the financial system. Note that the Committee did not recommend *full* CAC even at the end of the three-year horizon.

20. The discussion below picks up points of special relevance in the Indian context. For a more general discussion of CAC see Jagdish Bhagwati, (1998) 'The Capital Myth: The Difference between Trade in Widgets and Dollars', *Foreign Affairs*, vol. 77, no. 3 (1998); Richard Cooper, 'Should Capital Controls be Banished?' in William C. Brainard and George L. Perry (eds.), *Brookings Papers in Economic Activity: 1 (1999)*; B. Eichengreen and M. Mussa, *Capital Account Liberalisation – Theoretical and Practical Aspects*, Occasional Paper 172 (Washington, DC: IMF, 1998); J. Stiglitz, 'Capital Market Liberalisation, Economic Growth and Instability', in *World Development*, vol. 28, no. 6 (2000), pp. 1075–86; John Williamson, 'A Cost-benefit Analysis of Capital Account Liberalisation', in B. Fischer and H. Reisen (eds.), *Financial Opening: Policy Issues and Experiences in Developing Countries* (Paris: OECD Development Centre, 1993); John Williamson, 'Comment' (on Cooper, 'Should Capital Controls be Banished?'), in Brainard and Perry, *Brookings Papers in Economic Activity: 1* (1999), pp. 130–5.

21. India's financial sector is examined in Joshi and Little, *India's Economic Reforms*; James Hanson and Sanjay Kathuria (eds.), *India – A Financial Sector for the Twenty-first Century* (Delhi: Oxford University Press, 1999).

22. Since 1991 there have also been some important reforms in the non-bank financial sector. A regulatory body has been set up to supervise primary and secondary markets for equity. As a result, trading and settlement procedures have improved considerably. An important shortcoming that currently exists is the shallowness of debt markets. Progress in this area is closely connected with reform of insurance and pension institutions. These nationalised monoliths are mandated to invest 50–100 per cent of their funds in government securities. Unless they are reformed, it would not be possible to develop the deep debt market that a safe move to CAC requires. In the context of preparing for CAC, it is also a matter of high priority to improve India's primitive derivatives (including currency derivatives) markets.

23. Arguably, some prudential controls would be advisable even on a permanent, long-run basis, e.g. limits on banks' open positions in foreign exchange.

10 Learning to live without the Plan: financial reform in China

SHAUN BRESLIN

There was a time, not that long ago, when the leadership of the People's Republic of China (PRC) would have viewed international financial crises with a sense of glee and vindication – a sign of the vagaries of the global capitalist system and perhaps an indication of its impending demise. But contemporary China is no longer isolated from the global economy and wholly insulated against external shocks. A crisis in Mexico was of little more than academic interest to China's elites, but the crisis on China's doorstep in 1997 had immediate and direct significance.

This significance was primarily through the impact of the secondary or responsive stage of the crisis. The collapse of demand in Japan and other regional states, the dampening of international investment activities, and enhanced competition for export markets[1] combined to jolt the efficacy of China's export-led growth strategy after 1997. But while inward investment and export strategies had become more and more open and integrated, the Chinese financial system remained relatively closed and protected in 1997. And it was this relative lack of liberalisation that helped protect the Chinese economy from the worst excesses of the 1997 crisis.

Nevertheless, the pressures to reform the financial structure, which appeared to serve national interests so well in 1997, are enormous. These pressures partly come from without, most notably in the shape of meeting WTO standards and criteria. But they also come from a complex interplay between domestic and external forces as China incrementally reforms itself away from socialism. Financial systems and structures do not just emerge. They are constructed to serve specific ends and to privilege some political interests over others. In the Chinese case, the emerging and evolving financial system has been used to replicate some of those redistributive and social welfare functions that the old planning structure had previously served. In effect, it is used to maintain social stability by providing a palliative for those who have most to lose as the Chinese economy becomes more market oriented and more internationally open. In this respect, Chinese policy represents a compromise between the embedded residual socialist system, and the dictates of economic reform.

Perhaps most concretely, pressures for reform come from the simple fact that the cost of maintaining social stability has been the insolvency of many of China's financial institutions. For example, by the end of 2000, all four of China's major state-owned banks were unable to meet the minimum adequacy rate required by the Basel Agreement, and more than 40,000 rural credit co-operatives were technically bankrupt.[2] Reforms implemented after 1994 to restructure the financial system were designed to deal with the consequences of incomplete transformation from the old state-planned political economy. But while the incomplete nature of the transformation is in itself the perceived cause of the problem, the residual power, political alliances and paradigms that remain from the old system also provide the biggest obstacles to reform. Effective financial reform (in its own terms) is not just a matter of technical changes, but a fundamental reform of the Chinese polity.

Dismantling the Plan and replacing the Plan

At the risk of oversimplification, we can divide financial reform in post-Mao China into two phases. The first, from 1984, essentially entailed the gradual and incremental dismantling of the old state-planned system. The second, from 1994, represents the (as yet) incomplete gradual and incremental attempt to build a new market-oriented financial system. This lack of synchronisation is often cited by Chinese researchers as a major cause of financial instability. For example, Zhou Shaohua argued that 'The central government's comprehensive management system has been dismantled while new economic pillars have not yet been erected.'[3] Similarly, Gao Zhanjun and Liu Fei argued that

China is now in an important historical period during which an old financial system is shifting to a new one and the two are hitting each other ... New financial institutions and business lines are constantly emerging, whereas the old financial system has not been broken up completely, nor has a brand new financial system taken shape.[4]

Zhou's analysis was made in 1987, just three years after the central party-state leadership started to dismantle the old state-planned financial system. Gao and Liu were commenting some twelve years later, and five years after Zhu Rongji began to build a new integrated financial system. The similarity of these two assessments is testament to the size of the challenge to reformers and the strength of political constraints on economic reform. It is also a consequence of the assessment of some Chinese leaders that the Chinese Communist Party (CCP) should not abandon the state-owned working class[5] – either from ideological or more pragmatic considerations.

The key reforms implemented after 1994 are most closely identified with Zhu Rongji. First as vice-premier with specific responsibility for banking reform, and subsequently as premier, Zhu has been the most visible proponent of reform. Zhu's initiatives are often referred to as a process of 're-centralisation'.[6] While they are indeed intended to increase the power of the central authorities, we should be careful not to associate these processes with previous attempts to re-centralise the economy in the 1980s. The intention was not to draw back from the market, as was the case with the last serious attempt at re-centralisation in 1988–9. While the then Premier Li Peng also recognised that financial problems existed because 'the old structure coexists with the new', he saw the solution in restoring some elements of the Plan.[7] By comparison, Zhu Rongji's solution in 1994 was to create new mechanisms of macroeconomic control over the Chinese economy – to regulate rather than dictate. Zhu's attempts to 're-centralise' the economy in the 1990s was intended as one step on the way to greater economic liberalisation, not a retreat from it.

Even though Zhu Rongji has overseen the appointment of a number of his followers into key ministerial positions, these policies have faced considerable opposition from within the broadly defined Chinese party–state leadership itself. In particular, Zhu was accused of over-zealously attacking inflation after 1994, at the cost of urban employment. He had set a target that through its secondary consequences placed price stability as a more urgent priority than job creation. It is notable that the loudest voices of criticism came from those areas of China where the residual state-owned system still dominated the economy. These areas had most to lose (in the short term at least) from the liberalisation of the Chinese economy. The case for liberalisation did not, and (notwithstanding China's entry into the WTO) still does not, have the full support of Chinese elites. Even though the ideological battle over the need to liberalise might have been more or less won, there remains a lack of consensus over how to do this whilst not jeopardising social stability.

In many respects, isolating different areas of policy change misses the point that the post-1994 reforms were intended finally to replace the Plan with a new integrated and holistic system. It was a direct response to economic fragmentation and built on the premise that financial reform, fiscal reform, enterprises reform and international liberalisation had to be co-ordinated. Nevertheless, for the sake of simplicity, the following analysis is divided into two sections. The first deals with the growth of local economic control and the second with the subsidisation of employment and the growing debt crisis.

Redressing the balance in centre–local relations

There is now a relatively well-developed literature on the growth of local financial revenues in the post-Mao era vis-à-vis centrally controlled finances.[8] Suffice
it to say here that while Lardy argued that the key to – perhaps the defining characteristic of – the old financial system was that there was no correlation between
collecting and controlling finances,[9] post-Mao reforms deliberately and consciously created a link between local collection and control of finances. Indeed,
as the central authorities consciously devolved considerable financial authority
to local governments, it might seem strange that they have subsequently spent
so much time and effort in attempting to regain this power. But as Wong notes,
while a loss of central revenues relative to the provinces was considered not
only inevitable, but desirable, 'the magnitude and rapidity of this decline appear
to have caught officials in China by surprise'[10] – largely because of the unanticipated and unintended impact of the combination of revenue-sharing
reforms with changes to China's banking system.

1994 fiscal reforms and centre–local relations

This loss of central control over the economy was a key impulse for financial reform, and particularly for fiscal reform. The reforms were intended to
redress the balance of fiscal power between centre and provinces by creating
three fiscal categories – central taxes, local taxes and shared taxes. Crucially,
for Zheng Yongnian, the central government established its own national tax
service to collect not only central taxes, but also those taxes that are subsequently shared with the local governments. The link between local collection
and control of finances that the earlier reforms had created was (partially)
removed.[11]

The immediate result of the fiscal reforms was first to increase the total
amount of tax revenue, and second to increase the proportion accruing to the
central authorities, from around 30 to 50 per cent of all fiscal revenues.[12] By the
end of the decade, the balance of centre–province shares of total tax revenue
reached 58:42.[13] On the face of it, then, the fiscal reforms were successful in
that they increased the total volume of fiscal resources and partially redressed
what the central leadership perceived to be a structural imbalance in the division of finances between centre and locality. However, tax revenues are only
part of government income in China – indeed, only 40 per cent of all government revenue. The majority of government income is termed 'extra system'
revenue, which Gao Peiyong defines as '[those] revenues whose regulations are

formulated independently by various departments and localities and which are collected and disposed of by them as well'.[14]

Local control of financial institutions

The importance of fees as a source of local revenue is just one example of how the Chinese financial system has proved difficult for the central authorities to control. Another example – perhaps more important for an understanding of financial reform – is the way in which banking reforms altered the relationship between central and local authorities. In 1984 the People's Bank of China (PBC) was designated as the central bank, and four large specialist banks were introduced, each channelling capital for different sectors of the economy. Thus, the Industrial and Commercial Bank was responsible for channelling finances into state owned enterprises; the People's Construction Bank of China was responsible for new investment projects; the Agricultural Bank of China was responsible for agricultural procurement and rural investment (including rural industry); and the Bank of China took control of foreign exchange business.

This was followed in 1985 by a key transition from the plan, in that China switched from a grant based to loan based investment system. In order to facilitate the transition from central grants to bank loans, the power of specialised banks in the localities was increased in 1985. But in setting the investment quota for the new banks, the central authorities announced that the 1985 investment quota would depend on the amount of loans extended in 1984.[15]

The move to bank loans sponsored a huge boom in investment in capital construction by local governments. While investment in state planned projects recorded a 1.6 per cent year-on-year increase in 1985, investment in unplanned projects by local governments increasing by 87 per cent.[16] Crucially, while state planning agencies and financial authorities controlled the provision of 76.6 per cent of internal national investment capital at the start of the reform process, this proportion fell to 33.2 per cent in 1986 as a result of the new banking reforms.[17] It was not until Li Peng replaced Zhao Ziyang as Premier (in 1987) and implemented an economic retrenchment campaign in autumn 1988 that investment spending began to come under control.

Here we need to focus on the notion of dual control of local level organisation in China. Administrative organisation is built on twin and simultaneous functional and geographic channels. Thus a provincial branch of a bank is vertically responsible to the bank's central offices and at the same time horizontally responsible to the provincial finance bureau and the provincial government. The latter has the advantage of hands-on contact with the branch, since it is in direct day-to-day contact with bank officials. Furthermore, it possesses considerable power in terms of allocating goods, services and personnel to the banks. Thus, while not formally an agency of local government, local branches of banks often act as if they are part of the local government structure.

The power of local authorities[18] to collect and impose fees and to influence (if not control) local banks contributes to the characterisation of many local governments as running 'dukedom economies' (*zhuhou jingji*).[19] Through control of investment finance and controlling access to raw materials, distribution and markets, local governments have retained close control over local economic affairs despite the transition from state planning and state ownership. Furthermore, theoretical checks and balances on local government power provided by the legal system can also be discounted; 'Since courts and judiciary departments are subject to local governments, justice cannot be brought along in many fields.'[20]

While fiscal reform went some way to restoring the central authorities' ability to control the national economy, it was in itself not enough. Both the levying of fees and control of local branches of central financial institutions shifted the balance away from the centre to the provinces. Furthermore, we have to consider the financial 'chaos and mismanagement' resulting from the expansion of local financial institutions.[21] Despite a policy of encouraging mergers in the light of the failure of the Guangdong International Trust and Investment Corporation (ITIC) and the decision to cut the number of central ITICs to three in September 2000, there were still around 240 locally controlled ITICs operating in China in 2002. In addition to the ITICs, there are over 50,000 small-scale locally controlled rural and urban credit co-operatives in China today. By the end of 2001, outstanding deposits from all rural credit co-operatives stood at about RMB 1.3 trillion, accounting for 12 per cent of total deposits in financial institutions, while outstanding loans by rural credit co-operatives were about 11 per cent of the national total.[22]

Taken as a whole, China's rural credit co-operatives are insolvent. But they play an important role in maintaining employment and social stability in the countryside. This was particularly so after 1997, when growth generated by small-scale township and village enterprises dropped off sharply. In the three years from the first quarter of 1997, the People's Bank of China lent RMB 30 billion (about US$3.6 billion) to rural credit co-operatives, and then 're-lent' a further RMB 33.3 billion in September 2000,[23] followed by yet another refinancing to the tune of RMB 20 billion in the first half of 2001.[24]

In essence, like support for loss-making state-owned enterprises (SOEs), the financial system was being used in the short term to buy social stability. But even when the central government wants to constrain the activity of local governments, thanks to local control and horizontal dictatorship many of the actions of local authorities are beyond the reach of central macroeconomic control and central financial regulatory institutions. This quotation from Xie

Ping provides a succinct assessment of the impact of localism on the financial system:

a considerable number of financial institutions to be restructured are jointly invested by local governments and controlled by them. It is local government's intervention of senior management and business that cause the loss and difficulties of these financial institutions. Consequently, upon merger, restructuring and closure or even bankruptcy of these financial institutions, on the one hand local governments are only responsible for liabilities up to the amount of their investment, but on the other hand for the local interest their intervention in the described processes are severe. Even judicial justice can not be guaranteed since local judicial departments have to obey the orders of local governments.[25]

Indeed, the majority of urban credit co-operatives are actually illegal, as they are controlled by local governments below the prefecture level.[26]

It is this concern with local control over local financial institutions that led the PBC to undertake a major structural reform in August 1998. The central bank abolished its 49 provincial branches and replaced them with nine multi-provincial regional offices. The purpose of these reforms was to put an end to local government disturbance in monetary policies and financial supervision of the central bank and to set free state-owned commercial banks from the intervention of local government.[27] In a similar vein, the PBC announced in summer 2000 that each province would be allowed only one ITIC.[28] In addition to reducing sources of local financial autonomy, this move was also part of a wider attempt to deal with the technical insolvency of many of China's financial institutions. Whilst this is partly a result of imprudent lending decisions and misplaced gambles on foreign currency futures,[29] it is also in large part a result of the leadership's strategy of providing a soft landing on the transition from socialism.

Safety net socialism and financial reform

If the decentralisation of economic power is one defining characteristic of the Chinese reform process, a second is what we might call 'safety net socialism'. The leadership's desire for rapid economic growth has been tempered by a recognition that rapid growth can be as politically destabilising as no growth at all. The issue of decentralised control is also relevant here, in that the central authorities have faced constant pressure from representatives of those areas that have not developed as fast as the coastal areas. But the main emphasis in this section is on the perceived relationship between unemployment (particularly urban unemployment) and social stability.

Government debt and the subsidy cycle in the 1980s

In the initial period of reform, one of the major political tasks associated with reform was assuring key sectors that the new era would not harm their interests. Thus, for example, rather than liberalise grain production and supply, the government retained central pricing and allocation to ensure relatively equitable supplies of basic foodstuffs. With the price of other produce increasingly set by the market, the government essentially controlled incentives for grain production by increasing the procurement price. In most cases, an increase in the grain procurement price subsequently led to an increase in urban subsidies to offset the impact on urban purchasing power.

By the end of the 1980s, official Chinese figures showed that subsidies constituted almost a quarter of total central government expenditure. The political logic of reform was creating a subsidy cycle that was proving difficult to overcome. And while subsidies to maintain purchasing power were an important component of this subsidy cycle in the 1980s, debt to maintain employment became a characteristic of the 1990s.

It is difficult to overestimate the importance that the Chinese leadership attaches to maintaining employment. Particularly in urban centres, maintaining employment is seen as the prerequisite for the maintenance of social stability, and perhaps even the CCP's continued grip on power. Whilst not wishing simply to repeat the work of researchers such as Hu Angang here,[30] it is worth making a brief summary of China's employment statistics to reiterate why employment comes so high on the list of the leadership's concerns.

The PRC had a labour force in 2001 of roughly 718 million people – around a quarter of the world's total labour force and around one and a half times the combined workforce of all developed states. In the countryside, mechanisation and the replacement of collective socialist motivations with private and profit motivations resulted in the loss of an average of six million jobs a year in the 1990s, and it is widely accepted that around 120 million rural workers are without work for most of the year.[31]

One of the more notable consequences of this increased rural unemployment is the growth in migration – both state sanctioned and supported, and illegal. Not surprisingly, China's poorest provinces are the major sources of migrant workers.[32] Neither is it surprising that many have made their way to the cities in search of jobs – to the extent that people with rural household registrations accounted for 29.85 per cent of the new urban workforce in 1996. Rural unemployment is now very definitely an urban issue.

The extent of the unemployment problem in rural China is clearly significant. But for the purposes of this chapter, we need to turn our emphasis to the issue of urban unemployment. The official urban unemployment rate remains below

4 per cent. But these figures ignore laid-off (*xia gang*) workers – and workers can be laid off for up to three years before they count as officially unemployed. While urban unemployment increased by about 8 per cent per annum in the 1990s, the number of laid-off workers increased by around 40 per cent a year.

Thus while in 1993 laid-off workers accounted for around 3 per cent of the total urban payroll, the figure had risen to 8 per cent by 1996. Two thirds of these laid-off workers are from state-owned enterprises (SOEs), and, as with all things in contemporary China, there are large geographic variations. In essence, the old industrial bases have both the highest levels of unemployment and the highest levels of laid-off workers – 14.2 per cent of the payroll in Liaoning, 13.8 per cent in Heilongjiang, 11.2 per cent in Hunan and so on.[33]

Non-performing loans and institutional debt

We should also bear in mind that China does not have a national system of social security. China developed a system of workplace socialism after 1949, through which the *danwei* (work unit) in urban centres and the collective in the countryside provided health, education and welfare. Thus, the costs of maintaining employment can in some respects be considered to be disguised social welfare payment.

Throughout the reform period, the government has devoted a considerable amount of government spending on subsidies to keep loss-making enterprises in operation. Latterly, it has also relied on loans from the banks to serve the same function. As these loans are influenced by political considerations and often ordered by government officials, they can effectively be considered to be quasi-government spending – or as Wang, Liu and Liu term it, 'para-fiscal' investment.[34]

This understanding that loans constitute a form of government debt has important implications for how we consider the consequences of reform. From a political viewpoint, we return to the idea that financial systems are designed to serve specific purposes. Having created a state-owned working class through the plan, the CCP has acted to defend the interests of this class while the old system is dismantled – the interests of the state-owned working class have been privileged above the interests of other groups and classes. And the (mis)use of the financial system has been a key tool in achieving this objective.

From a technical economic viewpoint, we have to rethink the importance of debt. While the government debt balance as a percentage of GDP was only 8 per cent in 1997, the figure rises to 33.12 per cent if you include non-performing loans as part of the calculation.[35] Viewed as the price of ensuring social stability during a period of potentially destabilising economic reconstruction, this level of debt might be considered a price worth paying. But it is a process that cannot continue forever. As non-productive loans in support of political stability increased in the 1980s, then the ratio of bad loans to assets increased.[36] Returns on assets of China's specialised banks also dropped from around 1.4 per cent in 1986 to virtually nil by 1997.[37] And while the capital of state banks increased 1.88 times between 1987 and 1996, the balance of loans provided by state banks increased 5.25 times.[38]

It is difficult to come to an accurate assessment of the extent of bad loans in the four major state banks. The figures emanating from the PBC are widely re-garded as being politically constructed to present a positive confidence-building image, rather than being based on firm accounting. Furthermore, the official fig-ure of 25–30 per cent does not include the RMB 1.4 trillion of non-performing loans which had been transferred from the banks to the asset management companies by May 2002. So the real extent of non-performing loans in the big four banks in 2002 ranges somewhere from the official figure of 25 per cent, to the most pessimistic calculations of 50 per cent.[39] Perhaps it is best not to concentrate on finding the exact figure, and just accept Harding's as-sertion that 'China's banking system is insolvent: its bad debts exceed its capital.'[40]

Finding an effective solution to the debt crisis thus entails much more than technical reforms in the financial system. Rather, it entails a fundamental re-structuring of the Chinese economy and a fundamental change in the basis of communist party rule. The national leadership has to find new ways of creat-ing employment and providing social welfare, and has to accept and live with higher rates of unemployment. As reform of the financial system is inextricably linked with perceptions of the consequences of unemployment, processes of liberalisation and integration with the global economy are also brought into the equation.

The initial reforms of 1994, however, simply dealt with the symptoms, rather than the ailment itself. The banking reforms saw the four policy banks replaced as policy-based lenders by three policy banks.[41] The reforms highlight two key features of China's reform process. First, when new systems are introduced, they frequently, indeed typically, do not replace the old systems, but are grafted on top of (or alongside) the existing system. Thus, when the new policy-based banks were introduced, the four old specialised banks continued to operate, and retained responsibility for all their previous debts.

Second, despite repeated expressions of commitment to the independence of the banks (not least in the Central Bank Law and Commercial Bank Law, 1995), political interference remains a hallmark of lending decisions. Indeed, even the theoretical independence of the PBC is somewhat limited. Quite apart from the authority of Zhu Rongji over the bank whilst vice-premier in the mid-1990s, the PBC remains a government department under the State Council, and the

State Council is mandated to approve major policy initiatives. The autonomy of specialised commercial banks is also strictly limited.

The 1994 reforms, then, did nothing to deal with the existing bad debts of the new commercial banks, nor did they put an end to the extension of more bad debts in pursuit of political objectives. In an attempt partially to resolve the former, the government issued an unprecedented RMB 270 billion special treasury bonds on 18 August 1998 to replenish the capital of the four major state-owned banks.[42] The bonds allowed RMB 120 billion of bad loans to be written off, and were intended to keep capital adequacy at above 8 per cent for five to eight years. Another possible solution lies in the extension of 'debt to equity' initiatives. These initiatives simply convert some of the debt of selected SOEs and financial institutions into equities, which are then sold on to private and institutional investors. In the first instance, the equity is held and managed by four asset management companies established to help clear the debts of the four big commercial banks. But one of the problems with the scheme, according to the Bank of International Settlements, is that the initial capitalisation of RMB 10 billion each is too little for them to survive in the long run.[43] Furthermore, it is only really applicable to essentially healthy companies – those who took out loans before 1995 and whose deficits are 'mainly' a result of the burden of interest payments.[44] Thus, it is an attractive option for those that are basically sound, but does nothing for the hopeless cases. Indeed, the scheme is so attractive that it has given rise to intense lobbying from government organisations that want to help revenue-generating firms in their own sector. And as Zeng Paiyan argues, if the same political pressure that frequently led to the creation of bad debt in the first place is placed on the asset management companies, then 'the whole process will increase and not reduce financial risks and expenditures for the state'.[45]

Bad debts revisited: the politics of employment in the PRC

Again, these initiatives deal with some of the problems that are still affecting the solvency of state banks, but do not deal with the fundamental problem. Bad loans as a proportion of all loans remained high, and continued to increase. Effective reform is contingent on ending the strategy of using the banks as a means of subsidising employment in keeping with the party-state leadership's political goals.

In this respect, the most important reforms for the creation of a modern financial system are related to the position of SOEs within the Chinese economy – perhaps ultimately to the creation of a national social security system. As such, structural reforms, recapitalisation, debt-to-equity swaps and so on are all well and good, but rather ineffective without more fundamental changes, changes such as the announcement by Premier Zhu Rongji that politically directed lending would end in 1998, and Zhu's commitment to accelerating SOE reform.

The significance of SOEs cannot be underestimated for reform of the financial sector. In 1996 four major state-owned commercial banks held more than 90 per cent of all credit funds and extended 90 per cent of them to state-owned enterprises.[46] Even after the implementation of reforms at the end of 1998, SOEs still accounted for 63.5 per cent of all manufacturing assets, utilised 70 per cent of the national budget, and employed around 55 per cent of all urban workers. By the middle of 1999, the state-owned sector had an estimated US$200 billion worth of bad debts.[47]

The move towards final and fundamental SOE reform was tempered and at times put on hold as the leadership considered the social impact of rising urban unemployment. For example, when concerns over social instability resurfaced, new reactive policies were introduced to provide a temporary palliative. Indeed, rather than decrease, bank loans continued to grow.[48] This hesitation was partly a result of the delayed impact of the Asian financial crises on Chinese export growth noted in the introduction. Export growth had essentially been relied upon to provide the opportunity to deal with problems in the 'domestic' economy without jeopardising overall growth rates. It was a means of providing at least some new jobs to replace those being lost in the state sector. But falling demand in south-east Asia, South Korea and most importantly Japan, combined with increased competition from the south-east Asian states, undermined Chinese export growth in 1998.[49]

Opening to the global economy: external pressures for reform

The struggle to find a politically acceptable way of coping with unemployment provides the backdrop to an understanding of the relationship between the domestic and the external in financial reform. Viewed from within China (or by professional China watchers) there is a tendency to emphasise the relative openness of the Chinese economy. This is a valid view – China is relatively more open and liberalised than it was in the past. It is also arguable that the Chinese economy is more liberal than the South Korean or Japanese economies at similar stages of development.[50]

This gradual and partial liberalisation is clearly important and significant. On a very basic level, as China has re-engaged with the global economy, it has had to introduce mechanisms to facilitate international trade and inward investment. It has also developed policies in response to the demands of external actors, for example, to attract and retain (rather than just facilitate) investment. These responses take numerous forms – the city government in the southern city of Dongguan, for example, established a Taiwanese school in response to requests from the an association of Taiwanese businessmen who had invested in the city.[51]

Nevertheless, while China is much more open than it was before, liberalisation has been strictly limited: limited in terms of geographic areas,[52] of economic sectors, and in degrees of openness to the global economy. Indeed, in the financial sector, foreign actors are heavily restricted as to who can operate, where they can operate and how much they can do. In particular, the only partial and incremental process of opening resulted in a limited role for foreign capital. Strict capital controls, the lack of currency convertibility, and the underdeveloped nature of Chinese financial markets had helped to create a situation where 90 per cent of all foreign capital in China in 1999 was in the form of foreign direct investment (FDI) projects. And through a managed currency devaluation in 1994, the Chinese authorities massively increased the price competitiveness of exports compared with competing exports from the rest of Asia. The underdeveloped nature of Chinese capitalism allowed China to exploit its position as an 'even-later' developer and also provided a bulwark against the international economy when it was needed during the crises.[53]

Furthermore, in responding to the impact of the financial crises, the relatively closed nature of the economy gave the leadership a degree of autonomy and leeway in developing a response that was not available in other states. Witness, for example, the extent to which export tax rebates were used after 1997 as a means of promoting export growth.[54] Witness too the way in which the retention of capital and exchange controls allowed the Chinese authorities to reduce interest rates in an attempt to boost spending while maintaining the stability of the RMB.[55]

In the wake of the Asian financial crises, then, the strength of the arguments for further liberalisation seemed to have declined. Currency convertibility was delayed, export rebates increased, many institutions lost their rights to trade in foreign currency, and regulation and control of the stock exchanges were increased. As the Asian financial crises unfolded, and began to impact on China in 1998, then debates over liberalisation and globalisation were renewed.

In fact, the crises were interpreted in two different ways. For liberalisers like Zhu Rongji, the crises confirmed the need to overhaul China's financial institutions. China's financial institutions were far less stable than those of pre-crisis south-east Asian states, and it was essential to deal with this key and fundamental problem. For opponents, the crises undermined the examples of other developing states as models for China's development.[56] In addition, as strikes and demonstrations against the closure of factories and unpaid welfare benefits increased during 1998, the social and political environment appeared less conducive to economic reform than in 1997. Zhu's position, and the political profile of the liberalisers, was further weakened by the failure in spring 1999 of negotiations to broker a deal to join the WTO. Making considerable concessions to try and get a deal was bad enough for the sceptics – making considerable concessions and still coming back without a deal was even worse.

In the wake of this failure, Zhu's position as the key reformer came under threat. On a number of occasions, Western news sources ran stories about Zhu's impending resignation. As such, the deal signed with the US authorities in November 1999 that (eventually) paved the way for China's WTO entry marked a key political moment in China's post-Mao evolution. Here, a new alliance for reform seemed to appear – one in which the Chinese premier, Zhu Rongji, entered into an alliance with external actors and promoters of neo-liberalism in opposition to domestic Chinese forces for conservatism. The WTO deal was used by Zhu as a means of boosting the reform agenda. At the same time, the US representatives used the deal as a means of boosting Zhu within China, and promoting both him and the reform process at a time when domestic considerations seemed to be pulling China back (or at least, maintaining the status quo).

However, signing the agreement with the United States was not so much the end of the story as the start of a new chapter. China had to enter into bilateral negotiations with other WTO member states and groups of member states (most notably the EU), as well as with the WTO authorities in Geneva, which only concluded in September 2001, leading to China's formal entry at the Doha ministerial round in November. The delays were partly a consequence of the bilateral nature of negotiations, with US negotiators complaining that EU–China agreements sometimes contradicted agreements that had earlier emerged from US–China dialogue. But it was also a consequence of wariness of some in China's elites over the impact of membership on employment and social stability – leading to periodic backtracking or hesitancy on the Chinese side. The impact of the WTO deal on financial reform was and remains far from clear. This is not least because past experience suggests that new means of protecting chosen producers are likely to emerge once the WTO reforms have been implemented. However, in general terms, we can identify both direct and indirect implications for financial reform that were reflected in uncertainty within China over the short-term (at least) wisdom of joining.

In terms of the direct impact, the Standard Chartered Bank calculates that foreign banks in China can expect a 40 per cent annual growth in lending in China in the first decade after joining the WTO, with the four major commercial banks receiving the most competition.[57] The main indirect impact is on employment and in particular, employment in the state sector.[58] Indeed, a research report from the Chinese Academy of Social Sciences argued that 'structural unemployment may be China's chief adjustment cost for WTO accession'.[59]

Should the reforms be implemented in full, it seems likely that China's textile industry will gain through the phasing out of US import quotas. But these gains could be dwarfed by the losses in steel, automotive, chemical, machinery, computer and electronics industries. Notably, there is an expectation that industries where private ownership and (in particular) joint ventures dominate will benefit most, whereas those sectors where the residual state sector still dominates will be the main losers. In effect, there will be a move towards the desocialisation of the Chinese economy by other means, and a further transfer of economic power and political relationships and alliances.

For Pomfret, the reason for growing unease amongst the leadership over joining the WTO was simply that 'in March [2000], the price for corn on the Chicago futures exchange was less than $100 a ton. In China, the government-set price was more than $175'.[60] As such, WTO entry could lead to farmers losing considerable income as a result of increased agricultural imports. Given that social stability rather than financial prudence still seems to predominate in many lending considerations, it is possible (perhaps even likely) that as increased international competition leads to decreases in profits, the level of bad debts in China's financial institutions will increase.

Furthermore, though only potential, perceptions and fears are at least as important in shaping policy (and reactions) than concrete facts. There is already considerable social instability within China, and there is no political advantage in being wise after the fact. Even if there is an overall increase in jobs in the long run, there are still likely to be negative political consequences resulting from such factors as the time lag between losing and gaining jobs; uneven geographic, gender, age and sector balance between where the jobs are lost and created; and the issue of the type of jobs that are lost and created, and their associated welfare provisions.

Conclusions

When considering the international pressures on China to reform, it is tempting to concentrate on high profile and visible bilateral and multilateral negotiations. At the end of the process, we can (usually) see the details of the deal that has been hammered out and begin speculating on its implications (as I have done above). These negotiations, deals and treaties are clearly important. China is effectively negotiating re-engagement with an international system that has a set of rules and norms that it has had little part in shaping, and has for many years in large part opposed.

But there are many less overt channels of influence. International seminars of central bankers, research grants for Chinese officials and students to study abroad, the Temple University's legal training programme in China and so on all facilitate policy and ideational transfer from the West. So too do the contacts that Chinese banking representatives forge while working in overseas operations. And so too are simply the experiences of developmental states in east Asia. We have to take a holistic approach and analyse the political economy of contemporary China in total if we are truly to understand the nature of Chinese financial reform. And while much of the impulse to reform stemmed from internal pressures, rationales and thinking, the growth rates recorded in export-oriented developmental states in Asia also played their part in promoting a liberalisation agenda in China.

But the transfer from a politically to an economically based model of society remains incomplete. The old levers of state planning might have been dismantled, but elites, particularly at the local level, have used new economic instruments and institutions to fulfil many of the old functions of the planning system. Technical changes can be made to introduce a financial structure that appears to be market oriented and independent, but the way in which it actually functions depends on more than just technical changes. If financial reforms are to function as intended, they require a fundamental change – perhaps a paradigm shift – in the ideas and practices of key political actors.

This is not to say that what has happened in China is 'wrong'. Defending the interests of the working class is something that a ruling communist party should not be averse to doing. Indeed, the Chinese experiment has, by almost all criteria, been more successful than the shock therapy big bang away from socialism deployed elsewhere. Nevertheless, this has been achieved at a cost, and the Chinese leadership is now being forced to pay for its relative success in three ways – paying in financial terms in the guise of an insolvent banking system; paying in terms of increased obligations to, duties to and pressures from the international system; and paying in terms of the (delayed) growth in unemployment. While reforming the financial structure remains central to avoiding financial chaos, the success of these reforms are themselves dependent on wider change in political processes, strategies and practices – finally to learn to live without the Plan.

Notes

1. The collapse of south-east Asian currencies meant that exports from the crisis states were considerably cheaper on foreign markets after the crisis than they had been at the beginning of 1997.
2. *Zhongguo Jingying Bao*, 28 Nov. 2000.

3. Zhou Shaohua, 'Establishing a National Tax Reform System is Urgently Necessary for Continued Reform', *Shijie Jingji Daobao* (*World Economic Herald*) 24 Aug. 1987. Translated and reported in Publications Research Service, 3 Nov.

4. Gao Zhanjun and Liu Fei, 'The Closure of GITIC: Latent Financial Risks and Government Approach', *World Economy and China* vol. 7, no. 2 (1999), p. 55.

5. This concept refers to those workers employed in state-owned enterprises.

6. See, for example, W. Lam *The Era of Jiang Zemin* (Englewood Cliffs, NJ: Prentice Hall, 1999). Zheng refers to these processes as 'selective recentralisation'. Zheng Yongnian, 'Political Incrementalism: Political Lessons of China's 20 Years of Reform', *Third World Quarterly*, vol. 20, no. 6 (1999).

7. The failings of which had led to the decision to introduce economic reform in the first place. Li Peng 'Report on the Work of Government', 25 Mar. 1988 in The First Session of the Seventh National People's Congress of the People's Republic of China (Beijing: Foreign Languages Press, 1988) p. 17.

8. See, for example, Wang Huning, 'Zhongguo Bianhuazhong De Zhongyang He Difang Zhengfu De Guanxi: Zhengzhi De Hanyi (Ramifications of Changing Relationship Between Central and Local Government in China)', *Fudan Xuebao* (*Fudan University Journal*), 5; (1988) J. Tong, 'Fiscal Reform, Elite Turnover and Central Provincial Relations in Post Mao China', *The Australian Journal of Chinese Affairs*, no. 22 (1988); J. Unger, 'The Struggle to Dictate China's Administration: The Conflict of Branches Versus Areas Versus Reform', *The Australian Journal of Chinese Affairs*, no. 18 (1987); S. Breslin, *China in the 1980s: Centre–Local Relations in a Reforming Socialist State* (New York: St. Martin's Press, and Basingstoke: Macmillan, 1996).

9. N. Lardy, 'Centralization and Decentralization in China's Fiscal Management', *The China Quarterly*, no. 61 (1975), p. 57.

10. C. Wong (1991) 'Central–Local Relations in an Era of Fiscal Decline: The Paradox of Fiscal Decentralization in Post-Mao China', *The China Quarterly*, no. 128 (1991), p. 690.

11. Zheng, 'Political Incrementalism', pp. 1168–9.

12. The increase in the total revenue base is partly explained by previous lax tax collection and the deliberate under-reporting of local fiscal revenues to avoid making remittances to the central authorities.

13. *Xinhua Daily Bulletin*, 11 Jan. 2000.

14. Gao Peiyong, 'Further Improving China's Financial and Taxation System', *World Economy and China* vol. 7, no. 2 (1999), p. 41.

15. This move coincided with the extension of managerial responsibility in urban industrial sectors, which included lifting ceilings on staff wages and bonuses. As with the banking reforms, the amount of money allocated for wages in 1985 was based on the size of the 1984 wage bill and according to You 'Many enterprises, as a matter of urgency, distributed extra money to the workers'. You Ji, 'Zhao Ziyang and the Politics of Inflation', *The Australian Journal of Chinese Affairs*, no 25 (1991).

16. Huang Da (1985) 'Guanyu Kongzhi Huobi Gongjiliang Wenti de Tantao (Probe into the Problem on Money Issue Control)', *Caimao Jingji* (*Finance and Trade Economics*), no. 7 (1985), pp. 1–8.

17. Zhu Li, 'Zijin Fengpei de Zhuyao Gaibian (Major Changes in the Distribution of Funds in China)' *Jingji Guanli* (*Economic Review*), no. 9, (1987).
18. We should exercise care in assuming that there is a single local interest at work in each local authority. Duckett's investigation of Tianjin Municipality, for example, found that different departments within the local government were following their own independent policies which entailed independent strategies for raising capital. See J. Duckett, *The Entrepreneurial State in China* (London: Routledge, 1998).
19. For the earliest Chinese definition that I have come across, see Shen Liren and Tai Yuanchen, 'Woguo "Zhuhou Jingji" De Xingcheng Ji Chi Biduan He Genyuan (The Creation, Origins and Failings of "Dukedom Economies" in China)', *Jingji Yanjiu* (*Economic Research*), no. 3, 1990.
20. Xie Ping, 'Financial Reform in China: Review and Future Challenges', *World Economy and China*, vol. 7, no. 5 (1999), pp. 4–5.
21. Gao Zhanjun and Liu Fei, 'The Closure of GITIC', p. 53.
22. China's Rural Credit Cooperative Loans Rise', *People's Daily*, 5 February 2002. The RMB – renminbi – is the formal name of the Chinese currency, while the yuan is the denomination of the currency; the equivalent of sterling and pound. One US dollar is roughly equivalent to RMB 8.3.
23. *China Business Weekly*, 17 September 2000.
24. 'Refinancing Increased to Support Agricultural Production', *People's Daily*, 14 March 2001.
25. Xie Ping, 'Financial Reform in China', p. 13.
26. The prefecture is the intermediate level of local government between a province and a county. *Zhongguo Jingying Bao*, 28 Nov. 2000.
27. Xie Ping, 'Financial Reform in China', p. 4.
28. The decision was made in January 2000, but not formally announced until August. See *Commercial Daily* (Hong Kong), 9 Aug. 2000.
29. The Everbright Trust, China's second largest ITIC, was closed in August 2000 with huge losses that stemmed from disastrous investments in foreign currency futures in 1995. See *Hexun Caijing* (*Homeway Financial News*), 1 Aug. 2000.
30. Unless otherwise cited, the following employment statistics are all taken from Hu Angang, 'Employment and Development: China's Employment Problem and Employment Strategy', *World Economy and China*, nos. 3–4 (1999).
31. There are considerable regional variations – largely caused by the still very labour-intensive rice planting and harvesting periods.
32. For example, in Gansu, over 21 per cent of registered peasants working elsewhere; 20.6 per cent in Ningxia; 18.4 per cent in Sichuan; 18 per cent in Anhui and so on.
33. The major difference here is that the unemployed are the younger generation, while the older generation dominate the 'laid-off' category.
34. Wang Luolin, Liu Shucheng and Liu Rongcang, 'An Opportunity to Raise the Ultimate Consumption Rate while Restarting the Economy', *World Economy and China*, vol. 7, no. 3 (1999), p. 6.
35. Yu Yongding, 'China's Macroeconomic Situation and Future Prospect', *World Economy and China*, vol. 7, no. 2 (1999). And even these figures don't give the

full extent of the problem, as those non-performing loans that will not be paid off, but which aren't yet due, are not counted as bad loans. See Wang Dayong '270 Billion Special T-Bonds: What For', *ibid.*, p. 35.

36. Non-performing loans accounted for 20 per cent of the assets of Chinese banks in 1996. World Bank, *The Chinese Economy: Fighting Inflation, Deepening Reform* (Washington, DC: World Bank, 1997).
37. N. Lardy, *China's Unfinished Economic Revolution* (Washington, DC: Brookings, 1998) p. 100.
38. Wang Dayong, '270 Billion Special T-Bonds'.
39. For a pessimistic view, see G. Chang, 'China's banks on edge of disaster' *Taipei Times*, 21 March 2002; and G. Chang, *The Coming Collapse of China* (New York: Random House, 2001).
40. J. Harding, 'Jitters in Beijing', *Financial Times*, 10 Nov., 1997, p. 3.
41. These three policy banks are the State Development Bank of China, the Agricultural Development Bank, and the Import–Export Bank.
42. The bonds are for thirty years, are tradable and carry a 7.2 per cent annual interest rate.
43. All four received the same amount irrespective of the extent of bad debts in their area. See *China News Digest*, 7 Nov. 1999.
44. The idea was first put into practice on a large scale after the default of the China Everbright Trust and Investment Corporation in October 1996. The problem here was that as Everbright was not making any money, so those who took up the equity soon faced financial losses. Everbright was subsequently suspended for two years, and finally closed in 2000. Xie Ping, 'Financial Reform in China', pp. 11–13.
45. Zeng was Chairman of the State Development Planning Commission. See *China News Digest*, 7 Nov. 1999.
46. Gao Zhanjun and Liu Fei, 'The Closure of GITIC', p. 54.
47. *Hexun Caijing*, 30 Aug. 1999.
48. At the end of August 1999, the balance of loans in China's financial institutions had increased by almost 14 per cent year on year to RMB 9.2 trillion (US$1.11 trillion), with the value of new loans from January to August RMB 571.3 billion (US$69.1 billion). *Zhengquan Shibao*, 13 Sep. 1999.
49. Export growth for the year was 0.5 per cent in nominal terms – a decline of around 1 per cent in real terms. See S. Breslin, 'The Politics of Chinese Trade and the Asian Financial Crises: Questioning the Wisdom of Export Led Growth', *Third World Quarterly*, vol. 20, no. 6 (1999).
50. See, for example, 'China: World Trade Ordeal', *The Economist*, 4 Nov. 1995.
51. Katsuhiro Sasuga, (2002) 'Microregionalization Across Southern China, Hong Kong And Taiwan' in Shaun Breslin and Glen Hook (eds.), *Microregionalism and World Order* (Basingstoke: Macmillan, 2002).
52. Even though virtually all of China has now been formally opened to the global economy, international economic relations remain dominated by nine coastal provinces. These provinces account for over 85 per cent of all exports and around 80 per cent of all foreign direct investment.

53. We should also bear in mind that the relatively closed nature of the Chinese economy has also facilitated the maintenance of employment in SOEs, where increased
international competition could be fatal.

54. To the extent that China was accused of implementing a fiscal devaluation.

55. Despite the existence of these controls, Chinese academics and policy makers
are aware that China cannot make policy in isolation and simply ignore comparative real exchange rates. In particular, interest rate adjustments are unofficially
'pegged' above the US rate to prevent the sort of illegal capital flight that saw
US$20–40 million leaving China in 1998. As credit is now so cheap within China,
the fear is that illegal capital flight would see institutions borrowing money in China
and simply depositing it in overseas banks.

56. And in particular, proposals to build SOE reform on the model of the South Korean
chaebols lost much of its appeal.

57. *China News Digest*, 2 Jan. 2000. However, representatives of foreign financial institutions attempting to begin operations in China are much less optimistic. They fully
expect new barriers to be put in the way of foreign interests – with one expecting
to wait a further ten years after China joins the WTO before foreign institutions can
effectively compete with Chinese financial institutions.

58. It is notable that as the news of the WTO deal broke in Hong Kong, the Hang Seng
index surged by 127 points, and closed at a two-year high. However, the shares of
key mainland-related companies – the so-called 'red chip index' – fell by 2.8 per
cent. The high-profile Legend Holdings dropped 14.4 per cent as investors perceived
the company to be hurt by a price war from multinational computer firms. *China
News Digest*, 18 Nov. 1999.

59. Yu Yongding, Zheng Bingwen and Song Hong (eds.), *Zhongguo 'RuShi' Yanjiu
Baogu: Jinru WTO de Zhongguo Chanye* (*Research Report on China's Entry into
WTO: The Analysis of China's Industries*) (Beijing: Social Sciences Documentation
Publishers, 2000), pp. 1–2.

60. J. Pomfret, 'China's Poor Fear Cost of Free Trade', *Washington Post Foreign Service*,
24 Sep. 2000, p. A01.

11 The Asian financial crisis and Japanese policy reactions

MASAYUKI TADOKORO

Robert Rubin, the US Treasury Secretary, was reported to have bluntly criticised Japan for lacking a sense of urgency after his meeting with Kiichi Miyazawa, the Japanese Finance Minister, in September 1998.[1] In fact, the US–Japan dialogue on economic issues was highly acrimonious in early 1998, and American media were fraught with comments that ridiculed Japanese economic policy. In essence, they grumbled that the Japanese government was pursuing fiscal retrenchment and did nothing to rescue troubled banks, while the Japanese economy came under deflationary pressure and neighbouring countries were in the thick of the financial crisis. In view of the fact that the same media had, just four to five years before, described Japan as an invincible economic giant that even threatened the American economic supremacy, it is hard to believe that they were referring to the same economy.

In fact, the Japanese government was far from inactive during the Asian crisis. It made the largest financial contribution, organised a rescue package and even proposed a new regional mechanism for financial co-operation. Thus, it was surprising the United States, which was even unwilling to appropriate money for IMF resources through a quota increase, should criticise Japan. But Japan's international efforts were hampered by its poor economic performance. It had its own financial crisis at home, and was thus unable to help the crisis-stricken economies by absorbing more of their exports. It was well known that the Japanese financial system became increasingly fragile under the heavy load of bad loans. In autumn 1997 financial problems culminated in the collapse of two major banks.

This chapter attempts to examine how domestic constraints in Japan and changing Japanese–US relations affected Japanese responses to the Asian financial crisis. The major argument to be developed is that domestic financial difficulties, institutional rigidities and weak leadership limited the ability of the Japanese government to respond effectively to the crisis and to co-operate with its American counterpart to contain the tremors as they rippled across the Asian region. Equally, the same set of economic and political impediments also prevented Japan from playing a leading role in establishing regional mecha-nisms for policy co-ordination and crisis management, despite the heightened need for such mechanisms in the wake of the Asian crisis.

Initial rescue attempts under the IMF

The onset of the Asian financial crisis was early July 1997, when currency speculators battered the Thai baht into a drastic 18 per cent depreciation. It was widely known among experts that the Thai currency, which had been under attack during the first half of 1997, was overvalued. The decision to devalue the baht was thus regarded as an appropriate measure. However, the depreciation wrecked the balance sheets of Thai financial institutions, because they had enormous dollar-denominated external liabilities. Thai authorities requested financial assistance from Japan, and a Japanese mission was sent to Bangkok on 9–11 July to discuss the issue. Shortly afterwards, the Thai Finance Minister also visited Tokyo to seek financial assistance from his Japanese counterpart.[2]

The Japanese, however, declined the Thai request on the grounds that the Thais had disclosed insufficient information. At the same time, Japan was re-luctant to push for greater policy transparency in Thailand. Tokyo, therefore, thought that it would be better to deal with the matter within the policy frame-work to be established by the IMF so that it could play the tough guy.[3] The Thai government thus had no choice but to request assistance from the IMF, despite the harsh conditions attached.

The Japanese government, however, did play an active role in organising rescue packages. In an international conference held in Tokyo, Japan took the initiative in designing the rescue package totalling US$17 billion, and requested Asian participants to make as large a commitment as possible. Japan itself pledged $4 billion, by then the largest bilateral commitment, and other Asian countries, including Australia, promised to provide another $7 billion. However, the United States, which was present at the conference, did not make any money available.[4] Since this was the first major intra-Asian economic co-operation, it was then regarded as a successful Japanese diplomatic effort to strengthen regional co-operative mechanisms for financial management.

Japanese international monetary diplomacy, however, experienced a painful setback at the IMF annual meeting in Hong Kong in September 1997. Japan proposed to set up an Asian Monetary Fund (AMF) to help the crisis economies in the region. The proposal was strongly supported by the ASEAN countries but was vehemently opposed by the United States. It was partly because the regional fund would lessen the influence of the IMF, which was seen as effec-tively under American control, and partly because the United States was not prepared to let Japan take an initiative on this matter. In fact, the AMF proposal was first disclosed to the Americans during an OECD meeting in Paris in early September. The United States, represented by Larry Summers, then under secretary of the Treasury, did not express any objection to the idea, assuming that it would also be a member of the fund. Summers, however, became furious when he learned that the United States had been excluded from the proposed AMF. He called Eisuke Sakakibara, the Japanese vice finance minister in charge of international monetary affairs, at his home in the middle of the night on 14 September, saying 'I thought we were friends.'[5]

In the end, the United States effectively blocked the Japanese proposal for a regional monetary fund, and the Japanese were not prepared to go ahead without American blessing. In addition, China, which was suspicious about Japan's role in the region, did not support the proposal. As a face-saving measure, the United States allowed Asian countries to set up the so-called Manila framework. Although the framework was supposed to discuss monetary and financial cooperation among its members, it did not have any staff or financial resources. The framework, therefore, could not possibly be expected to be a meaningful mechanism for policy surveillance. The United States thus effectively dictated the course of events through its weighty position in the IMF.

Despite the international efforts to contain the financial crisis in Thailand, it rapidly spread to Indonesia in November and to South Korea in December. At the same time most ASEAN countries also came under increasing pressure to devalue their currencies. Indonesia and South Korea agreed to multi-billion-dollar lending programmes mandated by the IMF, to which Japan was again the largest bilateral financial contributor. Despite Japan's financial contribution, the IMF was structurally a US-dominated institution, and Japan did not have a big say in the contents of the rescue programmes. Japan's approach to the resolution of financial problems in the crisis economies was softer that that of the IMF, which pushed for structural reforms in line with the so-called Washington consensus. The Japanese approach was underlain by the fact that east Asia was of critical importance to its international security and political interests.

While Japan recognised that there was a need for structural reforms in the crisis economies, it also insisted that the priority should be to stabilise these economies by providing them with liquidity. On the other hand, both the IMF and the Americans emphasised the need for structural reforms, and obviously saw the financial crisis as a good opportunity to transform the policies and institutions of 'crony capitalism' in Asia. Nowhere were these differences more clearly demonstrated than in policy debates on the rescue package for Indonesia. A Japanese mission that visited Jakarta in October 1997 had a heated debate with an IMF team that supported major reforms in Indonesia. The IMF position was supported by US-educated technocrats within the Indonesian government, who saw structural reforms as the key to the resolution of various problems in the Indonesian economy. Japan eventually had to yield to pressure from the IMF and the United States, agreeing to the IMF rescue package that mandated sweeping reforms, including the cancellation of major national projects connected with the Soeharto family.[6]

The IMF and the United States also largely dictated the terms of the South Korean rescue package. The South Korean government first approached Japan for bilateral financial assistance in November 1997.[7] But it also referred the matter to, and eventually signed a standby agreement with, the IMF on 3 December. The IMF package, however, failed to restore market confidence. Moreover, South Korea was in the midst of a presidential election. Kim Dae Jung, one of the presidential candidates, called for renegotiation of the agreement with the IMF, further depressing market sentiment. South Korea, a member of the OECD and the eleventh largest economy in the world, was now on the verge of default. Japanese authorities attempted to persuade private bankers to maintain their credit lines with South Korea. Japan also provided South Korea with bridging loans until IMF rescue funds were actually disbursed.

Japan's failure in domestic economic management

While the three IMF packages were being implemented, and both Thailand and South Korea were going through painful structural adjustments, the financial crisis in Indonesia evolved into a major political crisis. It is now widely recognised that the IMF made major mistakes in Indonesia, at least at the initial stage of its reform programme. It decided to close sixteen banks without making any efforts to establish an effective safety net. This caused a financial panic that in the end completely destroyed the Indonesian financial system. Besides, Soeharto did not fully comply with the conditions of the IMF rescue packages, particularly with regard to the liquidation of his family businesses.

When Soeharto's resistance to the IMF-imposed reform became clear with his expansionary budget and his attempt to introduce a currency board, the Americans increased their pressure on him, demanding full compliance with the IMF programme and sending Larry Summers and Stanley Fisher to Jakarta in January 1998. In co-ordination with the IMF, Japanese Prime Minister Hashimoto also sent a mission to Jakarta. While the Japanese mission persuaded Soeharto to comply with the IMF demands, it also tried to modify those demands in a way that would be more acceptable to Indonesia. For the same purpose, Hashimoto himself visited Jakarta in March to meet with Soeharto, who was furious with the implicit American demand for his resignation. In the meantime, the economic disorder and sociopolitical unrest in

Indonesia continued. In May, large-scale violence against the ethnic Chinese took place in many cities. In the circumstances, Soeharto finally resigned on 21 May.

As initial efforts to control the crisis through IMF rescues did not work as had been expected, Japan came increasingly under harsh criticism, mainly from the United States. The criticism was directed primarily towards Japan's sluggish domestic economic performance and the weakening yen. Japanese macroeconomic policy was in fact still somewhat contractionary. The economic difficulties and the policy stance can be understood only in a larger context of political and economic developments in Japan during the 1990s.

Japan's problems represented the lingering effects of the slow-moving deflation of the asset bubble of the late 1980s. The Japanese government implemented several stimulus packages, and in 1995–6 Japan actually recorded the highest growth among the G-7 countries. This convinced Japanese policy makers that the Japanese economy was now back on the regular growth orbit. In retrospect, it was obviously a misjudgement. Once the fiscal stimulus was lifted, the Japanese economy started to slow down.[8] But deficit spending policies left the Japanese government with large public debts, particularly in comparison with those of the other G-7 countries.

During the 1990s the government also failed to solve the bad loan problem in an effective manner. The burst of the asset bubble in the early 1990s inflicted heavy damages on Japanese financial institutions, which saw their asset positions and balance sheets deteriorate rapidly. At the same time the heavily regulated Japanese financial system, which had provided financial institutions with protection against bankruptcy ever since the 1920s, was being liberalised, putting extra pressures on the ailing banking sector. Several attempts to strengthen the banking system through capital infusion by financial authorities were all unsatisfactory. Injecting public money into private banks was not a popular policy in Japan, as in any other country. Several factors contributed to the difficulty of resolving the problem promptly.

In the first place, banks, which often extended loans recklessly, were regarded as major culprits for having created the asset bubble. They were also rightly perceived to be enjoying protection by the Ministry of Finance (MOF), which helped them to secure oligopolistic profits. Bailing troubled banks out with public money was thus unacceptable to the general public, who also suffered heavy losses in their financial assets and had to deal with the problem under competitive conditions. Furthermore, the authorities' attempt to rescue ailing banks upset the public. The authorities had in fact decided as early as 1995 to use public money when liquidating insolvent housing loan companies whose shares were held by major banks. The decision to assist creditors of these companies with public money was questionable, since they did not collect deposits from the general public. In fact, the rescue was believed to have largely helped the banking arms of the politically powerful agricultural co-operatives that provided enormous funds to the loan companies. It was not surprising that the rescue efforts were highly unpopular and invited strong public criticisms. Using public money to rescue ailing banks then became the political nettle that nobody wanted to grasp again. Thus it was politically difficult to resolve the bad loan problem quickly, which only served to aggravate the problem. With the problem remaining unsolved, the MOF tried to strengthen the banks' balances gradually by helping them to secure profits to write off their bad loans and encouraging mergers to save weaker banks. Thus Japan's fragile financial system was wreaking havoc on its economy when the financial crisis hit Asia.

What also complicated official efforts to tackle structural problems in the Japanese economy were considerable changes in political leadership during the 1990s. In 1993, as a result of the general election defeat of the Liberal Democratic Party (LDP), Morihiro Hosokawa became the first non-LDP prime minister since the LDP was founded in 1955. One of the direct causes of the defeat was a scandal which involved bureaucratic elites, including MOF officials. The bureaucracy, which was regarded, rightly or wrongly, as the manager of the Japanese economic system, lost credibility with the general public because of its corrupt relations with the private sector which it supervised and its failure to lead the economy out of the protracted recession. Hosokawa's policy agenda focused on populist reform, which among other things aimed at reducing bureaucratic power. He also pushed for political and economic deregulation and decentralisation in Japan, which made him highly popular as a reformer both at home and abroad.

Strong public aversion to the bureaucracy continued beyond the Hosokawa cabinet. When Ryutaro Hashimoto came to power in January 1996, he announced that he would take strong measures to resolve the structural problems. Hashimoto also launched a major administrative reform and pledged to cut public spending to create a smaller government. The MOF naturally became a major target for administrative reform, and a proposal to split the ministry into two entities (financial and budgetary) was seriously discussed. Due to the MOF's strong resistance to the proposal, however, it lost only its authority over bank supervision.[9] Hashimoto also stressed the need for a budgetary reform. Assuming that the economy was now back on track, the government took a series of measures to balance its budgets, an effort that was inevitably deflationary. It actually called fiscal 1997 (which started in April) the 'first year for reconstructing a sound budget (*zaiseisaiken gannen*)', and planned to make deep cuts in expenditure in such sensitive areas as public works and overseas development assistance. Hashimoto increased the consumption tax in April 1997, and to demonstrate his strong resolve to reduce the budget deficit, introduced a new piece of legislation which would commit the government to contain the deficit within a certain limit. The legislation was passed by the Diet in November 1997, when the financial crisis was spreading rapidly across much of east Asia.

Believing that the Japanese economy had returned to normal and the bad loan problem had passed its worst, the Hashimoto government launched an ambitious programme for financial deregulation in June 1997. The following autumn, two major Japanese banks lurched to bankruptcy in the thick of the Asian crisis. Had this happened previously, the MOF would have bailed out the insolvent banks. With public opposition to official bail-outs becoming increasingly strong and the power of the MOF being weakened, however, the two banks were left to succumb to market forces. Although this episode was not directly related to the Asian crisis, the bank failure in Japan caused widespread concern in international financial markets.

It would be wrong, however, to attribute misjudgement and policy failure to a small number of political and bureaucratic elites. In fact, the Japanese intellectual mood of the 1990s, which had been influenced by neo-liberalism for a decade, was in favour of deregulation and liberalisation. Also, in the process of significant political changes in the wake of the LDP's defeat in the early 1990s and the ensuing reorganisation of political parties, administrative and political reforms along market-oriented lines became part of the orthodoxy of both the Hosokawa and Hashimoto cabinets. In addition, many influential economists in Japan also supported neo-classical reform. Some even argued that the reform did not go far enough. In 1997 a consensus emerged among policy makers and academia alike that the priority was structural reform rather than economic expansion.

Thus policies adopted by the Japanese government following the financial bubble in the 1990s did not contribute to economic growth. While the Japanese were preoccupied with political reforms, the bad loan problem remained largely unsolved under successive weak governments. When Hashimoto came to power, however, he made major efforts at structural reforms, which inevitably had a contractionary and somewhat destabilising impact on the economy. The move embodied a strange mixture of popular suspicions about public spending and the bureaucracy that controlled it, fiscal conservatism that emphasised budget cuts and intellectual thinking in favour of neo-classical reforms. In addition, despite the long-drawn-out recession, the Japanese economy did not reach crisis point, there being no social unrest and no general fall in living standards. The Japanese obviously had no reason to panic. Under such circumstances the government's priority was reform rather than expansion or stabilisation. Even after the government realised its policy mistakes, the prime minister was unable to change the course of economic policy in a timely manner, mainly because of the institutional rigidity of the budgeting process in Japan, which was partly attributable to Hashimoto's efforts to reduce budget deficits.

From reform to stabilisation

The US approach to the management of the Asian financial crisis through the IMF had its weaknesses. As the IMF was constantly called on to provide large-scale rescue funds, this caused a severe drain on its resources. Although the member countries of the IMF agreed to a quota increase, the US administration failed to persuade Congress to appropriate funds for the American contribution. While the Americans were busy preaching the virtues of the IMF programme and even blocked the regional efforts to manage the crisis, they themselves could not contribute to an increase in IMF resources. Moreover, the IMF programme did not work well. It was in this context that Japan increasingly became the target for American criticism. Because of the depreciating yen, weak economic conditions and failure to change domestic policies, Japan was blamed for having contributed to the worsening of the crisis.

But the Japanese perceived the situation differently. Japan, after all, was the largest contributor to all the rescue packages. The United States did not even contribute to a quota increase; it also blocked the Japanese initiative in establishing an AMF. At the same time, however, it wanted to dictate how Asian economies should be run without paying for its hegemony. Given these facts, it did not seem fair, in the eyes of Japanese policy makers, to blame Japan for the failure of the IMF programme. Thus, the increasingly vocal criticisms by the Americans deeply frustrated the Japanese.[10]

US President Clinton's visit to China in June 1998 represented the lowest point of US–Japanese relations during this period. The two countries had been working hard to strengthen their security ties since 1996, partly in response to an increasingly assertive China. A new defence guideline agreed upon between the two governments in 1997 was expected to encourage Japan to play a larger military role despite strong reactions from China. But now Clinton was in Beijing, praising the Chinese for not devaluing their currency while criticising, together with Chinese leaders, Japanese economic policy.

The diplomatic and political climate changed quite unexpectedly over summer 1998, however. First, Hashimoto stepped down as a result of the defeat of his party in the election to the upper house of the Diet in July 1998, and Keizo Obuchi succeeded him. The new prime minister appointed, quite unusually, a former prime minister, Kiichi Miyazawa, as finance minister. The appointment was widely interpreted to demonstrate Obuchi's determination to give first priority to economic recovery. He quickly froze the Budget Structure Reform Law and reoriented macroeconomic policy towards expansion. He also skilfully worked out a scheme to infuse public money into the troubled banking sector, despite strong public opposition.

Second, the financial crisis now seemed to spread beyond Asia as Russia practically defaulted on its international debts in August 1998. The Americans and Europeans treated Russia highly favourably in their efforts to facilitate its transfer to a market economy. The IMF was deeply involved in the formulation of structural reforms in Russia. In a sense, Russia set an example to other transitional economies in the process of neo-liberal reforms. It often contrasted with the Asian emerging economies, where political democratisation lagged behind economic liberalisation, a source of corruption and policy failure that was believed to have eventually led to the financial crisis. Such reasoning now sounded less persuasive after the financial crisis also hit Russia. As the crisis moved rapidly from regional disturbance to global threat, the argument that attributed the crisis to Asian cronyism or Japanese economic problems began to lose force.

Third, the financial turmoil spread even further, to Brazil. If a major financial crisis took place in Latin America, a powerful negative impact on the US economy would be unavoidable. For the Americans, the financial disorder now became their own problem rather than only that of the other countries with different models of capitalist development.

Furthermore, the serious financial difficulties of a major US hedge fund, the Long Term Capital Management (LTCM), surfaced in September 1998. Without any delay, American authorities came to the LTCM's assistance with the help of major financial institutions in Wall Street, rather than let it go bankrupt. The Americans might have had good reason for the bail-out, but it was perceived as strange by those countries that had been subjected to aggressive speculative attacks by hedge funds. While the Americans imposed painful reforms on the victims of speculative attacks, they lost no time in rescuing a hedge fund when it was in trouble. It was clear that the Americans rapidly shifted away from their efforts at the reform of 'crony capitalism' in line with the Washington consensus when the global financial disorder threatened the US stock market boom and the stability of the US economy.

Finally, while the Japanese economy did not show any rapid improvement, the yen started to appreciate at the same time as the LTCM crisis broke out. Some argued that this was caused by heavy purchases of the yen by hedge funds to repay low-interest yen-denominated funds following the LTCM crisis. Whatever the direct causes, the appreciation of the yen appeared to weaken the grounds for American criticism of the alleged Japanese manipulation of exchange rates.

It is in this context that a new Japanese proposal, the New Miyazawa initiative, was tabled for discussion during the annual meeting of the IMF and the World Bank in October 1998. The proposal aimed at setting up a regional scheme for financial assistance totalling $30 billion. Since the New Miyazawa initiative was basically a package of bilateral assistance from Japan mainly in the form of loans and credit guarantees, it differed from the aborted AMF proposal a year earlier. But this would be a regional mechanism led by Japan.

The United States, in sharp contrast to its attitude towards the AMF, warmly welcomed the new Japanese proposal. The American endorsement of the Japanese proposal seemed to be a quid pro quo for Japanese support for a new short-term facility established within the IMF to bail out Latin American countries. With a financial crisis looming large in Latin America, the US Congress also finally agreed on the appropriation of $18 billion for an IMF capital increase.[11] The new Japanese initiative appeared to have fitted well with shifts in American policy, which gave priority to stabilisation by providing public credit lines rather than imposing market disciplines on troubled countries.

A new start for regionalism in Asia?

It is obvious that Japan has a strong interest in maintaining stable relations with its neighbours. Since it is restrained both internally and externally from playing an active regional role in the military–strategic field, its efforts to create favourable regional environments are primarily focused on the economic realm. In addition, regional monetary co-operation is a step further towards the institutionalisation of Asian international relations, which would contribute to the stability of the region. An active foreign policy in Asia with regard to regional co-operation is thus an important policy goal for Japan that enjoys, unlike the official bail-outs of private banks, strong public support. As a major industrial economy, Japan's attention regarding international monetary diplomacy has long been concentrated on relations with the United States and European countries. The primary frameworks of Japanese international monetary co-operation were global institutions, such as the G-7 and the OECD, in which Japan could be easily isolated because of its non-Western identity and the lack of regional partners and groups with which to work.

With the impressive regional economic growth in the 1990s, however, Japanese monetary diplomacy attached more importance to Asia. Also, as economic globalisation went on there was a greater need for regionalism to cushion sometimes destructive and volatile global economic effects through co-operation among parties with closer relations and shared interests. Japanese policy makers, therefore, gradually intensified their efforts at organising macroeconomic and monetary co-operation in the region. The Bank of Japan, for example, strengthened its Asian monetary diplomacy by creating a new post of a board member who is exclusively responsible for Asia. It also played an active role in increasing the level of co-operation in the region by setting up swap networks, discussing settlement systems and launching technical assistance programmes among Asian countries.[12]

The co-operative trend within the financial circle also functioned at a higher political level as a result of the Asian crisis. The lesson that the Japanese learned from the bitter experiences of the Asian crisis was that stronger regional co-operative mechanisms were needed. Thus, regional monetary diplomacy became an agenda attracting strong commitment from political elites in Japan. For example, the prime minister sent a high-ranking mission led by the chief executive officer of Toyota to visit six Asian countries in August and September 1999. In its report submitted to the government in November 1999, the mission recommended a variety of measures ranging from human development to cultural exchange programmes. It also stressed the need for the internationalisation of the yen and for stronger regional monetary co-operation within the framework of 'ASEAN plus three' (namely China, Japan and South Korea). Thus the Asian crisis worked as a catalyst for more active Japanese regional monetary diplomacy by making the Japanese understand how closely the contemporary Japanese economy was tied to Asia and how humiliating it was to be dictated to by the United States through the IMF.

Japan's efforts to play a larger role in regional economic co-operation would be futile unless Asians welcomed such a role. In fact, the Asian crisis seems to have created an Asian pull for Japan's active role. While slow economic growth and the delayed shift in Japan's macroeconomic policy disappointed Asian countries, at the end of the day it would be only Japan that could provide the liquidity necessary to stabilise the regional economy in case of emergency. After all, Japan represents two thirds of total Asian GNP, and its economic strength is of critical importance for Asian countries. The New Miyazawa initiative proved to be quite popular among Asian countries. Setting up a regional fund like the aborted AMF also became a popular idea in the region. Support for it was certainly not limited to Malaysia and other ASEAN countries. Even South Korea, which had been highly suspicious of Japan's larger role in the region, surprised the Japanese by proposing a huge regional fund.[13] It also welcomed the internationalisation of the yen.[14] Under the Kim Dae Jung government, there have even been talks about the conclusion of a free trade agreement between the two countries.[15] China, which did not support Japan's proposal for the AMF, changed its position and agreed to 'strengthen self-help and assistance mechanisms in East Asia through the framework of ASEAN plus three'.[16]

These moves largely reflected Asian disillusionment with the United States and the IMF. While a robust Asian economic recovery in 1999 was very much helped by the strong American economy, American policy that imposed structural reforms left bitter memories in the minds of Asian leaders. While most countries in the region have realised that Asia needs more transparent financial systems and more effective supervisory mechanisms, many at the same time see the global financial market as too volatile and too harsh for emerging market economies. Besides, the Americans were seen to be taking advantage of Asian problems by extracting trade concessions from Asian countries through IMF conditionality and by buying Asian assets at depressed prices. Rightly or wrongly, the global financial system dominated by the United States never looked favourable to Asians. American policy during the crisis did not make the Americans look like a reliable friend, and Asians are prepared to accept alternative sources of financial assistance, and possibly leadership, to balance overwhelming American influence.

Asian regionalism was also stimulated by developments in Europe as well. There was a sharp contrast between Europe, which introduced the euro in 1999, and Asia, which made limited progress in regional economic co-operation. Asians tend to look to Europe as a model for solving their financial problems. All these factors – Asian pull, American push and Japanese willingness to play a larger role – have created a momentum for closer monetary co-operation in Asia. While the AMF was blocked, Asian regional monetary co-operation has seen noticeable developments. The New Miyazawa initiative, which consisted of a series of bilateral financial assistance packages to the countries badly hit by the financial crisis, was successfully implemented. Swap networks among Asian central banks were also broadened substantially.

There has also been momentum for a larger regional role for the yen. Japan is the second largest economy in the world, representing as much as 14 per cent of world GNP, and is the world's largest creditor. It is the world's largest official development assistance donor. But the international role of the yen has been disproportionately small. Some even argue that the current international financial system, by making Japan structurally dependent on the dollar-based financial market, has put Japan in a subordinate position.[17] By holding its international assets in the form of dollar instruments, Japan finances American deficits, facilitates the stock market boom in the United States and helps the American money game, including speculative attacks on the currencies of Asian countries. Whereas the conspiracy theory that claims that the United States controls everything behind the scenes does not merit much academic attention, it is important to note that many Japanese have started to question seriously the merit of following the dollar-based international monetary order.

More practically, as intraregional trade in Asia tends to grow more rapidly than trade with the United States, it is natural for Asian countries to desire more stable means of carrying out transactions among themselves. There is no reason to assume that the dollar is always more stable than regional currencies, and past records do not suggest that the United States will be very mindful of the need for stable exchange rates. In fact, the dollar and the yen have often been wildly misaligned, and from 1995 on there was significant under-valuation of the yen. This put Asian countries in an awkward situation because Asian currencies were in effect pegged to the dollar, and the under-valuation of the yen meant the over-valuation of Asian currencies vis-à-vis the yen, which made their exports to Japan difficult. It thus became a widely accepted view that the overdependence of Japan and Asia on the dollar was one of the causes of the Asian financial crisis. As intraregional trade becomes more and more important, Asian countries would hope for stable exchange rates among themselves and with their major trading partners. Japan is already as important an export market for Asian countries as the United States, and it is also a larger investor in Asian economies. In view of the importance of Japan to the regional economy, Japan and other Asian countries have strong incentives to conduct trade and capital transactions in yen.

From the Japanese viewpoint, it is hardly surprising that the Japanese might prefer using their national currency in international transactions. It would avoid exchange risks in their international transactions. They would prefer holding their international assets in their own currency rather than in other currencies. The internationalisation of the yen would mean more business opportunities for Japanese firms. What is surprising is how small the yen's international status has been despite the economic size and position of Japan as the largest creditor in the world. There could be many reasons for that, one of the major reasons lying in the tightly regulated Japanese financial system, which has made the Japanese financial market an unattractive place for foreigners as well as the Japanese to invest.

And yet the growing gravity of financial crises and Japan's humiliating experiences have contributed to changes in Japanese attitudes towards this issue. The MOF set up an advisory committee examining the internationalisation of the yen in autumn 1998. The committee, consisting of leading scholars and experts in the field, released a detailed report in April 1999 recommending concrete measures.[18] The Liberal Democratic Party also established a committee to examine the matter and recommended several measures to make Tokyo financial markets a more attractive place for foreign investors and borrowers.[19] The internationalisation of the yen was discussed frequently among politicians in the Diet. And the three major political parties – the LDP, the Liberal Party and Komei – formed a ruling coalition; they agreed to work on strengthening the yen as one of the four common economic policies.[20] The internationalisation of the yen, once a subject for experts, has been elevated to the political agenda in Japan.

Obstacles to regional monetary co-operation in Asia

In Asia there are many serious obstacles to regional monetary co-operation. Asian countries are too heterogeneous in terms of economic development, political regime, size and historical background to be a coherent group. The Asian economy is still more dependent on relations with the United States than is Europe. Japan's negative history has prevented it from taking bold initiatives, and while in Europe France can offer a balance to Germany's economic might, there is currently no comparable country in Asia to balance Japan at this stage in the region's history. Above all, Asians are aware that they are still critically dependent on the US military presence for regional peace and stability. While the United States disappointed Asians during the financial crisis, no country is prepared to shout 'Yankee, go home'. The Japanese will also continue to see it as crucial to gain American endorsement for their regional efforts in the foreseeable future.

American attitudes towards regionalism, however, may be changing. As was discussed above, when the Asian crisis was spreading to Russia and Latin America, the United States did not object to Japanese initiatives for regional financial stabilisation. Although the IMF may be a useful policy tool for the United States to project its policy to the rest of the world, it is highly unpopular in the American Congress, and its role may be reduced in the future. The Americans may also regard a larger role of Japan in the Asian regional framework as a contribution to global financial stability. After all it is not in the interest of the United States to isolate itself in Asia by continuing to oppose the policy initiative that all Asians support.

Thus, Japan, together with China and South Korea, agreed with ASEAN countries to set up the dollar swap mechanism with no objection from the Americans. This mechanism will allow these countries, in the event of crisis, to help each other by mobilising the large foreign exchange reserves of the regional countries. This is merely a mechanism for financial assistance, with no secretariat or other permanent structures. Regional co-operation has not been as institutionalised as was envisaged in the aborted AMF proposal. Besides, it is a dollar facility, not denominated in yen. Perhaps the Japanese themselves are not quite ready to make the strong political commitments necessary for a yen facility. Indeed, the internationalisation of the yen requires political courage, because, by making Japan the lender of the last resort in the region, it would require Japan to make tough decisions about when, how and to whom it would lend money. This would make it impossible for Japan comfortably to keep playing the role of good guys while having the Americans play tough guys.

Active Japanese monetary diplomacy and its efforts to promote the yen would, however, be ineffective unless the Japanese economy itself regains its vitality.

The Asian crisis, in this sense, will have had a serious negative impact on long-term Japanese economic recovery unless Japanese policy makers take a sensible policy line in the near future. First, the crisis practically forced the Japanese government to suspend some of its ongoing reform programmes for the sake of stabilisation. Budget reforms are obviously necessary as the Japanese public debt is piling up. Public works, which are not only increasingly inefficient and wasteful in terms of their effects on the economy but are also a hotbed for corruption, must be overhauled. The public pension system, which is doomed to go bankrupt as the Japanese population ages rapidly, has to be reformed so that people can start spending now rather than save for a long post-retirement period. But the Asian crisis caused the Japanese government to be preoccupied with emergency measures to defuse deflationary pressure, and necessary structural adjustments were shelved.

Because of alleviative measures taken by the government, private sector re-structuring was slowed down. Construction companies, which were criticised for their collusive relations with local authorities and politicians, were given more breathing space through public works programmes. The banking sector, whose weakness was one of the major causes of Japan's prolonged recession, was given financial support for the sake of systemic stability. The restruc-turing of insolvent banks, which had initially been planned to start in April 2000, was postponed for a year in order to accommodate weak banks. These moves could slow down the inevitable and indispensable reform of the private sector.

Second, the Japanese intellectual mood shifted considerably from embracing the neo-classical economic doctrine which had provided the major ideologi-cal basis for structural reforms under the Hashimoto government. While many scholars blamed the Asian crisis on the backwardness of Asian financial systems or collusive business–government relations, arguments that emphasised global financial instability as one of the causes gained influence in Japan, as the crisis spread to Russia, Latin America and even to Wall Street. While most Japanese scholars realise the shortcomings and vulnerability of the Japanese and Asian financial systems, the contemporary global financial market has been viewed as excessively volatile, so volatile that relatively minor policy errors such as mis-judgement of macroeconomic trends or pegged exchange rates, which might not have caused major crises in the earlier times, are likely to be severely punished by the global financial market. Calls for a new global financial architecture to prevent or manage growing financial market instabilities now sound persuasive to many Japanese.

Whatever the theoretical merit of those arguments may be, those who simply want to avoid painful reforms may use changes in intellectual mood as a con-venient excuse. Nevertheless, large-scale structural reforms can not only con-tribute to the Japanese economic recovery in the long run but also enhance the

economic leadership role of Japan in Asia. When the phase of emergency reflation ends, Japan will have to face a critical political and intellectual challenge –
how and when to tackle the structural weaknesses of the Japanese economy.

Conclusion

Japan's reactions to the Asian financial crisis were portrayed as a miserable
failure caused by bureaucratic rigidity and political incapacity. In fact, Japan
provided more liquidity than any other country in the world in a timely fashion.
Yet, in contrast to Japan's active efforts in external relations, its policy reactions
on the domestic front were slow and ineffective. This contrast is attributable to
weak leadership at both political and bureaucratic levels, the misjudgement of
economic conditions and the institutional rigidity of Japanese macroeconomic
policy making. More active Asian regional policy is widely supported by the
Japanese public policy community, particularly when both Asians and MOF officials welcome Japanese initiatives in Asia. Unlike the unpopularity of capital
infusion into private banks, external initiatives enjoy fairly strong public support. In other words, the Japanese find it politically easier financially to assist
troubled countries in Asia than to agree among themselves on how to put their
own domestic economic house in order.

Japan's external efforts, despite frustrating setbacks and clear limitations,
made some important progress in terms of closer regional monetary co-
operation. Historians in the future might mark the Asian financial crisis in
1997–8 as a first step for Asian regionalism in the monetary field, which was
and still is quite underdeveloped. The Asian financial crisis, painful as it was,
provided a stimulus to regionalism in Asia. The common painful experiences
and shared memories of working together to overcome the crisis among central
bankers and financial officials in the region have undoubtedly enhanced the
feeling that Asians are all in the same boat.

In comparison with Europe, however, there are many difficulties in regional
co-operation in Asia. The future of Asian regionalism depends very much upon
how successful Japan will be in reviving its domestic economy by shifting
its priorities from reflation to structural reforms in a timely manner. Efforts
at structural reforms were disrupted during the Asian financial crisis as the
government focused its attention on stabilising the shaky economy. They also
depend on how successful Japan will be at balancing its policy towards Asia
with that towards the United States. In any case, the institutionalisation of
Asian regional co-operation will be a long and difficult process. Despite all
these difficulties, the Asian crisis has strongly reminded both Japan and other
Asian countries of the need for closer monetary co-operation in the region.

Notes

1. *Asahi Shimbun*, 6 Sep. 1998.
2. *Mainichi Shimbun*, 19 July 1997. It was officially announced that there was no discussion about financial assistance.
3. Eisuke Sakakibara, *Sakakibara Memoir*, as quoted in *Yomiuri Shimbun*, 13 Nov. 1999.
4. According to Sakakibara, Assistant Secretary of the US Treasury Timothy F. Geithner, who participated in the conference, whispered to Sakakibara, 'How do you feel now about becoming a superpower?'
5. Sakakibara, *Yomiuri Shimbun*, 26 Nov. 1999.
6. Sakakibara, *Yomiuri Shimbun*, 13 Dec. 1999.
7. Sakakibara, *Yumiuri Shimbun*, 24 Dec. 1999.
8. For a macroeconomic analysis of the Japanese economy in the 1990s, see Chikashi Moriguchi, 'Doko e Iku Nihon Keizai', *ASTEION*, no. 48 (spring 1998).
9. Hashimoto later mentioned that if it had not been for the financial crisis, the dismantling of the MOF could have been completed. See *Nikkei Shimbun*, 15 Jan. 2000.
10. In May 1998, for example, Edward Lincoln, a well-known economist, suggested that the United States stop 'returning a call' to Japan. See his article, 'Japan's financial mess', *Foreign Affairs*, vol. 77, no. 3 (May–June 1998). On the other hand, the Japanese ambassador to the United States, Kunio Saito, in refuting American media reports criticising Japan for not making permanent tax cuts to stimulate domestic demands, was quoted as saying that 'the Japanese government is not a collection of idiots'. He questioned whether the US press knew that the multiplier of a tax cut in Japan was only 0.46 as opposed to 1.18 in the United States. See *Asahi Shimbun*, 30 April 1998.
11. *Mainichi Shimbun*, 16 Oct. 1998.
12. For example, in response to the Mexican peso crisis in 1994 Japan concluded a series of bilateral short-term credit agreements with Asian economies in 1996. They were designed to provide these economies with dollar reserves (with a limit of $1 billion for each economy) for intervention in foreign exchange markets at the time of crisis. The agreement was first concluded with Hong Kong, Singapore, Australia, Indonesia, Malaysia, Thailand and Philippines. See Eiji Yamamoto, *Kokusai Tsuka Sisutemu* (Tokyo: Iwanami Shoten, 1997), p. 224. Interestingly, the author, however, argued that it would be unlikely that Asian countries with stronger credit positions and huge amounts of foreign exchange reserves would be hit by a crisis similar to that in Mexico.
13. South Korean Premier Kim Jong Pil, when he visited Japan to see Prime Minister Obuchi in November 1998, suggested setting up the Asian Monetary Fund with as much as $30 billion. With the New Miyazawa Initiative just started, this idea just surprised the Japanese and did not develop into any tangible measures. *Mainichi Shimbun*, 30 Nov. 1998.
14. *Yomiuri Shimbun*, 23 May 1998.

15. *Asahi Shimbun*, 13 Nov. 1998. The Japanese Ministry of International Trade and Industry was also reported to have started to examine seriously bilateral free trade agreements, a move away from its prior position attaching primary importance to multilateral frameworks. *Asahi Shimbun*, 13 Dec. 1998.

16. The relevant part of the joint statement on east Asian co-operation, issued on 28 Nov. 1999, reads as follows: 'They agreed to strengthen policy dialogue, co-ordination and collaboration on the financial, monetary and fiscal issues of common interest, focusing initially on issues related to macroeconomic risk management, enhancing corporate governance, monitoring regional capital flows, strengthening banking and financial systems, reforming the international financial architecture, and enhancing self-help and support mechanisms in East Asia through the ASEAN+3 Framework, including the ongoing dialogue and co-operation mechanism of the ASEAN+3 finance and central bank leaders and officials.'

17. For example, Mototada Kikkawa argues that Japanese economic failure was caused by the dominance of the dollar in the global financial market. Despite the fact that Japan is the largest source of savings in the world, the United States, through its financial dominance, sucked up Japanese savings and even bought Japanese assets through sophisticated financial techniques. See Mototada Kikkawa, *Mane Haisen* (*The monetary defeat*) (Bungei Syunju, 1998).

18. See Gaikoku Kawase Shingikai (Council on Foreign Exchange and Other Transactions), *Nijuisseki ni Muketa Enno Kokusaika – Sekai no Keizai Kinyu Josei no Henka to Nihon no Taio* (*The internationalisation of the yen in the twenty-first century – Japan's response to changes in global economic and financial environments*), 20 April 1999.

19. LDP, Subcommittee on Yen's Internationalization and Research Committee on Financial Affairs, *En no Kokusaika ni Muketa Gutaitekisochi ni Tsuite (On concrete measures for the internationalisation of the yen)*, 14 Oct. 1998.

20. See documents on the agreement between the three ruling parties, 'Santo Renritsu Seiken Gouisyo', 4 Oct. 1999, http://jimin.or.jp/saishin/seisaku-66-2.html retrieved 29 Nov. 1999.

Part III

Private interests, private–public interactions and financial policy

12 Private capture, policy failures and financial crisis: evidence and lessons from South Korea and Thailand

XIAOKE ZHANG AND GEOFFREY R. D. UNDERHILL

Two sets of explanations have dominated academic discussions of the causes of the Asian financial crisis. One has attributed the crisis to external factors,[1] and the other has converged on weaknesses of economic fundamentals as the major causal factors.[2] What has largely been neglected in these explanations, however, is the role of domestic political factors. This chapter examines how one such variable – the changing balance of power between private interests and public authority – contributed to the onset of the financial crisis and affected its management. Focusing on South Korea and Thailand, we argue that the growing private capture of public policy processes not only led to an unsuccessful process of financial reform and to structural weaknesses which sowed the seeds of the crisis, but also generated serious problems of policy management in the lead-up to the outbreak of the crisis.

We begin by briefly outlining the argument concerning the institutional variables which shape the balance of private preferences and power versus public interests and authority with regard to public policy making in the domain of the financial system. We then develop this argument through a more detailed comparative examination of the financial crises in South Korea and Thailand. Our purpose is not to provide comprehensive accounts of what occurred in the two countries during the 1997–8 period, as such accounts can be found in more synoptic studies in this volume, but to explore the impact of institutional variables on the process of financial reforms and crisis management. We argue that if these variables were better understood, our expectations of financial reform and of global market integration would be more limited and realistic, and more caution would be exercised in financial liberalisation.

The argument

In both South Korea and Thailand a number of critical microeconomic problems came together during the early and mid-1990s to produce growing structural incompatibility between the characteristics of the respective domestic financial systems and the increasingly short-term nature of global capital markets. The rapid integration of domestic financial systems into the global financial and monetary order revealed tensions between the domestic policy-making processes and institutions on one hand, and the constraints of global capital markets on the other. The short-term nature of global capital flows was not compatible with the fundamental characteristics of the respective financial systems in the two countries, which had been associated with their unique developmental trajectories. As the systems were opened up in an adventure euphemistically labelled reform, domestic private and public interests not surprisingly shaped the process to their perceived advantage. Expectations of greater efficiency through liberalisation were not realised because the liberalisation process was not one of rational policy making to a desired model, but an interplay of interested parties carrying historical and institutional baggage.

In South Korea, microeconomic problems were primarily reflected in the rapid growth of short-term external debts and massive misallocation of funds to a cluster of manufacturing industries with increasing overcapacity but depressed investment returns. Thailand also experienced mounting foreign obligations and worsening debt structures, and saw excessive increases in institutional lending to property business and stock trading. These microeconomic problems, combined with international market shocks and domestic economic slow-down, contributed to significant decreases in corporate profits, rising levels of corporate leveraging and deterioration of balance sheets and asset positions in banks and many non-bank financial institutions (NBFIs). The untimely exposure of the structural characteristics of national financial systems to global market integration accompanied, and was compounded by, emerging macroeconomic difficulties during the same period, evidenced in export slumps and growing current account deficits.

The combined effects of structural weaknesses and macro difficulties clearly accentuated the economic predicament in which the two countries had found themselves prior to the crisis. What actually foreshadowed the impending financial turmoil were financial institution collapses in Thailand and a series of chaebol bankruptcies in South Korea over the 1996–7 period. When combined with capital account liberalisation, all of this revealed financial system characteristics unsuited to global integration. The governments failed to deal with the corporate failures and to restructure ailing financial and industrial firms because private interests integrated into the policy process tied their hands. Along with weakening economic fundamentals, the situation raised serious doubts about the ability of the governments to tackle mounting private sector troubles and invited speculative attacks on the currencies. The ultimately futile attempts to defend the dollar peg only served to deplete international reserves and aggravate external imbalances. As a result, the structural and external problems were quickly transformed into the sharp currency depreciation and the full-blown financial crisis.

The emergence of the financial crisis in South Korea and Thailand has deeper political and institutional roots. Financial and corporate sector weaknesses and macroeconomic difficulties stemmed, first and foremost, from the peculiar institutional arrangements and political constraints in the two countries. These manifested themselves primarily in the increased influence of the economically powerful and politically resourceful private actors – the Korean chaebols and Thai private bankers – and in the corresponding decline in state strength and capacity in economic governance. They facilitated extensive private penetration of the state apparatus and diminished the ability of government officials to act independently in line with public interests, impairing the coherence and credibility of economic policy and creating uncertainty about the policy environment. It is arguable that external pressures for liberalisation from IFIs and developed countries exacerbated this problem.

The ability of the South Korean chaebols and Thai private bankers to exercise growing control over policy processes derived, in the first place, from their strong organisational capabilities. The main source of this organisational strength was the spectacular concentration of their industrial structure, the direct result of previous government efforts to achieve specific industrial and financial policy goals. The high level of industrial concentration enabled big industrialists and private bankers to overcome collective action problems and increased the leverage that these powerful private actors had vis-à-vis state actors. Furthermore, oligopolistic firms were able to wield their influence over government policy from their sheer weight in the national economy. The chaebol had dominant positions across the South Korean economy. In Thailand, commercial banks had considerable control over the entire financial system and many other economic sectors. The fact that the performance of the national economy was closely tied to the fortunes of these industrial and financial groups tilted the balance of power strongly in favour of private actors, and had constraining effects on policy choice and implementation.

Private interests might not have exerted such negative impact on policy if weakened state institutions had not facilitated private capture. Most critically, the internal structure of the state in South Korea and Thailand became increasingly fragmented in the early and mid-1990s. Key state economic agencies did not possess the structural cohesiveness effectively to pursue policy goals, and lacked the sense of corporate purposes previously contained in the developmental ideology in South Korea and in the tradition of financial conservatism in Thailand. This produced co-ordination problems and bred inter-bureaucratic conflicts.[3] Conflictual interagency relations created the opportunity for private interests to gain access to the state apparatus and to influence the policy agenda. This was especially true where different state agencies attempted to mobilise social support in their rivalries with each other and therefore became more responsive to distributional demands from dominant private actors.

The weaknesses in the internal state structure reduced the capacity of economic bureaucrats to pursue their policy goals independently of private demands. In South Korea, major economic ministries found themselves increasingly susceptible to business influences, and the Bank of Korea (BOK) tried in vain to gain policy-making autonomy. Similarly, Thai financial technocrats, particularly at the Bank of Thailand (BOT), saw their policy authority being challenged by private financiers and politicians. The weak or weakened position of state economic and regulatory agencies provided the opportunities for particularistic rent seeking and for capture by narrow private sector interests, leaving disastrous consequences for financial policy making and for the management of systemic corporate distress. In Singapore and Taiwan, by contrast, independent and competent regulatory authorities contributed to the effective conduct of financial policies, enabling the two economies to withstand the deadly impact of the contagion.[4]

Growing private capture of public policy also had its source in macro-structural weaknesses in the political system. In South Korea, the ability of the president to insulate economic technocrats from private demands and to ensure bureaucratic stability was undercut by the increasingly divided ruling party and by frequent conflicts between the executive and the legislature. These constraints particularly plagued the Kim Young Sam government in 1997–8, although they had not been totally absent in the previous administrations. In Thailand, the problems were more fundamental and had their origins in the constitutional design that generated highly unstable coalition governments and internally weak and fragmented political parties.[5] Party divisions and weak political leadership, coupled with the heavy reliance by politicians on big business for campaign funds, allowed powerful private interests to wield undue influence over the policy-making process.

These institutional problems did not develop in isolation from changes in the broad political and economic context. In the late 1980s, the transition to democracy in South Korea and Thailand altered the political landscape by considerably expanding political space for societal forces. Dominant private actors seized growing control over political parties and parliamentary processes, and asserted themselves more aggressively in public affairs. Liberal democratic arrangements increasingly subjected economic bureaucrats to competing distributional claims and eroded the institutional underpinnings of their policy-making independence. Despite the emergence of political pluralism, big business, politicians and bureaucrats dominated socioeconomic policy arenas, largely to the exclusion of broad social forces. This left the position of powerful industrialists and financiers unchallenged by competing social groups and subjected government policy to their particularistic demands.

Equally important, the growing integration of the domestic economy with the international system in South Korea and Thailand imposed inherent limits on the ability of the governments to shape the behaviour of private market players. On the one hand, the integration helped to develop the knowledge and experience of the private sector to such an extent that it was now more capable than public officials of formulating business policies and making strategic choices. On the other hand, continued economic liberalisation enhanced private firms' access to alternative sources of finance, broadened their transnational linkages and strengthened their position as crucial economic agents. Structurally, these developments reinforced the economic dominance of the chaebol firms and private bankers, and deepened government dependence on big industrialists and financiers for policy implementation and economic growth.

In both South Korea and Thailand state economic agencies had traditionally maintained close and reciprocal relations with the private sector. Such relations, while contributing to economic performance in the past, now undermined policy efficiency and enhanced the play of particularistic interests, mainly due to the various institutional weaknesses depicted above. Rent-seeking activities on the part of private actors affected the coherent and effective conduct of financial policy. As the governments were more responsive to narrower constituencies than to broad public interests, they had difficulties implementing policies that would benefit the economy and society at large. Throughout the financial reform process of the 1980s and 1990s, the chaebols in South Korea and private financiers in Thailand constantly sought policy outcomes that protected their vested interests but led to serious problems with the reform process. As will be shown below, these problems led to the accumulation of structural problems in the corporate and financial sectors.

The same institutional weaknesses that had compromised financial reform also constrained the ability of the governments to respond to mounting micro- and macroeconomic policy difficulties on the eve of the financial crisis. South Korea and Thailand could not realign exchange rates with changing market conditions in a timely manner, partly because politicians and economic bureaucrats became captives of powerful private actors who carried huge foreign debts and thus had strong interests in keeping the dollar peg in place. For similar reasons the governments failed to restructure ailing corporate and financial firms, aggravating the various problems in the private sector and causing the profound loss of confidence on the part of local and foreign investors.

Thailand

As noted in the previous section, the rapid infusion of foreign capital, particularly short-term loans, into Thailand contributed directly to the build-up of financial sector weaknesses. The single most important cause was the significant opening of the capital account and, more specifically, the launch of the Bangkok International Banking Facility (BIBF) in early 1993. The forty-nine local and foreign banks with BIBF licences were allowed to borrow offshore and relend to domestic borrowers (out–in operations) or to foreign borrowers (out–out transactions). The creation of the BIBF had a complex of economic and political motives. Thai authorities viewed the facility as an important way of increasing the availability of capital for industrial expansion at home and of turning Bangkok into a regional financial centre as the linchpin of their efforts to initiate a new zone of economic co-operation in mainland south-east Asia against the backdrop of economic reform and opening in Indo-China.

Whether the BIBF achieved these objectives was a moot point, but it certainly opened the door to greatly expanded transnational banking activities and enhanced the access of Thai financial institutions to foreign-denominated short-term funds. While foreign creditors, lured by higher returns and seemingly bright growth prospects in Thailand, were eager to lend, demand-side factors were also at play. Thai banks used the BIBF to acquire foreign funds at an interest rate 4–5 per cent lower than domestic funds; low-cost foreign funds helped to mitigate competition among banks for depositors, depressing deposit rates and widening the interest rate spreads. In the meantime, foreign BIBF banks competed with one another to project themselves as significant players by expanding their loan portfolios in an attempt to obtain the few licences to operate full banking services in Thailand.[6]

Aware of the potential negative effects of rapid short-term capital inflows, the Thai financial authorities had initially intended the BIBF to bring in more long-term funds for industrial development and to engage mainly in out–out lending activities. Intense lobbying on the part of domestic and foreign banks to seek quick benefits through out–in transactions, however, overwhelmed the government's ability to contain BIBF operations within its original policy parameters.[7] As a result, BIBF operations were heavily skewed towards out–in rather than out–out lending. This led to the growing accumulation of external debts and aggravated the maturity structure of these debts, for the foreign funds borrowed via the BIBF were predominantly in the form of short-term loans.

While the launch of the BIBF resulted in massive inflows of short-term funds and growing financial frailty, failure to reform the oligopolistic structure of the Thai banking sector and to reduce its high level of ownership concentration also contributed to structural weaknesses, particularly with regard to corporate governance. Thai private bankers strongly resisted the competitive pressures associated with entry deregulation throughout the financial reform process. For nearly three decades until late 1996, no domestic commercial bank had been licensed and only one foreign bank had been allowed to establish a branch in Bangkok. Private pressures also frustrated the government's attempts to disburse the shareholding structures of banks and, to a lesser extent, finance companies, despite the existence of strict regulations on share disbursement. The result was that the high concentration of ownership and management persisted through strong family holdings in many Thai financial institutions.

Oligopolistic structure and concentrated ownership led to poor corporate governance in several ways. In the first place, Thai banks were not self-regulatory in that normal checks and balances among shareholders, directors and managers were lacking, mainly because they tended to be either the same persons or members of the same families.[8] The lack of internal controls provided scope for managerial malpractices and irregularities. The problem was particularly acute where restrictions were circumvented on the extension of credit to shareholders and directors as well as to affiliated businesses. Complex and personal cross-ownership and interlocking directorates enabled major shareholders and directors to finance their or their favoured clients' business undertakings, many of which neither had sufficient collateral nor were economically feasible. The oligopolistic banks also tended to follow high-risk, high-return strategies in their lending and investment activities, due largely to the problem of moral hazard. These institutions, which maintained the lion's share of total financial assets, capitalised on the belief that the government would bail them out to prevent systemic meltdown if their risk-taking behaviour landed them in rough water. The result was serious overinvestment in, and excessive exposure to, such volatile activities as real estate development and stock trading.

Imprudent lending and risk-taking behaviour, specifically on the part of Thai finance companies, also stemmed from the biased approach towards functional desegmentation – another poorly implemented reform measure that gave rise to financial sector problems. The Thai financial authorities invariably gave more attention and policy favours to the banking sector when removing the regulatory barriers that had underpinned segmentation between different types of financial institutions. The key reasons for the differential regulatory treatment rested not only with the desire of financial policy makers to control the pace of deregulation for the sake of financial system stability but also with the attempts by private bankers to maintain their dominant position in the financial sector. While some NBFIs were affiliated with banks, many operated independently and intensified competitive pressures on banks in the early 1990s.

The biased approach towards desegmentation, however, led to two interrelated developments in the behaviour of NBFIs, both of which proved detrimental to their financial position. First, operating at a competitive disadvantage, finance companies, especially those which were not affiliated with banks, were often forced to take in whatever clients were turned down by banks, many of whom had shaky capital structures and risky investment portfolios. When economic difficulties gripped the country over 1996–7, these clients bore the brunt and many went under, bringing down their creditors with them. Second, faced with competitive restraints, finance companies scrambled to establish themselves as big players in the domestic financial system, in the hope that they would be awarded full banking licences and compete with banks on a level playing field. The desire to grow fast caused finance companies to seek quick and high returns with a short payback period. With the property and stock markets booming during the early and mid-1990s, real estate and share price speculation became their favoured lending and investment options. Although finance companies did grow faster during this period, much of that growth resulted from their excessive involvement in the property and stock markets.[9]

A final problem in the reform process was the lax enforcement of regulation. Popular accounts have attributed the regulatory failure to the lack of sufficient rules and supervisory expertise on the part of financial authorities. These accounts appear to have missed an important point. The early 1980s financial crisis in Thailand provided the spur for attempts to overhaul its system of prudential regulation; further efforts were made to tighten controls over banks and finance companies in the mid-1980s. The regulatory reforms endowed financial authorities, specifically the Bank of Thailand, with wide-ranging legal powers and supervisory instruments.[10] The sequencing of financial reforms in Thailand also seemed to follow the 'conventionally right' wisdom: prudential regulations had been strengthened before controls over the financial sector were relaxed.[11]

The problem was not so much that of technical deficiencies or wrongly sequenced reform measures as that of ineffective implementation of existing regulatory rules. Continued ownership and management concentration led to inadequate information disclosure and opaque business procedures, making it easier for banks and finance companies to dodge lending restrictions but complicating regulators' efforts to assess the quality of their asset portfolios and to implement an efficient strategy for prudential regulation. Moreover, central bankers were sometimes not so strict with the enforcement of regulations as they were expected to be. The primary reason appeared to be their dependence on the private financial community for achieving important policy objectives. Time and again, they were unable to resist the temptation to relax regulatory standards as a way to secure private bankers' support and co-operation. This might have sent wrong signals to the private financial community and encouraged unscrupulous managers to defy regulatory standards.

This account underscores the dire consequences of poorly regulated liberalisation carried out in a sociopolitical milieu in which a banking oligopoly had long been a dominant feature of the economy and powerful private interests increasingly penetrated the state apparatus. The ineffectively implemented financial reform contributed directly to the outbreak of the crisis, particularly because it was implemented in a political economy that was not yet politically and socially prepared for the necessary adjustments. This suggests that if liberalisation and the benefits its ardent advocates proclaim are to be a sustainable policy, greater attention should be paid to the very political constraints on the liberalisation process. Liberalisation, which invariably implies the restructuring of legal, economic and political institutions, can result in instability and crisis if it happens too quickly.

The effects of the various structural problems associated with financial reform mistakes were clearly revealed in the traumatic collapse of the Bangkok Bank of Commerce (BBC), a medium-sized commercial bank, and a dozen finance companies prior to the crisis. The debacle of the BBC stemmed from years of mismanagement and fraudulent activities on the part of its senior executives. More importantly, it revealed the declining capacity of the Bank of Thailand to exercise its supervisory functions independently of political influences. The BBC had served many well-connected and powerful clients in the public and private sectors. As later revealed in press reports, between 1992 and 1995 the bank lent a colossal $2.8 billion to influential politicians and senior financial officials, much of which had no collateral or was backed by overvalued land.[12] Being the beneficiaries of large loans from the BBC, the politicians and officials were suspected to be among those pressing the BOT to grant the bank preferential treatment and to provide rescue funds to keep it solvent. In a published interview, the BOT governor, who resigned over the BBC scandal, suggested that opposition from prominent figures in the ruling coalition had overwhelmed central bankers' resolve to move in on the BBC and to press charges against its senior executives.[13]

The institutional handicaps of financial sector management ran much broader than just the failure to tackle the BBC malfeasance. On the heels of the BBC debacle, Finance One, the largest finance company in Thailand, suffered from serious liquidity problems and was on the brink of collapse. Its distress epitomised the woes of Thai finance companies, many of which were lumbered with weighty non-performing loans resulting in large part from their over-exposure to the troubled property and stock markets. In March 1997 financial authorities introduced a few measures to shore up the sector. They instructed all financial institutions to raise their provisions for bad debts and asked weak finance companies either to be absorbed into commercial banks or to increase their capital fully to cover doubtful loans.[14]

It should be noted that the measures announced were moderate and fell short of a wholesale approach to restructuring the sector. This might have reflected the concerns of financial officials that more radical measures would provoke opposition. Their concerns proved to be well placed, and even the implementation of the moderate measures was politically unattainable. Major shareholders in some of the weakest finance companies, ranging from private bankers to politicians and ministers from the Chart Pattana party, the second largest in the coalition government, strongly resisted the remedial action against their companies. Eager to hold his shaky multiparty government together, Prime Minister Chaovalit Yongchaiyut refused to take any firm action. Confronted with powerful resistance, financial technocrats virtually abandoned their efforts to restructure the problematic financial institutions.[15]

The failure to push through the restructuring measures demonstrates that financial authorities could no longer work above the political trenches of Thailand. The weakened institutional capacity of officials, particularly those at the central bank, assumed significance beyond its impact on policy-making efficiency. While the collapse of the BBC and Finance One in quick succession bolstered negative assessments of the Thai financial system, the BOT's inability to restructure the ailing banks and finance companies dealt a heavy blow to business confidence. Although the BOT tried to reassure the markets that most Thai financial institutions were healthy and solvent, investors apparently lost faith in the credibility of central bankers. Throughout the first half of 1997, foreign investors accelerated their withdrawal from Thailand, and many Thai companies and individuals also moved increasingly to US dollars. The result was that the value of the baht came under increasing downward pressure due to repeated speculative attacks.

By that time market conditions showed that the continued maintenance of the dollar peg was not a sustainable strategy. The BOT, however, rejected the alternative to defending the baht. From its perspective, devaluation could rarely be a good policy option, particularly when economic conditions were adverse. As global demand for many of Thailand's exports was sluggish in the mid-1990s, financial policy makers worried that devaluation would only inflict unnecessary damage on the already fragile economy if it failed to improve external imbalances. More important, by the end of 1996, commercial banks, finance companies and their industrial clients had carried over $60 billion dollars of foreign debts. Devaluing the baht would have immediately increased their debt-servicing burden and landed many of them on the rocks. They therefore lobbied hard against the devaluation of the baht.[16] Political pressures from dominant private interests, combined with the organisational inflexibility and factional conflicts within the BOT,[17] prevented the timely realignment of exchange rate policy and decisive response to the impending crisis.

In mid-1997, speculation intensified with growing evidence of the increasing fragility of financial institutions, mounting foreign debt and swelling current account deficits. This quickly overwhelmed the determination of the BOT to defend the exchange rate, leading to un-pegging of the baht and massive depreciation in early July. Following the devaluation, Thai banks and finance companies, already devastated by plunging asset prices and huge non-performing loans, saw their foreign debts multiply. Short-term dollar loans totalling more than US$40 billion borrowed by the private sector would fall due within the next twelve months. The central bank, which had squandered tens of billions of dollars in an ultimately futile bid to maintain the peg, now had alarmingly low foreign reserves and was in no position to act as a lender of the last resort. The government had no choice but to approach the IMF for assistance.

South Korea

As in Thailand, one important precursor of the financial crisis in South Korea was the excessive growth of short-term external debts in the financial and corporate sectors. While South Korea's economic boom in the late 1980s and expectations of a continued boom on the part of foreign creditors played a role, the more fundamental reason for the rapid inflows of short-term external funds was the highly selective approach to capital decontrols. Although the South Korean government was generally cautious with capital account opening, it moved more rapidly to reduce limits on short-term foreign borrowings by domestic commercial and merchant banks and by the privileged chaebol firms. At the same time, it maintained restrictions on foreign direct investment and gave foreigners only limited access to the bond market. Moreover, while trying to keep foreign investors at bay, the government encouraged large chaebol firms to expand their operations abroad. To finance their overseas investment projects, these firms borrowed an immense amount of short-term funds, resulting in large maturity mismatches in their balance sheets.

Selective capital decontrols, which biased capital inflows towards short-term maturity, in large part reflected the preferences of the chaebols and their powerful status in the South Korean political economy. While the chaebols were loath to see restrictions on FDI and on foreign participation in domestic equity removed for fear of increased competition and diluted ownership controls, they supported those deregulation measures that provided them with enhanced access to foreign capital and greater freedom to invest abroad. Chaebol firms relied heavily on short-term funds for financing their domestic and overseas investment activities, mainly because such funds were cheaper and easier to raise in international money markets. South Korean banking institutions, closely tied (mainly by lending portfolios) to the big business sector and concerned about its performance, were eager to channel external short-term loans to satisfy the financial needs of the chaebols.[18]

The increased exposure of South Korean financial institutions to short-term external debts and foreign exchange risks also resulted from a second reform policy mistake – the uneven-handed approach to functional desegmentation and the haphazard development of some NBFIs, particularly merchant banks. In their efforts to liberalise constraints on competition and institutional barriers between banks and NBFIs, financial authorities, specifically the Finance Ministry, tended to give the latter more policy favours to the disadvantage of the former. This was mainly due to the fact that the ministry had supervisory jurisdiction over the NBFI sector and that financial officials could benefit from the rapid growth of NBFIs in terms of bureaucratic power and personal interests. Equally important, the chaebols, which owned many NBFIs and relied on them increasingly for investment funds, had every interest in seeking regulatory favours for their financial subsidiaries.

As a consequence, the growth of the NBFI sector dwarfed that of the commercial banking sector, as non-bank financial firms saw restrictions on their operations being constantly reduced and their business scope rapidly expand. Merchant banks were among the NBFIs that gained most from this differential regulatory treatment. Their development was further facilitated between 1994 and 1996 when twenty-four finance companies were converted into merchant banks, drastically increasing their total number to thirty. Since merchant banks were allowed to engage in foreign exchange transactions – the very few NBFIs ever permitted to enter the business area – this deepened the integration of the South Korean financial sector with international financial markets. More significant, as most merchant banks were affiliated with the chaebols, they were understandably keen to bring in short-term funds at the behest of their industrial owners, contributing to the worsening of debt maturity structures in the corporate and financial sectors.

Corporate and financial sector fragility had its origins not only in the influx of short-term external debts into the private sector but also in the highly inefficient use of foreign funds. Foreign capital inflows may not be a curse if the borrowed money can be allocated and used efficiently. In South Korea, however, the financial system through which most foreign capital came failed this test. The bulk of foreign loans intermediated by commercial and merchant banks were over-invested in chaebol-favoured industrial sectors with large surplus capacity and declining returns. As a result, the efficiency of credit allocation was low and declining in the early and mid-1990s. A comprehensive study on the effects of credit policies in South Korea shows that credit flows were not directed to the profitable sectors and that the favoured industries failed to improve their productivity.[19]

The weak ability of banking institutions to allocate funds efficiently was mainly attributable to prolonged government intervention in their operations. Direct controls over financial prices and bank credit had long been the key instruments of the South Korean government for spurring industrial development. Such controls were largely maintained well after important financial liberalisation measures had been initiated in the late 1980s, primarily reflecting the desire of the Finance Ministry to manage industrial policy and preserve its regulatory power as well as the chaebols' efforts to obtain continued access to preferential credit. Even during the mid-1990s, when most interest rates were deregulated and policy loans phased out, the government still imposed, through administrative guidance, various restrictions on the portfolio management of banks and did not allow them to have full autonomy in their lending activities.

Continued government intervention contributed to the persistence of the moral-hazard problem in bank lending, which in turn hindered the emergence of a robust and independent banking sector. One of the lingering legacies of the state-directed financial system in South Korea was that the government was potentially responsible for all bank losses and implicitly undertook to rescue the ailing industrial firms that claimed a large amount of credit. In this 'coinsurance scheme existing among government, banks and industry',[20] lending risks were minimal and banks often accommodated the financial needs of chaebol firms without conducting strict creditworthiness checks. In the early and mid-1990s, heavy lenders to the big business sector no doubt felt secure in their position, confident that the odds of default were slim and that financial authorities would bail them out as they had always done in the past.

For these reasons, South Korean financial institutions, particularly banks, had little incentive to restructure their problematic asset portfolios and to avoid their traditional but dubious chaebol clients. The result was that their lending behaviour remained largely unchanged long after the financial reform process had got under way. As a clear indicator of this situation, credit allocation was still heavily skewed towards the big business sector, despite incessant government efforts to change it. By one account, the thirty largest chaebols received an annual average 33.1 per cent of total corporate borrowing (including bank, non-bank and foreign loans and debt securities) over the 1986–95 period and 40.3 per cent in 1996.[21] Credit concentration in the poorly performing chaebols exposed banks to excessive investment risks and saddled their balance sheets with growing delinquent debts.

One may ask why the South Korean government allowed huge short-term external debts to build into the economy and financial institutions to lend heavily to chaebol firms, given that this situation was seriously destabilising and was in large part responsible for private sector weaknesses. Apart from the above-mentioned reform policy mistakes, the lax enforcement of prudential rules offers much of the explanation. In South Korea, domestic financial dereg-ulation and capital account liberalisation were not matched by sustained and consistent efforts to establish an effective institutional framework of regulation and supervision. While financial authorities initiated some institutional and reg-ulatory reforms during the late 1980s and early 1990s, these tended to be partial in scope and inefficient in implementation.

Poor prudential supervision is about institutional constraints on the formulation and enforcement of rules as much as about technical deficiencies. One such institutional constraint was that commercial banks were supervised by the BOK whereas specialised banks and NBFIs operated under the oversight of the Finance Ministry. This fragmented system complicated the execution of supervisory duties, particularly when banks and NBFIs encroached on each other's business areas and resulted in the development of risky practices among financial institutions. In addition, the long-running conflicts between the BOK and the Ministry of Finance (later the Ministry of Finance and Economy) over the extended rights to supervise financial institutions undermined the government's efforts to establish a more unified regulatory system and to make its modes of prudential regulation compatible with a more liberalised environment.

Concomitant with the fragmented system of financial regulation was the lack of uniform supervisory standards imposed on the operations of banks and NBFIs. Reflecting the policy preferences and influence of the chaebols that owned many NBFIs and the asymmetrical power relations between the BOK and the Finance Ministry, banks and their non-bank counterparts operated under different regulatory regimes. While the normal banking operations of commercial banks were subject to credit controls, exposure limits and liquidity requirements, supervision of many NBFIs was much looser in terms of foreign exchange exposure, credit extension and liquidity management. So loose in fact that the authorities were not aware until too late of the rapid growth of their external debts, reckless lending to chaebol firms and large maturity discrepancies.[22]

Institutional weaknesses resulting in regulatory failure were complicated by the organisational deficiencies of the private sector. South Korean banks, which tied a dominant percentage of their assets to the big business sector, had strong incentives to continue providing the chaebols with fresh loans. Together with the moral hazard problem associated with implicit government support, this encouraged banks to dodge official limits on credit allocation and to lend heavily to chaebol firms. Similarly, the chaebols' ownership control over NBFIs, specifically merchant banks, also contributed to regulatory problems. Merchant banks often exploited close inter-corporate relations to leverage up their foreign exchange exposure and to channel short-term external funds to the related subsidiaries of their parent companies.[23] Intra-affiliate ties rendered opaque the financial transactions between NBFIs and their chaebol owners and made it difficult for regulatory authorities to monitor the borrowing and lending operations of NBFIs.

The foregoing analysis clearly shows that poorly managed reforms can have a powerful negative impact on financial governance, especially in a political economy where business–government relations, corporate practices, regulatory processes and policy-making rules were not compatible with the requirements of economic liberalisation. Driven by strong external pressures and by South Korean state elites' desire for OECD membership, the government rushed to policy changes without taking these problems into consideration. The resulting tensions between the nature of social, economic and political institutions and market-oriented reforms contributed directly to the outbreak of the crisis. This reinforces the main messages derived from the Thai case as well as the need to take account of compatibility deficits.

The reform difficulties which played a direct role in the build-up of the various structural weaknesses took their toll on the financial position of the corporate sector. Benefiting from implicit government support and the abundant supply of domestic and foreign funds, chaebol firms went on a borrowing binge and kept sinking money into capital-intensive investment ventures.[24] Heavy reliance on indirect financing aggravated the already fragile financial position of chaebol firms, and their ratios of debt to equity increased steadily during the early and mid-1990s. High leveraging rendered the chaebols vulnerable to sudden unfavourable changes in economic conditions. But their vulnerability was exacerbated in the mid-1990s: a substantial share of their newly incurred debts was in the form of short-term external loans, which overseas investors were clearly willing to provide. As these problems interacted with the sharp export slump in 1996 to cut export revenues and profits, many chaebols suffered severe liquidity difficulties and began to default on their maturing debts.

The first clear signs of the financial crisis in South Korea came during the early months of 1997, when several chaebols were on the brink of bankruptcy. In its efforts to tackle the troubled chaebols, however, the government adopted a highly selective and inconsistent approach for a combination of different economic and political reasons.[25] It let some crippled chaebols, such as Hanbo and Sammi, go under, while bailing the others out, if only temporarily. The incoherent approach sent contradictory messages to foreign creditors. While some foreign creditors were astonished to see the South Korean government allow Hanbo and Sammi to collapse, the broad international business community perceived the development in a positive light. The non-interventionist stance appeared to signal the intentions of policy makers to put an end to the implicit coinsurance scheme, to seize the opportunity for reform created by the crisis, and to push ahead with the long-overdue restructuring of the corporate and financial sectors.[26] Their expectations were, however, quickly betrayed by the South Korean government's decision to save the other ailing chaebols from bankruptcy. This policy inconsistency caused confusion among foreign creditors and significantly marred the credibility of official economic policy.

Another major source of discouragement to foreign investors and creditors was that the government failed in its efforts to restructure the rescued chaebol firms, specifically Kia Motors. After Kia was pulled back from the brink of bankruptcy, the creditor banks agreed to give the company a two-month breathing space to change its organisational structure. Among the many restructuring measures, Kia planned to reduce the number of group subsidiaries, sell redundant real estate and cut down the workforce. In return for these measures, Kia wanted its debts to be rescheduled. While the creditor banks, led by the Korea First, were willing to reschedule Kia's debts to avoid its complete collapse, the government opposed the request and demanded the resignation of Kia's top management. Senior Kia executives, however, refused to step down and had no intention of following through with their restructuring plan.[27]

In their attempts to pursue their respective interests, the chaebol management and economic bureaucrats refused to make any concessions and failed to find an effective solution to the Kia problem. While in deadlock, the predicament of Kia was causing havoc with the South Korean financial markets and the economy. Although the government finally decided to put Kia into court receivership and turned the firm into a public enterprise, the three-month policy stalemate over the restructuring of Kia caused irreparable damage. The international financial community was appalled at the irresolute, inconsistent and ineffective way in which the government had handled the corporate failures.[28] During mid-1997, shares on the Seoul exchange nose-dived, as foreign investors disposed of their stock holdings. At the same time, the won came under rising pressure, with enormous funds flowing out of South Korea.

This was a crucial juncture in the development of the financial crisis in South Korea. Clearly, there was an urgent need for an effective realignment of foreign exchange rate policy, with widespread concerns among local and foreign businesses about the country's growing corporate and financial vulnerability. Actually, market pressures for such realignment began to increase as early as late 1996, when the current account deficits began to worsen. But the South Korean government was reluctant to take any measures to readjust the exchange rate. The essential factors that prevented the timely devaluation of the won sprang from the political and institutional constraints on Korean economic management, the very constraints that led to the mishandling of the corporate failures.

Dominant private sector actors formed one important source of opposition to devaluation. During the 1996–7 period, the corporate and financial sectors were carrying massive and swelling foreign debts. Devaluing the won would have immediately increased their debt-servicing burden and wrecked their profits and balance sheets. Although the export earnings of the chaebols dwindled with the overvalued won, these costs were more than offset by the windfall profits that they obtained from borrowing foreign funds at low interest rates. Commercial and merchant banks, which had channelled most foreign funds to the big business sector, were as much concerned about the impact of devaluation on the fortunes of their chaebol clients as they were concerned about theirs. Together, the chaebols and banks formed a powerful anti-devaluation alliance and lobbied hard against any attempts to devalue.

The Ministry of Finance and Economy, which traditionally had close ties with the big business community and was increasingly penetrated by its rent-seeking activities, found itself only too ready to accommodate the demands from the chaebols and their financial subsidiaries. Economic officials, who were grappling with the unprecedented corporate failures during the first half of 1997, feared that devaluation would bring down more debt-stricken chaebol firms and, with them, financial institutions. Furthermore, the Kim government, which had come to power with a mandate to pursue price stability but failed to achieve the policy objective consistently, was eager to avoid cost-push inflation caused by the devaluation of the won. This consideration took on more political importance, particularly when the presidential election was drawing near. The government thus made comprehensive efforts to defend the won.

The won, however, was indefensible. Between early October and mid-November 1997, the won lost more than 30 per cent of its value against the US dollar, as local and foreign investors were all betting against it. South Korean financial and corporate borrowers, already weighed down by plunging profits and soaring non-performing loans, found it extremely hard to service external debts totalling some $60 billion that would mature in less than a year. The BOK, which had dumped its dollar reserves in an eventually futile attempt to defend the peg, had no foreign funds with which to help the cash-strapped financial institutions. As the exchange rate depreciated sharply and the domestic currency costs of servicing foreign debts mounted, foreign creditors, who already had investments and loans worth hundreds of billions of dollars in South Korea, were reluctant to extend new loans or roll over existing loans. With the spectre of national default looming large, the government called in the IMF for a bail-out in late November 1997.

Conclusion

The basic argument developed in this chapter has been that the financial crisis in South Korea and Thailand had important endogenous origins, among which were the interests of the private sector in the policy process. In both countries, severe weaknesses in the corporate and financial sectors corresponded to a problematic financial reform process. This in turn reflected the growing capture of public policy processes by powerful private sector interests. Equally, the same political constraints that had shaped the necessarily imperfect financial liberalisation process contributed directly to the persistence of an unsustainable exchange rate policy and to the inability of the governments to tackle mounting corporate and financial difficulties. The resulting policy failures ultimately caused a profound loss of investor confidence, provoked rapid withdrawals of foreign funds and triggered massive currency depreciation.

This comparative analysis of the political sources of the financial crisis in South Korea and Thailand underscores the importance of limiting the play of private interests in the financial system and of maintaining a balance between private power and public authority in the successful functioning of market economies. Financial and regulatory policy processes, characterised by technical complexity and close private–public interactions, are notoriously susceptible to particularistic rent seeking. There is thus an ongoing danger that structurally powerful and politically resourceful private actors can succeed in capturing the policy-making process and convert public interests into private gains, even under conditions of democracy.

The analysis also implies that external pressure for financial liberalisation should be exerted with caution. National financial systems undergoing reform need time to adjust not just economically, but politically and institutionally as well. Given that financial system design impinges on systemic stability and broader macroeconomic governance, the undue dominance of financial and regulatory policies by powerful private interests writing the rules and norms for their own convenience and profits can lead to government failures and economic crisis.[29]

The implications derived from the comparative study emphasise that the potential solution to the capture problem lies not so much in the mechanism of competition among private economic agents as in the constant restructuring of the market through state policy processes and institutional reforms. Financial market reform is likely to be less subject to political distortion and more growth-enhancing where the economic bureaucracy achieve a considerable degree of institutional autonomy from private actors and groups and where private–public interactions are kept oriented towards policy-making efficiency. Clearly, establishing and sustaining efficiency-oriented business–government relations and the politically independent bureaucracy is a difficult and costly process for many developing and emerging market economies. The daunting task of developing appropriate political institutions for improving the workings of markets suggests that we take a pragmatic and long-term approach to liberalisation, with greater attention to the risk of political capture and institutional development. If this argument can be accepted, financial market reform is likely to yield slower but better long-run results.

Notes

1. External explanations are exemplified in Steven Radelet and Jeffrey D. Sachs, 'The East Asian Financial Crisis: Diagnosis, Remedies, Prospects', *Brookings Papers on Economic Activity*, no. 1 (1998), pp. 1–90; Robert Wade, 'The Asian Debt-and-Development Crisis of 1997–?: Causes and Consequences', *World Development*, vol. 26, no. 8 (1998), pp. 1535–53; Jeffrey A. Winters, 'The Financial Crisis in Southeast Asia', in Richard Robison *et al.* (eds.), *Politics and Markets in the Wake of the Asian Crisis* (London: Routledge, 2000), pp. 34–52.
2. See, for example, Giancarlo Corsetti, Paolo Pesenti and Nouriel Roubini, 'What Caused the Asian Currency and Financial Crisis?' *Japan and the World Economy*, vol. 11 (1999), pp. 305–73; Graciela L. Kaminsky and Carmen M. Reinhart, 'The Twin Crises: The Causes of Banking and Balance-of-Payments Problems', *The American Economic Review*, vol. 89, no. 3 (1999), pp. 473–500.
3. These institutional weaknesses are discussed at length in Chung-In Moon and Sang-Young Rhyu, 'The State, Structural Rigidity, and the End of Asian Capitalism: A Comparative Study of Japan and South Korea', in Robison *et al.*; Xiaoke Zhang, *The Changing Politics of Finance in Korea and Thailand* (London: Routledge, 2002), ch. 7.
4. See Xiaoke Zhang, 'Domestic Institutions, Liberalisation Patterns, and Uneven Crises in Korea and Taiwan', *The Pacific Review*, vol. 15, no. 3 (2000), pp. 409–42.
5. For discussions that emphasis these variables as the direct causes of the financial crisis see Stephan Haggard, 'The Politics of the Asian Financial Crisis', *Journal of Democracy*, vol. 11, no. 2 (2000), pp. 130–44; Andrew MacIntyre, 'Political Institutions and the Economic Crisis in Thailand and Indonesia', *ASEAN Economic Bulletin*, vol. 15, no. 3 (1998), pp. 362–72.
6. Pasuk Phongpaichit and Chris Baker, *Thailand's Boom and Bust* (Chiang Mai: Silkworm Books, 1998), p. 98.
7. See William H. Overholt, 'Thailand's Financial and Political Systems', *Asian Survey*, vol. 39, no. 6 (1999), pp. 1013–4.
8. See Pedro Alba, Stijn Claessens and Simeon Djankov, 'Thailand's Corporate Financing and Governance Structures: Impact on Firms' Competitiveness', Policy Research Working Paper 2003 (Washington, DC: World Bank, 1998); Tull Traisorat, *Thailand: Financial Sector Reform and the East Asian Crisis* (The Hague: Kluwer Law International, 2000), ch. 2.
9. See Jonathan E. Leightner, 'Globalisation and Thailand's Financial Crisis', *Journal of Economic Issues*, vol. 33, no. 2 (1999), pp. 367–73; 'The Achilles' Heel of Thailand's Financial Market', in Tsu-Tan Fu, Cliff J. Hunang and C. A. Knox Lovell (eds.), *Economic Efficiency and Productivity Growth in the Asia-Pacific Region* (Cheltenham: Edward Elgar, 1999), pp. 287–307.
10. See Bank of Thailand, *Fifty Years of the Bank of Thailand: 1942–1992* (Bangkok: Bank of Thailand, 1992), pp. 300–2; R. Barry Johnston, 'Distressed Financial Institutions in Thailand: Structural Weaknesses, Support Operations and Economic Consequences', IMF working paper WP/89/4 (Washington, DC: IMF, 1989).

11. See Pakorn Vichyanond, 'Financial Sector Development in Thailand', in Shahid N. Zahid (ed.), *Financial Sector Development in Asia* (Hong Kong: Oxford University Press, 1995), pp. 303–70.
12. *The Nation*, 24 Aug. 1998 and 3 Sept. 1998.
13. *Far Eastern Economic Review*, 21 May 1998, p. 63.
14. The *Banker*, May 1997, pp. 70–1.
15. For a more detailed discussion, see MacIntyre, 'Political Institutions'.
16. See *Far Eastern Economic Review*, 27 March 1997, pp. 67–8; Pasuk Phongpaichit and Baker, *Thailand's Boom and Bust*, pp. 121–3.
17. *Bangkok Post*, 2 May 1998; *Bangkok Post Economic Review*, 30 June 1998, pp. 16–18.
18. See Zhang, *Changing Politics*, chs. 4 and 7.
19. Eduardo Borensztein and Jong-Wha Lee, 'Credit Allocation and Financial Crisis in Korea', IMF Working Paper WP/99/20 (Washington, DC: IMF, 1999).
20. Heather Smith, 'Korea', in Ross H. McLeod and Ross Garnaut (eds.), *East Asia in Crisis: From Being a Miracle to Needing One?* (London: Routledge, 1998), p. 74.
21. Borensztein and Lee, 'Credit Allocation', Table 5.
22. See Ha-Joon Chang, 'Korea: The Misunderstood Crisis', *World Development*, vol. 26, no. 8 (1998), pp. 1555–61.
23. See Joon-Ho Hahm and Frederic S. Mishkin, 'The Korean Financial Crisis: An Asymmetrical Information Perspective', *Emerging Markets Review*, vol. 1, no. 3 (2000), pp. 42–3.
24. By one account, nearly 70 per cent of annual increase in corporate investment in South Korea between 1993 and 1996 was financed by borrowed funds. See Michael Pomerleano, 'The East Asia Crisis and Corporate Finances: The Untold Micro Story', Policy Research Working Paper 1990 (Washington, DC: World Bank, 1998), Table 4.
25. A detailed discussion of these reasons cannot be accommodated here, but for the background see *Economist Intelligence Unit Country Report – South Korea*, 2nd Quarter 1997; *Far Eastern Economic Review*, 31 July 1997, p. 58; *The Korea Times*, 25 Jan. 1997.
26. *Far Eastern Economic Review*, 13 Feb. 1997, p. 53.
27. For detailed accounts of the process of corporate restructuring, see Stephan Haggard and Jongryn Mo, 'The Political Economy of the Korean Financial Crisis', *Review of International Political Economy*, vol.7, no. 2 (2000), pp. 197–218; Jongryn Mo, 'Political Culture and Legislative Gridlock: Politics of Economic Reform in Pre-crisis Korea', *Comparative Political Studies*, vol. 34, no. 5 (2001), pp. 467–92.
28. See Chung-In Moon and Jongryn Mo, 'Democracy and the Origins of the 1997 Korean Economic Crisis', in Jongryn Mo and Chung-In Moon (eds.), *Democracy and the Korean Economy* (Stanford: Hoover Institution Press, 1998).
29. This point is discussed more systematically in Geoffrey Underhill, 'The Public Good versus Private Interests in the Global Monetary and Financial System', *International and Comparative Corporate Law Journal*, vol. 2, no. 3 (2000), pp. 335–59.

13 Governance, markets and power: the political economy of accounting reform in Indonesia

ANDREW ROSSER

Over the past two and a half decades, increases in the international mobility of financial capital have generated pressures for the international harmonisation of financial sector regulations and practices. As finance capital has become increasingly mobile, controllers of financial capital have sought harmonisation of these regulations and practices in order to facilitate access to and exit from foreign markets and thereby reduce the risk and increase the profits associated with foreign investments. With enhanced mobility, controllers of financial capital have been able to threaten states that they will relocate their capital to alternative jurisdictions if they do not comply with demands for harmonisation. States have thus been severely constrained in terms of their policy options: if they do not pursue harmonisation they risk reduced access to international financial markets and the economic benefits that go with it.

One area in which these pressures have produced change has been accounting. Since its establishment in 1973, the International Accounting Standards Committee (IASC), a private sector policy-making body that is backed by a range of financial market players and other multinational corporations, has issued forty international accounting standards (IASs). Whilst this organisation does not have the formal authority to require countries to adopt its standards, it has had considerable success in persuading them to do so, especially in the developing world. Although the extent to which developing countries have adopted IASs has varied from country to country, there has nevertheless been a broad shift towards harmonisation throughout the developing world.[1] Some developing countries have also introduced changes to company and capital market laws which have given these standards legal backing and provided mechanisms by which minority shareholders can seek damages from public companies if they produce misleading financial information, further measures that are consistent with harmonisation.

At the same time, however, widespread concern has continued to be expressed about the quality of financial reporting in many developing countries. Rahman, for instance, has described accounting disclosure in many east Asian countries as 'inadequate' and has suggested that it 'contributed to the depth and breadth' of the recent Asian economic crisis. Further, he has argued that 'Accounting disclosures by financial institutions and corporations in most of the East Asian countries did not follow or comply with international accounting standards (IASs)', notwithstanding the widespread adoption of IASs throughout Asia.[2] Similarly, McKinsey & Co. have stated that the quality of financial reporting in many developing countries is 'poor' and has led to increased concern in business circles about the quality of corporate governance in these countries.[3] In short, it appears that whilst many developing countries may have revised their accounting regulations in accordance with global norms – and, in particular, IASs – the application and enforcement of these regulations has been weak.

How can this outcome be understood? Has it reflected the persistence of traditional cultural values in the face of globalisation and the changes unleashed by economic modernisation? Has it reflected a lack of institutional capacity on the part of states in developing countries and, in particular, a relatively low degree of state autonomy from political and social forces? Or has it reflected real limits on the capacity of the controllers of internationally mobile finance capital, their allies at the World Bank and the IMF, and other public and private sector actors to promote accounting reform in developing countries? What does it suggest about the prospects for global financial integration more generally? Does it imply that for all the talk about the erosion of national differences as a result of globalisation, national systems of financial regulation and the local systems of power and interest that underpin them are likely to survive?

This chapter attempts to shed some light on these questions by examining the dynamics of accounting reform in Indonesia since the mid-1960s. In brief, it suggests that globalisation is not leading to a complete erosion of national differences in the nature of accounting systems (and financial systems more generally) in the developing world. In Indonesia harmonisation has proceeded at the level of regulation – that is, the country has adopted IASs – but it has not proceeded at the level of accounting practice – that is, at the level of application and enforcement. Underlying this outcome, it is argued, has been the fact that controllers of internationally mobile capital and other political and social elements with an interest in neo-liberal economic reform have been unable to achieve direct control of the state. Whilst periodic economic shocks have dramatically increased the structural power of mobile capital controllers, direct control over the state has remained in the hands of elements opposed to accounting reform. In this context, the chapter suggests that we will probably not see a homogenisation of accounting systems (and financial systems more generally) throughout the developing world. Whilst developing countries will be persuaded to adopt Western accounting standards, the way in which many of them apply and enforce these standards will not accord with global norms.

The chapter is divided into three parts. The first examines the alternative ways in which accounting researchers have explained accounting reform in developing countries and outlines an alternative approach that focuses on state- and class-based interests. The second examines the Indonesian case of accounting reform in detail. The final section examines the implications of the argument for efforts to move towards a global financial architecture.

Understanding the dynamics of accounting reform in developing countries

In explaining accounting reform in developing countries, accounting researchers have generally relied on explanations that emphasise the economic rationality of accounting policy makers. Anglo-Saxon accounting policies, it is argued, represent a 'logical guide' for developing countries because they reduce the cost of capital, lower investment risk and promote a more efficient allocation of economic resources and higher rates of economic growth.[4] At the same time, traditional cultural values in developing countries are seen as being incompatible with the changing business environment and in conflict with the goal of economic modernisation.[5] In this view, then, accounting reform is simply a matter of accounting policy makers making rational choices. The only precondition for reform, it is implied, is the existence of policy makers who are able to overcome cultural obstacles to reform and put considerations of efficiency above all else.[6]

The problem with these explanations is that, like the neo-classical and modernisation theories on which they are based, they portray accounting reform as a purely technical process in which politics and power play no role. It is assumed that accounting policy makers make their decisions solely on the basis of considerations of efficiency and growth. Yet, as several scholars have pointed out, it is less a technical concern to improve efficiency and growth that drives the process of economic policy reform than a desire to protect, reinforce or gain social and economic power.[7] Economic policies, they have argued, not only influence the efficiency with which resources are allocated but also their distribution within society – that is, they influence 'who gets what, why and how'.[8] As such, they are embedded in systems of power and interest, and reform will only occur when there has been a prior shift in the balance of power away from elements who are opposed to change and towards those who are in favour of change.

A second way of understanding the dynamics of accounting reform in developing countries is suggested by the rational choice institutionalist work of scholars such as Stephan Haggard and Joan Nelson. At the heart of this work is the idea that economic policy reform concentrates costs on the beneficiaries of the existing system and disperses benefits to a broad range of actors. For this reason, it is argued, economic reform presents a serious collective action problem: whilst losers will have an incentive to engage in collective action to block reform, potential winners will have little incentive actively to promote reform because of uncertainty about the expected pay-off.[9] As a result, it is argued that an important prerequisite for reform is the existence of a state that is autonomous or is insulated from political and social forces. As Thomas Callaghy has put it, 'The success or failure of adjustment efforts to a large degree depends on a government's ability to insulate itself from – and buffer against and adjust to – threatening political, societal, and international pressures that might prevent the inherent economic logic of the adjustment process from coming into play to the extent necessary.'[10]

The problem with this approach is that it rests on a negative conception of politics. Politics enters the analysis only as an obstacle to reform, not as the process by which reform is obtained. As Hector Schamis has argued,

Theoretically, these claims are based on a profoundly negative view of politics characteristic of neoclassical economics (that is why whenever societal groups engage in political organisation, protectionism is invariably expected to follow) and on what appears to be an increasingly prevalent tendency in the field of political economy: to view political institutions – particularly the state – as autonomous structures with their own distinctive configurations, ideas, and interests, and take them as the independent variable that explains various socio-economic outcomes, government policy among them.[11]

The point is that all state action – whether it promotes or hinders reform – needs to be understood in terms of political and social interests, not just reform failure and intervention.

Argument

We argue that accounting reform in developing countries is best understood in terms of the extent to which structural changes in global and domestic economies shift the balance of power between competing interests (both foreign and domestic) and thus create a political climate conducive to accounting reform. States in developing countries, we argue, are not autonomous entities but ones that respond to a complex range of political and social interests. On the one hand, they respond to the particularistic interests of the dominant political and social coalitions in these countries – typically coalitions consisting of the strata of politico-bureaucrats that occupy the state apparatus and the dominant fractions of capital. On the other, because (in most cases at least) they exist within a capitalist context, they are also structurally compelled to provide a legal, political and fiscal environment conducive to the reproduction of capital-in-general.[12] Hence they are compelled to ignore the interests of the dominant political and social forces and make concessions to other fractions of capital or organisations such as the World Bank and the IMF if this will ensure the continued health of the capitalist economy. This in turn means that structural changes in global and domestic economies often translate into policy change because they strengthen the position of certain groups vis-à-vis other groups.

In the Indonesian case, we argue that accounting reform was not the product of rational choices by wise technocrats but rather of structural pressures generated by periodic economic crises. These crises, we argue, dramatically strengthened the position of elements – such as controllers of internationally mobile capital, the IMF and the World Bank – that favoured accounting reform because they significantly increased the country's need to attract greater amounts of foreign aid and investment. Within this context, influence over economic policy (and accounting policy in particular) shifted away from the politico-bureaucrats and their corporate clients and towards liberal technocrats within the government. At the same time, however, these crises did not dislodge the politico-bureaucrats and their clients from their position of political and social dominance – even in 1997–8 when the Indonesian economy virtually collapsed, they were to remain very influential. The result was that the technocrats were only able to push through a partial range of accounting reforms: whilst they were able completely to revamp the country's accounting regulations, they were unable to ensure the proper application and enforcement of these regulations through auditing and judicial reform.

The Indonesian case

The contending interests

Broadly speaking, two main sets of political and social interests have played a role in shaping accounting policy in Indonesia during the New Order period. The first of these has been controllers of internationally mobile capital and their allies at the World Bank and the IMF. Controllers of mobile capital have supported accounting reform because they have desired more reliable information on which to base their investment decisions and greater control over how Indonesian companies use the funds they give them. In short they have wanted to reduce the risk and thereby maximise the profits associated with Indonesian investments. The amount and reliability of financial information from Indonesian companies, they have argued, has been low compared with developed countries and even some developing countries. They have thus called on the government to introduce tougher disclosure rules and harmonise accounting practices with Western ones.[13]

The international aid agencies have supported these calls for accounting reform because of the neat fit between them and their own broader agenda. As Western governments and business groups have become increasingly concerned about the quality of governance in developing countries, these agencies have placed increased emphasis on the institutional foundations of economic growth. Markets, they have argued, require a broad array of institutional supports, including sound accounting and auditing systems, to operate efficiently and promote economic growth.[14] Because Indonesia's accounting and auditing regulations have been weak and its professional organisation under-developed, they have advised the Indonesian government to make reform in this area a priority.[15] Their views have carried considerable weight, not because they have been correct in any technical sense, but rather because they have embodied the interests of foreign governments and investors, and their control over aid money has given them enormous structural leverage over governments, especially at times of economic crisis.

Within the state these elements gained support from the liberal technocrats who have run key economic departments such as the Ministry of Finance and Bank Indonesia, the central bank. Drawn almost exclusively from the Faculty of Economics at the University of Indonesia and in many cases educated overseas in orthodox economics, the technocrats have been strong supporters of neo-liberal economic reform and accounting reform in particular. In their view, accounting reform has been essential for the country to create a more market-oriented and competitive economy. 'Good accounting standards', they have argued, 'generate confidence among investors that is absolutely essential to stimulate the flow of capital. Further, good accounting also helps insure [sic] the continued efficient use of capital once it has been accumulated.'[16]

The second set of political and social interests that have played a role in shaping accounting policy in Indonesia has been the 'politico-bureaucrats', a small cadre of senior state officials who have controlled many other sections of the state apparatus and their corporate clients. The central characteristic of the politico-bureaucrats has been their ability 'to appropriate the offices of the state apparatus and in their own right exercise authority over the allocation of resources and access'.[17] In contrast to the technocrats, they have been opposed to accounting reform because of their fear that, by making business enterprises more transparent, it could limit their opportunities to engage in rent-seeking activity.[18] In the absence of adequate transparency, senior government and military officials have been able to secure lucrative positions within state-owned enterprises (SOEs) for themselves, ensure that supply contracts for these enterprises are awarded to companies with which they have close connections, and use SOEs to raise extra-budgetary revenue for sections of the military and government departments.[19] One of their main concerns about accounting reform has thus been that – by making business enterprises more transparent and accountable – it could limit their ability to use SOEs as milch-cows.

Another has been that accounting reform could have negative implications for the private domestic conglomerates with which they are connected. Prior to the revival of the capital market and the introduction of accounting reforms in the 1980s and early 1990s, it had been commonplace for private companies in Indonesia to keep three sets of books – one which showed the 'true' state of the business and which was used for management decision-making, one which showed a positive result and which was used for raising loans from foreign and local banks, and one which showed a loss or small profit and was used for taxation purposes.[20] The politico-bureaucrats have thus been concerned that, by increasing and standardising the amount of financial information that is publicly available, accounting reform could reduce the ability of companies to avoid tax and manipulate lenders and other financial statement users. Another concern has been that, by exposing more information about these companies' wealth, it could also fuel populist criticism of their activities.

The relative influence that these groups have exercised over Indonesia's accounting policies during the New Order period has fluctuated according to the country's need for private capital inflows and inflows of foreign aid. When the country's need for these inflows has been high (as it was during the late 1960s–early 1970s, the period since the mid-1980s, and again during 1997–8), the New Order has had to be responsive to the needs of controllers of internationally mobile capital and the international aid agencies. The technocrats have thus been able to promote the process of accounting reform. When the country's need for these inflows has been low (as it was during the oil boom years of 1973–81), however, the New Order has been able to ignore the demands of these groups and act in a relatively autonomous manner. Within this context, the influence of the technocrats over accounting policy has declined and that of the politico-bureaucrats and conglomerates has risen. The result has been a significant slow-down in the process of accounting reform.

Accounting policy making in Indonesia: 1965–mid-1980s

When the New Order came to power in 1965, Indonesia was in the midst of the worst economic crisis that it had experienced since independence. Between 1961 and 1965, the economy virtually ground to a halt, with net domestic product rising only slightly from Rp. 407 billion to Rp. 430 billion (figures in 1960 prices). At the same time, the country's export earnings fell dramatically, from US$750 million to US$450 million, making it virtually impossible for the country to meet its burgeoning foreign debt commitments. Spiralling inflation, caused by excessive printing of money, provided the most obvious sign of economic distress. In 1960, inflation stood at 20 per cent per annum, but by 1965 it had risen to almost 600 per cent.[21] In this context, internationally mobile capital either fled overseas or was diverted into activities with quick returns, such as trade and currency exchange. The result, as Emil Salim, one of the New Order's most important economic ministers, has pointed out, was that 'Normal long-term investment stopped.'[22]

With the economy in disarray, the technocrats were to emerge as the most influential economic policy makers within the government. The leader of New Order, General Soeharto, recognised that the survival of his government depended at least in part on its ability to renegotiate debt, secure foreign aid, promote investment and stimulate economic growth. None of these goals could be achieved, however, unless his government could attract internationally mobile capital back into the country and gain the support of the IMF, the World Bank and other international donors. He was thus under enormous pressure to shift away from the radical populist and nationalist interventionism of the previous regime and towards the sort of policies advocated by the technocrats.[23]

Within this context, the government was to give increased attention to accounting reform as part of a broader attempt to revive the Indonesian capital market. The previous government's decision to nationalise all Dutch companies in 1958 and to suspend trading in shares of Dutch firms in 1960 had effectively made it impossible for the country's capital market to survive, and it was eventually closed down in 1968. The technocrats argued that the country needed a properly functioning capital market if it was to attract internationally mobile capital back into the country and, consequently, took steps to revive it. In 1968, they established the Money and Capital Markets Preparation Team under the Governor of Bank Indonesia to make recommendations to the central bank concerning money and capital market policy. In 1970 and 1972, they established another two bodies, again under the central bank governor, to begin the process of reactivating the capital market and to supervise its activities. As part of these bodies' work, they were to be responsible for producing, in conjunction with the professional accounting institute – the Indonesian Accounting Association (IAI) – Indonesia's first set of accounting standards in 1973.[24]

These standards, which were called Indonesian Accounting Principles (*Prinsip Akuntansi Indonesia* or PAI), were a compilation of basic accounting principles, practices, methods and techniques. Based on the American Institute of Certified Public Accountants' 1965 research study 'Inventory of Generally Accepted Accounting Principles for Business Enterprises', they were intended to address general accounting issues rather than provide detailed prescriptions for accounting practice.[25] Even in their revised 1984 form, they did not deal at all, for instance, with accounting practices for specific industries such as banking, insurance or mining, and their coverage of specific topics such as consolidations and the creation of allowances and provisions was either extremely limited or non-existent.[26] At the same time, they were not given legislative backing. At that time, Indonesia's company law, which had been inherited from the Dutch colonial period, simply required that 'adequate accounts' be kept.[27] It did not contain a specific requirement that financial reporting be done in accordance with the PAI or any other prescribed set of standards. For this reason, and because the PAI permitted companies to refer to other countries' accounting regulations where the PAI did not deal with a particular accounting issue, companies still had enormous latitude in the way in which they could account for their financial affairs.

Despite the technical weaknesses of the PAI, however, the government was to do nothing to further the process of accounting reform over the next decade. The main reason for this was the onset of the oil boom in the mid-1970s. International oil prices rose dramatically between 1973 and 1974 and again between 1979 and 1981, on both occasions more than tripling in value. As a result of this rise, Indonesia's oil and gas exports leapt from US$1.6 billion, or 50.1 per cent of total exports, in 1973 to US$18.4 billion, or 82.6 per cent of total exports, in 1982. At the same time, the government's oil and gas revenues rose from Rp. 382 billion, or 39.5 per cent of total government revenues, in 1973/74 to Rp. 8.6 trillion, or over 70 per cent of total government revenues, in 1981/2. Within this context, the conditions that had made accounting reform possible during the early New Order period evaporated. With vast sums of petrodollars flowing into government coffers, it was no longer necessary for the government to design capital market policies that would attract internationally mobile capital back into the country. Furthermore, the politico-bureaucrats' control over much of the government's new oil wealth meant that they, rather than the technocrats, came to exercise the dominant influence over economic policy.[28] In this context, accounting reform was simply dropped from the agenda.

When the government eventually re-established the Indonesian capital market in 1977, it did not introduce accompanying accounting reforms. Indeed, the main purpose for re-establishing the capital market as far as the government was concerned had changed entirely. The mid-1970s had seen a series of demonstrations by students, small businessmen and other marginalised groups when the government's economic policies were criticised and appeals were made for an end to foreign and Chinese domination of the economy. For this reason, the government decided to re-establish the capital market, not as a mechanism for attracting internationally mobile capital, but rather as a mechanism for redistributing wealth from large (especially foreign) companies to ordinary Indonesians.[29] In this context, there was no need for the government to address issues of accounting reform. Redistributing wealth through the capital market required the introduction of a range of restrictive regulations that in turn had the effect of reducing demand for Indonesian stocks.[30] With low demand for Indonesian stocks, there was also low demand for good accounting information and therefore for accounting reform.

It was to take the collapse of international oil prices in the early to mid-1980s – and the enormous structural pressures that it generated – to put accounting reform back on the agenda. The oil price collapse dramatically reduced both Indonesia's oil and gas exports and the government's revenues from the oil and gas sector. By 1986, the country's oil and gas exports had fallen to US$8.3 billion, or 56 per cent of total exports, and by 1986/7 government revenues from the oil and gas sector had fallen to Rp. 6.3 trillion or 39.3 per cent of total government revenues. Within this context, the government decided to reinvigorate the Indonesian capital market. This had grown extremely slowly between 1977 and the mid-1980s – only twenty-four companies had listed their shares on the Jakarta Stock Exchange (JSX) by late 1988 – largely because of the restrictive capital market regulations imposed by the government at its inception.[31] With the country in desperate need of new sources of investment funds, it was no longer possible for the government to continue with capital market policies that restricted the flow of portfolio capital into the country. Instead it was forced to pursue the capital market strategy advocated by the technocrats: deregulation and the introduction of measures, such as tougher financial accounting requirements, that would improve the institutional infrastructure of the capital market.

Accounting policy making in Indonesia since the mid-1980s

Initially, the government was to focus on deregulation of the capital market rather than accounting and other institutional reforms. Its main concern following the collapse of oil prices was to revitalise the capital market, and it was consequently reluctant – at least at first – to introduce any measures, such as tougher financial accounting requirements, that might discourage the conglomerates from going public.[32] Thus between December 1987 and September 1989, when it introduced its first major capital market reform packages, it did nothing in the area of accounting. The main purpose of these packages was to deregulate the capital market by eliminating restrictions on share price movements, granting permission for foreign investors to purchase shares in publicly listed companies, establishing a new over-the-counter market, simplifying procedures for issuing and listing securities, equalising the tax treatment of interest and dividends, and reducing the role of the state-owned investment trust in buying and selling shares, underwriting and operating mutual funds.

Over the next few years, however, the government was to come under increasing pressure to push ahead with the process of accounting reform. First, the World Bank was to become increasingly critical of the government's accounting policies, arguing that reform in this area was necessary if the country was to continue the process of economic development and capital market development in particular. In its 1993 report on the Indonesian economy, for instance, it argued that the country needed 'a sound accounting and auditing system . . . to instil financial discipline'.[33] With the Bank's structural leverage greatly enhanced by the country's need to attract internationally mobile capital and foreign aid, the government was under enormous pressure to heed its advice. Second, the capital market was to be shaken by a series of financial reporting scandals that seriously undermined investor confidence.[34] Although a large number of conglomerates rushed to go public following deregulation – by the mid-1990s, there were more than two hundred local companies listed on the JSX – few of them were willing to provide the level of disclosure and transparency that mobile investors were demanding. The result was that the capital market was only able to attract highly volatile, speculative flows of capital. In the wake of these scandals, it became clear to government policy makers that the government had to do something to improve the quality of financial reporting within the country if the capital market was to be transformed from a casino into a mechanism for mobilising long-term investment flows.

In this context, the technocrats were able to push through a series of measures aimed at overhauling the country's financial accounting regulations. In late 1994 the government introduced a new set of financial accounting standards, known as Financial Accounting Standards (PSAKs), to replace the old PAI. Issued formally by the IAI, they represented the product of a co-operative project between that organisation, the Capital Market Supervisory Agency (Bapepam), the international accounting firm Arthur Andersen and the World Bank, which had funded their production.[35] In contrast to the PAI, they were based largely on IASs and consequently were a much more comprehensive set of accounting regulations.[36] Around the same time the government also launched a joint project with the World Bank to develop further Indonesia's accounting regulations and train accounting professionals. Known as the 'Second Accountancy Development Project', this project required almost US$34 million to be spent over a six-year period on improving the quality of financial reporting within both the government and the private sector. A key objective of the project was to be the production of another forty financial accounting standards.[37]

In March 1995 the government continued the process of reform when it introduced several provisions related to accounting in its new Companies Code. Article 58 of the new Companies Code made it mandatory for all companies to prepare their annual accounts in accordance with PSAKs, except where they had just cause not to do so. Article 59 required publicly listed companies to have their accounts audited by a public accountant. Article 60 made company directors and commissioners personally liable for any losses incurred by any persons as a result of untrue or misleading information contained in financial reports.[38] Later that year the government introduced further legal requirements for accounting as part of its Capital Markets Law. This law contained general provisions specifying the format of financial reports and forbidding public companies from providing untrue or misleading information to the public. It also contained provisions that dealt with more specific disclosure matters. Public accountants who discovered that a company was breaching the law or felt that a company was in financial crisis were required to report their concerns to Bapepam. And company directors, commissioners and major shareholders were required to report important events that might affect share prices or else incur a fine of up to Rp. 100,000 per day. The law also introduced a requirement for bond issuers to report how funds raised from going public were to be used.[39]

The 1997–8 economic crisis and further reform

With the collapse of the rupiah during 1997–8, pressure on the government to improve the quality of financial reporting in Indonesia increased even further. The rupiah crisis virtually destroyed the political and economic bases of the New Order. By early 1998 most of the country's conglomerates were technically bankrupt, the banking system was on the verge of collapse, a serious fiscal crisis was looming, rising inflation and unemployment had driven millions of people into poverty, and the government had been forced to call in the IMF and negotiate a rescue package. At the same time political and social unrest was spreading rapidly as a result of rising prices and growing opposition to President Soeharto.[40] Within this context, influence over economic policy making was to shift even more decisively in favour of the controllers of internationally mobile capital and their allies at the IMF and the World Bank. Only by pursuing a more market-oriented economic agenda did the country have any chance of stemming the flight of mobile capital and securing critically needed foreign aid.

At the same time, much public analysis of the Asian economic crisis was to blame poor accounting practices for fuelling the crisis. Foreign investors, it was argued, had 'risked their money on deals that wouldn't have looked so appealing had the books been prepared to international standards'.[41] The head of the US Federal Reserve, Alan Greenspan, was to be amongst the most important critics of Asian accounting practices, telling the US Congress that the Asian crisis would not abate until countries within the region adopted better and clearer accounting rules.[42] The World Bank was also to make accounting a major issue by calling on the Big Five international accounting firms – PricewaterhouseCoopers, Deloitte and Touche, Arthur Andersen, KPMG Peat Marwick and Ernst and Young – to withhold their brand name imprimaturs if their affiliates in developing countries did not meet international accounting and auditing standards.[43] With the country desperately needing to restore mobile investor confidence in the economy and attract foreign aid, the government had little choice but to pay attention to these criticisms.

Within this context, the government was to push ahead with the process of accounting reform. In February 1998 it announced that all limited firms with assets of Rp. 50 billion or more would be required to publish financial statements and have them audited by external auditors.[44] In July 1999 this was followed by a decision by the nominally private but effectively government-controlled Jakarta Stock Exchange Company to introduce a new set of corporate governance regulations for publicly listed companies. Among the main provisions of these regulations were a requirement for publicly listed companies to reserve at least 30 per cent of positions on their boards of directors for 'independent' individuals and for these individuals to form and lead companies' internal audit committees. 'Independent' individuals were defined as those who had no connections to majority shareholders, other directors or other companies within the group.[45]

Resistance to reform

Despite the enormous structural pressures for accounting reform that emerged after the mid-1980s, however, the government was prevented from pursuing a number of key accounting reforms. Although the collapse of oil prices in the mid-1980s weakened the politico-bureaucrats and the conglomerates, they continued to dominate Indonesia's political system. The government electoral vehicle, Golkar, continued to win national and provincial elections with resounding majorities, Soeharto's position as president remained secure despite an apparent challenge from elements within the military in the late 1980s, and bureaucratic pre-eminence vis-à-vis parliament was maintained. It was only with the sudden collapse of the rupiah in 1997–8 that the position of the politico-bureaucrats and the conglomerates came under serious threat. Even then, however, they remained a powerful force. When Soeharto stepped down as president in May 1998, he did so in favour of figures who were closely associated with his regime. Many of the country's new leaders, including the president, Habibie, the senior economics minister, Ginandjar Kartasasmita, and the head of the armed forces, Wiranto, were products of the political and institutional structures of the New Order. Even after the election of opposition figures Abdurrahman Wahid and Megawati Soekarnoputri as president and vice-president respectively in October 1999, figures associated with the New Order remained influential.

Several were given key ministerial and bureaucratic positions in Wahid's first cabinet, and Golkar remained an important constituency in parliament and the MPR (the body that elects the president and vice-president), despite a relatively poor showing at the 1999 national elections. At the same time, the new political parties which contested these elections and came to dominate parliament had few reformist credentials. Most were defined by a commitment to primordial attachments such as religion or radical populism and nationalism rather than by liberal market values.[46]

Within this context, the ability of internationally mobile capital controllers and their allies at the World Bank and the IMF to achieve their reformist agenda within Indonesia was constrained. Although the structural power of international mobile capital controllers had increased significantly as a result of the crisis, direct control of the state remained in the hands of elements that were, for the most part, opposed to liberal market reform. This in turn was to impair their ability to ensure the proper application and enforcement of the country's new accounting regulations.

One important area in which they were to experience difficulties was auditing. In the mid-1980s the government had officially prohibited foreign accountants from practising in the country, forcing international auditing firms to operate through domestic affiliates over which, in most cases, they had little control. This combined with the conglomerates' ability to change auditors if they desired, meant that there was great scope for the conglomerates to pressure local auditor firms into signing off on financial reports that were incomplete, misleading or both.[47] In early 1997, following World Bank calls for Indonesian auditors to be more independent of their clients, the government announced that it would permit foreign accountants to practise within the country on an individual basis. It did not, however, give permission for foreign accountants to establish their own auditing firms, effectively forcing international firms to continue operating in Indonesia through their affiliates. The result, then, was that there was virtually no further scope for improved auditing within the country.[48]

At the same time, the government also did nothing to reform the country's notoriously corrupt judiciary. In the absence of an independent judiciary Article 60 of the Companies Code concerning the personal liability of company directors and commissioners for losses incurred as a result of misleading information was effectively unenforceable. Any minority shareholder who launched legal proceedings against a director or commissioner of a major conglomerate would have little hope of winning, given that the judiciary would probably side with his or her opponent. This also suited the conglomerates for obvious reasons. As with auditing, the reason for the government's inaction in this area was that it was simply too difficult politically. The authority of the politico-bureaucrats and the conglomerates was based to a considerable extent on their ability to control judicial outcomes.[49] Judicial reform would have given their political opponents a much stronger chance in court and thus severely undermined their own political and social position.

Not surprisingly, then, serious concerns continued to be expressed about the quality of financial reporting in Indonesia during the mid- to late 1990s. Business consultants and analysts continued to claim that Indonesian financial reports were unreliable and misleading.[50] Even figures associated with the IAI acknowledged that manipulation of financial reports was still widespread despite the regulatory changes.[51] At the same time, more financial reporting scandals were exposed. In May 1997, for instance, it was revealed that a leading listed property company, Summarecon, had produced two sets of financial accounts that reported contradictory results for one of its subsidiaries. The first set of accounts, which had been prepared to fulfil legal obligations in case the subsidiary was liquidated, reported that the subsidiary had made a loss of Rp. 70 billion. The second, which had been prepared for public shareholders, reported that the subsidiary had made a large profit. Concerned that the company had doctored its accounts to mislead investors, both Bapepam and the IAI announced that they would launch investigations into the matter.[52]

Conclusion

What, then, does this analysis suggest about attempts to move towards a global financial architecture? Much academic writing on the effects of globalisation has suggested that it is leading to increasing homogenisation in the nature of economic regulations and institutions across the globe. Several scholars, for instance, have suggested that the east Asian economic crisis – which is widely seen as having been a product of globalisation – has signalled the end of the Asian development model and created conditions for growing convergence between east Asian economic systems and the Western neo-liberal model.[53] At the same time, much academic writing on accounting systems in developing countries has tended to assume that these systems will inevitably become more Western in character. Scholars such as Chow *et al.* and Han, for instance, have suggested that developing countries will shift away from traditional accounting practices and towards Western ones as the former become incompatible with an increasingly complex and competitive business environment and globalisation creates a need for more efficient accounting systems.[54]

The analysis presented here, however, suggests that there is nothing inevitable about homogenisation in this area. It is certainly true that, as in the Indonesian case, many developing countries are adopting IASs (or other Western accounting standards) in order to access global financial markets. And it is likely that as long as developing countries need capital from these markets, they will at least try to look as if they are doing something to improve the quality of financial accounting within their borders. But, at the same time, governments within developing countries are embedded in domestic political and social interests that, in many cases, are opposed to the introduction of measures – such as auditing and judicial reform – that are essential for accounting systems to operate according to Western standards. In short, what is required for the emergence of a truly global financial architecture is fundamental political change. Only if the controllers of internationally mobile capital – or perhaps domestic forces with a neo-liberal agenda – are able to establish instrumental control over the state will the political and social conditions for auditing and judicial reform prevail.

What this analysis suggests, then, is that prospects for global financial integration and homogenisation will be a function of two variables: (i) the extent to which controllers of internationally mobile capital can transform their structural power into direct control over particular states; and (ii) the extent to which there exist pro-reform coalitions at the domestic level that might also be able to seize direct control over the state. In the Indonesian case, it is apparent that neither variable has been conducive to complete convergence on the Western financial model, at least in the area of accounting: direct control over the state has remained in the hands of elements opposed to accounting reform. But this need not be the case in other developing countries. Even within south-east Asia, there are marked differences in terms of the coalitional structure, institutional character and ideological make-up of countries within the region.[55] This suggests that progress towards global financial integration will be uneven and that there is a real prospect that national differences in the nature of financial systems will endure.

Notes

1. C. Hoarau, 'International Accounting Harmonization: American Hegemony or Mutual Recognition with Benchmarks?' *The European Accounting Review*, vol. 4, no. 2 (1995), p. 219. See also C. Nobes, 'Harmonization of Financial Reporting', in C. Nobes and R. Parker, *Comparative International Accounting* (New York: Prentice Hall, 1995; R. Ma (ed.), *Financial Reporting in the Pacific Asia Region* (Singapore: World Scientific and Singapore Institute of Management, 1997) P. Pacter, 'International Accounting Standards: The World's Standards by 2002', *The CPA Journal*, vol. 68, no. 7 (July 1998), pp. 14–21; C. Roberts, C. Adams, R. Woo and X. Wu, 'Chinese Accounting Reform: The Internationalization of Financial Reporting', *Advances in International Accounting*, vol. 8 (1995), pp. 201–21.
2. M. Rahman, 'The Role of Accounting Disclosure in the East Asian Financial Crisis: Lessons Learned?' mimeo, UNCTAD, Geneva (1998) p. 13.
3. *Business Day*, 31 Aug. 2000.

4. R. Graham and C. Wang, 'Taiwan and International Accounting Standards: A Comparison', *The International Journal of Accounting*, vol. 30, no. 2 (1995), p. 150. See also K. Han. 'Setting Accounting Standards in Singapore', *Advances in International Accounting*, 6 (1994), pp. 147–161.

5. See L. Chow, G. Chau and S. Gray, 'Accounting Reforms in China: Cultural Constraints on Implementation and Development', *Accounting and Business Research*, vol. 26, no. 1 (1995), pp. 29–49; L. Graham and C. Li, 'Cultural and Economic Influences on Current Accounting Standards in the People's Republic of China', *The International Journal of Accounting*, vol. 32, no. 3 (1997), pp. 247–78.

6. Several accounting researchers have argued that cultures in developing countries present a serious obstacle to accounting reform. See, for instance, Chow et al., 'Accounting Reforms'; Graham and Li, 'Cultural and Economic Influences'; and S. Hamid, R. Craig and F. Clarke, 'Religion: A Confounding Element in the Internationalization of Accounting?', *ABACUS*, vol. 29, no. 2 (1993), pp. 131–48.

7. See P. Bardhan, 'The New Institutional Economics and Development Theory: A Brief Critical Assessment', *World Development*, vol. 17 (1989); K. Chaudhry, 'The Myths of the Market and the Common History of late Developers', *Politics and Society*, vol. 21, no. 3 (1993), pp. 245–74; 'Economic Liberalization and the Lineages of the Rentier State', *Comparative Politics*, vol. 27, no. 1 (October 1994), pp. 1–25; A. Rosser, 'The Political Economy of Institutional Reform in Indonesia: The Case of Intellectual Property Law', in K. Jayasuriya (ed.), *Law, Capitalism and Power in Asia: The Rule of Law and Legal Institutions* (London: Routledge, 1998; S. Sargeson and Zhang Jian, 'Reassessing the Role of the Local State: A Case Study of Local Government Interventions in Property Rights Reform in a Hangzhou District', *The China Journal*, no. 42 (1999); T. Tinker, 'Theories of the State and the State of Accounting: Economic Reductionism and Political Voluntarism in Accounting Regulation Theory', *Journal of Accounting and Public Policy*, vol. 3 (1984), pp. 55–74.

8. Chaudhry, 'The Myths of the Market', p. 247.

9. S. Haggard and R. Kaufman, 'Institutions and Economic Adjustment', in S. Haggard and R. Kaufman (eds.), *The Politics of Economic Adjustment* (Princeton: Princeton University Press, 1992), pp. 18–20; J. Nelson, 'The Politics of Economic Transformation: Is Third World Experience Relevant in Eastern Europe?' *World Politics*, vol. 45 (April 1993), pp. 434–5; H. Schamis, 'Distributional Coalitions and the Politics of Economic Reform in Latin America', *World Politics*, vol. 51 (1999), p. 237.

10. T. Callaghy, 'Towards State Capability and Embedded liberalism in the Third World: Lessons for Adjustment' in J. Nelson et al., *Fragile Coalitions: The Politics of Economic Adjustment* (New Brunswick: Transaction Books, 1989), p. 120.

11. Schamis, 'Distributional Coalitions', p. 266.

12. See, for instance, R. Robison, *Indonesia: The Rise of Capital* (St Leonards: Allen & Unwin, 1986); R. Robison, K. Hewison and G. Rodan, 'Political Power in Industrialising Capitalist Societies: Theoretical Approaches', in K. Hewison, R. Robison and G. Rodan (eds.), *Southeast Asia in the 1990s: Authoritarianism, Democracy and Capitalism* (St. Leonards: Allen & Unwin, 1993); D. Rueschemeyer and P. Evans,

'The State and Economic Transformation: Toward an Analysis of the Conditions Underlying Effective Intervention', in P. Evans, D. Rueschemeyer and T. Skocpol (eds.), *Bringing the State Back In* (Cambridge: Cambridge University Press, 1985); Rosser, 'The Political Economy of Institutional Reform in Indonesia'.

13. See, for instance, The Tokio Marine and Fire Insurance Company, 'Indonesia's Securities Market: Institutional Investor's Perspective', in Institute of Global Financial Studies (ed.), *The Stock Markets in Asia* (Institute of Global Financial Studies, 1994) *Asian Wall Street Journal* (hereafter *AWSJ*), 28 Sep. 1989; and *Neraca*, 15 Nov. 1995.

14. M. Camdessus, 'Asia Will Survive with Realistic Economic Policies', *Jakarta Post*, 8 Dec. 1997, p. 5; International Monetary Fund, *Experimental Case Studies on Transparency Practices.* (Washington, DC: IMF, 1999); World Bank, *World Development Report 1997: The State in a Changing World* (Washington, DC: World Bank, 1997).

15. See, for instance, World Bank, *Indonesia: Sustaining Development* (Washington, DC: World Bank, 1993).

16. R. Prawiro, 'Accounting Development for Economic Development', speech delivered at the South-East Asia University Accounting Teachers Conference, 21–23 January 1991. See also I. Suta, 'Perlu Solusi Cepat Untuk Atasi Tantangan Yang Dihadapi AP', *Bisnis Indonesia*, 15 Dec. 1993; *Jakarta Post*, 22 Sep. 1990.

17. R. Robison, 'The Middle Class and the Bourgeoisie in Indonesia', in R. Robison and D. Goodman (eds.), *The New Rich in Asia: Mobile Phones, McDonalds and Middle Class Revolution* (London: Routledge, 1996), p. 82.

18. Many politico-bureaucrats – or more commonly their relatives – have been given minority shareholdings or senior executive positions in major private domestic conglomerates. In other cases, politico-bureaucrats have gone directly into business themselves by establishing family-owned companies. See R. Robison, 'Politics and Markets in Indonesia's Post-Oil Era', in G. Rodan, K. Hewison and R. Robison (eds.), *The Political Economy of South-East Asia: An Introduction* (Melbourne: Oxford University Press, 1997); A. Schwarz, *A Nation in Waiting: Indonesia in the 1990s* (St Leonards: Allen & Unwin, 1994).

19. H. Crouch, *The Army and Politics in Indonesia* (Ithaca: Cornell University Press, 1998); Robison, *Indonesia*.

20. K. Kwik, *Analisis Ekonomi Politik Indonesia* (Jakarta: Gramedia Pustaka Utama, 1994).

21. See H. Arndt, 'Economic Disorder and the Task Ahead', in T. Tan (ed.), *Sukarno's Guided Indonesia* (Brisbane: Jacaranda, 1967); H. Hill, *The Indonesian Economy Since 1996: Southeast Asia's Emerging Giant* (Cambridge: Cambridge University Press, 1996).

22. As quoted in J. Winters, *Power in Motion: Capital Mobility and the Indonesian State* (Ithaca: Cornell University Press, 1996), p. 47.

23. See H. McDonald, *Suharto's Indonesia* (Blackburn: Fontana, 1980); K. Thomas and J. Panglaykim, *Indonesia: The Effects of Past Policies and President Suharto's Plans for the Future* (Melbourne: CEDA, 1973); Winters, *Power in Motion.*

24. Sumantoro, *Pengantar Tentang Pasar Modal di Indonesia* (Jakarta: Ghalia Indonesia, 1990).

25. Prawit Ninsuvannakul, 'The Development of the Accounting Profession of the ASEAN Countries: Past, Present and Future', in Zimmerman V. (ed.), *Recent Accounting and Economic Developments in the Far East* (Urbana-Champaign: Center for International Education and Research in Accounting, 1988).

26. R. Briston, 'The Evolution of Accounting in Developing Countries', *The International Journal of Accounting*, vol. 14, no. 1 (1978), pp. 105–20; H. Yunus, 'History of Accounting in Developing Nations: The Case of Indonesia', mimeo, 1998.

27. World Bank, *Indonesia*.

28. A. Rosser, 'Creating Markets: The Politics of Economic Liberalisation in Indonesia Since the Mid-1980s', unpublished Ph.D. dissertation, Murdoch University, 1999, p. 72.

29. *Ibid.*, p. 141.

30. These regulations included restrictions on share price movements, a ban on foreign investment in the capital market and a requirement for the state-owned investment trust to purchase up to 50 per cent of all issued shares and then resell them in the form of cheap bearer certificates.

31. Rosser, 'Creating Markets', p. 42.

32. J. Mackie and Sjahrir, 'Survey of Recent Developments', *Bulletin of Indonesian Economic Studies*, 25 (December 1989), pp. 3–34.

33. World Bank, *Indonesia*, p. xxi.

34. For a detailed discussion of these scandals and their impact on the JSX, see Rosser, 'Creating Markets', pp. 162–9.

35. Interviews with Indarto, Head, Accounting Standards Bureau, Bapepam, 8 Oct. 1998; and Unggul Suprayitno, Operations Officer, World Bank, 5 Oct. 1998.

36. J. Diga and H. Yunus, 'Accounting in Indonesia', in N. Baydoun, A. Nishimura and R. Willett, (eds.), *Accounting in the Asia–Pacific Region.* (Singapore: John Wiley & Sons, 1996).

37. See World Bank, 'Staff Appraisal Report: Indonesia: Second Accountancy Development Project', unpublished report, 29 July 1994.

38. See D. Cole and B. Slade, *Building a Modern Financial System: The Indonesian Experience* (Cambridge: Cambridge University Press, 1996).

39. *Info Finansial*, October 1995; *Jakarta Post*, 18 Jan. 1996.

40. R. Robison and A. Rosser, 'Surviving the Meltdown: Liberal Reform and Political Oligarchy in Indonesia', in R. Robison *et al.* (eds.), *Politics and Markets in the Wake of the Asian Crisis* (London: Routledge, 2000), pp. 171–91.

41. *AWSJ*, 20 Oct. 1998.

42. *AWSJ*, 3 May 1999.

43. *AWSJ*, 20 Oct. 1998.

44. Previously only publicly listed companies and certain financial institutions were required to publish audited financial statements. See *Jakarta Post*, 23 Feb. 1998.

45. I wish to thank Felia Salim, a director of the JSX, and others at that institution for providing me with information concerning these regulations.

46. Robison and Rosser, 'Surviving the Meltdown', p. 190.

47. Interviews with former employee of a major international accounting firm, 28 Aug. 1998; an official in the listing division of the JSX, 6 Oct. 1998; and two journalists who regularly cover the capital market, 6 Oct. 1998. See also M. Backman, *Asian Eclipse: Exposing the Dark Side of Business in Asia* (Singapore: John Wiley & Sons, 1999).

48. *Media Akuntansi*, June 1998.

49. D. Bourchier, 'Magic Memos, Collusion and Judges with Attitude: Notes on the Politics of Law in Contemporary Indonesia', in K. Jayasuriya (ed.), *Law, Capitalism and Power in Asia: The Rule of Law and Legal Institutions* (London: Routledge, 1998); T. Lubis, *In Search of Human Rights* (Jakarta: PT Gramedia Pustaka & SPOS, 1993); H. Thoolen (ed.), *Indonesia and the Rule of Law*. A study prepared by the International Commission of Jurists and The Netherlands Institute of Human Rights (London, Pinter, 1987).

50. Comments made by James Castle, a leading business consultant in Jakarta, Centre for Strategic and International Studies, 28 July 1995. See also Backman, *Asian Eclipse*, pp. 42–51.

51. See, for instance, comments by Soedarjono, the then head of the IAI in *Kompas*, 14 July 1995.

52. *Gatra*, 21 May 1997.

53. M. Beeson, 'The Political Economy of East Asia at a Time of Crisis', in R. Stubbs and G. Underhill (eds.), *Political Economy and the Changing Global Order* (Oxford: Oxford University Press, 2000), pp. 352–61; F. Fukuyama, 'Asian Values and the Current Crisis', 1999, http://wbln0018.worldbank.org/ eap/eap.nsf/

54. See Chow *et al.*, 'Accounting Reforms in China'; K. Han, 'Setting Accounting Standards in Singapore'.

55. K. Jayasuriya and A. Rosser, 'Economic Crisis and the Political Economy of Economic Liberalisation in Southeast Asia', in G. Rodan *et al.* (eds.), *The Political Economy of Southeast Asia: An Introduction*, 2nd edn (Oxford: Oxford University Press, 2001).

14 The private sector, international standards and the architecture of global finance

GEORGE VOJTA AND MARC UZAN

Recent financial crises in emerging market economies have heightened the importance of prevention as the better part of cure. Crisis prevention has become central in current efforts to reform the international financial architecture, partly because of growing systemic disturbance caused by regional contagion and partly because of the increasingly constrained ability of the IMF to rescue crisis countries. From architecture debates and discussions there has emerged a consensus on the essential policy measures needed to prevent future financial crises. Emerging market governments and private sector institutions have been required to change their interactions with domestic and international financial markets through greater transparency in various policy arenas. They have also been urged by the IMF to implement minimally acceptable and harmonised standards in supervision, accounting and corporate governance.[1]

Concrete steps to enhance transparency and to design international financial standards have been centred on the Bretton Woods institutions as well as on national governments. The IMF, the World Bank and other international financial institutions have encouraged and helped domestic regulatory authorities to develop and implement good principles and practices for sound economic management and to improve their capacity to make timely and accurate assessments of the vulnerability of financial and corporate sectors to external shocks. The core of national government responsibilities has rested with the compliance with these principles and practices under the surveillance of the IMF and other international groups. Given prevailing interpretations of the causes of currency and financial crises in emerging market economies, important measures have been undertaken to refine standards of good behaviour across a wide range of issue areas, including timely data provision, policy transparency and external debt management.[2]

Regulatory and supervisory tasks in these areas have been rendered increasingly difficult and complex by capital account liberalisation, corporate innovation and global market integration. National governments have been caught in a tide of international transactions beyond their capacity to supervise and regulate. Attempts by national regulatory agencies to co-operate with their overseas equivalents in order to design more effective regulatory standards and to fulfil their respective legal mandates have borne fruit but have often proved problematic. This is due not only to the difficulties of co-operation in an international system of competing state jurisdictions but also to variations in domestic market structures, financial institutions and legal systems.

Policy initiatives and reform efforts on the part of official domestic and international institutions, while important, may not be sufficient for the effective design and implementation of international financial standards in emerging market economies. The task of standard setting and enforcement, therefore, should not be left entirely to official sector institutions. Norms and standards must also involve the private sector in two ways. First, private sector actors must be encouraged to integrate the use of official standards into their risk management techniques to a greater extent than is currently the case. Second, private sector institutions must be encouraged to develop best practice standards of corporate governance and behaviour in the financial sector. These goals may be achieved either through private–public collaboration or by private sector institutions themselves, although official institutions may possess political resources to induce emerging market economies to implement such codes and norms.[3]

All this points to the importance of getting the private sector involved in the formulation and implementation of international financial standards. As a matter of fact, the transnational nature of market structures and the difficulty of mastering the changing dynamics of international financial and corporate activities have led national regulatory officials increasingly to recognise the importance of private firms and market forces in risk management. Furthermore, private firms and their associations can help to enhance the increasingly limited policy expertise and capacity of public officials, given that they have played an important role in developing and shaping financial market structures. More significant, private sector institutions have been instrumental in identifying and refining international standards for minimally acceptable practices in accounting, auditing, insolvency provision and corporate governance.[4] By dint of their broad transnational linkages and networks, they have already gone some way towards formulating and promoting the good principles and practices of financial management and corporate governance.

Private involvement and private–public co-operation in the process of standard setting and enforcement are crucial but problematic. The private sector is far from being monolithic and homogeneous. The banking sector, particularly in emerging market/developing economies, usually consists of commercial, specialised and development institutions. Different types of banking institutions tend to have dissimilar business activities, varying degrees of international exposure and divergent preferences for the design of standards for sound managerial practices. The political difficulty of co-ordinating different private institutions and their respective interests in standard formulation and implementation within a transnational context is likely to be considerable. This problem grows more severe when we turn from banks to non-bank financial institutions, capital markets and corporate firms, as these latter sectors are more diverse than the banking sector in terms of business scope, external linkage and policy preference.

Furthermore, private involvement in standard formulation is also related to broad normative questions. A more active role for market institutions and closer co-operation between the public and private sectors raise the spectre of public policy being captured by private interests. To the extent that private interests dominate public purposes, financial standards are likely to be aligned to the preferences of powerful market players. Given that these standards should promote market stability and public interests, the greater participation of private sector actors in the standard-setting process may run counter to its purported objectives and, more important, may be in tension with the capacity of democratic governments to maintain their political legitimacy. The argument is not that the private sector should be excluded from standard formulation, but that regulatory authorities should find a way constructively to involve private institutions without being captured by particularistic interests. This old dilemma highlights the importance of maintaining a politically sustainable balance between private market interests and broad public concerns in financial policy making.

This chapter seeks to address the role of the private sector in standard setting and enforcement and to examine the real and potential problems of private involvement in that process. The arguments will be developed in five main sections. The first two sections will examine how deficiencies in domestic regulatory systems contributed to economic crises in emerging market countries and briefly describe the codes and institutional reforms endorsed by the current architecture exercise. The third and fourth sections will look at the role of international financial institutions, discuss the reasons why the private sector should be involved in standard formulation and explore the political and normative implications of private involvement. The final section will summarise the arguments and conclude the chapter.

Informational failure, confidence collapse and capital crisis

In the second half of 1997 four east Asian countries – Thailand, Malaysia, South Korea and Indonesia – experienced a massive reversal of large foreign capital inflows that they had enjoyed during much of the 1990s. The swing from net inflows to outflows amounted to more than US$100 billion and exceeded some 11 per cent of their GDP. This capital flight precipitated large falls in their currencies, dramatic declines in stock market and other asset prices, deep domestic financial crises and severe economic recession – rivalling those in the worst years of the debt crisis in Latin America. In a matter of months, countries in east Asia that had experienced unprecedented growth and prosperity over the previous three decades were suddenly in deep trouble.

Subsequent events in the world economy were no less remarkable. With surprising speed and succession, the Asian crisis spread to Russia and the former Commonwealth of Independent States countries, the Middle East and other oil-producing countries, Brazil and the rest of Latin America. The effects of the Asian crisis were most severe in countries that were heavily dependent on private capital inflows to finance current account deficits or on primary commodities for export earnings, as commodity prices plummeted some 30–40 per cent in 1997–8, and/or relied on manufactured exports to Asian markets. Adding to these problems, the continuing recession and financial turmoil in Japan led 1998 to record a significant decline in aggregate growth in developing countries. The Asian crisis demonstrated once again how interconnected the global economy has become. Interventions by international financial institutions and G-7 governments were notable in their failure to stem the general contagion.

A central question is what caused the failure of the global economic architecture to prevent and/or deal with the consequences of the crises effectively. Although the Asian crisis was similar in some respects – most notably the negative consequences flowing from overvalued, pegged exchange rates – to previous crises in Chile and Mexico, there were elements of a new pattern of pathology. The Asian crisis was a capital crisis as opposed to a crisis caused by fundamental general macro imbalances.[5]

The trigger event of massive portfolio investment outflows reflected a loss of confidence in the countries affected, resulting, as noted, in a depression of currency values and asset prices, and a staggering increase in non-performing assets in indigenous financial sectors as a result of private sector defaults on foreign and domestic debt obligations. It became evident that weaknesses in the financial systems of affected countries, owing to a lack of transparency, inadequate risk management disciplines, inappropriate lending to local firms and currency mismatches in liability structures, compounded and magnified the crisis of confidence. The ensuing deep recessions in the affected countries followed from the depressed currencies, punitively high domestic interest rates, cessation of credit extension, and corporate and financial sector defaults, bankruptcies and liquidations.

There is no doubt that the international policy community did not and could not anticipate the crisis. To some extent analysts were misled by the apparent reasonableness of fiscal and monetary policies in the affected countries and were victimised by the absence of usable information about the true state of the external position, the deterioration of asset quality and solvency in the corporate and financial sector. Furthermore, the extensive contagion, which resulted from the strong positive correlation of markets, with increased volatility and illiquidity, was also unanticipated.

Failure to anticipate the crisis was largely attributable to an inability to access and analyse pertinent information. Although the 'overhang' risk of excessive reliance on short-term capital flows to finance external deficits was well known, the absence of transparency about external assets and liabilities and the state of affairs in the banking system were not well understood. Failure by local governments to tackle promptly troubled financial institutions and to promote effective processes of private credit restructuring and bankruptcy became clearly evident. Contrary to popular perceptions, IMF and World Bank financial packages, tied to agreements on macro and structural reform, were not intended to bail out private creditors. They were designed to break the psychology of panic 'run for the exit' behaviour and stem the excessive loss of official reserves and short-term credit from the private sector. Nonetheless, the efficacy of these programmes has been questioned. It is widely held that more timely, effective private sector involvement in crisis prevention and management is needed. As the crisis spread, public sector default (in Russia and Brazil, for instance), again owing to a lack of transparency about the true state of the fiscal position, could be expected.

It is generally recognised that the understanding of financial crises must start with careful analysis of specific country conditions in order to ascertain the causes of the problems at that level. No one pattern prevails; the pattern of crisis at the country level has not moved from one broad 'paradigm' to another. Causal patterns can involve fundamental illiquidity,[6] insolvency as a result of misdirected investments and mis-priced assets,[7] structural financial and corporate sector weaknesses and excessive leverage as well as traditional mismanagement of fiscal and monetary policies.[8] Irrespective of causation at the country level, the systemic risk and loss experience arising from whatever crisis occurs are now significantly magnified by the contagion phenomenon, ultimately due to the continuing spread of information technology throughout the world.

Proposals to reform the global financial system

The international community has passed through phases in thinking about appropriate future changes to the international financial architecture. Some initial, radical thoughts – a global central bank, a world bankruptcy court, and an international regulatory authority – while worthy of some consideration, have been rejected as impractical. A coalescence of thinking on more pragmatic measures subsequently occurred.

More feasible proposals, particularly those advanced by Eichengreen, Goldstein and the Institute of International Finance, propose short-term measures. These include, among others, limiting short-term borrowing to the extent covered by international reserves, improved creditor clauses in debt financing, avoidance of fixed exchange rates during crises, and the establishment of investor relations functions by emerging market countries.[9] Beyond this set of short-term measures there has also emerged a consensus on desirable medium-term initiatives. These have mainly focused on greater policy transparency, sound financial systems, the correct sequence of temporary restrictions on capital account liberalisation, private sector involvement in crisis prevention and management, the reform of IFIs and more appropriate exchange rate regimes in emerging market countries.

To move this agenda forward, the G-7 has adopted a pragmatic path of change. The group has maintained its strong commitment to an open global economy, supported by free movement of capital, technology and skill, and reinforced by increasingly liberalised foreign trade and investment regimes as the most desirable course to maintain global growth under stable conditions. It proposes an approach which involves the establishment of comprehensive standards, representing best global practices towards which all countries participating in the global system would strive. With the immediate crises abating, the sense of urgency has slowed progress to a degree. The recently issued G-7 communiqué has strongly endorsed this approach to the improvement of the global architecture. There has been enough evidence to suggest that the path of architectural reform has now been established.

IFIs and global financial standards

A new role for the Bretton Woods and other international institutions has begun to emerge as a result of the crisis in emerging market economies. Tremendous efforts have been under way to establish international standards and codes of good practice that build on and offer the potential to globalise the standards that exist within the most advanced states. New standards are being defined and existing ones refined. The IMF has been formulating standards or codes of good practice for governments in its core domain of responsibilities, which are already well advanced or being implemented. Many agencies have been working to develop standards in their areas of expertise: accounting, auditing, corporate governance, payment and settlement systems, insurance and bankruptcy.

In their efforts to strengthen domestic financial sectors, the IMF and the World Bank are co-operating closely to help promote stronger financial systems, in line with the internationally accepted basic core principles. The Financial

Stability Forum (FSF) that has been established to encourage dialogue among the many relevant national and international agencies will make an invaluable contribution to harmonising global standards for regulation and supervision.

The Fund began to formulate standards for adequate data dissemination shortly after the onset of the Mexican crisis. These are now fully operational, and the more demanding Special Data Dissemination Standard (SDDS) has now been adopted by about one quarter of member countries, the large majority of which participate actively in capital markets. The Fund, working together with the BIS, a representative group of central banks, the World Bank and the OECD among others, has also prepared a draft Code of Good Practices on Transparency in Monetary and Financial Policies.

Equally important, there have been the relevant private sector bodies that are active in developing financial standards in various areas. In some cases they co-operate with official international institutions in formulating and implementing good practices for sound financial management. For insurance there is the International Association of Insurance Supervisors (IAIS). In accounting and auditing there are the International Accounting Standards Committee (IASC) and the International Federation of Accountants (IFAC). The United Nations Commission on International Trade Law (UNCITRAL), the World Bank and the Basel Committee on Banking Supervision (BCBS) have been working on corporate governance. And the Committee on Payment and Settlement Systems (CPSS) has made efforts to improve payment systems in developing and emerging market economies.

With many agencies now preparing or updating their standards, principles and codes of good practices, attention is shifting to a more difficult challenge – implementation. Although the IMF does not yet have the expertise to assist in implementing many of the new standards, its mandate does enable it to have regular – usually annual – contacts with all member countries for policy discussions. International institutions will need to play a significant role in encouraging and monitoring the implementation of the new standards.

It is obvious that the Bretton Woods institutions, in executing these new tasks, will have to enhance and supplement their in-house expertise by relying heavily on the skills, resources and advice of the many agencies engaged in defining standards as well as the private sector for implementing them. In this emerging context for a reformed, global architecture, the role of the IMF surveillance function is envisioned to expand to a considerable degree. For the IMF to play this role more effectively, a number of important issues need to be carefully addressed.

To begin with, effective surveillance depends, ultimately, on the responsiveness and co-operation of members. Surveillance will not be effective if members regard the IMF as an adversary rather than a partner, and do not take account of the Fund's views in their policy-making process. It is also important to avoid a reduction in the intensity of the dialogue and analysis, as happened in Mexico after the expiration of an IMF-supported programme. The burden is placed on the Fund for the quality of its analysis, the way it is conveyed to authorities, and the persuasiveness with which the international perspective is presented to the authorities, which are typically biased by domestic economic and political considerations.

Furthermore, strengthening surveillance depends on regular and timely provision of data to the Fund, by all members. There has been an explosion in the availability of such data and it now needs to be better incorporated into the policy analysis of the IMF and better presented to authorities in a user-friendly way so that right decisions can be made. In an environment of global interdependence, well-informed financial markets can contribute to efficiency and provide a useful discipline on policy makers. The other side of the coin, of course, is that delays in providing basic information to markets can detract from both efficiency and the associated policy discipline. The greater the transparency and information, the earlier and more effectively resources can be mobilised, and the less severe market adjustments will be. There also needs to be greater continuity in policy discussions among the IMF's members to bring to the surface in a timely manner important questions regarding their economic developments or policy changes. New mechanisms are being put into place within the Fund to facilitate this process.

Finally, IMF surveillance needs to be more selective and focused. Better attention must be given to countries at risk. And better processes are needed to identify those countries as early as possible. Strong resistance exists against anything like a list of countries at risk, but clearly the IMF in its own operations needs to know every day which countries those are. A big issue is that assigning to the Fund the role for gaining information determines what it could do that informed markets cannot. And if the IMF has privileged information, it is worth asking why it should expect to have that information. The Fund's comparative advantage in surveillance has been in identifying issues where one country's actions had important spill-over effects on others and allowing a country to cite the IMF authority as a cover to do what it wanted to do anyway.

If more information is provided, it is neither necessary nor desirable for the IMF to put itself in the position of being the assigned warning bell. Also, it is questionable whether the markets are good enough at using the information when available. The fact is that markets overshoot both on the up side and on the down side. There is very little differentiation, in fact, in risk spreads between those countries that provide relatively more information – and more reliable information – and those that do not. Nevertheless, greater transparency is a public good. It will reduce, over time, the cost of capital to countries that are active market borrowers. That may not be in the interest of brokers but it is certainly in the interest of the public and the international community. Over time there will be less volatility in capital flows if there is more and better information on a continuous basis.

Vigorous efforts on the part of international financial institutions to encourage the adoption of minimally acceptable standards are most likely to reinforce growing pressures for policy harmonisation among many developing and emerging market economies. The process of policy harmonisation embedded in the current attempts to reform the global financial architecture, however, would be a long-term evolution. The political and institutional obstacles at national and regional levels to the convergence of financial systems, corporate structures and legal frameworks are expected to be considerable. On the one hand, the diversity of national socioeconomic systems continues to shape the responses of domestic state and societal actors to external pressures for policy changes and institutional reforms. On the other, the particular patterns of financial regulation and corporate governance are deeply rooted in distinctive domestic social milieus and unique national development experiences. Differences among national market systems and development models are likely to persist, particularly where these systems and models have contributed to economic successes and sociopolitical stability.[10]

International efforts to seek financial and corporate changes in line with harmonised standards and practices, which entail institutional reforms of crucial importance to emerging market polities across the different aspects of economic governance, will inevitably face substantial national incentives to resist or deviate from these standards and practices. If the adoption of harmonised financial standards is to be a politically sustainable effort, international policy makers should make sufficient allowance for local financial, corporate and legal practices. While it is desirable to implement institutional reforms needed to improve financial systems, the difficulties that even advanced industrial countries had in establishing their financial and corporate institutions (which are arguably far from perfect) suggest that these reforms would remain a long-term challenge in developing and emerging market economies. Countries active on global financial markets must meet minimally acceptable standards, but they should be allowed to do so by different routes and through divergent institutional arrangements.

The private sector and standard formulation and enforcement

The formulation of internationally acceptable standards represents a significant (if not the only) element of efforts to reform global financial architecture. Following the financial crisis of 1997/8, the international community reached a consensus that elaboration of best practice standards in key policy areas and the

Table 13. *Standards for sound financial systems designated as key by the Financial Stability Forum.*[1]

Standard-setting bodies	Key policy areas Macroeconomic fundamentals
IMF	Code of good practices in monetary/financial policy transparency
IMF	Code of good practices in fiscal policy transparency
IMF	Special data dissemination standard/general data dissemination system[2]
	Institutional and market infrastructure
World Bank	Insolvency procedures[3]
OECD	Principles of corporate governance
IASC[4]	International accounting standards (IAS)[5]
IFAC[4]	International standards on auditing (ISA)[5]
CPSS	Core principles for systematically important payment systems
FATF	The forty recommendations of the financial action task force (FATF)
	Financial regulation and supervision
BCBS	Core principles for effective banking supervision
IOSCO	Objectives and principles of securities regulation
IAIS	Insurance supervisory principles

Notes:
[1] While the key standards are categorised here by policy area, some of them are relevant to more than one area.
[2] Economies with access to international capital markets are encouraged to subscribe to the more stringent SDDS and all other economies are encouraged to adopt the GDDS.
[3] The World Bank is co-ordinating a broad-based effort, involving relevant institutions and legal experts, to develop a set of principles and guidelines on insolvency regimes. The United Nations Commission on International Trade Law (UNCITRAL), which adopted the Model Law on Cross-Border Insolvency in 1997, will help facilitate implementation.
[4] The International Accounting Standards Committee (IASC) and International Federation of Accountants (IFAC) are distinct from other standard-setting bodies in that they are private sector bodies.
[5] The IAS and ISA are used in some jurisdictions but are not endorsed by all jurisdictions. The IAS are currently being reviewed by the BCBS, IAIS and IOSCO.
Source: International Standards and Codes – *Financial Stability Review*, December 2000, p. 165.

creation of public and private incentives to achieve compliance were desirable. To their credit, international institutions and other standard-setting bodies, encouraged by the G-7, have in fact succeeded in articulating these standards (see Table 13).

The ongoing standard-setting process, however, has suffered from important weaknesses. In the first place, non-G-7 countries have had little effective participation in the standard-setting process. If non-G-7 countries are excluded from that process and therefore do not have the incentives to embrace and implement international financial standards, the process may come to little consequence. Broadening the number of countries actively involved in identifying and developing financial standards (and other norms that have bearings on financial system stability) in the institutional form of the G-20, which includes G-7 countries and many non-G-7 emerging market economies, has been an important step in the right direction.

Second, the burden of designing institutional reforms and developing international financial standards has so far fallen primarily on international financial institutions, the IMF in particular, and national governments. At the heart of the reforms are *national* policy changes: better data yielding greater informational transparency, better IMF monitoring, more clarity in terms of insolvency and supervisory procedures. National policy changes and institutional reforms promoted by the Bretton Woods institutions have not always been responsive to the needs of the private sector in many emerging and developing economies. And it follows that the inputs from private market actors have not been fully incorporated into the process of standard formulation.

This leads to the third and most critical point. Private sector involvement in the process of standard formulation and implementation has been insufficient and is particularly weak in the context of emerging market economies. As mentioned in the previous sections, one major lesson derived from recent financial crises suggests that institutional reforms needed to minimise the incidence of such crises should extend beyond macroeconomic management policies. Without greater efforts to integrate the information and norms developed through these standards into the investment and risk management decisions of private firms, the process remains incomplete. The private sector as such constitutes the 'front line' in terms of risk management and financial supervision in the global financial order. Market-oriented and prudent private sector behaviour is central to the containment of systemic risk.[11] Trends in Basel Committee banking supervisory standards recognise this important element of private sector responsibility.[12] In this sense the next stage of the standard-building process in emerging market economies is to integrate better the information provided by the new official standards into the decision-making processes of private firms, and to encourage better standards of corporate governance and behaviour in the financial sector. This can be viewed from two angles: providing information for companies seeking to measure the investment climate in a particular country; and to ensure that the risk management, corporate governance and investment behaviour of the financial institutions of a particular country (and therefore its financial sector) are sound.

The position of the private sector relative to the standard-setting process is nonetheless problematical in emerging market countries. 'Given their recent origin, most market participants are not very familiar with either the 12 standards recognised by the FSF as key to sound financial systems or the [International Monetary] Fund–[World] Bank *Reports on Observance of Standards and Codes* (ROSCs)', observed a report published in connection with the September 1999 meeting of the Forum. 'Few market participants to date explicitly take account of an economy's observance of standards in their lending and investment decisions or use ROSCs directly for risk-assessments leading to pricing and allocation decisions.'[13]

The report also notes that market incentives are more likely to be effective if market participants use information on the economy's observance of standards in their risk assessments and reflect this in pricing or allocation of credit or investment to that economy or institutions in that economy. Furthermore, preconditions for market incentives to work are also needed. As suggested in the report, for market incentives to work, market participants need: (1) to be familiar with international standards; (2) to judge them to be of relevance to their risk assessments; and (3) to have access to credible and timely information on the observance of standards.

Currently, however, there is no source of credible, timely information available to the private sector (from either public or private sectors) which profiles the country observance of standards. The ROSC process has not been comprehensive or updated to stay current. The information generated from the reports on the observance of standards and codes is not organised and presented in a form that is usable by market participants. Concerning the role that the private sector should play in generating information on the observance of standards, these reports have noted that views are 'mixed'. The balance of this section focuses on the desirability of private activity in generating usable information on standard compliance and on the importance of such information for risk management functions in private institutions, including rating agencies.

At present, country risk assessment in the private sector, including rating agencies, concentrates on macroeconomic analysis and forecasting. Recently efforts have been made to improve the efficiency of macro-models, particularly by complementing them with scenario analysis and 'stress testing conventions',[14] and to improve both predictive capabilities and crisis preparedness. The rating agencies seem to be better acquainted with and pay more attention to observance of standards. They claim that their direct access to national authorities (and sometimes confidential data) provides them with a more in-depth understanding of the quality of supervision and regulation, policy and data transparency and market infrastructure.[15] Very little specific information about standards compliance appears in the country rating reports by rating agencies.

Concentrating on enhanced macro-models and the issues concerning utilisation of confidential information have drawn the attention of private sector institutions away from a comprehensive and ongoing monitoring of compliance with standards. Nonetheless, this chapter argues that there is a strong case to be made for private sector initiatives to generate comprehensive, timely, userfriendly information, based on public information only concerning country compliance with the standards in the twelve key policy areas.[16]

These particular standards are important because national experiences with recent crises have demonstrated that when a country came under financial stress and headed towards crisis, it usually resulted from a combination of macro-imbalances, market risks and the effects of regional contagion. To the extent that there were deficiencies or a poor state of affairs in these key policy areas, the crisis, which was magnified in terms of exposure to risk and losses sustained, became more complex to manage and more difficult to resolve. Examples abounded in Asian financial crises of 1997–8. Publication by the Thai government of heretofore unreported foreign exchange forward sales changed the market perception that the country had abundant exchange reserves to one of an alarming near zero net reserve balance. The lack of a workable bankruptcy and corporate reorganisation regime in Indonesia has made it impossible to resolve the massive private sector debt defaults and bring the country out of the crisis. Most recently, reports of the hidden $26 billion deficit in the Daewoo Group of South Korea in its net worth has frustrated resolution of the debt problem of this conglomerate. This problem occurred because local accounting and auditing standards were deficient. In fact, numerous notable deficiencies existed in each of the key policy areas during this period, with widespread negative consequences.

Even though the private sector had some knowledge of standard deficiencies in many countries, they relied on an ability to anticipate macroeconomic performance and trusted to the willingness and ability of governments to manage during crises. Painful experience made it clear that these assumptions were fallacious. It can be argued that today governments' intent and capability to accept and comply with global standards have become the critical factor in determining the true and ultimate risk of taking on exposure of any kind by lenders and investors.

It is sometimes claimed that the standards articulated in the twelve key policy areas are 'Anglo-Saxon' in character, and therefore not relevant or applicable to many countries for one reason or another. While the characterisation of the standards is correct, the standards are appropriate because they represent the fullest elaboration of disciplines that should be observed to protect the *fiduciary responsibilities* of lenders and investors. Lenders and investors conduct their activities with third party resources – capital, deposits, borrowings and fiduciary funds. They are accountable for the consequences of putting these resources at risk to earn a return. This standard applies to all markets. It applies to both domestic and cross-border activities, covers both public and private sector activities, and transcends any cultural value system. Simply put, any party using funds sourced from third parties for any purpose has the obligation (legally and morally) to deploy those funds prudently, within the best attainable risk parameters. This is why the articulated standards are both right and deserving of compliance. In the long run, progress in standards compliance by countries in the global economy is the best path to improving the global financial architecture in terms of risk management and transparency. Also, improved risk management and transparency are the surest path to crisis prevention and the best option to managing crises in a timely and effective manner.

Now let us assume that the private sector has access to timely, comprehensive and usable public information concerning country compliance with standards. Why should this information be utilised in credit and allocation decisions, *as additional key inputs* to these processes? This question deserves specific answers. First, no country in the world is in full compliance with the twelve recognised standards; regrettably, many countries have made no progress whatsoever in moving towards compliance. The important point is that any country which moves from non-compliance towards compliance with these standards improves its risk and transparency profile relative to lenders and investors.

Second, based on public information only, some countries have not stated any position on the adoption of and compliance with standards. Some countries have stated publicly that they will not adopt and/or comply with global standards as a whole or in part. Although some countries have stated that they are adopting and/or moving towards compliance with particular standards, they are silent as to their approach to the body of standards as a whole. Countries that articulate a public programme of implementing all standards signal a strong desire to improve their risk and transparency position vis-à-vis global benchmarks. The significance of these responses is that they are a gauge of a country's declared intent relative to the enactment and implementation of standards. Intent relative to the standards is an accurate proxy for a country's desire or lack thereof to be a full participant in the global economic system. We have learned that responsible country behaviour in the global community requires both the *willingness* to accept the responsibilities for investment and debt commitments as well as the *ability* to discharge these responsibilities.

Public silence on the standards by a country implies that that country either does not know about the standards or does not care about standards, an important point for investors and lenders to consider. Countries that publicly state their intention not to comply with standards have serious reservations about becoming responsible members of the global economy. Countries that publicly communicate relative to specific standards but omit consideration of other standards or only state a view towards total compliance with standards lack comprehensive coherence in their efforts to adopt standards. Countries that express a coherent view of intent to adopt and comply with standards actually commit themselves to be responsible members of the global economy. It is possible therefore to establish a country's *intent* or *lack thereof* from the sources of public information. Again this is a key point for market participants to consider in their risk assessment concerning the credibility of countries.

Third, a publicly available profile of country attitudes and programmes relative to standards adds a significant additional dimension to the process of assessing country risks. It strongly enhances the conventional macro-analysis-based models (which attempt to assess the ability of countries to service their debts). This enhanced public profile will be an important step towards the establishment of a more effective 'market discipline' on countries. More effective market discipline is a powerful force for positive changes in the global economy.

Fourth, a public profile of a country's positions on standards allows an explicit examination of specific important risks involved in conducting private investment and lending activity in that country. Since governments can no longer be relied on to bail out private investors and lenders, careful analysis and understanding of these risks becomes vital to risk management and investment decisions in private institutions. Lack of compliance with the macro-data standards for national macro-statistics and lack of transparency in fiscal and monetary policies imply that the private sector is exposed to hidden risks that can compromise, seriously and suddenly, the country's macro-performance. Non-compliance with international auditing and accounting standards means that risks are opaque in all institutions within a country. Lack of an appropriate bankruptcy regime means that workable restructuring or exiting from troubled investments/loans is nearly impossible, exposing private loans and investments to total write-off. Absence of adequate corporate governance standards creates uncertainty concerning the quality of management of all institutions in a country. Non-compliance with international standards for regulating banks, insurance companies, securities companies and the payments mechanism makes it impossible to determine whether or not a country's financial system is safe and sound. The poor state of financial institutions in many Asian countries compounded the magnitude of each crisis to a major degree, and is responsible for the fact that in several countries (such as Indonesia, South Korea and Japan) the crisis remains unresolved.

Finally, private investors and lenders may be able to improve risk and transparency in the global financial system (which redounds to their direct material benefit) if they require accurate, timely information about standard compliance from counter-parties that are potential recipients of investments and loans from them, and if they can differentiate terms, pricing and allocation decisions to reward counter-parties that comply with the standards and to penalise those which do not. If private investors and lenders act in this manner, there will be the most powerful stimulus to compliance with standards. Compliance with standards will then be a critical factor (together with sound macro-performance) in determining the degree and terms of access of countries to private markets which control the preponderance of resources they need to support their trade and development. This linkage is totally lacking today; if it can be achieved the global economy is more likely to be in a considerably better condition.

We have so far confined ourselves to the discussion of technical details concerning private sector involvement in standard formulation and enforcement. The issue of private involvement, however, escapes the bounds of technocracy.

It is linked to the broad questions of important political and normative implications. Although private market actors and institutions need to be integrated into the process of policy changes and regulatory reforms, the private sector itself is diverse and far from uniform. This diversity implies the political complexity of interactions between public officials and a wide range of market players who have conflicting interests and are marked by different relationships to state agencies. This difficulty has raised the critical question of how regulatory authorities can effectively co-ordinate different private sector actors and interests when trying to set and enforce harmonised standards that are supposed to be applied across the various financial and non-financial sectors. Policy makers at national, regional and international levels should take account of these political constraints in their efforts to fashion new market codes and norms.

Private involvement in the regulatory process also has significant implications for democratic governance. As mentioned earlier in this section, financial standards, which are designed to ensure market stability on which the economic prosperity of the millions depends, should be regarded as the public good. For financial standards to maintain their 'publicness', there should be an unambiguous distinction between private and public interests in the standard-setting process. The clear definition of public interests seems to be difficult, however, when private actors and interests influence or dominate the making of financial policies. Empirical studies demonstrate that there is an ongoing danger that structurally powerful and politically resourceful market players can succeed in defining and indeed capturing the definition of public interests in the regulatory process.[17] Private domination means that regulatory standards are most likely to be aligned towards the particularistic interests of powerful private actors and institutions. This can crucially alter the notions of public good which underpin the formulation of regulatory standards, compromise the capacity of democratic governments to maintain their political legitimacy, and pose a fundamental problem of democratic accountability.

Threats posed to democratic accountability by the undue private dominance of public purposes become more severe in the transnational domain. The intensifying process of global monetary and financial integration has weakened public controls over private capital flows and transactions, rendered policy makers increasingly dependent on market forces for various regulatory functions, and changed the balance between private power and public authority strongly in favour of the former.[18] Crucial decisions about the structure of international financial markets have often been taken within narrow and closed transnational policy networks where there is a risk that private interests dominate, to the exclusion of broad segments of society and beyond traditional legislative oversight. In the absence of strong public authority over private market power, international regulatory standards may not only become incompatible with the imperatives of economic development and political stability in developing and emerging market countries but also lead to serious problems of policy management. Under these circumstances, the institutional and policy-making arrangements through which these countries are integrated into the standard-setting process are more likely to facilitate the interests of private actors and institutions than to address the major policy concerns of the developing world.[19] The real issue about private involvement in standard formulation is thus a normative one about who can and ought to benefit from new regulatory standards and about whose interests these standards are to serve. Failure to address this issue can call into question present efforts to reform the international financial architecture.

Conclusion

This chapter has explored the respective roles of the official community and the private sector in the formulation and implementation of international standards for minimally acceptable practices in financial management and corporate governance, widely recognised as the core measures of crisis prevention. It has argued that the task of identifying and developing financial standards should not be left entirely to national governments, the Bretton Woods institutions, and other official international bodies. This is partly because regulatory authorities have been caught in a tide of transnational market changes which are beyond their effective capacity to monitor, and partly because domestic and international policy makers do not have sufficient resources and expertise with which to design the codes and norms of good behaviour that can be applied in a wide range of policy areas across different national socioeconomic systems. The corollary of this argument is that private actors and institutions, which have played an increasingly important role in shaping market practices and rules in cross-border financial and non-financial transactions, should be fully incorporated into the standard-setting process. If they are not, market disciplines may fail to play their role in financial governance.

Private sector involvement in the making of financial and regulatory standards is not merely a technical issue. Rather, it is linked to important political and normative questions, given the difficulty of co-ordinating different private sector actors and interests in regulatory processes and, more important, the ongoing danger of public purposes being dominated by private market interests in the financial sector. The formulation and enforcement of regulatory standards are the very public domain in which private sector inputs and participation are necessary but strong public controls over the play of particularistic interests are essential. If global regulatory processes serve not merely to protect the interests of private investors and lenders, but also to ensure financial market stability and improve the welfare of the millions in developing and emerging market

economies, a politically sustainable balance between private power and public
authority has to be maintained.

Notes

1. For more detailed discussions of these policy changes see Alan S. Blinder, 'Eight
   Steps to a New Financial Order', *Foreign Affairs*, vol. 78, no. 5 (1999), pp. 61–2;
   Barry Eichengreen, *Toward a New International Financial Architecture: A Practical
   Post-Asia Agenda* (Washington, DC: Institute for International Economics, 1999),
   pp. 19–36.
2. More comprehensive discussions on official efforts in these issue areas can be
   found on the IMF website on architecture reforms at http://www.imf.org/external/
   np/exr/facts/arcguide.htm. See also Miles Kahler, 'The New International Financial
   Architecture and its Limits', in Gregory W. Noble and John Ravenhill (eds.), *The
   Asian Financial Crisis and the Architecture of Global Finance* (Cambridge: Cambridge University Press, 2000).
3. The proper role of the Bretton Woods institutions in the process of standard setting
   and enforcement is examined in a more detailed manner in Barry Eichengreen, 'The
   International Monetary Fund in the Wake of the Asian Crisis', in Noble and Ravenhill,
   The Asian Financial Crisis, pp. 182–6; Peter B. Kenen, 'The New International
   Financial Architecture', *International Journal of Finance and Economics*, vol. 5,
   no. 1 (2000), pp. 1–14. For an excellent summary of the recent literature on the role
   of the IMF in crisis prevention and management see John Williamson, 'The Role of
   the IMF: A Guide to the Reports', Policy Briefs No. 00–5 (Washington, DC: Institute
   for International Economics, 2000).
4. These institutions include the International Accounting Standards Committee, the
   International Organisation of Supreme Audit Institutions, Committee J of the International Bar Association and the International Corporate Governance Network.
5. See Masaru Yoshitomi, 'Capital-Account Crisis and Credit Contraction', ADBI
   Working Paper 99–02 (Tokyo: Asian Development Bank Institute, 1999).
6. See Steven Radelet and Jeffrey D. Sachs, 'The East Asian Financial Crisis: Diagnosis, Remedies, Prospects', *Brookings Papers on Economic Activity*, no. 1 (1998),
   pp. 1–90.
7. See Paul Krugman, 'What Happened to Asia', at http://web.mit.edu/krugman/
   www/DISINTER.htm.
8. These points are discussed at length in Roberto Chang and Andrews Velasco, 'The
   Asian Crisis in Perspective', unpublished manuscript, Federal Reserve Bank of At-
   lanta, 1998; Gerardo Esquivel and Felipe Larrain, 'Latin America Confronting the
   Asian Crisis', paper presented at the Reinventing the Bretton Woods and the World
   Bank Conference, Washington, DC, 1998.
9. See, for instance, Eichengreen, *Toward a New International Financial Architecture*;
   Morris Goldstein, *The Asian Financial Crisis: Causes, Cures, and Systemic Implica-
   tions* (Washington, DC: Institute for International Economics, 1999).

10. The tensions between harmonising pressures and continued national diversity are discussed more systematically in Louis W. Pauly, 'National Financial Structures, Capital Mobility, and International Economic Rules: The Normative Consequences of East Asian, European, and American Distinctiveness', *Policy Sciences*, vol. 27, no. 4 (1994), pp. 343–63; Geoffrey R. D. Underhill, 'Transnational Financial Markets and National Economic Development Models: Global Structures versus Domestic Imperatives', *Économies et Sociétés*, Série 'MonnaieGt', ME, n° 1–2, 9–10/1999, pp. 37–68; Chapter 4 by Underhill and Zhang in this volume.

11. See Group of Thirty, 'Global Institutions, National Supervision and Systemic Risk', A Study Group Report (Washington, DC, 1997); Ulrich Cartellieri and Alan Greenspan, 'Global Risk Management', William Taylor Memorial Lecture 3 (Washington, DC, 1996), available at http://www.group30.org/publications/allPubs/Pubs96.htm.

12. See Basel Committee on Banking Supervision, *The New Basel Capital Accord* (Basel: Bank for International Settlements, Jan. 2001). Other related documents can be found at http://www.bis.org/publ/bcbsca.htm.

13. *The Financial Stability Forum Report* (Washington, DC: The Financial Stability Forum, September 1999).

14. As an example, the Council on Foreign Relations recently concluded 'Roundtable on Country Risk in the Post-Asian Crisis Era: Identifying Risks, Strategies, and Policy Implications', summarising work covered from Oct. 1999 to Sep. 2000.

15. *The Financial Stability Forum Report*, p. 7.

16. See Table 13 in this chapter for a detailed description of these twelve key policy areas.

17. See Geoffrey Underhill, 'Keeping Governments out of Politics: Transnational Securities Markets, Regulatory Co-operation, and Political Legitimacy', *Review of International Studies*, vol. 21 (1995), pp. 251–78; 'Private Markets and Public Responsibility in a Global System', in Underhill (ed.), *The New World Order in International Finance* (London: Macmillan, 1998), pp. 17–49; Chapter 12 by Zhang and Underhill in this volume.

18. These points are discussed at length in Louis Pauly, *Who Elected the Bankers: Surveillance and Control in the World Economy* (Ithaca: Cornell University Press, 1997); Geoffrey Underhill, 'The Public Good versus Private Interests in the Global Monetary and Financial System', *International and Comparative Corporate Law Journal*, vol. 2, no. 3 (2000), pp. 335–59.

19. See Pauly, *Who Elected the Bankers*; Tony Porter, 'The Transnational Agenda for Financial Regulation in Developing Countries', in Leslie Elliott Armijo (ed.), *Financial Globalisation and Democracy in Emerging Markets* (London: Macmillan, 1999), pp. 91–114.

Part IV

Building the new financial architecture: norms, institutions and governance

15 The legitimacy of international organisations and the future of global governance

JEAN-MARC COICAUD AND LUIZ A. PEREIRA DA SILVA

One way to examine global governance – that is, its present and future situation – is to analyse international organisations (IOs). Given their important position and mandate in the international arena, they provide a convenient entry point of analysis. However, their number, variety of purposes and contradictions provide strong evidence against a vision of international socialisation seen as a natural and smooth process of progressive integration of states into a peaceful international society under the guidance of universal values and rules. The tension between goals, charts, intentions and realpolitik, far from being an object of naive lamentation or hypocritical contempt, is precisely the interesting empirical material with which one can study the components of their legitimacy. The main purpose of this chapter is to examine the legitimacy of international organisations where this tension plays a visible and important role. The examination will not only provide a good indication of their standing and evolution but also allow us to take stock of the present situation and explore the future of the international system and global governance.

This chapter contends that the legitimacy of IOs stems from an awareness and an acceptance of the need of mechanisms and institutions of global regulation for the common good. In turn, this awareness feeds a political rhetoric and a system of ethical values which are then 'operationalised' by the political ruling elites in nation states. In short, the Wilsonian principles after the Second World War became accepted by an increasingly large number of nation states, despite (and perhaps because of) the Cold War. While there was competition between 'socialist' and 'capitalist' systems to determine the 'best' economic system, all nations agreed that stability has to be preserved. There is more: the legitimacy of IOs also arises from what IOs do and how they do it. The key issue is the recognition that IOs carry a body of technical knowledge, international rules and procedures that can prove to be effective. Thus the legitimacy of IOs is also dependent on the interaction between the Wilsonian ideals and the observable capacity of IOs to enforce them. A corollary of our thesis is that a crisis of legitimacy in IOs emerges as soon as the perception of a divide between affirmed principles and reality, between the ideology of international stability and the capacity of IOs to enforce it creeps in and settles down. And, naturally, a crisis in the legitimacy of IOs affects global governance as well. This chapter will focus more specifically on the legitimacy of international financial institutions (IFIs).

These points will be developed in three main sections. First, we will assess the current legitimacy of international organisations, particularly the Bretton Woods institutions – the World Bank and the International Monetary Fund. We start with a brief history of the legitimacy of IOs. Second, the chapter will examine the contribution of IOs to international socialisation, which is another word for global governance. We will explore what problems arise in the context of the current reflections on the new international financial architecture. Finally, the chapter will attempt to map some of the possible key issues which are likely to influence international organisations and their legitimacy, and the future of the international system and global governance.

The legitimacy of IOs: history and crisis

To some extent, the creation of international institutions in the United Nations' galaxy after the Second World War was related to lessons learned from the 1930s. The establishment of the World Bank and the International Monetary Fund was a consequence of a greater awareness of the negative social consequences of economic slumps. Furthermore, given the disastrous consequences of the post-First World War German resentment, the Allies understood after the Second World War that it was important to rebuild the economies of Germany, Japan and Europe through aid and in particular through the Marshall Plan. Simultaneously, the postwar reconstruction of the international economy encountered two challenges. One was the establishment of rules for the development of a system of equal free trade and exchange rate stability. The other was the competition between the West and the East in peaceful terms which implied the demonstration of the economic superiority of one system over the other at some point.

Naturally, the legitimacy of IFIs had a narrower basis than global peace. This is mainly because the IMF and the World Bank were created under the stewardship of the most powerful nations of the Western world, particularly the United States, to shape global finance. In the immediate postwar period, the supremacy of the United States was indisputable, although many ideas about the international financial architecture came from the United Kingdom. It was proposed that a world of free trade, free capital movements and stable currencies would be the best insurance against renewed episodes of crises and global slumps. The corollary of that was an institutional set-up that would reduce trade impediments and mechanisms to avoid global financial crises. In these two areas, there was opposition from the United States, and eventually a much more modest agenda was agreed upon, which nevertheless worked well for about twenty to twenty-five years. Ironically, because of the economic dominance of the United States and the Cold War, the developments in the 1950s–60s unexpectedly fulfilled the unattained original ideal. Traditional high US tariffs and the appetite for fast US export expansion – an impediment to a balanced expansion of world trade – was countervailed by the Cold War-induced long-term view that growth and expansion of US trade partners was important. Liquidity was indeed provided, not so much through, as originally planned, the newly created IFIs as through the direct lines of credit of the Marshall Plan. Hence, in such a system, the US dollar played the role of an international currency (whose management was denied to the newly created IMF).

While the world economy expanded and developed around the strong US base, there was a gradual increase in the economic might of the countries composing the restricted club of the advanced industrialised countries. This re-balancing of power came with a strengthening of the regulatory role of IFIs in the international financial sphere. Progressively, while serving as its source of authority, particularly because of their voting powers in its boards of directors, the G-7 also assigned to IFIs a second criterion of legitimacy. IFIs would be under the obligation to go beyond the interest of each member state and disseminate general principles of management of international economic relations that should apply to all countries to avoid worldwide slumps. This task resulted in the constitution of a body of technical principles. This body of knowledge evolved significantly from the 1950s until the 1980s, when it resulted in what John Williamson summarised as a 'Washington consensus' regarding the management of national economies.

One of the reasons why the legitimacy of IFIs depended on their capacity to provide 'growth and financial stability' rested with the Cold War. One should remember that from their creation until the 1990s, IFIs were operating in a divided world. A significant portion of countries were embracing (by true ideology or a strategic political alliance) institutions to run their economies that were closer to, or at least influenced by, non-market principles ranging from a bit of state intervention in social sectors to the centrally planned allocation of resources. The competition between these two systems was particularly acute when political and economic crises triggered the possibility of countries shifting from one side to the other of the two 'rival' systems and prompted the development of a 'market-based' development agenda.[1] That agenda included an explicit reference to the social challenges of reducing poverty and inequality by fostering economic growth and development.

And truly, during the three decades of 1945–1975, in what Eric Hobsbawn called the 'Golden Years' of capitalism – a period of extraordinary success of a system that seemed to be on the brink of collapse in the 1930s – there was an accumulation of good news that strengthened the mandate and the legitimacy of IFIs.[2] After the reconstruction of war-devastated Europe and Japan in the 1950s, new challenges emerged against the backdrop of the complex decolonisation process and socioeconomic developments in the Third World during the 1960s and 1970s. IFIs made good use of the quite optimistic vision of the development process produced by the first generation of development economists.[3] They were very confident in the grand models of development and strategies formulated in the 1950s. The basic point was that development was about high per capita growth, driven by capital accumulation and by structural change in the economy, from an agrarian economy towards an urban and industrialised one. The immensity of the task required a central and powerful actor to conduct the process, namely the state, through extensive government involvement in investment, planning and allocation of resources. This vision was certainly influenced by what had happened in the Soviet Union in the 1930s–1940s and in some industrialised countries (notably France and Japan) during the reconstruction years of post-Second World War. State intervention led also to the development of planning and programming agencies and macroeconomic models and corresponded in the economic literature to the spread of all forms of Keynesianism.

The legitimacy crisis in IFIs

The IFIs' crisis of legitimacy emerged because of a gradual shift in the perception of their effectiveness. Over the 1980s it became increasingly clear that IFIs were failing to explain, prevent and solve major challenges that they were supposed to address. The lack of convergence in the levels of income between developing and industrialised countries, the economic stagnation or even regression in many developing countries and the growing severity of financial crises in the 1990s illustrated the shortcomings of IFIs.

In the first place, development strategies, which were designed along an overly simplified version of the Solow–Swan neo-classical growth model and were actively promoted by the Bretton Woods institutions in Third World economies, did not resolve many of the pressing development issues. This was particularly true with regard to the convergence between rich and poor countries and income inequality and poverty within poor countries. Moreover, sometimes they contributed to creating new socioeconomic problems such as massive migration to overcrowded cities and the production of a number of negative externalities. The legitimacy crisis worsened when policies designed to resolve the debt crisis of the 1980s were put in place under the label 'structural adjustment'. These policies corresponded to new developments in the economic literature regarding the relationship between economic growth, trade openness and the role of macroeconomic balances, and thus required developing economies to change their incentive structure, that is their relative prices. These new ideas portrayed strategies that were less pro-active and public sector-driven, leaving a more important role for private investors and their 'expectations' of profits. They were at odds with the former import-substitution strategy that in many cases had led to public sector indebtedness and relatively inefficient domestic industries. These novelties demanded significant changes in state institutions modes of economic governance and government policies, which had social consequences and altered the perception of IFIs. The 1980s saw most of this new agenda being implemented with increasing political upheavals in developing countries.

The legitimacy of IFIs crumbled further because of dramatic changes in the international economy. Even with the conceptual problems mentioned above, the legitimate function of IFIs, of channeling savings from the North to the South, played its role during the debt crisis. During the subsequent decade, however, the intensifying process of financial globalisation posed an increasing threat to the role of IFIs, as private flows far exceeded public flows in international capital movements. While in the 1950s capital flows to developing countries totaled about $22 billion (of which about $9 billion were private flows), in the mid-1990s total capital flows jumped to $282 billion (of which $247 billion were private flows)! An illustration of this change in the relative importance of the private sector vis-à-vis IFIs is the role of private meetings such as the World Economic Forum in Davos, which attracts more media coverage than all the economic studies produced by IFIs. The private sector's expectations today are increasingly shaped by declarations by either private sector CEOs or actors that are well beyond the sphere of influence of IFIs and national financial authorities. All these prompted IFIs to restructure themselves and address the emerging issues that were much beyond the ken of pure macroeconomics. In a sense, the crisis of legitimacy forced them to evolve towards a much more fragmented and complex vision of the development process. This, however, did not facilitate the relationship with their own shareholders: greater sophistication in the analysis of development and its norms was associated with increasing scepticism about the usefulness of IFIs.

Finally, the last element of IFIs' crisis of legitimacy is their inevitable 'clientelism'. Suspicion and criticism arise from the belief that international organisations, especially IFIs, operate in a clientelist mode. That means that, despite the rhetoric, economic interventions will inevitably benefit specific groups with more influence.

The perception of 'clientelism' created problems of legitimacy for the IFIs because of the discrepancy between the values they claimed to defend (justice, equity, protection of the poor) and the vehicles of their practical actions and programmes. For example, the economic support for authoritarian governments in the aftermath of right-wing political coups (such as in Brazil and Indonesia in the mid-1960s, Chile in the 1970s, and so on) or the financial backing of anachronic regimes such as Mobutu's in former Zaire or the apartheid system in South Africa became increasingly difficult to justify on the grounds of helping the poor irrespective of taking sides in domestic politics. For a while these problems were manageable, *inter alia*, by invoking the principle of non-interference in the internal political affairs of member countries.

The 1990s, however, saw the emergence of challenges to this principle concomitant with the collapse of the Soviet Union and the de facto establishment of a world dominance by the Western democratic industrialised countries on both political and economic principles. The idea of legitimate 'international political interference' in internal affairs gained ground in the aftermath of the Gulf War. The end of the Cold War also meant that the social rhetoric of IFIs could be taken much more seriously without undermining governments that were strategic allies of the G-7. In this context, the 1990s saw a series of political revolutions at the periphery of the First World (South Africa, Zaire, Indonesia) and the transition to 'market-based' economic institutions in former members of the socialist camp. But then, and quite logically, the 'burden of proof' shifted in economic terms. The commitment of IFIs to their 'social agenda of reforms' and poverty reduction became thoroughly 'testable', irrespective of 'politics'. Geo-strategic and political considerations were no longer an acceptable excuse for not rocking the boat. Would IFIs get 'tough' with former allies of the West? In that sense, the pressure mounted for IFIs to become more transparent, more accountable to their own affirmed principles and more capable of demonstrating their usefulness.

While these criticisms were taking hold, there were two quite opposite trends. 'Political intervention' on the grounds of a set of universally agreed upon democratic principles can be acceptable. 'Economic intervention' on the grounds of 'technical' rules to manage economies tend to be 'bad'. On the one hand, international organisations dealing with security issues have had a history of internationally somewhat accepted interventions, legitimised by values and policies to preserve global peace. There is at least some kind of agreement over the general humanistic values upon which the international political order should be built, even if the United Nations' role has been criticised on suspicion that 'some interventions' are still being dictated by the strategic objectives of the few dominant (Western) countries. On the other hand, the Bretton Woods IFIs never managed to sell a complete consensus over policies to intervene in countries in economic and financial crises. All programmes had to be 'imposed', and were never considered fully 'appropriate' by the international community.

Consequences of the legitimacy crisis

The legitimacy crisis that we described for IFIs is faced by other international organisations and is not peculiar to them. States and national governments themselves face the challenge of having to universalise particular interests. Even when functioning properly, that is, when integrated and producing public goods reasonably well, they never succeed completely in this enterprise. Their decisions and actions are seldom able to generate full qualitative consent. They, too, have clients and detractors in their national realm. However, due to the derivative status of international organisations vis-à-vis states, the tendency to tailor policies to client interests becomes a central impediment to their legitimacy. Instead of placing multilateral qualities at their core, on which their legitimacy primarily depends, this tendency leaves such qualities at their periphery, hence the low level of multilateral institutionalisation of international organisations.

The lack of proportionality between international organisations' charters and the means at their disposal to accomplish the mandates and goals specified in these charters provides a good illustration of the low level of institutionalisation. Of course, charters and the mandates and objectives they dictate have rhetorical, inspirational and mission-establishing functions that exceed any plans that they should ever be entirely realised. This is especially true for the wide mandate of international organisations such as the United Nations (global security and prosperity) and the World Bank (eradication of poverty), much as it is for those delineated by the constitutions, declarations of rights and principles on which most modern nations are based. Moreover, the mandate of an international organisation does not necessarily imply that it falls exclusively to that organisation to achieve the designated goals. Their implementation is part of a systematic effort in which states, developed and developing countries, corporations, and individuals have a role to play. Considering this role, some argue that the responsibility of international organisations is mainly to occupy the interstices between the contributions of these other actors. No matter how sensible these arguments are, it remains the case that if the charters, mandates, and goals of international institutions are really going to be taken seriously, the means provided to fulfil them need to be adequate, even if in a minimally reasonable way. There is a threshold under which the lack of resources prevents any effort from being successful.

In the end, the low level of institutionalisation that characterises international organisations is reflected in the fact that, rather than being global institutions with both worldwide integration of the institution proper and effective operational reach, they tend to be headquarters organisations. In this context, the head is likely to be remote from the rest of the organisation and its activities on the ground. At times, the two hardly recognise each other as parts of the same entity. As internal deficiencies usually result in poor power projection, this situation largely accounts for the inadequate cohesion of decision-making processes and erratic implementation of operations in the field. As a consequence, what international institutions have built so far is less a thick multidirectional web or matrix than a thin network with a relatively meagre normative, operational, and political grip on or 'pull power' over developed and developing countries.[4]

Do member states, particularly the most powerful ones, feel compelled to engage internationally to satisfy a sense of solidarity and responsibility beyond their borders, while never really expecting or seeking significant, actual results or improvements? If this is so, the relatively low level of institutionalisation of international organisations and the international integration and socialisation that go with institutionalisation appear as key factors of explanation.[5]

International organisations and international socialisation

We suggested earlier that the crisis of legitimacy of IOs has stemmed partly from the perception of a growing discrepancy between professed universal values and norms that IOs propose and their narrow, clientelistic behaviour. One illustration of such a discrepancy is the absence of 'international socialisation'. We can define international socialisation as a state where there is a perception of agreed upon norms and principles that can be enforced. International socialisation can be a cross-boundary version of the rule of law that serves to secure the life of national citizens. This concept implies that international actors see (and believe in) norms and rules that are complied with by all willingly. Conversely, the weak reference to international law can be a symptom of a failure of international socialisation. The absence of the rule of law reveals a low degree of socialisation.

How does this apply to our discussion? We argued in the previous section that history was at the origin of international organisations, and that history too brought about their crises of legitimacy. The progressive disappearance of agreed upon principles or norms can be a symptom of a weakening international socialisation. This section examines the problems of creating and enforcing norms associated with international economic and financial organisations.

For international economic and financial organisations, socialisation can be defined as the recognition of the rights and duties associated with the status of the international economic order and architecture. A major difference between IFIs and other types of international organisations comes when there is a need to 'enforce' rules. Coercion has a different meaning when it comes to 'economic' decisions. The 'enforcement' of UN principles by means of an explicit (political or military) intervention demands greater efforts because of the much higher visibility of international political crises. By contrast, there is a much greater number of 'interventions' by the economic and financial IOs, where countries are 'forced' to abide by what is 'defined' as sound 'economic laws'. The leverage, as we shall discuss below, comes from the pressure of *conditionalities* imposed by IFIs. Individual states do not enter into these 'programmes' voluntarily, and it does usually requires a crisis situation.[6]

IFIs' contribution to international socialisation

One piece of evidence for international socialisation in economic terms would be to find the acceptance of general rules agreed upon by all economic actors – private and public, powerful and weak, poor and wealthy – designed by actors that are equals, and to improve the functioning of the international financial architecture for the common good. Needless to say, we are far from that. For example, the United States, the European Union or Japan are unwilling to accept the constraint of macroeconomic co-ordination aimed at, say, reducing the volatility of exchange rate fluctuation between the dollar, the euro and the yen. Although most politicians agree that co-ordination would be a 'good' thing, it comes at the expense of the independence of their monetary policies. Can socialisation nevertheless occur in a more limited way, that is, through a simple process where countries accept common 'technical rules' for their external economic relations?

If all countries followed 'rules' of good 'financial governance' at home, then that was supposed to be capable of preventing world recessions such as the Great Slump of the 1930s, even if IFIs were not lenders of last resort. The rules also applied to other economic policies. For example, world economic progress required the development of free trade under a regime of fixed – but adjustable – exchange rates. They also allowed countries facing temporary external shocks and unable to meet their balance-of-payments obligations to be assisted. A country that relied on exports of a given primary commodity whose price fell for some reason totally independent of the country's policies was eligible for assistance. And these rules were not arbitrary. They addressed the fear that balance-of-payments crises could spread and thus create international crises, and were based on the better understanding after the Second World War of the transmission mechanisms of the Great Slump. A country with a fixed exchange rate facing payments difficulties and losing reserves could be tempted to solve its temporary problems by 'devaluing' its currency and shifting the burden of adjustment to its trade partners. The role of IFIs was precisely to use commonly agreed upon techniques to identify the nature of a crisis. Then they would point to the remedies to correct the problems. The underlying principle relied on the acceptance by all countries of the legitimacy of 'IFIs' economic skills' to distinguish crises that were 'external' or 'exogenous' from crises that were 'endogenous', namely those caused by domestic economic mismanagement. IFIs developed several tools and analytical instruments that were aimed at understanding the nature of external imbalances and designing the appropriate programme of assistance. Such programmes were part of an agenda of preventing a local crisis from spreading to the rest of the world and producing a snowball negative effect.

In addition, among IFIs, the IMF had the responsibility of constantly monitoring – through periodic consultations (the IMF's Article IV consultations) – the vulnerability of member countries' balance of payments. From the 1950s to the end of the 1980s, there was limited capital mobility, and the major role for the IMF was (a) to solve balance-of-payments (BoP) crises by financing temporary gaps which were usually small (because of the limited mobility of capital and the existence of controls); (b) to make sure that countries followed policies (fiscal and monetary) that were consistent with their exchange rates; and (c) to recommend changes in the exchange rate (devaluation) when external imbalances persisted. This 'golden age' for the IMF corresponded to a concept of 'surveillance' of the international order where the monitoring and policy recommendations were based on a very simple 'analytical' model of how imbalances were created and transmitted. In simple terms, a BoP gap (say an excessively high level of imports) had to have a monetary equivalent (somebody was financing it) under a system of a temporary fixed exchange rate. The Polak model provided the basis for the development of the financial programming,[7] the frame upon which the IMF would construct its programmes and give recommendations to member countries. Under a fixed exchange rate regime, excessive domestic credit growth (usually originating from growing public sector deficits) would eventually run down foreign exchange reserves by eroding the credibility of the exchange rate regime. The strength of 'financial programming' in a world of low capital mobility came from the fact that in most cases it was an effective solution to a BoP crisis. The combination of a 'devaluation' with 'fiscal restraint' would usually succeed in bringing the BoP of a given country back to equilibrium.[8]

The important point is that the emergence of 'development economics' as a research field and the practical experience of IFIs dealing with crises were instrumental in creating two things: first, a body of technicians whose expertise in crisis management and knowledge of cross-country development experiences served as a vehicle to strengthen the legitimacy of these IFIs and their solutions to crises; second, the idea of conditionality as the mechanism to 'enforce' these solutions that necessitated in many cases harsh decisions by governments (such as reducing fiscal imbalances and hence affecting the country's political economy). The modus operandi of IFIs, or in other words their contribution to a process of international socialisation, was to define the strict conditions under which they would agree to assist a country. For example, if the identified source of a balance-of-payments problem was excessively expansionary domestic macroeconomic policies, the usual set of 'conditions' under which IFI liquidity support that would allow a country to remain solvent and avoid defaulting on its external obligations would be provided, would be to request, quantify and enforce a significant contraction in domestic demand, through 'austerity' measures. Conditionality soon became a synonym for 'interference' in domestic macro policies, and was criticised for its consequences on the local social fabric, since most of these programmes implied cuts in expenditure for both the private and the public sectors.

But in the 1990s, many of the assumptions underlying the IMF's diagnosis of a crisis no longer held. Imbalances originating in the capital account of the BoP came to play a much more important role in international crises. For example, the 'financial programming' tool paid little attention to the determinants of capital flows and their mobility that were at the centre of the Asian crisis and also of the new type of crises that started preoccupying IFIs in the middle of the 1990s. These crises were preceded by a long period of economic and financial prosperity described as an economic and financial 'boom'. It was a period of coexistence of high growth with sound macro fundamentals that did not require any IMF 'intervention'. The crisis came, at some point, after the prosperity turned into a 'financial bubble' that eventually collapsed. It was a blow to IFIs. Although many of their technicians (together with academics and risk analysts) were fully aware of the 'dangers' of 'financial bubbles' and documented the 'early warning signals' of a (possible) crisis in Asia, there was no real capacity to impose a 'change' in policy in due time. This is partly because of the 'lack of leverage'. Ironically, IFIs were designed to be able to 'intervene' only in a post-crisis mode, once the bubble collapses. There is very little they can do during prosperity, even if they detect worrying signals. They are still 'emergency rooms' of financial hospitals rather than 'preventive medical care'. In any event, their inability to prevent the Asian crisis contributed to a further deterioration of their image.

These sudden and devastating crises are the types of crises of the twenty-first century; IFIs are much less equipped, intellectually and practically (in terms of the required liquidity assistance needed), to deal with them. In particular, the 'conditions' to be imposed upon countries are much more difficult to design. De Gregorio *et al.* examine precisely the role of the IMF in the face of the new types of crises that are related to the globalised financial world.[9] These crises are difficult to detect and different from the old balance-of-payments crisis originating in trade and competitiveness problems. In this context the IMF has been forced to increase dramatically the scale of its lending and to add to the design of its programmes areas of structural reforms such as the financial and banking sectors with which it is relatively unfamiliar. The size of the rescue packages and the relative opaqueness of the final destination of funds have created another area of tension between the IFIs and their legitimacy. To make things worse, with much more leverage (i.e. more lending, more areas of controls), the IMF was unable to prevent the two episodes of similar crises that followed the Asian flu, namely Russia (1998) and Brazil (1998–9).

It is after these 1997–8 Asian crises that politicians, NGOs and economists pointed out that many of the tools applied to understand these crises were misused and were possibly responsible for sending countries in wrong directions.[10] Critics argued that IFIs based their analytical work on tools – the 'old' Polak model – that were largely obsolete to interpret the nature of modern economic interactions between countries. It might be easy to point out that many underlying relations and assumptions in IFI models had little to do with the observed behaviour of modern economic agents in the globalised financial world.

In addition, programmes have been questioned on the grounds that despite IFIs' assurances, they were harming the country's poor. Ironically, these criticisms were supported by a general mood of 'political correctness' in the G-7 countries, advocated by many NGOs and activists that positioned themselves as allies of the developing countries' poor but were sometimes also critics of lifting the protectionist barriers in their own countries. Those were admittedly a major obstacle to the integration of the poor into the flourishing world economy of the 1990s. This criticism prompted a recent transformation of IFIs. They created a drive towards (at least) a different rhetoric and expressed more concerns about the social consequences of economic reforms and political correctness. The pressure for such an analysis confirms that the legitimacy of IFIs' policies is challenged and that the previous benign neglect with which social consequences were treated is now challenged. It also shows that the G-7 countries, through their representatives on the boards of the IFIs, are now pushing for quite a different agenda. Interestingly enough, in some cases, this agenda corresponds to their own need to strengthen the legitimacy of their 'bilateral' aid policies vis-à-vis their own domestic constituencies while abandoning their commitment to supporting the IFIs' multilateral approach.

International rules, values and norms: what has been left over?

We therefore are left with a problematic sense of legitimacy, if not a sense of a decline in the legitimacy of international norms and rules. Political principles of justice find little international applicability, principally because of the lack of consistency and consensus.[11] And regarding economic principles, there is much greater perplexity regarding the rules that can be seen as governing the complex process of development. We are in a world where it is tempting to adopt a cynical attitude regarding the legitimacy of many international interventions to protect global peace, despite the rhetoric and an emphatically supportive media coverage.[12] And certainly we are far away from the simplistic views under which IFIs operated from the 1960s till the 1990s, to the point where some now argue that only charitable organisations are truly legitimate.

IFIs certainly now have less room for imposing 'conditions' and their vision of 'socialisation' on developing countries. Nevertheless, they remain and still have somehow a 'technocratic' legitimacy. Even fierce critics remain fascinated by the internal 'culture' and 'discipline' of these institutions, claimed to function as a medieval Church or a typical Leninist party.[13] This internal culture is grounded on 'economics' claimed to represent empirically tested theories that allow societies to make rational choices. A body of 'scientific' knowledge is used to legitimise these choices and actions.[14] Indeed, many critics still see the IFIs as capable of imposing a vision of the development process based on an ideological and technocratic view of economic and social transformation.

So, we are facing a paradox. The critiques of IFIs are equally virulent from both the left and the right of the international and domestic political spectrum. From the left's viewpoint, the technocratic power of IFIs is excessive and they still manage to bend the policies of developing countries. From the right's point of view, IFIs are simply incapable of altering significantly and influencing enough the policies of countries (and of other economic agents). Hence the left wants to shut IFIs down because of their excessive power to affect national policies in a non-democratic, technocratic way, and their recipes based on an ideological a priori for the 'free market'. And the right wants also to shut them down because they are not strong enough to change decisively national policies and truly implement the same 'free market' principles. Or, conversely, because IFIs' interference in international crises creates 'more bad than good'. Their interventions allow the 'survival of the unfit' and produce 'moral hazard' that perpetuates inefficiencies. In short, IFIs are not effective and cost too much for national taxpayers.

For a Marxist critic, IFIs are nothing but a sophisticated piece of machinery through which the modern (and now dominant) capitalist elite in the G 7 coun tries expands the 'rules of the game', imposing when it can (and crises are surely a good opportunity) changes in the behaviour of other fellow (but sometimes reluctant) elites in less developed countries. In that sense, IFIs contribute to the modernisation of capitalism, its continuous process of integration and self-regulation, that is, they are simply instruments of an acceleration of capitalism's historical trends to become truly a global system (including in its cultural and philosophical dimensions). IFIs are the guardians and enforcers of a set of rules that are by definition biased, where there will always be a 'dominant' centre of the system and a 'dominated' periphery. Now for liberal-democrats, IFIs can also be seen as the (imperfect but promising) embryo of a future civil service in a future democratic global world of equal partners. The rules that they set are a prelude for a global system of governance. In that sense, IFIs, together with other international organisations, contribute to the economic and financial regulation of the international order. They try to impose precisely in all quarters the same set of legitimate principles. These two visions are contradictory only in the perspective of a search for an imperative relationship between ideas and the truth.

Scenarios for the future of global governance

Should we thus look at the long-term future for IFIs with a cynical perspective, or with an optimistic Kantian view of the Enlightenment? What combination of forces and values would there be at play? It is increasingly difficult to see clearly the future of the issues that were mentioned earlier. But we can suggest that the international system and global governance will most likely err between one of the following visions that we will examine in turn. On the optimistic side is the achievement of a form of universal constitutionalism; on the pessimistic side is the breakdown of the international process of socialisation and perhaps the triumph of technocratism and cynicism.

Universal constitutionalism

Under this optimistic vision of the future of the international order, there is a progressive integration of states into a process of international socialisation, symbolised by 'Western constitutionalism'. In this context, international organisations are key to the gradual establishment of international constitutionalism – being understood here as a theory whose central focus at the international and the national level is the relationship between the source of authority of political power and the practical control of its exercise (which is, incidentally, one possible definition of the social–philosophical problem of legitimacy). Nevertheless, the need for international organisations is not a guarantee that their existence and legitimacy will automatically be secure. For them to be actors of strategic importance to international constitutionalism in the making – including the limitation of unequal distribution of power (economic, political and cultural) as well as the defence of individual rights – they must rise to four major challenges.

Adjusting diversity without annihilating it is the first of these challenges. This entails tackling the fact that at the international level, plurality lies much deeper – in terms of cultural differences, levels of developments, and aspirations – than it is at the national level. Here, the question is how to implement a multilateral culture without having it become a tool of Western extension and neo-colonisation. The problem also encompasses the means of bringing about an international order that is not, in its regulation of openness, a veiled monopolisation of power. Answering this problem particularly involves looking for ways further to democratise the cultural, political and economic hegemony of which the multilateral project is a part.[15] It is, namely, according to this condition that access to and circulation of power will not be opposed by multilateral arrangements themselves.

Second, it will be necessary for international organisations to address the weak sense of international community. In order to overcome this weakness, stronger mechanisms of global identification, participation, representation, responsibility and solidarity than the present ones will have to be imagined and implemented. However, strengthening the sense of global community must not be envisioned as the construction of a war machine against national or even regional realms. For if the development of a legitimate international community cannot be reduced to the imposition of one cultural model, neither can it be based on the unilateral exclusion or elimination of existing forms of political association. Forms of synergy and complementarity among the various layers of contemporary politics are advisable. In this context, the democratic qualities of national, regional and international political arrangements constitute an asset, one that can be capitalised on in negotiating and facilitating the establishment of an international consensus.

This presupposes that international organisations will revisit the nature of their co-operation with the actors that are both their partners and competitors, especially states, regional arrangements, private actors, non-governmental organisations and individuals. This is the third challenge that must be confronted. Improving the nature of collaboration with these actors is destined to be a complex task, particularly because each tends to have an agenda that does not necessarily coincide entirely with those of the others. Fine-tuning the co-operation of international organisations with these actors will therefore mean not only the adaptation of international organisations but also an adjustment in how these actors see themselves and function.

States will have to become less protective of their sovereign powers: more willing, for instance, to share power with international organisations and non-governmental organisations, and more open to claims from individuals. In addition, demonstrating institutional flexibility without adopting an attitude of copy-catting the economic ideology of corporations will help. Regional arrangements will have to clarify the aims and modes of their operation of their multilateral strategies and relations. For example, the European Union will probably have to find a workable balance between using the European project as a tool of international competition and making it an integral part of the multilateral network. Non-governmental organisations will be required to become more aware of the imperatives of representation and delegation attached to the exercise of public responsibilities. Self-appointment does not serve here as a substitute. Corporations will have to be more oriented to the public good. As for individuals, it may be necessary to come to terms with the fact that the defence of individual rights cannot equate strictly to a culture of entitlement and, as a result, should not be accomplished at the expense of a sense of responsibility.

The fourth challenge for international organisations is handling the effects of the paradox of contemporary democratic culture. The increased sense of responsibility at the international level and the simultaneous proliferation of a culture of individual entitlement at the national level (in particular through the diffusion of the American version of democracy) that is apt to be allergic to solidarity is, indeed, a riddle for institutions committed to international socialisation. What is to be made of these two trends, and can they continue to develop in parallel? Will the evolution of contemporary international democratic culture pursue the liberal quest of entitlement, or will it follow a more republican path – in which modern democratic culture as a whole is historically and ideologically rooted – with greater sensibility to the global social and citizenship concerns that it could bring about?

Regionalism, particularism, technocratism and cynicism

There are all too many pessimistic contributions supporting a view of the future that is at odds with the previous optimistic projection. In a world where particular interests prevail, there are many reasons for that scenario to unfold. For example, Ohmae suggests that economic specialisation and progress will bring about – at not too distant a future – the end of nation states.[16] The dramatic changes in the world economy are now driven increasingly by regions or groups of interest (investors, consumers, networks) that operate across national boundaries. According to such a vision there is little scope for international organisations, whose purpose is to represent all sovereign nation states, to play any useful role. On the contrary, the meaningful units of the future, capable of creating values and playing world politics, would be transnational corporations in alliance with specific regional political entities that are by definition absent from current representation in IOs.

Would this be a 'better' world than the one projected by the vision of the Enlightenment? It is naturally difficult to see, but one can point out that the world of particularisms poses itself challenges that are much more difficult. For example, a world of transnational corporations hardly needs to be concerned with all mankind as a 'universal project' and as a reference 'value'. In fact, this world can set limited objectives in its version of 'international socialisation', by, for instance, guaranteeing only a partial and 'regional' order over its partial area of interest, while leaving the rest of the world to violence and banditry. And indeed, when one observes trends where entire regions such as central Africa or countries such as Colombia and Russia are run (in part) by warlords and mafia one can foresee bits and pieces of this scenario unfolding.

To make things even darker, the world of regional particularisms and transnational corporate power is also a world of cynicism and technocratic rhetoric where the dominance of specific groups can be hidden behind the rationality of science.[17] It is a totalitarian Brave New World but it is one where the 'civilised' places that are preserved from 'chaos' are run rationally and within the rule of law. There is even a role for IOs and IFIs there, provided that they abandon their pretence of universalism and concentrate on the limited scope of the brave new world. There, the extensive use of 'social sciences' in a manipulative way (economics, sociology, political science, statistics, etc.) would certainly help to control and administer the equilibrium of this world. And moreover, the role of IOs can even be extended. The administration of aid, the provision of advice to less developed countries can still exist on this divided planet. However, this would be done in a context of increased cynicism, a view of the international order and of the international socialisation where countries are not equal, and where there are entire regions and populations that are left behind and explicitly ignored. Suffice to say that the evidence supporting each of the two visions outlined above can be found in today's world.

Notes

1. The emergence of a 'social' agenda of 'equality', 'justice', 'development of poor countries' for IFIs (and particularly the World Bank) became more pronounced after R. McNamara, a former US Secretary of Defense, took over as the World Bank president in 1968 (and held that post until 1981). While undoubtedly many prominent economists recognised the need to think about the relationship between growth, development and equality (starting with Nobel prizewinner S. Kuznets), the agenda of IFIs became heavily charged with social democratic insights partly because of the need to manage the rivalry between the West and the East during the Cold War.

2. See E. Hobsbawn, *The Age of Extremes: A History of the World, 1914–1991* (New York: Pantheon Books, 1995).

3. Among a vast literature, these issues are discussed in N. Stern 'The Economics of development: a survey', *The Economic Journal*, vol. 99 (September 1989), pp. 597–685; and more recently in G. M. Meier and J. Stiglitz (eds.), *Frontiers of Development Economics* (Washington, DC, Oxford and New York: World Bank and Oxford University Press, 2001).

4. On pull power, see Thomas M. Franck, *The Power of Legitimacy among Nations* (Oxford: Oxford University Press, 1990), p. 204.

5. The term 'socialisation' is used to qualify the process of social integration, taking into account the imperatives of justice, that is, the importance of reciprocity and the dynamics of rights and duties among actors.

6. John Williamson, *The Political Economy of Reform* (Washington, DC: Institute for International Economics, 1993).

7. The Polak model, named after the IMF's economist and head of its research department, is a typical old (1953) but long-living instrument that still functions as the backbone of IMF programmes. The basic idea is that a country's external imbalance – a change in international reserves under a fixed exchange rate regime – has somehow to be financed by money and credit creation. Hence the way to correct such an imbalance is to find the 'creator' of excess liquidity in the economy (usually the public sector through fiscal deficits) and stop the bleeding (usually by imposing conditions on the Fund's assistance based on public deficit cuts and reductions in domestic credit).

8. It should be noted, however, that the way to engineer a 'fiscal contraction' rested entirely on the political economy of the country itself. Whether the government would decide to cut social expenditure or military expenditure remained an open question. Naturally, the relative strength of ministers in developing countries, the Cold War, and other domestic political factors were neglected by the IFIs' analytical programming tools. However, the manner of achieving stabilisation is now required to be more explicit in the current programmes and agreements reached with governments.

9. J. De Gregorio, B. Eichengreen, T. Ito and C. Wyplosz, *An Independent and Accountable IMF* (Geneva: International Centre for Monetary and Banking Studies, 1999).

10. These points are discussed at length in J. Stiglitz, 'The Insider: What I Learnt at the World Economic Crisis', *The New Republic*, 17 April 2000.

11. See, for instance, the debates generated by the NATO intervention in Kosovo and its problematic endorsement by the UN Security Council.

12. There was scepticism regarding the true motivation that lay behind the recent military interventions in the form the UN peace-keeping operations.

13. S. George and F. Sabelli, *Faith and Credit: the World Bank's Secular Empire* (London: Penguin Books, 1994).

14. Jürgen Habermas, *La Technique et la Science comme Idéologie*, trans. into French from German (Paris: Denoel-Gonthiers, 1978).

15. Following this route does not put the burden exclusively on developed countries. It encompasses the expectation that developing countries will take responsibilities

themselves. The privileged few in the developing countries would, for instance, have to move away from the victim/dependant mentalities vis-à-vis the West that are frequently combined with being the co-responsible and prime local beneficiaries of the unequal development of their countries.

16. See Kenichi Ohmae, *The End of the Nation State* (New York: Free Press, 1995).
17. Habermas, *La Technique et la Science*.

16 The G-7 and architecture debates: norms, authority and global financial governance

ANDREW BAKER

Since the 1980s, a regular round of meetings between finance ministers and central bank governors from the G-7 countries has been one of the principal mechanisms for formulating international financial and monetary policy.[1] This chapter traces the contribution of the G-7 finance ministers and central bank governors to debates on the design of the international financial system, and draws conclusions on the collective role these agencies play in global financial governance. Such an exercise takes us right to the very heart of questions concerning the exercise of power and authority in the international system. Over the last decade, G-7 finance ministries and central banks have shared and refined ideas and drawn collective lessons against a backdrop of widespread financial turmoil that has posed questions about the sustainability of the current system and the authority of the state.[2]

It is argued in this chapter that the G-7 finance ministries and central banks have developed a narrow, technical belief system. This belief system has not only constrained the finance ministries' and central banks' ability to respond to financial crises, but it has also generated a series of very modest incremental proposals for reform of the global financial system. Rather than challenging the finance ministries' and central banks' belief system, the principal impact of the financial crises of 1997–8 and the subsequent response has been to reinforce, refine, deepen and extend the belief system into new countries and new policy areas. The likely net result of these activities is further capital account liberalisation. A further consequence of recent reforms is the increasing prominence of a pattern of three-dimensional diplomacy, in which the structural dynamic of the market dominates, but according to which also long-term financial stability ultimately fails to be guaranteed.

The chapter is divided into four sections. The first section illustrates how the G-7 finance ministries and central banks have progressively cultivated and refined a shared belief system on matters concerning macroeconomic policy, exchange rates and the general design of the international financial system over the last decade. The second section argues that this belief system has led to a pattern of three-dimensional diplomacy where global financial governance is concerned. The third section examines the G-7 finance ministers and central bank governors' proposals on financial architectural issues after the financial crises of 1997–8. The fourth and final section concludes the chapter by summarising the major arguments and discussing their implications for the governance of international financial relations.

The shared belief system of the G-7

Over the last fifteen years, finance ministries and central banks from the G-7 countries have progressively cultivated and refined a shared belief system in the areas of macroeconomic and monetary policy, exchange rates and the design of the international monetary and financial system. Belief systems consist of a whole series of explicit causal hypotheses relating to a specific area of policy. They emerge when policy makers develop a series of interconnected intellectual premises, involving a clearly articulated and supposedly empirically verifiable chain of causal factors and variables. In this respect ideas can be said to 'go together' to form a belief system, yet international financial matters affect a wide range of social groupings well beyond the financial sector.

Within the state apparatus finance ministries and central banks enjoy a monopoly of expertise and competence in international financial affairs Efforts to emphasise the technical nature of macroeconomic and financial governance have had the effect of depoliticising financial and monetary policy by insulating the finance ministries and central banks from societal pressures, as evidenced by fiscal rules and independent central banks. It is largely the finance ministry and central bank deputies (senior officials) who have cultivated the current G-7 belief system. They undertake preparations for G-7 meetings and meet about ten times a year in the G-7 setting, as well as in other settings such as the G-10 and the OECD. Several deputies have been academic economists of similar intellectual outlook, or private sector financial analysts. Others are career officials who have acquired technical expertise over time. Most of these officials have also previously held either staff positions at the IMF, have performed the role of national executive directors at the IMF, or other international institutions such as the EBRD. In other words, they have been progressively socialised into the beliefs of a prevailing intellectual orthodoxy on macroeconomic and financial matters.

As finance ministries and central banks have acquired more autonomy within their domestic policy-making process, so the process of G-7 agenda setting has become greatly circumscribed and this is reflected in the form and content of the G-7 belief system. The range of interests represented at G-7 meetings is unduly narrow. Officials view their natural constituency as the financial centres located in their national territory. The interests of Wall Street, the City of London, Tokyo, Paris and Frankfurt accordingly translate into officials' conception of the 'national interest'. Furthermore, societal consultations prior to G-7 meetings are invariably restricted to the occasional seminar with representatives of some of these financial interests on specific issues or initiatives.[3] In other words, the G-7 process operates as a relatively self-contained elite network. The consequence of this is that issues such as a return to a system of capital controls, managed exchange rates, increased public sector investment or redistributive macroeconomic policies based on criteria other than financial and monetary ones never get on to the G-7 agenda.

Macroeconomic policy

Throughout the G-7 countries and beyond, macroeconomic policy increasingly revolves around the notion of 'credibility', based on 'sound' long-term policies. In relation to monetary policy national inflation targets are being adopted by central banks throughout the industrialised world. Inflation targets are said to result in a form of 'constrained discretion',[4] and are justified on the grounds that they make announced intentions believable to a watching audience of international investors.[5] In this respect, timely data release is seen to reduce the possibility of market turbulence, as well as reducing suspicions about authorities' intentions. It is on this basis that finance ministries and central banks have justified multilateral surveillance exercises. Such exercises are based on the notion of 'transparency'. In accordance with this, finance ministries and central banks have attempted to establish peer-reviewed standards for international data release. It is believed that data release prevents unsustainable policies from being hidden from view by making more information available to market participants on the state of an economy.

Authorities have also attempted to signal a strategic 'pre-commitment' to a tough anti-inflationary stance by legislating to make central banks independent. Central bank independence has been justified on the good anti-inflationary track record of existing independent central banks and the view that central bankers are less likely than politicians to cheat and dash for growth ahead of elections.[6] In this regard, panels of senior central bank officials and independent experts increasingly make interest rate decisions with the objective of meeting a specified inflation target. This is becoming the dominant model across the G-7 and is being promoted as an example of good practice.

With regard to fiscal policy, similar principles of credibility through constrained discretion and pre-commitment also reign. This has been evident in the introduction of fiscal rules designed to stabilise debt-to-GDP ratios, involving legally constituted targets for budget deficit reduction programmes such as the Maastricht Convergence criteria and the fiscal stability pact in the EU, efforts to pass a balanced budget resolution in the United States and a 'golden fiscal rule' in the United Kingdom. As well as pre-commitments to long-term targets to ensure that current expenditures will not exceed current revenues, there have been moves to publish more information on the state of countries' public finances. Independent audit bodies are increasingly recommended as a means of reaching judgements on the quality of a government's fiscal data. These institutional adaptations are all based on the fundamental belief that contractionary fiscal policy leads to economic growth, because it reduces government debt, bringing down long-term interest rates and ultimately reducing the cost of capital.

Exchange rates and the international financial system

The current G-7 belief system holds that the only way to have an exchange rate policy is through national monetary policy. But national monetary policies are exclusively directed towards the objective of low national inflation throughout the G-7.[7] Proactive exchange rate management is therefore eschewed. The focus is on getting national macroeconomic policies right as a means of delivering exchange rate stability. Former US Treasury Secretary and G-7 Deputy Larry Summers argued that:

What we've learnt is that the idea that you can have a monetary policy, a fiscal policy and an exchange rate policy is a profound confusion. There is no enduring exchange rate policy that is independent of monetary or fiscal policy. I feel that there are very real costs when monetary policies are directed at exchange rate objectives rather than at growth or price stability objectives. Without monetary policy changes there are real limits to how much governments can affect exchange rates – I think that's the lesson of the EMS period, that's the lesson of the bubble period in Japan.[8]

In effect, the G-7 belief system acknowledges that exchange rates are the market's verdict on the conduct of national monetary and fiscal policies. However, officials deny that they ignore exchange rates altogether.[9] The view is that exchange rate misalignments result in resource misallocations within and between economies, but that correct exchange rate valuations change on a daily, even hourly basis.[10] The G-7 surveillance process therefore focuses on the identification of sustained exchange rate misalignments caused by market volatility. When the finance ministries and central banks agree that the value of a particular currency represents a misalignment, they release a statement the markets are expected to interpret. Such statements represent monetary authorities' collective expression of opinion and are essentially a form of code.[11] At the same time, exchange market interventions are viewed as a policy instrument of increasingly limited utility in the context of increased international capital flows and are therefore used sparingly.[12] Officials openly acknowledge that these activities give the G-7 process the character of little more than a pressure group in relation to foreign exchange markets.[13] In effect, market actors are engaged in an ongoing and continuous referendum on the anti-inflationary credentials of domestic macroeconomic policies.

On the question of international capital mobility, the deputies start from the position that 'greater capital mobility and increasing integration of world capital markets are good for the world economy, increase overall global welfare and provide the basis for settled policy throughout the OECD'.[14] Capital mobility is seen to lead to a greater realisation of the efficiencies available from specialisation, from more rapid technology transfer and more productive allocation of resources, from comparative advantage and from the spur of competition. Benefits are believed to show up in higher rates of economic growth, leading to higher wages and higher returns on capital, and higher standards of living.[15]

On the whole the G-7 finance ministries and central banks have rejected capital controls. Such controls are seen to induce economic distortions and macroeconomic costs which far outweigh the benefits. The exception to this rule are cases where inadequate prudential regulation of the banking system may justify the maintenance of capital controls on short-term inflows into banks for prudential reasons.[16] Even the US Treasury accepted this caveat as early as 1996. The use of capital controls has become a controversial issue. As Benjamin Cohen's chapter in this volume illustrates, a number of prominent economists effectively changed their position following the financial crises and began to advocate the use of controls. However, none of these individuals occupied key positions in G-7 finance ministries, central banks or international institutions. The only openly dissenting voices within the international policy-making community, Joseph Stiglitz at the World Bank (on the issue of capital controls) and Oskar Lafontaine, the German finance minister (on exchange rates and macroeconomic policy), were rapidly marginalised by their colleagues.

The belief system and the G-7 process

Despite some differences between the G-7 countries on the issue of defining financial systems in terms of capital or credit markets, the G-7 finance ministries and central banks do have certain common shared objectives relative to other sections of the state apparatus, notably financial liberalisation and macroeconomic discipline.[17] Commitment to the basic principles of sound money and open markets is partly rooted in national social formations, or the close relationships finance ministries and central banks have with financial sectors, and a shared professional ethos. The relatively narrow career background of most G-7 deputies augments this commitment to monetary and financial criteria. Furthermore, the equivalent of a Wall Street–Treasury axis exists to varying extents in all G-7 countries, although this is clearly most prominent in the United States. Consequently, whilst differences may persist on the regulatory significance of information exchange and the regulation of certain financial instruments such as hedge funds, the broad principle of capital liberalisation is on the whole supported and is even seen as virtuous. In this respect, the G-7 process has the characteristics of a trans-governmental coalition. The constituent agencies build co-operative relations with like agencies in other states, to provide endorsement for their mutually shared objectives, enhancing their influence in domestic policy debates and a whole host of decision-making settings throughout the global political economy.[18]

The belief system in practice: three-dimensional diplomacy

The constituent premises of the G-7 belief system effectively result in a pattern of three-dimensional diplomacy in macroeconomic, exchange rate and, increasingly, financial regulatory matters. Simultaneously, this pattern of three-dimensional diplomacy serves to reinforce and maintain the G-7 belief system. Dimension I diplomacy involves interactions at G-7 meetings such as efforts to arrive at a consensus and activities such as multilateral surveillance (an informal, frank and candid exchange of information and opinion, as countries expose their policies to collective scrutiny and comments). Dimension II diplomacy involves efforts by participants at G-7 meetings to influence domestic policy making. Domestic politics and institutional arrangement also affect G-7 agenda setting and the possible courses of action open to the G-7. Dimension III diplomacy involves policy makers' collective attempts to communicate with financial markets as a transnational structure or global cross-border space, as well as the process through which markets scrutinise domestic policy and G-7 statements. In the week leading up to a G-7 meeting the public statements of policy makers and prominent market spokespeople intensify. Each expresses an opinion based on their own calculations and data. An ongoing form of coded diplomacy is played out quite publicly in global publications such as the *Financial Times*.

In the dimension I setting, the G-7's surveillance process is designed to act as a form of peer review to discipline domestic macroeconomic policies, and to temper the worst excesses of the financial bubbles and panics that characterise a system of floating exchange rates in an era of liberalised capital. Surveillance leads to the release of coded statements if the G-7 authorities agree upon an exchange rate misalignment. Dimension III diplomacy therefore involves direct efforts to communicate collectively with financial markets as global cross-border spaces in an effort to modify some of their more extreme destabilising tendencies. However, the markets remain in a position to accept, or reject G-7 views. One of the consequences of these activities is that domestic macroeconomic policies implemented in the dimension II setting are disciplined and focus on the criteria most monitored by global financial markets – current and projected rates of inflation and fiscal deficits.[19] In other words, the search for credibility involves playing to an audience of international investors. It also involves establishing domestic dimension II institutional arrangements that are based on the dimension I belief system and therefore have 'credibility' with the markets. The result is a dynamic interlocking form of triangular or three-dimensional diplomacy, involving multilateral surveillance, domestic policy making and scrutiny by global markets.

However, the institutional products of the current G-7 belief system pose some problems in terms of responding to financial crises. Paradoxically, whilst central banks and finance ministries have seen their powers and degree of autonomy increase, simultaneously their capacity to co-operate with one another has diminished. This is mainly because independent central banks remain subject to legal and constitutional constraints such as national inflation or monetary targets to which they are 'pre-committed'. Their room for manoeuvre in accordance with international negotiations is highly constrained in practice. Moreover, central bank decision-making processes relating to interest rates often involve committees of independently minded technocrats such as the Federal Reserve's open market committee, the board of the Bundesbank, the new governing council of the European Central Bank (ECB), or the Bank of England's monetary policy committee reaching decisions collectively. This means that central bank governors have difficulties in giving international commitments on the future direction of monetary policy at international meetings. They cannot speak on behalf of their colleagues.

The type of international co-operation that results from these institutional arrangements was evident in the G-7 central banks' response to the global financial crisis of 1998 and the 11 September 2001 terrorist attacks. Fears of global deflation, as a consequence of the financial turmoil in Asia, Latin America and Russia, reached their peak in November and December 1998. This compelled the G-7 central banks to undertake some sort of joint interest rate easing in response, but the response taken indicates the sort of difficulties central banks face in such circumstances. In September and October 1998, G-7 meetings in London and Washington led to reports that these meetings would result in a round of co-ordinated interest rate cuts to stave off a global recession. However, such reports manifestly overstated the capacity of the central bank governors to deliver such pledges.[20] Central bank governors have to protect the independent status of their institutions as well as collaborate with international counterparts to maintain the integrity and stability of the international financial system, while it is accepted that making specific demands of one another's policies at G-7 meetings constitutes inappropriate behaviour.

It was in this context that the acknowledgement from the London G-7 meeting that the balance of risks in the global economy had switched from inflation to deflation should be understood.[21] It was a signal to national monetary policy committees to move the focus of their debate – a form of suasion. Subsequently, first the United States, then the United Kingdom and Canada cut interest rates. This was followed by a co-ordinated rate cut amongst European central bankers some three months later as part of preparations for the euro. Therefore whilst the G-7 meetings did not produce an international agreement involving specific national commitments, they did shape the subsequent course of monetary policy debate throughout the industrialised world. A similar pattern followed the 11 September attacks in 2001. Central banks decided for themselves on the timing and size of the interest rate cuts. Crucially, global financial crises often necessitate a temporary co-ordinated monetary easing, but current national institutional arrangements are not conducive to this and there is no higher authority in existence to compel such an easing. In 1998, G-7 meetings acted as a useful safety valve mechanism, but the approach employed was haphazard and cannot guarantee the necessary national policy shifts.

The G-7 process and the architecture of global finance

The issue of global financial architecture became a prominent one for G-7 finance ministers following the Mexican peso crisis of 1994–5. Finance ministries and central banks prepared a report on financial architectural questions for inclusion in the communiqué of the Halifax summit the following year.[22] It is important to note that there is a basic continuity between the contents of that report and the response to architectural questions, following the financial crisis of 1997–8. The basic principles outlined in the Halifax report, which emphasised crisis prevention, crisis management and system improvement, subsequently informed the position of G-7 finance ministries and central banks on the issue of designing a stable global financial system. Significantly, wider societal input into proposals on the global financial architecture was almost non-existent.

Finance ministry and central bank officials dominated the process through the secretive deputies and deputy deputies networks, enabling them to promote and reinforce their shared belief system. These individuals invariably have a narrow technocratic financial background and little interest in, or awareness of, the impact of financial and macroeconomic governance upon wider society. However, the narrow input into the Halifax report, both in terms of countries and social groupings, was in many respects its crucial weakness, impeding its subsequent implementation.

In the minds of G-7 officials, the Asian crisis revealed that the problem with the Halifax strategy was the process of implementation, rather than the fundamental approach itself.[23] The first and most important lesson drawn from the crisis was that the work done after Halifax was fundamentally sound.[24] Halifax was viewed by officials as having moved the system along, ensuring that they were 'one or two steps behind instead of three or four'.[25] The whole issue was viewed as being 'less of one of approach and more of a question of persuading countries to actually do certain things'.[26] For this reason, US officials were quite openly referring to the process of scrutinising the global institutional architecture in the aftermath of the Asian crisis as Halifax II.[27]

In this respect, for G-7 officials the Asian crisis revealed that Thai, Indonesian and Malaysian authorities had been less than truthful in the release of data. For example, surveillance and data release, highlighted at Halifax under the heading of crisis prevention, had not worked as well as they might because of the requirement for countries to engage voluntarily in data release. There was therefore a need to investigate ways of improving, deepening and extending surveillance and the pattern of three-dimensional diplomacy upon which it rested. However, officials remained upbeat about what Halifax had actually achieved. Their initial verdict on the crisis was that problems in the crisis countries were picked up relatively quickly and that the new 'Emergency Financing Mechanism' worked relatively well.[28] At the same time, however, the reckless private sector investment that a G-10 report of 1996 had attempted to discourage was acknowledged as a contributory factor in the Asian situation.[29] In retrospect, officials acknowledged that the transparency issue, particularly concerning data standards, had not been pushed hard enough and the message should have been given more loudly and more consistently.[30] Essentially, the Halifax II exercise was an investigation of ways of doing this.

There were two major outcomes to the G-7 finance ministries' and central banks' work on proposals for improving and adjusting the existing global institutional architecture during 1998–9. The first of these consisted of three codes of good practice relating to good economic governance covering the areas of monetary policy, fiscal policy and corporate and financial sector governance. The second outcome was the creation of two new bodies (the Financial Stability Forum and the G-20) designed to foster dialogue between macroeconomic policy communities, various financial regulatory bodies and authorities in emerging market economies.

Areas that were identified as being particularly important for incorporation under the new codes of practice were forward transactions in foreign exchange transactions, foreign currency liabilities of foreign banks and indicators of the health of the financial sector. The code of practice for corporate governance was to involve principles for auditing, accounting and disclosure in the private sector. The codes of practice had no formal enforcement mechanism. Rather they operated through the threat of a withdrawal of market actors if countries failed to comply with the data standards spelt out in the codes of practice. The codes therefore gave markets a clearly stated standard by which to judge countries' macroeconomic policies and financial sectors. The codes provided some degree of institutionalisation of the pattern of three-dimensional diplomacy, that both stems from and reinforces the G-7 belief system. The IMF's role in relation to the codes was to publicise concerns about gaps in information disclosure where the public sector was concerned. The Basel Committee was to do likewise for the banking sector and the International Organisation of Securities Commissions (IOSCO) for securities markets. In this respect, the IMF has been publishing country reports on the observance of standards and codes (ROSCs), while joint IMF–World Bank teams have been preparing financial sector assessment programmes (FSAPs), which are expected to lead to the voluntary publication of financial system stability assessment (FSSA) reports. Both of these developments have had the effect of placing processes of peer and market review of national macroeconomic policies and financial sectors on a firmer foundation.

Throughout 1998, US Treasury officials were effectively engaged in a form of multi-dimensional diplomacy. First, they were engaged in dimension I negotiations with G-7 partners to agree an increase in the United States' quota contribution to IMF funds. Second, they bargained with Congress to persuade them to release the financial resources required to raise the IMF's capital base.[31] As a concession to Congress, a coalition had to be built to support increased transparency and the promotion of core labour standards by the IMF. This was pursued in further G-7 dimension I negotiations. A third dimension to their diplomacy involved attempts to calm market sentiment by presenting an optimistic assessment of the prospects for congressional approval of the IMF bill in public statements. The messages that the quota increase was a sufficient level of financing, and that the private sector would not be bailed out, were also repeatedly sent out to the markets. Finally, the Treasury communicated bilaterally and collectively through the G-7 with the IMF, urging it to improve transparency in its operations and develop more effective channels of communication with the World Bank, IOSCO and the Basel Committee.

Likewise efforts to persuade authorities in emerging economies to open their markets further, to adopt sound money macroeconomic policies and to engage in further structural reform of labour and financial sectors, were pursued through bilateral channels, and through the G-7 and the IMF. The US Treasury also established a new Group of Twenty-Two (G-22) countries, including a number of developing countries. This was to broaden the input into the review of the institutional architecture beyond G-7 countries. The rationale behind the G-22 was alluded to by US Deputy Larry Summers when he stated that the crucial task remained one of 'building an institutional architecture that links the industrialised and developing world and unites them in the way the industrialised world is already united'.[32] In effect, the aim has been to create the basis for agreement on the desirability of sound money policies and open capital markets, whilst broadening the constituency for transparency. The G-22 was an example of a group of powerful states, the G-7, creating a body in an effort to obtain the voluntary compliance of weaker states through an active process of consultation and discussion.[33]

During 1998 work on the global institutional architecture by finance ministries and central banks was taken forward in three G-22 working parties. Reports were prepared on transparency, strengthening financial systems and involving the private sector in crisis resolution. The consensus amongst the G-7 finance ministries and central banks was that the principal cause of the Asian financial crisis was the disclosure of previously withheld data. In particular, the South Korean central bank was criticised for not disclosing the extent of short-term borrowing by South Korean banks until December 1997. The transparency and data release issue was therefore a principal focus for the G-7 finance ministries and central banks. Behind the promotion of transparency was the belief that authorities in emerging markets had to establish lasting relationships with private sector investors and achieve an honest and open dialogue in which hard questions could be asked and bad news was difficult to conceal.[34] The private sector, it was argued, also had a duty to engage, although the onus was placed firmly on authorities in emerging markets to provide private sector investors with data.

The overwhelming rationale behind the G-7 finance ministries' and central banks' activities as they continued to prepare their proposals on the global institutional architecture was 'to assist emerging markets in their preparations for the process of liberalisation'.[35] Contrary to some commentaries there was no serious division on the issue of capital account liberalisation.[36] There was a universal recognition that this could proceed too quickly, that it needed to be appropriately sequenced and that further financial liberalisation needed to be preceded by adequate financial regulatory and supervisory structures, on which the IMF, in consultation with the Basel Committee, could provide advice.

Apart from the codes of practice, the other issue was how to foster increased communication and interaction between various international regulatory bodies. There were two major institutional innovations, but neither constituted fundamental reform. Rather they have been incremental and piecemeal adaptations designed to institutionalise further a system based on sound money policies, liberalised capital markets, a floating exchange rate regime and market-oriented forms of regulation. One of the reasons for this incremental reform path is that fundamental reform of the international financial system requires repeated crises, broad agreement that an existing situation is unsatisfactory and a consensus on what constitutes a feasible alternative.[37] Despite repeated crises, there remains a consensus on the desirability of the current system among G-7 finance ministries and central banks, and there are no universally accepted proposals for fundamental reform. Fundamental reform is further impeded by the fact that finance ministries and central banks have monopolised the process for formulating proposals, with little or no input from wider societal interests. The G-7 belief system has to some extent provided the justification for this lack of wider societal input.

The first institutional innovation resulted from a proposal from a working group chaired by Hans Tietmeyer, president of the Bundesbank. It was aimed at bringing the IMF and the World Bank together with bank, insurance and securities market supervisors, thus enhancing exchanges of information between macroeconomic and financial regulatory communities. The Financial Stability Forum (FSF) was created as a result of Tietmeyer's efforts. Emerging market economies were also to be invited to join the new forum. Initially the forum was to be an initiative of the G-7 countries, with additional national authorities to be invited to join the forum over time. Tietmeyer's proposal was formally endorsed by the G-7 in Bonn in 1999. Each G-7 country was to be allowed three representatives on the forum, one each from the finance ministry, central bank and senior supervisory authority. The IMF, the World Bank, the Basel Committee and IOSCO were to have two members each. The BIS, the OECD, the Committee on Payment and Settlement Systems and the Committee on the Global Financial System (under the auspices of the BIS) were to have one member each. Overall this added up to thirty-five participants. For an initial period of three years, the forum, convened in April 1999, was chaired by Andrew Crockett, General Manager of the BIS. The forum has a small secretariat located in Basel, reflecting Tietmeyer's belief that sweeping changes are not required. The FSF meets twice a year. Since its inception the Netherlands, Australia, Hong Kong and Singapore have each been allocated one representative. Despite this, the FSF remains G-7-centric in terms of its membership and uses its technical expertise to set agendas for global financial governance.

The overall aim of the forum, according to the G-7 communiqué issued after the Bonn meeting, is to ensure that national authorities, multilateral institutions, relevant international supervisory bodies and expert groupings can more effectively foster and co-ordinate their respective responsibilities.[38] Tietmeyer maintains that the forum is intended to improve the pooling of information and help develop early warning indicators of crises. Additional reporting and the disclosure of hedge funds and other highly leveraged investors were highlighted by Tietmeyer, but the G-7 has yet to reach any decision on this matter. The FSF's first two initiatives were the publication of a report on highly leveraged institutions and offshore financial centres, and a report on the implementation of codes of practice. The FSF's crucial findings on highly leveraged institutions (HLIs) came in a report published in March 2000. The principal FSF conclusion was that direct regulation of HLIs was unnecessary if FSF recommendations were implemented, but that this would be reconsidered if financial market instability persisted. Improved disclosure practice, together with enhanced national surveillance of financial market activity and review of good practice guidelines for foreign exchange trading were seen to suffice in the quest to reduce the risks associated with hedge fund activity. The FSF is continuing to monitor progress. In effect, the FSF is the culmination of efforts to improve communication between national authorities, overlapping multilateral bodies and private investors. Ultimately, the objective is to enhance information exchange between these various bodies and the private sector and to promote transparency and market discipline.[39]

The second institutional innovation has been the creation of the G-20 finance ministries and central banks. This has been an effort to broaden the informal dialogue between systemically significant countries and facilitate a broader consensus on international issues.[40] Once again the lessons of Halifax appear to be being learned in the sense that participation in consensus formation appears to be being broadened to include authorities from emerging markets.[41] However, the G-7 will remain dominant because it has firm control of the chair, and because crucially the G-20 is only to meet once a year, against the G-7's three meetings a year. Consequently, the G-20 will not have the same momentum as the G-7 process and will for the most part find itself discussing G-7-generated agendas. In effect, the G-20 appears to have been motivated by a desire to secure a broader consensus for G-7-generated ideas in much the same way as was the G-22.

Conclusions

This brief review of the G-7 finance ministries' and central banks' proposals on the global financial architecture has revealed that they have attempted to deepen and extend their shared belief system in three ways. First, by introducing codes of practice on transparency in fiscal and monetary policy and corporate governance, the finance ministries and central banks have institutionalised a pattern of three-dimensional diplomacy. Under three-dimensional diplomacy, market operators are given key data on these policy areas, enabling them to engage in a continuous ongoing referendum on the viability of national policies and structures. A series of technical standards, practices and principles have been spawned as a response to the Asian financial crisis. The net impact of this is the extended influence and oversight capacity of the technocrats connected to the G-7 finance ministry and central banking community who monitor the implementation of these standards, practices and principles, as well as financial market players whose ability to scrutinise policy and practices in emerging markets has become more precise. A series of interlocking three-way interactions between multilateral standards, national structures and policies, and a global audience of investors characterise contemporary global financial governance. Multilateral surveillance has been placed on a firmer institutional footing and extended to new countries and new policy areas. Market-disciplined national macroeconomic and financial policies are the result.

Second, there have been efforts to broaden the support for the G-7 belief system, as the G-7 finance ministries and central banks have consulted more actively with sympathetic authorities. Primarily, these authorities have been finance ministries and central banks from selected emerging markets in created groups such as the G-22 and the G-20. Officials from these institutions often sympathise with the premises of the G-7 belief system as a consequence of their educational background and close involvement with foreign financial institutions.

Third, there have been efforts to strengthen the system by increasing the consultations between financial regulatory and macroeconomic policy communities. The aim of these efforts is to ensure that finance ministries and central banks are better able to assess the risks to the global financial system and publicise those risks, where necessary, to the watching audience of markets. The aim is to make the world safer for a liberalised financial order by improving the quality of information on which market actors base their decisions. The culmination of these efforts has been the creation of the new Financial Stability Forum. Once again three-way interactions between domestic practices, multilateral settings/international standards and global markets are evident. The trajectory of reform after the financial crises of 1997–8 has therefore been incremental and piecemeal, and has been informed by and simultaneously institutionalised the G-7 belief system.

Ultimately, the G-7 finance ministries' and central banks' prescriptions on the issue of the global financial architecture and macroeconomic and exchange rate policy, indeed their entire belief system, has been premised on the desirability of financial liberalisation. The finance ministries' and central banks' subsequent reform proposals have led to the creeping institutionalisation of the pattern of three-dimensional diplomacy in macroeconomic and financial governance. The ascendancy within this three-sided process quite clearly lies with the market.

Three-dimensional diplomacy is used as means of bringing government policies into conformity with transnational market preferences. Governments are now effectively more responsive to non-citizens – international investors and foreign currency traders, other finance ministries and central banks, and international organisations in various multilateral settings – for their national financial and macroeconomic policies. Consequently, the notion of national accountability is being incontrovertibly diluted and dispersed in two directions simultaneously. Direct coercion is avoided, but the three-way interactions are having the effect of propelling emerging markets towards further liberalisation and marketised governance structures. Any other national objectives become secondary and are subordinated to the ultimate goal of complete financial liberalisation. The emphasis for authorities in emerging markets is on building a sustained and open dialogue between both market actors and international bodies such as the IMF and the Basel Committee, or risk being shut out of international capital markets. This is premised on the fundamental belief that if they are provided with more accurate and timely information, financial markets will behave in a more rational and orderly fashion.

As the experiences of the 1990s have shown repeatedly, however, rather than fulfilling human wants, needs and desires, finance tends to feed off and nourish itself, resulting in spectacular overreactions and gyrations that disrupt the workings of the productive economy. Unfortunately, the ascendancy of the market in the process of three-dimensional diplomacy means that mobile and speculative finance has the capacity to determine the fortunes of citizens and governments across the globe. The question that the G-7 finance ministries and central banks have left unanswered is one posed by Jonathan Story in Chapter 1 of this volume. If global markets are capable of failure on such a grand scale, by what right are they judge and jury over the lives of millions of people?

The reason for finance ministries' and central banks' neglect of this question lies in the fact that they have been motivated by a desire to protect the integrity of the principle of capital liberalisation at all costs. They have done so not simply for intellectual reasons, but also because a return to capital controls, as Benjamin Cohen's chapter demonstrates, would have damaged the profits of important financial constituents. This was evident in the G-7's abandonment of plans to amend the articles of the IMF so as to promote capital account liberalisation. The reason for this was not outright rejection of the principle of capital account liberalisation, but fear that hasty liberalisation might result in further financial crises, discrediting the whole concept of a liberal financial order. G-7 finance ministries and central banks have supported financial liberalisation because it has provided a justification for independent central banks and fiscal rules, thus enhancing their institutional position in national policy processes. As Cohen points out, this has also made financial liberalisation appear attractive for elites connected to finance ministries and central banks in emerging markets.

The promotion of the principles of price stability and financial liberalisation by finance ministries and central banks has also been a reflection of the fact that the application of these principles primarily benefits the financial sector, because they enlarge the area in which and improve the terms on which global financial concerns can make money.

Unfortunately, the evidence from the last decade reveals that the global financial system remains prone to reckless investment and repeated dislocations and disruptions. Under the current system, market sentiment appears all-powerful, whilst the loose steering of the system by the G-7 finance ministries and central banks through their shared beliefs, technocratic standards and the incremental nature of reform proposals have all given the system the character of a 'durable disorder'.[42] With the prospect of future financial crises only marginally reduced by recent G-7 proposals and initiatives, the question of how central banks will respond to the likelihood of future crises needs to be addressed. When the 1997–8 crises reached their peak in autumn 1998, the situation was certainly eased by collective interest rate reductions by the G-7 central banks. Yet, as already explained in this chapter, it is not easy for central banks to respond rapidly in such circumstances. Their current decision-making procedures are not conducive to such co-ordinated interest rate reductions, which can ease pressure on crisis countries, because governors have difficulty in giving assurances on the future course of policy at international meetings. Therefore it may be necessary to write provisions into the mandates of central banks that allow governors to take discretionary interest rate decisions in conjunction with international counterparts, in the event of a universally acknowledged financial crisis. At the same time, if the G-7's current narrow financial and monetary perspective is to be transcended, then the annual leaders' summits need to have their membership extended to include emerging markets. The summits should also become more active in addressing financial questions. This would at least re-politicise the issues of exchange rates and capital flows, because it would bring them within the reach of a broader range of societal groupings, allowing elected politicians to challenge the technocrats' current monopoly of the debate and their restricted approach.

Finally, little has been done to resolve one of the principal problems in the global financial system, namely the speed with which capital can be moved across borders. Despite this, some proposals have emerged from within the finance ministry–central banking community, notably from Wolfgang Fillic of the German Finance Ministry, who suggested that the period between the execution of a foreign exchange transaction and its settlement should be lengthened. This could deter large-scale betting on currency movements, given that problems in financial sectors often manifest themselves through exchange rate crises, without challenging the G-7's cherished principle of financial liberalisation. However, an almost ideological attachment to free capital movements evident in the G-7 belief system has prevented serious consideration of such 'guard rail' proposals. Given the likelihood of further financial crises, the continued sustainability of such a position is questionable.

Notes

1. For a historical perspective on the G-7 process and its relationship with the summits see R. Putnam, and N. Bayne, *Hanging Together: Co-operation and Conflict in the Seven Power Summits* (London: Sage, 1987).
2. On the challenge to state authority posed by globalisation see S. Strange, *The Retreat of the State: The Diffusion of Power in the World Economy* (Cambridge: Cambridge University Press, 1996). P. Cerny, 'Globalization and the Changing Logic of Collective Action', *International Organization*, vol. 49, no. 4 (1995), pp. 595–625.
3. Confidential interviews with US and UK officials, February 1997, March, April, July 1998.
4. E. Balls, 'Open Macroeconomics in an Open Economy', Scottish Economic Society, Royal Bank of Scotland Annual Lecture, *Scottish Journal of Political Economy*, vol. 45 (May 1988), pp. 113–32.
5. M. King, 'The Inflation Target Five Years on', LSE Financial Markets Group Lecture, 1997.
6. A. Alesina and L. Summers, *Central Bank Independence and Macroeconomic Performance: Some Empirical Evidence*, Harvard International Economic Research Discussion Paper 1496 (Cambridge, MA: Harvard University Press 1990).
7. Confidential interview with official, July 1997.
8. L. Summers, 'US Policy Towards the International Monetary System on the Eve of the Lyon Summit', Remarks to Emerging Markets Traders' Association, 24 June 1996.
9. Confidential interview with official, February 1998.
10. N. Wicks, 'The Development of International Institutions and the G-7 Co-ordination Process', speech at the Groucho Club, Soho, London, 1995. Confidential interview with official, March 1998.
11. Confidential interview with official, February 1997.
12. Summers, 'US Policy Towards the International Monetary System'. Wicks, 'Development of International Institutions'. J. Stark, 'The G-7 at Work', *The International Economy* (July / August 1995).
13. Confidential interviews with officials, February 1997.
14. *Ibid.*
15. L. Summers, 'Reflections on Managing Global Integration', Distinguished Lecture on Economics in Government, *Journal of Economic Perspectives*, vol. 13, no. 12 (Spring 1999), pp. 3–18.
16. See Summers, 'US Policy Towards the International Monetary System.'
17. See J. Story, 'The Emerging World Financial Order and Different Forms of Capitalism', in R. Stubbs and G. Underhill (eds.), *Political Economy and the Changing*

Global Order (Oxford: Oxford University Press, 2000), pp. 129–40. I am grateful to Randall Germain for highlighting this point.

18. R. Keohane and J. Nye, 'Transgovernmental Relations and World Politics', *World Politics*, vol. 27, no. 1 (October 1974).

19. L. Mosley, 'International Financial Markets and Government Economic Policy: The Importance of Financial Market Operations', paper presented at the Annual Meeting of the American Political Science Association, Duke University, 1997.

20. *Guardian*, 15 September 1998. Both Alan Greenspan and Hans Tietemeyer rebutted these suggestions in the days following the London meeting.

21. Communiqué of G-7 Finance Ministers and Central Bank Governors, London, 30 October 1998.

22. Background Document, Halifax summit 1995.

23. Confidential interviews with officials, February and March 1998.

24. *Ibid.*

25. *Ibid.*

26. Confidential interview with official, April 1998.

27. Point made repeatedly in confidential interviews with officials in 1998. Note that the second principle at Halifax of improved crisis management was also revisited and the IMF given new financing mechanisms after the financial crises of 1997–8. These include the Contingent Credit Line (CCL) and the Extended Fund Facility (EFF). Space prevents a detailed treatment.

28. Confidential interviews with officials, March, April 1998.

29. Report on the Orderly Resolution of Sovereign Liquidity Crises to G-10 Ministers, prepared under the auspices of the Deputies, May 1996.

30. Confidential interview with official, January 1998.

31. Involvement with Congress doubled for staff in the Treasury's IMF office, from 25 per cent of their time to 50 per cent of their time being spent dealing with congressional matters in the first half of 1998. Confidential interview with official, February 1998.

32. Summers, 'US Policy Towards the International Monetary System'.

33. For an application of this argument to the FSF and the G-20 see T. Porter, 'The G-7, the Financial Stability Forum and the Politics of International Financial Regulation', paper presented at the International Studies Association Annual Meeting, Los Angeles, March 2000.

34. Speech by Gordon Brown, UK Chancellor of the Exchequer, to the Kennedy School of Government, Harvard University, December 1998.

35. Central Bank Official, *Financial Times*, 31 October 1998.

36. One commentator misinterpreted Oskar Lafontaine's calls for a system of target zones as the beginnings of a large difference between the United States and Europe. In actual fact other European authorities and even those within his own government dismissed Lafontaine's calls as unworkable. The main differences between G-7 finance ministries and central banks were on the issue of the extent to which hedge funds could be regulated, whilst Japanese authorities were more willing to accept the short-term use of controls on capital inflows than the United States, although the United States did accept this in principle. For an alternative interpretation see

R. Wade, 'The Coming Fight over Capital Controls', *Foreign Policy*, vol. 113 (Winter 1998–9), pp. 41–53.

37. G. Bird, 'From Bretton Woods to Halifax and Beyond: The Political Economy of International Monetary Reform', *The World Economy*, vol. 19, no. 2 (1996), pp. 149–72.

38. Communiqué of G-7 Finance Ministers and Central Bank Governors, 20 February 1999.

39. Greater private sector burden sharing and responsibility have been a repeated feature of post-Asian crisis G-7 initiatives. The most recent is an action plan announced in April 2002 whereby governments in emerging markets add special clauses to all their bonds which specify what will happen in the event of the need for a sovereign debt restructuring, including descriptions of how creditors will engage with borrowers. The aim is to develop private sector responsibility and lending in crisis situations. This recommendation was first made in 1996 in a G-10 follow-up report to the Halifax summit's initial exploration of architectural issues. Already Mexico, G-20 member, has expressed opposition to the proposal.

40. G-20 membership includes Argentina, Australia, Brazil, China, India, Indonesia, Mexico, Russia, Saudi Arabia, South Africa, South Korea and Turkey, together with the G-7 countries

41. R. Germain, 'Global Financial Governance and the Problem of Inclusion', *Global Governance*, vol. 7 (2001), pp. 411–26.

42. A. Minc, *Le Nouveau Moyen Age* (Paris: Gallimard, 1993).

17 Bail-outs, bail-ins and bankruptcy: evolution of the new architecture

MANMOHAN S. KUMAR AND MARCUS MILLER

> The problem is that we have no accepted framework in which a country *in extremis* can impose a payments suspension or standstill pending agreement with its creditors ... [This is] compounded by the absence of an accepted legal framework in which the debtor and its creditors can work to seek to restore viability.
>
> Stanley Fischer[1]

Legal and institutional aspects of global economic governance, particularly the management and resolution of financial crises, are the focus of this chapter. To avoid ever-larger public sector bail-outs (and their adverse incentive effects), increased involvement of private bankers and investors in resolving sovereign debt crises is called for. In the short term this may be achieved by standstills and other 'bail-in' devices such as forced roll-overs, collective action clauses and bond swaps. In the longer term, however, an International Bankruptcy Procedure accompanied by private arrangements for contingent credit provision and debt restructuring will probably be required.

   We begin with an interesting historical precedent. When the United States left the Gold Standard in 1933, the dollar price of gold rose by almost 70 per cent and the Gold Indexation Clause embedded in most private long-term debt contracts – and in much of the public debt – mandated a matching increase in the dollar value of debt. To prevent a credit crunch, President Roosevelt secured a resolution of Congress suspending the Gold Clause; but this was challenged by creditors going to the law, all the way to the Supreme Court. But on the day the Court handed down its judgement in favour of the president and against the creditors, the private sector debt for which the Gold Clause had been cancelled went up in value. How could this be? The answer suggested by Randall Kroszner in his fascinating account of the episode is that creditors as a whole were better off with their pre-existing nominal claims on viable corporations than they would be with greater claims on companies driven into liquidation.[2] This episode essentially involved domestic debt, but the principle applies to sovereign debt externally held: even the finest debt contracts may sometimes need to be restructured.

While the sanctity of US bond contracts was overruled in this case,[3] it was stoutly defended in other ways. Supreme Court Judge William O. Douglas in particular championed the deletion of majority voting rules in debt bond covenants (on the grounds that they were being used to write down debt values so much during the Great Depression as effectively to reverse the priority of bondholders over shareholders). Before long, however, US bankruptcy law was revised to assist debtor rehabilitation, with debt restructuring handled under court-ordered insolvency procedures; and the Chandler Act of 1938 included a Chapter XI allowing for corporate management to keep control when debt was being restructured.[4]

The absence of restructuring provisions – other than those ordered by the courts – has remained a distinctive feature of bonds issued under New York law to this day. Although Mark Roe describes this as an historical anachronism,[5] it applies to much international debt. More than half of all international bonds and more than two thirds of all emerging market issues do not include collective action clauses (CACs).[6] *For sovereigns, however, there are no court-ordered procedures to act as an alternative.*

This is why, hard upon the heels of the Mexican crisis of 1994/95, Barry Eichengreen and Richard Portes made a persuasive case for changing the status quo.[7] To permit the restructuring of externally held sovereign debt, they recommended the adoption of collective action clauses – backed up with a Bondholders Council to promote creditor co-ordination.[8] This call for *ex ante* measures for orderly resolution procedures was taken up by the G-10 deputies in their report on *Sovereign Liquidity Crises* in 1996 and re-echoed later by the G-22 in 1998. But the markets have, by and large, ignored the call for voluntary inclusion of collective action clauses, and financial crises have continued.

In response to the East Asian crises, there were large official 'liquidity injections'[9] accompanied, in the case of South Korea, by a substantial *bail-in* of Western banks. Subsequently there was a voluntary roll-over of interbank credit lines in Brazil; and events in Russia, Ukraine and Latin America have involved *standstills on bondholders*, followed by bond exchanges. But as yet there has been no fundamental shift in the structure of sovereign debt contracts.[10] Why not?

The reason, we believe, is 'strategic behaviour'. Creditors who agree to debt restructuring, with or without write-downs, have to accept some restrictions on their freedom of action. So the incorporation of *ex ante* provisions in debt contracts has to be motivated by the view that the alternatives will be worse. But the prospect of constant liquidity injection or bail-outs has until recently removed that threat.

Treating the provision of support for debtors as a sequential game, where the creditors move first and the IMF acting as lender of last resort (LOLR) moves next, it appears that the IMF could be 'gamed' into providing bail-outs: creditors have only to move out for the IMF to get sucked in.[11] But what if the LOLR retains some discretion in the provision of liquidity support – offering its services as crisis manager as a substitute? And what if emerging market countries were encouraged to write down their debts in cases of insolvency? Given the uncertainty facing creditors under this discretionary approach – including the possibility of outright default – they may be ready to accept some bailing in. And this could promote the adoption of the bond clauses that Eichengreen and Portes have been calling for.

While bail-ins involving no loss of value (no 'haircuts') seem to have proved broadly acceptable, this has not been true of bail-ins with haircuts. Thus most banks were happy with a 'voluntary' roll-over arranged in late 1997 when South Korea faced a severe liquidity crisis; but the debt restructuring in Russia, Pakistan, Ukraine and Latin America has proved much more controversial. Some say that they threaten the continued flow of capital to emerging markets and they should be deliberately scaled back.[12] And others have argued that bail-ins have simply been enjoying a short honeymoon, to be ended as soon as the private sector learns how to avoid haircuts – a 'Lucas critique' of policies for private sector involvement.[13]

If efforts to bail in the private sector are indeed to be blocked by a vigorous response on the part of creditors, the international system will return to the *status quo ante* where the IMF is 'gamed' into providing liquidity to pay off the creditors. Avoiding this is a prime reason for an orderly international bankruptcy procedure.[14]

Beginning with liquidity crises, in section two of this chapter we discuss the role of LOLR at the domestic and global level, indicating how creditor co-ordination has been used to complement liquidity provision. Next, we report on the debate about collective action clauses as a mechanism to restructure and write down sovereign debt. Comparing debt which can be restructured with that which cannot suggests that the moral hazard effect of these clauses are offset by efficiency gains for high quality debtors: for low quality debtors, the rise in the risk premium reflects the increased hazard of strategic default. Section four considers the recent history of efforts to 'bail in' the private sector by means of involuntary bond exchanges and how the private sector has responded. Section five restates the strategic case for improving legal procedures and discusses the interim solutions. Section six concludes.

LOLR, liquidity provision and creditor co-ordination

The opening of emerging markets to external capital flows has raised at the global level key issues already faced by nation states in the course of economic development: how to regulate financial markets to achieve financial stability, and with what institutional mechanisms. By acting in accordance with Bagehot's recommendation – to act as a lender of last resort (LOLR) to prevent contagion – the Bank of England 'prevented incipient crises in 1878, 1890 and 1914 from developing into full blown panics'.[15] Meanwhile, in the United States, there were twenty-one bank panics between 1890 and 1908; and it is estimated that, prior to the founding of the Federal Reserve Board in 1914, *the probability of having a bank panic in the United States in any given year was 0.32*.[16] But 'The founding of the Federal Reserve Board provided the US economy with a lender of last resort, and the frequency of bank panics immediately decreased ... between 1915 and 1928, the banking system experienced no financial panics.'[17]

There was, however, a sharp increase in financial panics in the years following the Great Crash of 1929 – which would seem to provide an argument against the effectiveness of the LOLR. Milton Friedman and Anna Schwartz convincingly argued on the contrary, that the Fed had failed to act as LOLR in that period.[18] Meltzer's more recent assessment took the same view: that 'the worst cases of financial panics arose because the central bank did not follow Bagehotian principles'.[19] This episode was of course the main impetus for the founding of the Federal Deposit Insurance Corporation in 1934, designed to avoid panics not by cash but by value guarantees for creditors.[20]

What message might this history of institutional evolution hold for the global financial system? The first is surely that laissez-faire may on occasions be *laissez paniquer*! The second is that mechanisms for preventing panics can be mishandled. That, at any rate, is the verdict of Friedman and Schwartz on Fed policy in the Depression; and, more recently, the collapse of many savings and loans institutions (S&Ls) showed how deposit insurance without regulation can be the cause rather than the cure for financial crisis. These messages have naturally coloured the debate and affected the evolution of institutions to deal with global financial panics. In lending to countries facing external payments crises, Stanley Fischer has emphasised that the IMF has increasingly come to play the role of crisis manager and quasi-international lender of last resort.[21] The Meltzer Commission pushed for a Bagehotian role for the IMF, lending only to countries that met criteria related to the stability of their domestic financial systems: 'except in unusual circumstances where the crisis poses a threat to the global economy, loans would only be made to countries that met preconditions that establish financial soundness' and 'there would be no need for detailed conditionality'.[22] In other words, lending with prequalification and no conditionality.

But the straightforward application of Bagehot's doctrine at the international level has been questioned on two grounds. First, it may no longer be the best guide even for national central banks. As Curzio Giannini puts it: 'Bagehot's doctrine, perhaps appropriate in the context of the London capital market in the second half of the nineteenth century, is no longer relevant to describe national practices in this area – essentially because the distinction between illiquidity and insolvency has proven a poor guide for action by central banks.'[23] Second, and more fundamentally, because of national sovereignty: 'An international LOLR is likely to have a hard time because the ultimate source of power and legitimacy in the present institutional context is still the nation state' and 'surrendering part of sovereign powers to a truly universal institution is still an unpalatable option'.[24] Others have argued that the IMF's resources are in any case too limited.

If not Bagehot, what else? The answer is to put greater emphasis on *creditor co-ordination* than on liquidity provision per se. Historically, as both Charles Goodhart and Dirk Schoenmaker[25] and Curzio Giannini[26] have indicated, central bank lender of last resort operations often took the form of concerted rescues, with private banks not immediately at risk playing an important role. This has, in fact, been a characteristic of two recent crises. First is the roll-over of short-term South Korean liabilities in December 1997 where, with a lack of multilateral resources and uncertainty about the contribution from the bilaterals, G-7 central banks engineered a roll-over to avoid a sovereign default. Second is the handling of the near-bankruptcy of Long Term Capital Management (LTCM) in the Fall of 1998. Though the US Federal Reserve lowered interest rates to signal its willingness to supply liquidity on demand, the rescue of LTCM itself involved no public funds: it came about through a 90 per cent takeover by other market players, orchestrated by the Federal Reserve Bank of New York. Both episodes demonstrate the importance of creditor co-ordination for crisis resolution and the lead role played by the central banks, and both are prime examples of what is now referred to as private sector involvement (PSI). South Korea was a roll-over to deal with a liquidity crisis, while for LTCM there was recapitalisation to avoid the collapse of a failing firm.

Given the difficulties that would face any fully fledged international LOLR, an alternative is to involve private sector creditors directly, both to supply liquidity and, if necessary, capital. In the case of banks and near banks, the IMF can call upon the powers of 'moral suasion' possessed by central banks to secure creditor co-ordination, as was the case in Latin America during the 1980s, as well as South Korea in 1997. But bond-holders, who are likely to be numerous and widely dispersed and more prone to 'free ride', present a more challenging problem. Before discussing in some detail how bond-holders may nevertheless be bailed in, it may be useful briefly to classify the various mechanisms available to involve all creditors, be they banks or bond-holders.

The most attractive mechanism in theory is the use of *ex ante* financial contracts which specify explicitly what is to happen in adverse circumstances. These may take the form of innovative new contracts for the provision of hard currency on a short-term basis in the event of a liquidity crisis, as in the case of Argentina and Mexico's arrangements with private banks, or the IMF's Contingent Credit Lines. Or they may involve incorporating new clauses in debt contracts providing for restructuring in liquidity or solvency crises. Examples are the sharing, majority voting and collective representation clauses advocated by Eichengreen and Portes,[27] and the amendment giving all sovereign debtors the right to one roll-over (of limited duration) proposed by Willem Buiter and Anne Siebert.[28]

The second mechanism takes the form of debt standstills, that is, temporary measures to reduce the net payment of debt service. As the IMF report on standstills indicates, these can take several forms, running from voluntary agreements for maintaining exposure (Brazil, 1999), moral suasion to maintain bank exposure (South Korea, 1998), sovereign state default (Ecuador, 1999), exchange controls (Malaysia, 1998) and capital controls.[29] Like the bank 'holidays' in the United States in the early 1930s, some standstills are essentially means of co-ordinating creditors to avoid liquidity crises. Where a debt write-down is unavoidable, the role of standstills, like the automatic stay provisions of Chapter 11, is to provide negotiating time for debt work-outs.

Last is a formal mechanism for debt write-down and restructuring which exists for corporate debtors but not currently for sovereign states. Though there have been calls for legislative changes to remedy this,[30] up-coming cases will have to be handled with existing procedures, including, for example, bond exchanges by 'exit consent'.[31]

The debate about CACs: theory and evidence

Why do so many emerging market bonds fail to include collective action clauses? Eichengreen suggests two reasons.[32] First is *institutional inertia*. Because they were being used to reverse the priority of bond-holders over equity, CACs were taken out of US bond contracts during the Great Depression: and reinserting them involves overcoming the lock-in effect of historical convention. The second reason why an existing contract structure may stay in place even though it is not socially efficient is a significant *externality* – systemic financial risk – which is not 'priced in'.

Consider this logic as it applies to bank deposits. A key aspect of a demand deposit 'contract' is its capacity for checking moral hazard on the part of deposit-taking institutions. The contract is so attractive to both parties (the borrower gets cheap finance and the lender gets both liquidity and the means to police the borrower) that it is universally used. But, because it is so exposed to bank runs and bank panics, it is not efficient in the absence of public intervention – as the pervasive runs and panics in the United Kingdom and the United States before public policy intervention testify.[33]

By analogy, bonds contracts with non-renegotiable terms are more efficient at checking moral hazard, but they are more exposed to financial collapse in the presence of exogenous shocks. The need for provisions to cope with such shocks was dramatically illustrated by Roosevelt's wholesale repudiation of the Gold Clause in 1933. More commonly of course, it is the bankruptcy courts which oversee *ex post* restructuring for commercial debt and use their powers to limit moral hazard. Under US law, for example, these renegotiations take place under Chapter 11 of the bankruptcy code. Since there is no Chapter 11 for sovereign states, Eichengreen and Portes propose that encouragement be given for the incorporation of CACs into all bond contracts, by making emergency assistance for those who use renegotiable bonds cheaper or more readily available.[34]

Making debt restructuring easier clearly runs the risk of increasing 'moral hazard' on the part of borrowers, that is, strategic default. In his paper on PSI, William Cline expresses concern that 'a default-friendly international regime deprives international lenders of their quasi-collateral: heightened economic difficulty for the defaulter'.[35] By comparing recent flows and prices with what happened before recent bail-ins, moreover, he concludes that the evidence strongly supports the presence of moral hazard effects. Specifically he notes first that there has been a very marked *slow-down in net capital flows* to emerging markets (which the Institute of International Finance forecast at $26 billion for 2000, compared with an average of $157 billion in 1995–7).[36] Second, there has been a considerable *widening of sovereign spreads* – up from 360 basis points in 1996 to 680 basis points in 2000 for Argentina and Brazil, for example.[37]

As Barry Eichengreen and Ashoka Mody point out, however, the effect of increased private sector involvement on sovereign spreads is ambiguous.[38] Any increase in borrowers' moral hazard will tend to raise them; but avoiding messy defaults and raising 'recovery rates' can be expected to reduce spreads. These two effects can be seen after decomposing the sovereign spread, s, into two components, the hazard rate of default per unit of time, denoted π, and the loss on default $(1-R)$, where R is the recovery rate, so $s = \pi (1-R)$.[39] Increased efficiency of resolution procedures raises R and so cuts spreads: but this may be offset by a rise in the probability of default, as π rises.

The authors find this theoretical ambiguity reflected in cross-section data. As an ingenious way of testing for bail-in effects, they use the difference in spreads at launch between UK and NY bonds to estimate the impact of CACs. Eichengreen and Mody find that 'the presence of collective action clauses, so measured, raises borrowing costs for countries with poor credit [ratings] while reducing costs for countries with relatively good ratings. The coefficients on

UK governing law shift smoothly from large positive to . . . large negative as we move up the credit ratings gradient.' Focusing on sovereign debt alone, they conclude 'It would appear that the market's pricing of these provisions is no different for sovereigns than for other borrowers.'[40]

What they find, therefore, is some evidence of moral hazard being priced into spreads, but, for better rated borrowers, any moral hazard losses are more than offset by efficiency gains.

Recent bond exchanges: was it a 'standstill honeymoon'?

Recent bail-ins have shown that bond restructuring is easier to do than might have been expected: it can be achieved by bond exchanges with 'exit consent' by those willing to restructure. Under the New York law, where unanimous agreement is required to alter the *payment* structure, only a simple majority is required to change the *waiver of sovereign immunity* provisions, however. So creditors threatening to hold up proceedings (e.g. vultures) can be threatened with actions which will deprive them of their rights. As Gabrielle Lipworth and Jens Nystedt put it, 'the use of "exit consent" amendments in a sovereign bond context (a "poisoning the well behind you" strategy) . . . makes it less attractive for hold-out creditors to remain in the old bond and not tender'.[41] (There is always the risk that aggrieved creditors might go to court, but so far this has not occurred. The risk of such proceedings is indeed one of the main arguments in favour of CACs.)

Salient features of four bond exchanges are briefly summarised in Table 14. Lipworth and Nystedt note that the hit to be taken in Ecuador and Russia was exaggerated beforehand (as is suggested by the subsequent strong recovery in bond prices) and that in Pakistan and Russia creditors were seduced by

Table 14. *Post-1998 bond exchanges.*

	Comment	'Haircut' face value write-off	Subsequent gain	'Sticks': use of CACs	'Carrots': use of sweetener
Pakistan	No default	0			Yes
Ukraine		0		Yes	
Russia		1/3 plus	58 per cent return		Yes
Ecuador		40 per cent average	60 per cent return		
(Peru)	Failed default	Big write-up			

Source: Gabrielle Lipworth and Jens Nystedt, 'Crisis Resolution and Private Sector Adaptation', paper presented to the IMF First Annual Research Conference, Washington, DC, 9–10 November 2000.

persuasive sweeteners. They warn that 'it is unlikely with private creditors up-dating expectations of recovery, that it will be as easy to offer similar carrots ... in the future', and conclude that these easy bond exchanges will not continue. They argue that what we are seeing is a 'standstill honeymoon', to be followed by efforts by the private sector to avoid being bailed in altogether.[42]

As evidence for this 'Lucas Critique' of the recent policy of PSI, they note how creditors switched from medium- to short-term debt following the Brady deals: and how derivatives and related instruments may be used to offset PSI.[43] They also quote the conclusion of Eric Lindenbaum and Alicia Duran that 'Elliot's seemingly credible threat of attaching Peruvian interest payments has tilted the scales back towards creditors, and will encourage others to do the same.'[44]

In the case of *Elliott* v. *Peru* – the failed default shown at the foot of the table – 'vultures' (hedge funds or large individual investors) were able to redeem distressed bonds at par by threatening interruption of servicing on other external debt. As a recent article in *Euromoney* described it: 'The winner of the *Peru* case, Elliott Associates, didn't even need an oil receivables fund to attach. Once it received its court judgement against Peru, it simply attached Peru's next Brady bond coupon payment, thereby preventing it from making any debt payments before it settled.'[45]

This view, that the incentives for creditors to hold out have dramatically increased and the prospects for debt restructuring has correspondingly fallen, was endorsed by Stanley Fischer, till recently Deputy Managing Director of the IMF. In his Lionel Robbins Lectures on *The International Financial System: Crises and Reform*, he asserts that 'Right or wrongly, probably rightly, debtor governments see the costs of a debt default as extremely large – and recent legal developments, including the Elliot Associates case in the Peruvian debt restructuring, have raised the likely costs.'[46]

The strategic case for improving legal procedures

The systemic implications of the current situation and the strategic case for pay-ments standstill and bankruptcy procedures have been examined elsewhere.[47] In a two-player strategic game between creditors and the IMF representing debtors, Miller and Zhang describe a 'time consistency trap' facing the IMF (and its partner institutions who supply emergency funds). The IMF is trapped because, without standstills, the prospect of 'asset grabbing by the creditor is so disas-trous for both the creditor and the debtor that the IMF will be forced to act ... [so] there is only one Nash equilibrium – constant bail-outs'. As a consequence, 'there will be no incentive for the latter to monitor their investments and the probability of failure will go up...[leading to] a degradation of the global financial system due to moral hazard'.[48]

To escape from this time consistency trap, it was argued that 'the IMF must be able credibly to threaten not to bail the debtor out...[This could be achieved by] changing the rules of the game to enable the IMF to act like a bankruptcy court – by protecting debtors from premature liquidation, and by allowing for financial restructuring – including possible debt write-down – subject to the conditionality needed to ensure appropriate effort on the part of debtor – as well as lender of last resort'.[49]

Despite much discussion on improving the global financial architecture, there has been little significant progress in this specific area, and prospects for debt restructuring by sovereign debtors who are effectively insolvent remain shrouded in uncertainty. As Stanley Fischer puts it in his Robbins Lecture:

The problem is that we have no accepted framework in which a country in extremis can impose a payments suspension or standstill pending agreement with its creditors to support the restoration of viability – and that accordingly any country contemplating a standstill faces enormous uncertainties about what will happen to the economy if it does so. Those uncertainties are compounded by the absence of an accepted legal framework in which the debtor and its creditors can work to seek to restore viability.[50]

Though he warns of the dangers of debtor moral hazard, Fischer is quite explicit on the need for legal changes. He reasons as follows:

the absence of procedures for dealing with situations where debts have a very high probability of becoming unsustainable, distorts the aggregate behaviour of the international system. Under present circumstances, when a country's debt burden is unsustainable, the international community – operating through the IMF – faces the choice of lending to it, or forcing it into a potentially extremely costly restructuring, whose outcome is unknown. I believe the official sector should go very far to help countries that are willing to take the necessary measures to avoid defaults, but debts will sometimes have to be written down. That should be costly for the country concerned, but not as costly as it is now.'

He concludes: 'So we should get on with work on this topic, but we should recognise that it is likely to take many years to change the legal framework.'[51]

What if anything can be done in the meantime? Start from the principle that bankruptcy procedures offer (a) protection against creditors in the form of an automatic stay; (b) temporary, debtor-in-possession finance; and (c) debt restructuring with 'cram-down clauses'[52] to prevent 'holdouts' and possible management changes to check moral hazard. What can be achieved with existing technology in cases of 'insolvency' where debt restructuring is inevitable? Consider the following procedures: first, the IMF could signal approval of a standstill by initiating a policy of lending into arrears – accompanied, of course, by appropriate conditionality to check moral hazard. This will achieve objectives (a) and (b) above. In the negotiating time provided by standstill, it is vital that creditors engage with debtors on the terms of debt restructuring, (c), which may, for example, take the form of a bond exchange. Finally, it is important that bond-holders who tender into exchange be asked to agree to 'exit consents' designed to punish vultures and others who refuse to go along with the restructuring.

The strategy of lending into arrears has already been established in previous cases, so no new issue of principle is involved there. What is new is how to handle recalcitrant bond-holders: and the mechanism is exit consents. We believe the procedures outlined above avoid the two main pitfalls observed in recent restructuring – the lack of creditor involvement in the use of exit consents on the one hand and the lack of cram-down control against vultures on the other. In the case of Ecuador, for example, bond-holders became very nervous because the bond exchange came as a unilateral take-it-or-leave-it offer from a sovereign debtor, with no monitoring by the IMF and no representation by the creditor committee in designing the restructuring. IMF finance plus creditor involvement in negotiations should limit the moral hazard that made creditors so nervous. Since *Elliot* v. *Peru*, however, the boot has been on the other foot; and debtors live in fear of creditor power. The use of exit consents is a legal device to outwit such strategies and punish the free-riding creditors.

Summary and Conclusion

As Giannini has observed,

To make the constrained discretionary regime more credible, the international community should lay greater emphasis on institutional adaptation, especially as regards legal practices in the area of contract law and international bankruptcy.[53]

The canonical case of the South Korean rescue in 1997 persuaded many in the public and private sector that 'prompt collective action' by creditors can play a key role in resolving *liquidity* crises. Evidently creditor involvement can act as a supplement to – or even as a substitute for – officially orchestrated liquidity provision. History provides an equally dramatic episode, when many of the finest bonds in issue in the United States were restructured by the Supreme Court without creditor agreement.

Unlike the case of domestic debt, however, there is no court to handle sovereign debt restructuring. This is why Eichengreen and Portes have, since 1995, promoted the incorporation of collective action clauses in sovereign debt instruments worldwide. Despite the logic of their arguments and the explicit support of G-10 and G-22 reports,[54] such clauses are not included in most debt instruments.

Nevertheless, bond exchanges with 'exit consent' have permitted restructuring in a number of cases; and concern has been expressed that unilateral bail-ins will promote debtors' moral hazard and could severely reduce capital flows to emerging market countries.[55] Recent events, however, seem to have tipped the balance decisively in favour of creditors. With the court decision on Elliot Associates, vultures have effectively become a protected species. Giving creditors the power to seize assets is no guarantee of social efficiency, however: it can promote creditor grab races which destroy value. Avoiding this requires the rights of creditors to be circumscribed, as they face debt standstills and restructuring. The case for a sovereign bankruptcy procedure is to restrain creditor power in these ways without permitting easy default by debtors. In his recent survey, Kenneth Rogoff observed that 'over the longer term ... the prospect of benefits of global market integration will likely prove a powerful incentive for enhancing global and regional political institutions. Then, ideas like a global bankruptcy court or an integrated system of financial regulation may not seem so far fetched.'[56] Problems facing emerging market debtors have made it clear that the time for action is now.

Bond-holders (the 'buy side') are well aware that there are risks involved in lending to emerging markets: what they want are predicable procedures for debt restructuring.[57] Pending the implementation of legal changes, we have discussed how standstills plus bond exchanges may be used to effect restructuring in the meantime. What is needed are procedures where the private sector bears its fair share of the burden – and where the risk to which it is exposed can be priced into the spread demanded of debtors. In that case, the private sector will not be 'cheated' and there need be no threat to international capital flows. A beneficial side-effect of standstills – followed by haircuts – may be to give creditors the incentive to adopt collective action clauses in new debt contracts.

Postscript

Since the chapter was written, prospects for institutional and legal reform have improved. In particular, Anne Krueger, first Deputy Managing Director of the IMF, has proposed a sovereign debt restructuring mechanism (SDRM) to help countries with unsustainable debt resolve them promptly and in an orderly way. While the initial version involved a key role for the IMF, a revised version gives creditors a greater role.[58] The reaction of the US Treasury to this proposal has, however, been to recommend the inclusion of collective action clauses in sovereign debt instead.[59] These seemingly discordant approaches to the issue may be viewed as complementary elements of a two-track approach which involves trying collective action clauses first and moving forward with SDRM only if necessary.[60] It seems that having the prospect of an SDRM is necessary to get things moving with collective action clauses. But for an SDRM to be a 'credible threat', one has to be sure that the United States will support it if necessary, since the United States alone can block the amendments of the IMF Articles that would be needed to implement the mechanism.

This increased focus on reforming the financial architecture may well reflect the disastrous situation in Argentina where – in the absence of orderly procedures for restructuring its dollar debt – the peso has sunk to a quarter of its previous value in less than a year and the economy is dropping in a dangerous downward spiral. Will the use of innovative bond swaps to secure collective action as proposed by New York financiers secure sensible restructuring? This would greatly strengthen the case for collective action clauses. Or will 'vultures' hold things up to secure rich pickings for themselves? In that case the United States will surely have to get more involved to avoid widening financial instability in Latin America, as it did in the 1980s with the Baker and Brady plans.

Notes

This chapter was prepared when Marcus Miller was a Visiting Scholar at the Research Department of the IMF. We are grateful for comments from participants at the conference 'From Naples to Genoa: A New World Of Finance and Development' organised by the Reinventing Bretton Woods Committee in May 2001; and to Pongsak Luangaram for research assistance funded by CSGR. The views expressed are solely the responsibility of the authors and should not be interpreted as reflecting those of the IMF or its Executive Directors.

1. Stanley Fischer, 'The International Financial System: Crises and Reform', Robbins Lecture, mimeo, London School of Economics, 29–31 October 2001.
2. Randall S. Kroszner, 'Is it better to forgive than to receive? Repudiation of the Gold Indexation Clause in long-term debt contracts during the Great Depression', mimeo, Graduate School of Business, University of Chicago, 1999.
3. The Court argued that the creditors protected by the Gold Clause stood to make a large unanticipated capital gain from the surprise devaluation of the dollar: so they would suffer little material loss by its cancellation.

4. In the Bankruptcy Reform Act of 1978 this was absorbed into Chapter 11 of the current US code. This chapter – on corporate reorganisation – has generated much debate, being lauded for keeping businesses going and derided as too debtor-friendly. See Kevin J. Delaney, *Strategic Bankruptcy: How Corporations and creditors Use Chapter 11 to their Advantage* (Los Angeles: University of California Press, 1992).

5. Mark Roe, 'Chaos and Evolution in Law and Economics', *Harvard Law Review*, vol. 109, (1996), pp. 641–68.

6. See Barry Eichengreen, *Can the Moral Hazard Caused by IMF Bailouts be Reduced?* Geneva Reports on the World Economy, Special Report 1 (London: Centre for Economic Policy Research, 2000).

7. Barry Eichengreen and Richard Portes, *Crisis? What Crisis?* (London: Centre for Economic Policy Research, 1995).

8. For subsequent updates see Barry Eichengreen, *Toward a New International Financial Architecture: A Practical Post-Asia Agenda* (Washington, DC: Institute for International Economics, 1999) and Richard Portes, 'Sovereign Debt Restructuring: the Role of Institutions', World Bank/IMF/Brookings Institution Conference on Emerging Markets and in the New Financial System, March/April 2000.

9. Although popularly known as 'bail-outs', this is a misnomer as official lenders, such as the IMF, typically get repaid in full. See O. Jeanne and J. Zettelmeyer, 'International Bailouts, Moral Hazard and Conditionality', *Economic Policy*, vol. 33 (October 2001), pp. 407–32.

10. Canada and the United Kingdom are the only exceptions, as they introduced these clauses early in 2000.

11. See Marcus Miller and Lei Zhang, 'Sovereign Liquidity Crises', *Economic Journal*, vol. 110 (2000), pp. 305–62.

12. See William R. Cline, 'The Role of the Private Sector in Resolving Financial Crises in Emerging Markets', paper presented to Conference on Economic and Financial Crises in Emerging Market Economies, National Bureau of Economic Research, Washington, DC, October 2000.

13. Robert Lucas of Chicago University is famous for arguing that the effectiveness of policy rules should be judged only after private sector responses to those rules have been taken into account. In this case, some argue that the private sector response might nullify private sector involvement. This is the Lucas critique. As it is in the interest of creditors to have restructuring provisions, we disagree.

14. See Fischer, 'The International Financial System'.

15. Michael D. Bordo, 'The Lender of Last Resort: Some Historical Insights', NBER Working Paper 3011 (Cambridge, MA: National Bureau for Economic Research, 1989), p. 14.

16. Jeffrey A. Miron, 'Financial Panics, the Seasonality of the Nominal Interest Rate, and the Founding of the Fed', *American Economic Review*, vol. 76, no. 1 (1986), pp. 125–40.

17. Xavier Freixas and Jean-Charles Rochet, *Microeconomics of Banking* (Cambridge, MA: MIT Press, 1997), p. 209.

18. Milton Friedman and Anna Schwartz, *A Monetary History of the United States, 1867–1960* (Princeton, NJ: Princeton University Press, 1963).

19. Freixas and Rochet, *Microeconomics of Banking*, p. 209.

20. When creditor panics and policy response were analysed in a classic paper by Douglas Diamond and Philip Dybvig (see 'Bank Runs, Deposit Insurance and Liquidity', *Journal of Political Economy*, vol. 91, no. 3 (1983), pp. 401–19), the focus was on deposit insurance rather than on LOLR.

21. Stanley Fischer, 'On the Need for an International Lender of Last Resort', *Journal of Economic Perspectives*, vol. 13, no. 4 (1999).

22. The Meltzer Commission, *Report of the International Financial Institution Advisory Commission* (IFIAC) (Washington, DC: IFIAC, 2000).

23. Curzio Giannini, 'Pitfalls in International Crisis Lending', in C. Goodhart and G. Illing (eds.), *Financial Crises, Contagion, and the Lender of Last Resort: a Reader* (Oxford: Oxford University Press, 2002), p. 29.

24. *Ibid.*, p. 22.

25. Charles Goodhart and Dirk Schoenmaker, 'Should the Functions of Monetary Policy and Banking Supervision Be Separated?' *Oxford Economic Papers*, vol. 47, no. 4 (1995), pp. 539–60.

26. Curzio Giannini, 'Enemy of None but a Common Friend of All: An International Perspective on the Lender-of-Last-Resort Function', Essays in International Finance No. 214 (International Finance Section, Department of Economics, Princeton University, 1999).

27. Eichengreen and Portes, *Crisis?*

28. Willem Buiter and Anne Siebert, 'UDROP: A Small Contribution to the New International Financial Architecture', *International Finance*, July 1999.

29. IMF, *Involving the Private Sector in the Resolution of Financial Crises – Standstills* (Washington, DC: IMF, 1999).

30. See, for example, Fischer, 'The International Financial System'; Miller and Zhang, 'Sovereign Liquidity Crises'; Jeffrey Sachs, 'Do We Need an International Lender of Last Resort', mimeo, Frank Graham Lecture, Princeton University, 1995; John Williamson, 'International Monetary Reform and Prospects for Economic Development', in J. J. Teunissen (ed.), *Fragile Finance: Rethinking the International Monetary System* (The Hague: FONDAD, 1992).

31. In bond exchanges, the use of 'exit consents' involves those tendering into the exchange voting in favour of amendments which make the original bond much less attractive. They effectively penalise those who 'hold out' against restructuring, which may include those who have bought a straight debt in the hope of claiming full value (so-called 'vultures').

32. Eichengreen, *Can the Moral Hazard Caused by IMF Bailouts be Reduced?*

33. Nor is simply providing deposit insurance the answer. For, as soon as the insured depositors stop monitoring, the latent moral hazard will promptly reappear with costs that fall upon the insurance agency: cf. the S&L crisis in the United States. As insurance agencies are well aware, deposit insurance must be complemented by prudential regulation. (The same logic applies to the unconditional supply of liquidity and/or bank holidays.)

34. Eichengreen and Portes, *Crisis?*

35. Cline, 'The Role of the Private Sector', p. 5.

36. It is worth noting that the historical comparison that Cline uses to measure the effects of moral hazard relies on the choice of 1995–7 as an appropriate base when capital markets were functioning normally: but for many observers, these were years when investors were investing without due diligence, and emerging market countries were building up dangerous short-term debt exposure.

37. In 2001, sovereign spreads for Argentina spiralled above 2,000 basis points as forced restructuring of internally held government debt made sovereign default look highly likely.

38. Barry Eichengreen and Ashoka Mody, 'Bail-ins, Bail-outs and Borrowing Costs', IMF Annual Research Conference, *IMF Staff Papers*, vol. 47 (2001).

39. William Cline and Kevin Barnes, 'Spreads and Risk in Emerging Markets Lending', IIF Research Paper No. 97–1 (Washington, DC: Institute of International Finance, 1997).

40. *Ibid.*

41. Gabrielle Lipworth and Jens Nystedt, 'Crisis Resolution and Private Sector Adaptation', IMF Annual Research Conference, *IMF Staff Papers*, vol. 47 (2001).

42. *Ibid.*

43. As in the case of Brazil, where the creditors, having agreed to maintain their currency exposure, promptly shorted the real. Eric Lindenbaum and Alicia Duran, 'Debt Restructuring: Legal Considerations – Impact of Peru's Legal Battle and Ecuador's Restructuring on Nigeria and other Potential Burden-Sharing Cases', Merrill Lynch, New York, October 2000.

44. Along the same lines, Felix Salmon quotes an unspecified IMF report to the effect that 'The recent success of the litigation strategy employed by a distressed debt purchaser against Peru may have the effect of encouraging creditors to hold out in future debt restructuring.' See Felix Salmon, 'The Buy Side Starts to Bite Back', *Euromoney*, April 2001, pp. 46–61.

45. *Ibid.*

46. Fischer, 'The International Financial System'.

47. See, for instance, Miller and Zhang, 'Sovereign Liquidity Crises'.

48. *Ibid.*

49. *Ibid.*, pp. 353–4.

50. Fischer, 'The International Financial System' (emphasis in original).

51. *Ibid.*

52. Cram-downs are provisions enforcing majority decisions on all creditors – including those voting against them.

53. Giannini, 'Pitfalls in International Crisis Lending'.

54. G-10, *The Resolution of Sovereign Liquidity Crises*, a report to the Ministers and Governors prepared under the auspices of the Deputies, May 1996; G-22, *Report of the Working Group on International Financial Crises* (Washington, DC: G-22, October 1998).

55. Cline, 'The Role of the Private Sector'.

56. Kenneth Rogoff, 'International Institutions for Reducing Global Financial Instability', *Journal of Economic Perspectives*, vol. 13, no. 4 (1999), p. 40.

57. Salmon, 'Buy Side Starts to Bite Back'.

58. See Anne Krueger, *A New Approach to Sovereign Debt Restructuring* (Washington DC: International Monetary Fund. 2002).

59. See John Taylor, 'Sovereign Debt Restructuring: A US Perspective', Washington DC, Department of the Treasury, April 2002.

60. Marcus Miller, 'Sovereign Debt Restructuring: New Articles, New Contracts – or No Change?' International Economic Policy Brief, No. PB02-3, Institute for International Economics, Washington DC, April 2002.

Conclusion: towards the good governance of the international financial system

GEOFFREY R. D. UNDERHILL AND XIAOKE ZHANG

Reflecting on the causes of recent financial crises, former World Bank chief economist Joseph Stiglitz observed by analogy that when so many accidents occurred on the same road one needed to re-examine the design of the road.[1] And indeed, the growing frequency and severity of financial crises have fostered a re-examination of the international financial architecture. The recent episodes of currency and financial crises in east Asia, Russia, Latin America and Turkey have provided the same watershed opportunity for rethinking the architecture of global finance as did the breakdown of the Bretton Woods order. In the wake of the Asian episode in particular, there has been a flurry of proposals on how the policies and institutions of the global financial regime should be reformed.

These reform proposals on the official 'new financial architecture' agenda, however, have remained limited in their intent and extent. While there has been progress in the development of international financial standards, efforts at exploring the optimal exchange rate regime, defining and encouraging private sector responsibility in crisis resolution and improving multilateral policy surveillance have been patchy and uneven.[2] The modesty of proposed reforms to the global financial system have not been restricted to technical issues. The apolitical terms in which financial architecture debates have been couched serves to obfuscate the political dynamics that underlie and limit international efforts to restructure the global financial regime. Three years after the outbreak of the Asian financial crisis, the robust economic recovery in some crisis countries appeared to lull governments and international institutions into complacency about the long-term weaknesses of global financial structures. As the architecture exercise ran out of steam, many of the structural problems that threatened international financial stability have remained dangerously unresolved and are suddenly rendered urgent once again.

It should be noted that the manuscript for this volume was essentially completed before the outbreak of either the current Turkish or Argentine crises, both of which remain unresolved at going to press. In Turkey and Argentina (now Latin America more generally), as in other crisis countries, capital mobility, external market pressures and domestic policy choices and failures once again conspired to produce capital flight, collapsing exchange rates, banking system fragility, and unsustainable levels of debt. Post-11 September 2001, Turkey remains a fragile but strategic NATO ally embedded in the Islamic world as war looms large, but also a crucial test for IMF-led reform on the Washington consensus model, and thus remains a safe bet for some sort of rescue. Yet the Argentine crisis in particular represents the sort of prototypical event which we and a number of our authors most feared. We significantly underestimated its scale and potential for contagion. In Argentina the political legitimacy and normative basis of market-oriented reforms in a relatively young democracy appear to be seriously challenged. The politics of the street cast a shadow, and it is unclear whether eventual elections will resolve either the internal or external political impasse over reform and further IMF rescue packages. Surely the extraordinary hardship of the population and the risk of political meltdown must be priorities for national government *and* IFIs alike. Yet despite the growing debate within the IMF and G-7 and G-10 themselves over debt work-out policy, Argentina has not yet prompted a major turnaround in the approach of either creditor countries or the Fund itself.

In this conclusion, we evaluate the ongoing official attempts to establish a new international financial architecture against the central conceptual and policy issues discussed in the various chapters of this volume. We first summarise the major empirical findings that have emerged from the volume and the implications of those findings for architectural reform. We then outline the ways in which a fairly complacent official consensus on the redesign of financial architecture came to be challenged, and explore how and why the consensus has failed to address the fundamental dilemmas and problems that existing arrangements in the international financial system have posed to public authorities at national, regional and global levels. Recent noises are promising, but there is a long way to go.

Empirical findings and policy implications

In this section, we focus on the findings of the various contributors relative to the six sets of conceptual and policy issues that were raised in the introduction and examined in the volume in a variety of ways. The first set of issues concerned national responses, particularly in developing and emerging market economies, to the problems of financial liberalisation and capital mobility. In many crisis-hit countries, the rush to capital account opening and other forms of liberalisation played a significant role in the development of financial and corporate difficulties that were to follow. To add to the difficulties, emerging market authorities often opened their capital accounts without improving regulatory frameworks, due as much to administrative incapacity as to political impediments. External pressure for rapid liberalisation from both developed country governments and IFIs also played their role, often with little understanding of local conditions. The result was that capital flows were liberalised but the necessary institutional mechanisms that might have acted as shields against the real and potential dangers of market integration were weak or non-existent. And this was a crucial causal factor behind the ensuing regional financial turbulence in Asia and elsewhere.

Emerging market economies may hope for the reform of financial architecture to ease the pains of increased capital mobility, but eventually they must equip themselves better with policy instruments to deal with those pains. There has emerged a strong consensus among the various contributors to this volume that capital controls should be, and indeed are, a workable policy instrument to that effect. Capital controls, if implemented with caution, can give governments the much-needed running room to compensate for the discretionary errors of policy which all governments make and, more importantly, for financial market volatility. While few have endorsed comprehensive capital controls and some, concerned about costs to such controls, have emphasised the use of Chilean-style taxes on short-term inflows, all appear to concur that proper restrictions on volatile cross-border capital movements are the prerequisites for financial stability and sustained economic growth.[3]

Politics have figured prominently in the design and implementation of capital controls. As clearly revealed in the two case studies on China and India (both of which have shaky financial systems), they managed to escape the regional contagion mainly because of the presence of capital controls. Their 'heterodox' policy orientations reflected ideological predilections and political considerations on the part of state elites. Similarly, the revival of capital controls also has its political logic. Emerging market governments have been hesitant to embrace capital controls despite the evidence that they can indeed contribute to financial stability. In his contribution to this volume, Benjamin Cohen has argued that it has been primarily political constraints – the phalanx of the US government, global investors and powerful domestic interests – that lie behind such hesitancy. To reinstall capital controls as a legitimate tool of financial governance, Cohen contends, it is necessary to build a more effective transnational coalition of proponents.

At the national level, another important consensus that has emerged from this volume is that achieving economic stability in the context of high capital mobility goes beyond policies towards capital controls and requires the design and adoption of minimally acceptable financial standards. One valuable lesson from the Asian crisis is that emerging markets are likely to succumb to external tremors again if structural weaknesses in their financial systems are not rectified.

Institutional reforms have been proposed in the various chapters to facilitate the implementation of effective bank supervision and adequate auditing and accounting practices. More importantly, the standards implemented must be transparent and consistently applied. This allows investors to be sure of the business environment in which they are operating and helps to prevent the widespread financial panic that devastated many Asian economies.

Implementing internationally acceptable financial standards is vital, but remains problematic. What has been demonstrated in this volume is that the national differences in socioeconomic structures and institutions that underpin existing practices complicate the process of identifying and enforcing minimally acceptable standards. This implies that there should be some latitude for the domestic implementation of international standards in such a way as to leave sufficient room for local practices and traditions and to allow countries to reform by different routes. Moreover, there is often entrenched domestic resistance by politically powerful actors who identify their interests with the status quo and thus attempt to convince regulators to interpret international standards generously. Given the high political stakes involved, global financial standards should be implemented cautiously and domestic political and institutional constraints taken seriously. Agents external to these systems should be careful to understand the complexity of national contexts.

The second set of conceptual and policy issues addressed in this volume has focused on the tension between the harmonising forces of global market integration and the prevailing diversity of financial systems and corporate practices in emerging market countries. As has been made clear in several chapters, there have been strong pressures for the convergence of economic policies and development models towards market-oriented liberal practices throughout the global system, primarily as the result of state policy capacity being severely compromised and national institutions of economic governance eroded in the process of globalisation. Such pressures intensified in the wake of recent financial crises, as the leading financial power centres and international institutions pushed vigorously for the reform of macroeconomic policy, financial regulation and corporate governance along the neo-liberal and harmonised principles in developing and emerging market economies.

If convergence has indeed been taking place in the world economy, this is most likely to be a long-run and uneven process. The principal reason lies with the fact that individual countries integrate into the global system from different starting points, and that the institutional diversity of their economic systems continues to shape the responses of the relevant domestic policy communities to external market and political pressures. While the pressures have yielded some progress in terms of harmonisation, the patterns of adaptation to changing market forces have remained individual. Economic and political complexity makes a clear calculation of the costs and benefits of harmonisation difficult to determine for the actors involved. Differences among national financial practices and market systems are thus likely to persist, particularly in those countries which have only accepted limited transnational integration.

The tension between harmonising pressures and continued national variations and its consequences for policy management have clear implications for efforts to design a new financial architecture. Promotion of market reforms and policy harmonisation, which entail institutional changes of crucial importance to emerging market countries across the different aspects of economic governance, will invariably face substantial national incentives to resist or temporise with harmonised practices. If harmonisation – with the benefits its ardent advocates proclaim – is to be a sustainable effort, it should make sufficient allowance for local legal, financial and corporate practices and give national political economies enough time to make necessary adjustments. Where externally imposed reforms clash severely with domestic development models and associated institutional arrangements, they may fail to take root and even increase the potential for economic and political instability. Equally, policy harmonisation implies restructuring processes, and if these happen too quickly, changes in financial and economic systems are likely to backfire. Developing societies, for better or worse, may become more at home with market-oriented practices, but it will take a while. If harmonisation really is as good as advertised, we should proceed with it slowly, and be prepared for lots of turns and stops along the way. Let us remember that G-10 governments, especially the US administration and Congress, jealously guard their right to choice in these matters. Their own reform programmes happened over decades, and there were important mistakes made along the way. Developed countries should extend the same luxury to emerging market economies.

Continued national differences in market systems and economic models have important implications for international co-operative efforts at global monetary and financial governance – the third set of conceptual and policy issues examined in this volume. Such governance requires, first and foremost, that there exist institutions that can exercise the capacity to command compliance similar to the public authorities of nation states, albeit in limited policy domains. Following recent financial crises, international initiatives sought to create such institutions and attempt to give them sufficient power to enforce bankruptcy laws and to conduct financial regulation at the global level. National governments, however, have relatively little enthusiasm for initiatives that would further compromise their policy autonomy. Even if they are willing to cede additional prerogatives, it would be almost impossible for an international bankruptcy court to achieve co-ordination among countries that have very different bankruptcy procedures and for a global regulator to set the rules that can work effectively in different financial systems.[4]

Also, prevailing variations in national financial practices continue to complicate policy co-operation through international institutions. The key IFIs remain far more accountable to the wealthier G-10 member countries than to emerging market economies, an asymmetry which poses legitimacy problems for these institutions. Thus key international institutions, particularly the IMF, generally rely on their member governments to offer support for an international policy consensus on the modalities of global economic governance. However, beyond agreement on the long-term policy goal of reducing financial market risks and instabilities, international institutions have been unable to obtain broad consensus on such crucial issues as exchange rate arrangements and regulations over capital flows. Hesitancy on the part of national governments to reform their financial systems and economic institutions, a hesitancy which reflects the interests of dominant domestic policy constituencies, has impeded uniform understandings of the means to achieve the long-term goal. The persistent failure of national governments to collaborate effectively thus reduces prospects for the successful restructuring of the global financial regime through international co-operation based on harmonisation.

Given the difficulties of institutional collaboration at the international level, many contributors to this volume have emphasised the importance of building regional co-operative processes for managing the global monetary and financial system. At the regional level, emerging market governments, which tend to face similar problems with market integration and have similar interests in financial policy management, may be more prepared to establish collective mechanisms for dealing with systemic instability. Given the risks of contagion effects, regional neighbours have more incentives to co-ordinate macroeconomic policy, follow common rules over capital flows, contribute to the provision of contingency liquidity and apply peer pressure to ensure compliance. By developing institutional arrangements for economic management, regional collaboration can attenuate some of the difficulties of international co-operation at the same time as it helps member states to confront the pressures of financial globalisation.

The effects of financial contagion and the growing pressures of global market integration appear to have pulled east Asian economies ever more strongly together. The harsh conditions of IMF rescue packages made the governments actively seek the possibility of establishing regional facilities for the provision of international liquidity. The subordinate position of individual east Asian governments vis-à-vis their US and European counterparts in the structure of global financial governance has also prodded the former to strive for a cohesive and strong representation of their interests in international policy arenas through more effective regional co-operation.[5] Ever since the onset of the crisis, regional central bankers and financial regulators have redoubled their efforts to build institutional linkages in a series of intergovernmental forums. Some elements of an Asian Monetary Fund have been in the process of formation and more ambitious long-run proposals for monetary co-operation seriously discussed. It is hoped that these moves may strengthen the kind of collaborative ties that will support more ambitious programmes of regional financial and monetary co-operation in the near future.

Structural reforms, economic governance and regional co-operation involve not only official policy makers but also private sector actors and their inter-actions with public authorities at national and international levels. These are the central themes of the fourth set of conceptual and policy issues explored in this volume. The various contributors have concurred that the private sec-tor is crucial to policy making and institution building in the management of global money and finance. Given that private financial firms have led the way in product development and innovation and have played an important role in shaping market rules and structures, they can help to enhance the increasingly limited expertise and capacity of public officials. On the other hand, the vol-ume has also demonstrated that the frenetic trading operations of investment houses, hedge funds and asset managers can contribute to financial crises. By implication, they should share the costs of such crises and should be integrated into the process of crisis prevention and management, just as they benefit more than most in times of growth. This is done at the national level all the time, so that firms can hardly object.

Private sector actors, while crucial to financial management, can have po-tentially perverse effects on policy processes, particularly against the backdrop of increased global market integration. It has been made clear in this volume that financial globalisation has strengthened the position of private actors and shifted the balance of power increasingly in favour of market interests over pub-lic authority. The resulting asymmetry, in which powerful private actors come to dominate the formulation of economic policies and states are increasingly interested in facilitating market processes, has critically changed the notions of public interest that underpin the operation of financial systems. The problem has become more acute in the transnational domain. The process of acceler-ated financial integration has undermined the institutions of public control over capital flows and transactions that were established in accordance with the orig-inal Bretton Woods agreement. Crucial decisions about the structure of global financial markets have often been made in transnational policy communities that are dominated by private interests, to the exclusion of broad segments of society and beyond traditional legislative oversight.

The growing dominance of national and international policy processes and the closed nature of such processes have meant that market rules and regu-latory standards have been increasingly aligned to the preferences of global market players. These rules and standards have facilitated the transformation of the global financial structure in ways that have greatly constrained the capac-ity of democratic governments to maintain their political legitimacy through macroeconomic and social policy mechanisms. More importantly, the private domination of public purposes has not only posed a fundamental problem of political legitimacy and democratic accountability, it has also resulted in financial instability and crises. Several chapters in this volume have presented strong evidence that the growing private penetration of the state apparatus severely compromised policy efficiency and contributed directly to financial mismanagement and crises in some Asian countries.

These empirical findings have heightened the real and potential dangers of private capture and the constant need of restructuring the market through state policy processes and institutional reforms, in addition to the traditional (often neo-liberal) emphasis on market competition as a means to prevent particularistic rent seeking. This suggests that the clear definition of public interests distinct from the necessarily particularistic claims of private market actors is the key to ensuring the predominance of such interests in the financial system. Maintaining strong public authority over private market power lies in the considerable strengthening of democratic institutions of accountability in the national, regional and global levels of governance. The implication for the reform of the global financial regime is robust and clear: the behaviour of major private financial firms should be firmly placed under the surveillance and control of such institutions.

The fifth set of conceptual and policy issues examined in this volume concerns the relationship between the regulatory and supervisory aspects of financial policy on the one hand, and the effectiveness of social and macroeconomic policies on the other. The general conclusion reached here is that there are extensive micro–macro linkages in the governance of the global monetary and financial system. Regulatory changes and supervisory adaptations have important ramifications for the management of exchange rate and monetary policies and for the realisation of a range of social policy goals. Similarly, corporate governance, pertaining to the mode of corporate financing and the relationship between state, finance and industry, is integral to the systemic dimensions of economic governance and national development strategies. Policy-making processes at regional and global levels should therefore take full account of these linkages. The more global financial integration proceeds, the more these linkages will be essential to the design of social and economic policies.

Implementing regulatory changes in isolation from macroeconomic policy considerations exerts powerful negative influences over not only the institutions of the monetary and financial order but also the functioning of the civic democratic order. Regulatory policy changes in favour of deregulation have led to the liberalisation of financial transactions across national borders. The resulting structural transformations in financial markets and tremendous growth in short-term capital flows and portfolio investments have greatly complicated the problems of economic governance. Under the impact of capital account liberalisation, states, particularly in emerging markets, have found it increasingly difficult to achieve their monetary and exchange rate policy goals, finance their social and health programmes and continue pursuing their chosen development strategies. As a result, major policy commitments of democratically elected governments have often been thrown into disarray, and their credibility and legitimacy increasingly put in jeopardy.

To a large extent, this has been a problem not just of structural changes, but of institutional design and vision in terms of policy. Recent financial crises are the best indication of the extent of the problem. Driven by external pressures and the demands of powerful domestic private interests, emerging market governments rushed to deregulate their financial systems without giving adequate attention to the effects of policy changes on prudential regulation and macroeconomic management. The result was the piecemeal adaptation of domestic institutions to the liberalised environment, the misalignment of exchange rate policy and financial crises. Global financial markets are clearly rendering more difficult the adjustment of national political economies to the exigencies of rapidly changing market forces. These market forces stem from the ability of financial institutions and investors instantaneously to move vast sums of capital rapidly across political jurisdictions and across different market segments. And this ability has no doubt been enhanced by national and international policy changes in conformity with liberal mantras embodied in the 'Washington consensus' which largely prevailed in the 1990s.

The imprudent separation of regulatory and supervisory policy processes from macroeconomic policy making has impeded the smooth adjustment of domestic sociopolitical institutions to rapid transformations in the global financial regime. More market-oriented regulatory practices have demonstrably constrained the macroeconomic policy options of states and their societies in the international system, with a potential for the growth of protectionist reactions from vulnerable but influential socioeconomic groups. In the long run, the fragmentation of micro–macro linkages may eventually turn the global system towards the destructive economic nationalism of the 1930s, an unprecedented social and economic crisis triggered, need one be reminded, by a market-oriented system of short-term capital mobility.

This last point heightens the looming importance of distributional questions in relation to existing world economic arrangements and of fairness and legitimacy issues in the international financial order – the final set of conceptual and policy issues addressed in this volume. These issues are not simply matters of social nicety with respect to the disadvantaged, but of smooth sociopolitical management and successful economic development as well. When substantial segments of the population find their economic security threatened by a bewildering array of volatile signals, uncertainties and risks from the financial system, the political ground can shift rapidly. Governments, increasingly hamstrung between global financial constraints and domestic demands for effective policy measures to counteract the impact of those constraints, have growing difficulty in maintaining credibility with the general public. The tension between their often vulnerable domestic constituencies and the dominant forces of the transnational market economy are difficult to square as the efficacy of the policy instruments of national economic management has diminished.

Furthermore, international financial policy changes have increasingly been formulated in the interactive networks of regulatory and supervisory authorities and powerful private agents. These policy changes, in the form of domestic and external financial deregulation, often place severe strains on fragile regulatory frameworks and induce inflows of speculative funds in emerging market economies, leading to financial instability and crisis. When liberalisation goes awry, international financial institutions effectively compel crisis-stricken countries to adopt budgetary austerity and severe adjustment programmes by making their adoption a precondition for the receipt of credits. Harsh adjustments are imposed to restore 'market confidence' with costs for the economic interests and welfare of society at large. The crucial question is: how do the interests of investors and investor confidence relate to the sacrifice of ordinary citizens in a situation of dramatic economic adjustment, particularly in a democratic context? The most urgent example is Argentina, which went through three presidents in a few months, the streets are in turmoil and the parliament appears paralysed on issues central to crisis management, and elections loom like a poisoned chalice to politicians of all parties.

All this points ultimately to the unavoidable normative content of the choices involved in the governance of global financial markets. The financial order and its dramatic transformations are not merely technocratic matters but are linked to questions of what sorts of societies we want to live in. A consistent inability of democratic processes to generate legitimacy in the eyes of their constituents in this regard can increase the fragility of democracy itself. The legitimacy of the international financial order may be called into question if emerging market economies are forced to accept rules over which they have little effective control and if vulnerable people are made to bear the costs of regulatory change for which global investors and the policies of major creditor countries may be primarily responsible. Policy makers must address this normative dimension in a serious manner, for the failure to deliver a more just international financial order can lead to the breakdown of global markets as a form of governance.

Limits of the new financial architecture

Current international efforts to reform the global financial system originated from the G-7 Halifax summit in the wake of the 1994–5 Mexican peso crisis.

These efforts continued through the IMF Interim Committee meetings in 1996 and culminated in a host of reform proposals in the aftermath of the 1997–8 Asian financial crisis. What became the official consensus on the new financial architecture evolved through policy debates and deliberations initiated and dominated by the US Treasury, the G-7/G-10 and the IMF.[6] During the first two years of the Asian crisis, the IMF laid down the core ingredients of architectural reform.[7] These involved the promotion of standards for good behaviour and transparency in private and public sectors, implementation of internationally acceptable practices for sound financial systems, flexible management of exchange rates, private sector involvement in debt restructuring and cautious liberalisation of capital accounts. In the meantime, the US Treasury and the G-7 made declarations and issued reports, all echoing the IMF architectural themes and emphasising the importance of national policy and institutional changes and orderly debt work-outs as the linchpins of effective crisis prevention and management.[8]

The formulation of new norms and rules was accompanied by some institutional changes in the international decision-making structure. The new architecture mainly focused on the IMF, the G-7 and the G-10 'Basel Process' as the essential institutional mechanisms for global financial management. Realising the need to enable 'systemically important' emerging market countries to acquire a genuine stake in the reform agenda, however, the architects moved to make the policy-making process more inclusive; the mechanisms of inclusion centred on several institutional developments. In the first place, the IMF Interim Committee was converted into the International Monetary and Financial Committee, a multilateral forum in which members of the IMF could raise and debate issues of their concerns. More significantly, leading industrial powers created the Financial Stability Forum (FSF) in Basel, comprising the G-7, the Bretton Woods institutions and major intergovernmental organisations in the domain of banking and finance, and in 1999 formed a new international grouping of countries known as the G-20.[9] The formation of the FSF and the G-20 represented an attempt to monitor and enforce the implementation of architectural reforms as well as to broaden the basis of the policy process and render it more accountable to emerging market economies.

The new financial architecture has fallen short of a fundamental restructuring of the ways in which global finance is governed.[10] The crucial shortcoming of the prevailing official consensus on architectural reform manifests itself in the apolitical approach to global financial governance. Although the new architecture has emphasised national policy changes, it has tended to ignore the political and institutional factors that underlie their implementation. The growing tension between the harmonising pressures of global market integration and the prevailing diversity of national economic systems has received little attention in the reform package endorsed by the IMF and major industrial nations. Despite the fact that neo-liberal market reforms and regulatory changes have important, often negative, bearings on socioeconomic management and democratic governance, these critical issues have been given little priority on the reform agenda. Equally important, the new architecture debate has been conspicuously devoid of normative discussions of global governance issues. While private market actors and agencies are increasingly integrated into international policy processes, how to fashion a politically sustainable balance between public authority and private power at national and international levels is essentially omitted from the agenda. By the same token, there has been a failure to address explicitly the questions of inequality and injustice in connection with the reform of the global financial regime.

Political constraints on national policy changes

One of the defining features of the new financial architecture is its emphasis on crisis prevention, given increased systemic instability caused by regional contagion and the enormous economic and social costs of tackling financial crises. Central to crisis prevention are national policy changes that not only range across a large number of micro and macro policy areas but also require institutional reforms. Successful efforts to enhance policy-making transparency and to improve financial regulation and corporate governance are not simply a matter of implementing a set of standards and codes of good conduct. Rather, they are contingent upon the transformation of longstanding domestic norms and rules and of their institutional underpinnings. Changes in these underpinnings would, in turn, impinge directly on the prevailing configuration of power and interests among state actors and societal groups.

Policy changes required to implement the agenda of transparency and best practice thus have high political stakes. Many of the economic policy-making rules and regulatory standards sanctified in the new financial architecture do not represent new reform measures; they embody the practices that international institutions and intergovernmental forums have been promoting in emerging markets for quite some time.[11] As has been made clear in recent financial crises, however, national governments often failed to adopt recommended policy-making rules and regulatory standards. This was due as much to administrative incapacity on the part of financial authorities as to persistent resistance from powerful political actors who identified their interests with existing policy rules and regulatory frameworks. Given this record, the current approach to the new financial architecture, which apparently assumes this to be an essentially technical problem admitting of universal solutions, has obscured the underlying political logic of financial policy reforms. Beyond improving economic governance through greater efficiency, there is the further problem of strengthening state institutions and managing political coalitions that underpin the ongoing process of governance.

It has been established in this conclusion that economic policy changes and market reforms are difficult to disentangle from political processes. Particular regulatory frameworks and governance modes confer asymmetric benefits on private and public actors and create vested interests. Reform is likely to alter the existing distributional arrangements that involve the interests of powerful groups in both private and public sectors. Corporate restructuring often requires the transformation of bank–industry relations and of the oligopolistic practices through which business groups maintain their ownership and managerial control. Similarly, regulatory tightening is likely to diminish the opportunity for powerful financiers to exploit supervisory loopholes for private gain. Corporate and regulatory reforms do not simply involve the substitution of new and stringent standards for old and lax ones, but entail fundamental shifts in the nature of power relations that underlie existing policy regimes. Beneficiaries of the status quo are unlikely to cave in to external pressures for reform without a fight, and difficulties in implementing policy changes are therefore acute in emerging markets.

This implies that governments and international institutions should pay close attention to both the economic optimality *and* the political feasibility of policy changes. Reforms represent an assault on established modes and institutions of policy management, and can cause dislocations that involve welfare loss and social unrest. In view of the possibility that reforms may lead to political instability, there is likely to be conflict between promoting sound financial practices through reform and pursuing redistributive policies necessary to maintain stability. The resolution of these conflicts will necessarily require patience and compromise. No one can seriously argue against institutional reforms required to improve policy-making efficiency and prudential regulation, but the reforms would have to be formulated and implemented in the imperfect world of political constraints and compromises.

Given international institutions' experience in promoting structural reforms in developing countries during the 1980s and the widespread awareness of their political difficulties,[12] the politically insensitive approach to the new financial architecture is rather perplexing. Whether the reform programmes endorsed by international institutions can be effectively carried out depends on the extent to which national governments are able to build political coalitions that support those programmes.[13] In some crisis countries such as South Korea and Thailand, reforms of regulatory practices and corporate structures have mainly been propelled by growing populist demands for clean government, social justice and economic stability in the aftermath of devastating economic crisis.[14] Garnering enough political support for institutional reforms so that new financial policies and practices can take root in emerging markets remains crucial to the long-run legitimacy of governments and of international institutions, particularly the IMF among others.

Harmonising pressures versus national diversity

Structural reforms promulgated in the context of the new international financial architecture will no doubt reinforce pressures for the convergence of financial systems and corporate structures towards market-oriented neo-liberal practices in emerging market economies. As inducements for adopting harmonising rules and standards, international institutions have given a central role to instruments of external influence – conditionality and policy surveillance.[15] The official consensus on the new financial architecture has set the bottom line of structural reforms as consisting of transparent macroeconomic policies, open financial markets, arm's-length bank–industry ties, Anglo-Saxon-style corporate governance, and market-led industrial adjustment strategies. Regardless of national differences in financial and economic systems, these prescriptions have been seen as having an essentially universal application.[16]

While there has been increased pressure for policy harmonisation, the convergence of economic models is far from inevitable. As discussed in the previous section, policy-making modes, financial systems and corporate practices have always remained embedded in the fabric of local legal, social and economic institutions, nationally defined for the most part at the moment. Variations among national forms of capitalism persist to some degree as each local economy continues to refract external market and political constraints in its own way. Historically, few paths to capitalist development have converged for long. Where the tensions between harmonising liberal market structures and local contexts and institutions become overwhelming, capitalist development and a market-based society as such are unlikely to be politically sustainable. If the harmonisation of financial policies, regulatory frameworks and corporate structures conflicts with domestic political and economic imperatives, the legitimacy of the reform programmes ardently promoted by international institutions may be called into question.

We are not arguing against the introduction of sounder regulation and corporate practices. But we do argue that international policy makers must take local conditions fully into account when designing and implementing structural reforms in emerging market countries. As it stands, however, the new financial architecture has made little explicit reference to national legal, business and political practices and institutions. While recognising differences in national

financial and economic systems, the architects have not given adequate attention to the real and potential conflicts between those differences and their efforts
to promote policy harmonisation. Nor have they fully realised the implications
of those conflicts for national economic development, political legitimacy and
democratic governance.

Financial systems and the patterns of corporate governance, as an integral part
of any political economy, are closely linked to the interactions between financial institutions, industrial firms, labour markets and the state. In other words,
differences in financial and corporate practices are central to what makes different models of capitalism different. It can therefore be argued that financial
and corporate reforms mandated in the new financial architecture may unravel
these institutions to yield transformations in the relationship between finance,
industry, labour and the state, and thus an associated change in the distinguishing features of economic development models themselves. To the extent that
structural reforms lead to the convergence of financial and corporate practices,
this is likely to preclude some development strategies that have contributed to
economic growth and social progress in emerging market economies.[17]

The more serious challenges that structural reforms have presented for emerging market governments lie in the arena of political stability, legitimacy and
democratic governance. Policy harmonisation along the line of neo-liberal practices is expected to have important consequences for the patterns of gains and
losses among various actors and groups in the economy. More market-oriented
reforms are likely to result in intensified competition among domestic firms
and between them and their foreign rivals. Open and transparent financial markets may favour multinational firms and mobile asset holders over domestically
based enterprises and internationally immobile factors of production. This will
lead to social and industrial restructuring, which one may well argue is beneficial in a long-term sense, but involves significant short-term costs for the more
vulnerable market actors and social groups and creates the potential for political
conflicts. If they are not managed properly, these situations may develop into
serious sociopolitical instability.

Furthermore, the process of policy convergence, which has disturbing effects
on the patterns of welfare gains and losses, has also posed a serious problem
to the existing mechanisms for income distribution. Complex institutions have
emerged over time to manage distributional conflicts, with different degrees of
success in different historical epochs and national settings. Rapidly increasing
exposure of structural adjustment processes to external market and political
pressures, however, risks displacing those institutions too rapidly for them to
cope or survive. To the extent that these institutions have contributed to sociopolitical stability and the legitimacy of national governments, radical institutional reforms can deprive governments of their political credibility. If emerging
market economies are forced to accept rapid and significant liberal restructuring,

which may threaten the very domestic arrangements that have underpinned their accumulated successes, this is likely to undermine the nascent democratisation process in these economies.

That the new financial architecture has given little attention to the clashes between policy harmonisation and national differences and to their economic and political consequences should not be seen as benign neglect on the part of international policy makers. Rather, it may have represented deliberate efforts to overhaul the institutions of development policies that have been deeply embedded in many east Asian and developing societies. In the wake of the Asian crisis, many economists of neo-classical persuasion breathed a sigh of relief that these once-successful exceptions to economic orthodoxy had finally met their come-uppance. For IMF leaders and US Treasury officials, the new financial architecture has been a means of altering the longstanding models and institutions of economic policy making and development strategies that often proved impenetrable to Western corporate entities.[18] The destructive effects of structural reforms on the Asian financial systems and corporate practices may have been exactly what they hoped for.

The new financial architecture reflected not only the ideological orientation of leading financial centres and international institutions but also the interests of their major constituencies. The liberal reform agenda conforms with a broader set of policy and institutional preferences of global investors who favour open financial sectors, liberal industrial policies, deregulated labour markets and transparent business practices (of their competitors but not always their own). It is not beyond plausibility to argue that there may have been the interpenetration of interests among powerful financiers, the US Treasury and the IMF in the closed, club-like policy community created through the 'Wall Street–Treasury–IMF complex'.[19] But the danger is that structural reforms that have catered to the preferences of global investors in the name of 'sound' financial practices may be implemented at the expense of economic growth and political stability in emerging market countries.

Regional co-operation: the neglected option

Global market integration, regional contagion and financial crisis have all heightened the need for enhancing international co-operative efforts at monetary and financial governance. The new financial architecture, which involves significant national policy and institutional changes of central importance to developing and emerging market economies, also requires close collaboration between international institutions and national governments. But prevailing differences in national financial systems and regulatory frameworks have contributed to divergent understandings of, and varying approaches to, global financial problems, not only between industrial and developing countries but also among key international institutions (the tensions between the twin Bretton Woods institutions during the Asian crisis are the prima facie evidence), defying comprehensive global co-operation in financial policy management.[20] Conflicting interests and political disagreements have reduced the prospects for effective international co-operative arrangements for crisis prevention and management.

As international economic co-operation continues to be difficult, many countries, particularly developing countries, have shown growing interest in regional institutional co-ordination. They have increasingly realised that regional co-operation, despite its real and potential problems, would be better able to prevent or contain financial market instability and to insulate vulnerable economies from negative spill-over effects from crises. International institutions and their most powerful members, however, have not shown much enthusiasm for such developments. The new financial architecture tended to view the IMF, the Basel process and the OECD as the fulcrum of global monetary and financial governance. Institutional reforms advocated by the architects emphasised the improvement of co-operation among international financial institutions; only recently have regional co-operative efforts been encouraged.[21]

Given that international institutions have demonstrated little aptitude for effective co-operation in the past, the bias against regional efforts embedded in the new financial architecture has placed in jeopardy an important alternative which could operate alongside global monetary and financial governance. One may rightly argue that regional economic co-operation is not immune to the political and economic difficulties that plague global-level collaboration. Yet the successful regional economic and monetary integration experiences of European countries and now NAFTA-level collaboration offer valuable lessons. During and after recent financial crises, Asian governments were able to move fairly quickly towards greater regional co-operation, particularly in the monetary and financial realms. Various proposals, ranging from modest ideas on more effective co-ordination among financial regulators and joint efforts to create more extensive Asian capital markets to more ambitious plans for a regional monetary fund and a currency unit, have been put forward and some partially implemented.[22]

So far, among the greatest obstacles to regional co-operation in east Asia have come from outside the region itself. These in large part account for the relative lack of official regional co-operation proposals on the financial architecture agenda. Most critically, greater regionalisation is likely to reduce the control and influence of international institutions over Asian monetary and financial affairs. Through a more active and extensive Asian capital market, for instance, countries with strong monetary reserves can finance the investment needs of others which may otherwise seek outside assistance. A regional monetary fund can provide countries with contingent credits during crisis periods under much more favourable conditions than those mandated by the IMF. All this would make Asian governments more independent and less subject to the policy demands of international institutions, rendering the latter strongly opposed to stronger regional economic co-operation.

Furthermore, the current moves towards the development of east Asian regional institutions, particularly in the domain of financial policy management, appear to be limited to Asian countries only and would thus exclude such major Western powers as the United States. Some regional leaders have viewed such moves as an important or even primary means of avoiding deference to Washington.[23] This may not be surprising, given that the US Treasury largely dictated the course of policy responses during the Asian crisis and imposed, through the IMF, structural reforms that many crisis countries found economically counterproductive, socially costly and politically intrusive. Apparent desires on the part of Asian countries to escape domination by the United States (despite the fact that they also need the country for economic and security reasons) has underpinned US opposition to such proposals for enhancing regional co-operative efforts as the Asian Monetary Fund.

To the extent that strengthening regional co-operation threatens to reduce the economic and political influence of the United States and the IMF, this is likely to make it more difficult for them to reduce Asian independence in policy-making and development strategies. In other words, more effective regional collaboration may provide Asian governments with the political resources that they need to resist pressures for policy harmonisation and to maintain their distinctive economic models. Already, many countries in the region, inspired by the examples of India, China and Malaysia, have become more supportive of using capital controls not only to avoid future financial crises but also to regain autonomy in their development policies. The US Treasury and the IMF have thus opposed the regional co-operative initiatives that would harbour policies inimical to their ideological and political preferences and to the interests of their Wall Street constituents.[24] Yet regional solutions may help to attenuate some of the tensions between national economic development models and global pressures for harmonisation, a goal supported by the evidence presented in this volume.[25]

Failure to forge micro–macro linkages

One of the central themes developed in this volume is that there are extensive linkages between regulatory change, supervisory adaptation and corporate restructuring on the one hand, and the effectiveness of macroeconomic and social policies on the other. Perhaps the most important policy challenge in the domain of global financial governance is to maintain these micro–macro linkages. Fragmenting the linkages could have serious economic and political consequences. For many years, regulatory change and rapidly adapting corporate strategies together have led to a less segmented, and more market-oriented, financial system. Tremendous growth in short-term capital flows and portfolio investments have greatly complicated the problems of macroeconomic policy management. States have struggled to achieve their exchange rate and monetary policy objectives in a new and increasingly unstable global financial environment. Major socioeconomic policy commitments of democratically elected governments have often been thrown into disarray as a result of financial liberalisation, structural changes and the aggregate behaviour of global investors.

In the shadow of recent financial crises in emerging market countries, the various policy problems of de-linking micro–macro relations have been felt acutely. Nonetheless, there has been a genuine loss of direction in policy terms. National governments have been trying to learn about the changed international financial environment and to deal with its risky and volatile characteristics. They have realised that on their own they are unable to return to the segmented and repressed international financial system, as the seemingly irreversible process of financial globalisation greatly circumscribes policy options. Although there has been considerable questioning by policy makers and scholars of the principles embodied in the Washington consensus,[26] novel approaches to forging micro–macro linkages and to managing the problems of market integration are lacking. The architects have failed to address the misconceived separation of regulatory and corporate governance issues from macroeconomic policy concerns. Even capital account liberalisation, albeit 'cautiously and in an orderly fashion', has still remained a key element on the new policy agenda.

Not only has the new approach to financial architecture failed to forge micro–macro linkages, it has reinforced the growing separation and the associated policy difficulties in many respects. Efforts to promote the convergence of financial practices and to enhance regulatory and supervisory co-operation, crucial for policy harmonisation and risk management, have a perverse effect. By reducing national differences and thus financial transaction costs and risks through the harmonisation and co-ordination of standards, they are most likely to accelerate further structural transformations in international financial markets, with a commensurate impact on the making of macroeconomic and social policies. One may ask whether this accelerating pace of harmonisation and change would permit adequate time for political systems to adjust and cope. Without a link between financial regulation and corporate governance on the one hand and socioeconomic policy making on the other, the piecemeal and inadequate adaptation of domestic political institutions to the new and rapidly changing realities looks likely to continue.

Inadequate attention to normative dimensions

The foregoing analysis suggests that the complexities of structural reforms, institutional collaboration, private sector involvement and micro–macro linkages point ultimately to the normative dimensions of policy options and choices involved in global financial governance. One of the central arguments advanced in this volume is that the international financial order derives its legitimacy not only from its potential contribution to improved investment opportunities and economic efficiency but, more fundamentally, from its ability to ensure redistributive justice, social fairness and democratic accountability on a global scale. The key issues in the international financial architecture go beyond policy transparency, regulatory adequacy and risk management, and concern the broader questions about the ends of public policy in the domain of global money and finance. Failure to address these questions may lead to the loss of legitimacy and even the breakdown of the global economic order.[27]

The language of the new financial architecture, however, is a primarily technocratic discussion of policy management by national governments and international institutions. Questions of social justice and of the legitimacy of international policy-making institutions have received scant attention from within the emerging consensus on the reform of the international financial regime.[28] By the same token, the new architecture pays little attention to the long-term problems of redistributive justice and political legitimacy that financial integration and structural transformations have presented for governments, democratic or not. That the current global debates on architectural design were thoroughly thrashed out at Bretton Woods so long ago, and workable compromises reached, has apparently been forgotten. There appears to have been limited concern for the proper balance between on the one hand financial globalisation and on the other the ability of states to ensure economic security among broad segments of society and the efficacy and credibility of (hopefully democratic) governance.

The marginalisation of the normative dimensions of global financial governance has reflected the narrowness of the institutional processes by which the agenda has been formulated. While the formation of the G-20 and the Financial Stability Forum (FSF) might have rendered the international decision-making process more inclusive, the membership and structural hierarchy of these forums have left no doubt that the global financial system will continue to be run by the leading industrial nations.[29] The G-20 and the FSF still excludes the majority of developing countries. Even the emerging markets that are included realise that they have different interests from and lack collective bargaining power vis-à-vis the dominant members. Institutional changes in the new architecture thus have not altered the uneven distribution of voting power in the international political economy; at the epicentre of global financial governance remains the G-7. The key components of the reform agenda have actually resulted from the compromise and conflict of interests among the most powerful members of the global economic system, in spite of the fact that the implementation of the agenda would affect the lives and livelihood of millions of people throughout the developing world.[30]

Existing institutional arrangements in the global financial system have also privileged the representation of powerful private interests. Financial policy and regulatory practices are formulated in policy communities consisting of regulators and private agencies from the leading industrial nations. In these networks, private market interests find respondents in finance ministers and central bankers and have thus been able to influence the global agenda for financial policy changes. International institutions involved in the reform of the international financial regime have explicitly advanced the interests of their most influential members and powerful market players at the expense of those of developing and emerging market economies. The rules and standards sanctified in the new architecture have been designed more to facilitate policies of liberalisation than to address problems for those economies regarding financial globalisation and increased capital mobility. Their governments have found it increasingly difficult to deviate from the preferences of powerful market players and agencies, no matter how important particular policies may be for resolving their individual problems of economic development and sociopolitical stability.

There is therefore little doubt concerning for whom the new financial architecture has been 're'-designed. It is no coincidence that the main ingredients of the new architecture have been so consonant with the broad policy preferences of the leading financial centres and global investors for regulatory harmonisation, reduced financial transaction costs and the continued liberalisation of capital accounts. They have enhanced the particularistic interests of private financiers and firms in those nations at the expense of socioeconomic equality, political stability and, potentially, the democratisation process in the developing world. Private sector burden sharing and responsibility issues have been notable for their absence in the policy debate, despite the clear need for a more rational and balanced debt restructuring process which, like domestic level procedures, is less creditor friendly. Hopefully recent IMF statements endorsing orderly debt work-out arrangements will prove fruitful in short order,[31] but the difficulties of Argentina's negotiations with the IMF, despite the ominous political instability, do not give cause for optimism.

The new architectural agenda has thus further weakened the autonomy of developing countries in managing capital flows and in choosing the financial governance regimes they deem appropriate to their development needs and circumstances. Emerging market countries face enhanced conditionality attached to liquidity provision, without significantly enhanced participation and voice in the relevant policy processes. Unless the wider issues of this volume are addressed, the outcome of the architecture exercise will lack widespread legitimacy. It may also aggravate the existing strains in the global financial and monetary arena, with considerable costs for those whom it currently benefits the most.

Notes

1. Joseph Stiglitz, 'Capital Market Liberalisation, Economic Growth, and Instability', *World Development*, vol. 28, no. 6 (2000), p. 1075.
2. Two prominent technical assessments of the new financial architecture are Barry Eichengreen, 'Strengthening the International Financial Architecture: Where Do We Stand?' paper presented to the East–West Center Workshop on International Monetary and Financial Reform, Honolulu, 1–2 October 1999; Morris Goldstein, 'An Evaluation of Proposals to Reform the International Financial Architecture', paper presented to the NBER Conference on Management of Currency Crises, Monterey, California, 28–31 March 2001.
3. Even the IMF has recognised this with characteristic caution; see IMF, *Reforming the International Financial Architecture – Progress through 2000* (Washington, DC: IMF, 2001). See also Daniel Citrin and Stanley Fischer, 'Strengthening the International Financial System: Key Issues', *World Development*, vol. 28, no. 6 (2000), pp. 1133–42.
4. See Barry Eichengreen, *Toward a New International Financial Architecture* (Washington, DC: Institute for International Economics, 1999), pp. 79–95.
5. For detailed discussions of these issues, see articles on regionalism in the Asia–Pacific region after the financial crisis in *The Pacific Review*, vol. 13, no. 3, 2000.
6. For comprehensive discussions on the origin and evolution of the architecture exercise see Andrew Baker, 'The G-7 as a "Global Ginger Group": Plurilateralism and Four-Dimensional Diplomacy', *Global Governance*, vol. 6, no. 2 (2000), pp. 165–90; Peter B. Kenen, 'The New International Financial Architecture: Reconstruction, Renovation, or Minor Repair?' *International Journal of Finance and Economics*, vol. 5, no. 1 (2000), pp. 1–14.
7. The official documents that elaborate systematically on these ingredients include 'Managing Director's Opening Address', *IMF Survey*, 19 October 1998; 'Toward an Agenda for International Monetary and Financial Reform', 1998, at http://www.imf.org/external/np/speeches/110698.htm.
8. The proposal of the G-7 is exemplified in 'Declaration of G-7 Finance Ministers and Central Bank Governors', 1998, at http://www.imf.org/external/np/g7/103098dc.htm; that of the US Treasury is represented in Secretary Robert Rubin,

'Remarks on Reform of the International Financial Architecture to the School of Advanced International Studies', *Treasury News*, RR-3093, 21 April 1999.

9. The G-20 has brought together finance ministers and central bankers from Argentina, Australia, Brazil, China, India, Indonesia, South Korea, Mexico, Russia, Saudi Arabia, South Africa and Turkey, as well as from the G-7.

10. For other reviews and evaluations of the new international financial architecture, see articles contained in a special issue of *Global Governance*, vol. 7, no. 4 (2001).

11. What is seldom recognised is just how long it took for G-7 countries to develop the existing consensus – several decades of postwar development, the collapse of Bretton Woods, and subsequent policy disagreement and change at the least. Emerging market economies are apparently expected to go through this process at an accelerated pace.

12. The political dynamics of structural reforms in developing countries and their major policy lessons for national and international policy makers are discussed systematically in Stephan Haggard and Steven B. Webb (eds.), *Voting for Reform* (New York: Oxford University Press, 1994); John Williamson (ed.), *The Political Economy of Policy Reform* (Washington, DC: Institute for International Economics, 1993).

13. The importance of building domestic political coalitions for structural and policy reforms is also emphasised in Miles Kahler, 'The New International Financial Architecture and its Limits', in Gregory W. Noble and John Ravenhill (eds.), *The Asian Financial Crisis and the Architecture of Global Finance* (Cambridge: Cambridge University Press, 2000), pp. 255–6.

14. See, for instance, Stephan Haggard, *The Political Economy of the Asian Financial Crisis* (Washington, DC: Institute for International Economics, 2000), chs. 3 and 4.

15. The pros and cons of these instruments are examined at length in Devesh Kapur and Richard Webb, 'Governance-related Conditionalities of the International Financial Institutions', G-24 Discussion Paper No. 6 (Geneva: United Nations Conference on Trade and Development, 2000).

16. These reform measures are discussed at length in Goldstein, 'An Evaluation'; Dani Rodrik, 'Governing the Global Economy: Does One Architectural Style Fit All?' paper presented to the Brookings Institution Trade Policy Forum conference on Governing in a Global Economy, Washington, DC: 15–16 April 1999.

17. For discussions on how IMF-mandated reforms have impinged on national policy choices that have proved to be growth-enhancing in the past see Martin Feldstein, 'Refocusing the IMF', *Foreign Affairs*, vol. 77, no. 2 (1998), pp. 20–33; Rodrik, 'Governing the Global Economy'.

18. See Joseph E. Medley, 'The East Asian Economic Crisis: Surging US Imperialism?' *Review of Radical Political Economics*, vol. 32, no. 3 (2000), pp. 379–87.

19. See Jagdish Bhagwati, 'The Capital Myth: the Difference between Trade in Widgets and Dollars', *Foreign Affairs*, vol. 77, no. 3 (1998), pp. 7–12; Robert Wade, 'The Asian Crisis: the High Debt Model versus the Wall Street–Treasury–IMF Complex', *New Left Review*, no. 228 (1998), pp. 3–23.

20. For a recent discussion of the difficulties of international co-operation in global economic governance see Ngaire Woods, 'The Challenge to International Institutions', in Ngaire Woods (ed.), *The Political Economy of Globalisation* (London:

Macmillan, 2000). See also Kahler, 'The New International Financial Architecture', pp. 235–60.

21. See IMF Issue Briefs for 2001, 'Reforming the International Financial Architecture – Progress through 2000', at www.imf.org/external/np/exr/ib/2001/030901.htm.

22. Recent progress in regional co-operation in east Asia is reviewed in C. Fred Bergsten, 'The New Asian Challenge', Working Paper 00–4 (Washington, DC: Institute for International Economics, 2000).

23. *Ibid.*; Gregory Noble and John Ravenhill, 'Causes and Consequences of the Asian Financial Crisis', in Gregory Noble and John Ravenhill, *The Asian Financial Crisis and the Architecture of Global Finance* (Cambridge: Cambridge University Press, 2000), pp. 23–32.

24. It should be noted, however, that the IMF appears to have changed its rhetoric, if not its policy, on regional financial and monetary co-operation since Horst Kohler was made Managing Director in early 2001. See an interview given by Kohler in *Far Eastern Economic Review*, 14 June 2001.

25. See, particularly, Chapter 5 by Phongpaichit and Baker and Chapter 11 by Tadokoro.

26. See Charles Gore, 'The Rise and Fall of the Washington Consensus as a Paradigm for Developing Countries', *World Development*, vol. 28, no. 5 (2000), pp. 789–804.

27. The normative dimensions of global economic and financial governance are discussed more thoroughly in Richard Devetak and Richard Higgott, 'Justice Unbound? Globalisation, States and the Transformation of the Social Bond', *International Affairs*, vol. 75, no. 3 (1999), pp. 483–98; the various articles in Geoffrey Underhill (ed.), *The New World Order in International Finance* (London: Macmillan, 1998).

28. Some minority voices on these issues include Alan S. Blinder, 'Eight Steps to a New Financial Order', *Foreign Affairs*, vol. 78, no. 5 (1999), pp. 50–63; George Soros, 'On Measures to Encourage Sound Long-Term Lending to Emerging Economies', in Council on Foreign Relations Independent Task Force, *Safeguarding Prosperity in a Global Financial System* (Washington, DC: Institute for International Economics, 1999), pp. 141–3.

29. Even those who perceive these institutional changes in a relatively positive light would concede that the international decision-making structure remains G-7-centred. See Randall D. Germain, 'Global Financial Governance and the Problem of Inclusion', *Global Governance*, vol. 7, no. 4 (2001), pp. 411–26.

30. See Yilmaz Akyüz and Andrew Cornford, 'Capital Flows to Developing Countries and the Reform of the International Financial System', UNCTAD Discussion Paper No. 143 (Geneva: United Nations Conference on Trade and Development, 1999).

31. See Ann Krueger (First Deputy Managing Director, IMF), 'International Financial Architecture for 2002: a New Approach to Sovereign Debt Restructuring', address to the National Economists' Club, 26 November 2001, at www.imf.org/external/np/speeches/ 2001/112601.htm.

Index